Learning from Difference

Christopher Balfour

Learning from Difference
Christopher Balfour

Design ©131 Design Ltd
www.131design.org
Text & images © Christopher Balfour

ISBN 978-1-1909660-27-4
A CIP catalogue record for this book
is available from the British Library.

Published 2014 by Tricorn Books
131 High Street, Old Portsmouth,
PO1 2HW
www.tricornbooks.co.uk

Printed & bound in UK

Acknowledgements

This book would not have been possible without an enormous amount of help and encouragement from the family. Ann's support is incalculable, coping with so many hours I have spent on research and composition, and sacrificing her social life and enjoyable eating to provide my basic food. Max, Juliet and Kate (and Max's wife, Ay, and Juliet and Kate's husbands, Jonathan & Harry) initially expressed some concern about the project. I think and hope they have come to realise that much can be learnt from a better understanding of the past. Despite all their other activities they have read the text, corrected mistakes and made helpful suggestions. Jonathan's skill was responsible for the fiftieth anniversary photograph. Of their children, Samuel Morley, with all his computer skills, has generously used precious hours of his holiday time to upgrade my word processing knowledge. Tom and Sebastian Bench have willingly debated political issues. If they have not been able to directly contribute, Hugo Bench, Rose Morley and Alexander and Josephine Balfour have put up with and accepted the immersion in the project. My sister Karen, supported by her husband Fabyan Evans, has taken time out of her busy life to carefully read the whole text. Her incisive brain made many valuable suggestions, most of which have been incorporated. She was also one of those who convinced me that the original Balfour family chapter was too complicated and needed to be split into three sections. Her sons Nigel and Alexander and daughter Jessica have confirmed their wish to know more about their background.

Of cousins consulted, Charles Balfour in Italy has bombarded us with emails full of family history of which I knew nothing. It is through his efforts that there are pictures of family buildings in Fife and much else. He has pointed to the uncertainty about earlier family history which I hope future generations will solve. It is through Charles that we have had contact with and photographs from Michael Balfour and Penny Moran. Charles's daughter, Beatrice, has also helped with pictures. Stuart Balfour has generously let me use all the information which his family have put together for their Balfour family tree. Louise Balfour Goodman, besides constant encouragement, has let us have a copy of her great-uncle, Sir Philip Balfour's, war memoir, told us something of her father Hugh's achievements and interests and of the little she knew about her great-grandfather Fred in India. Hugh's sisters Jenifer Phillips and Ursula Mackenzie passed on their family knowledge and also encouraged. Mark Goldsmith, present site manager at Pfaudler Balfour, Leven, has allowed me to use pictures from their bicentenary history There was conversation with Betty Balfour before she died and her solicitor, John Clifton, kindly rescued and gave us her photograph albums with pictures of her parents and her brother Ken in Africa. Sir Robert's grand-daughter, Margaret Ashbrook, and her daughter, Susan Ashbrook, filled in other details.

On the Joachim side Catherine King Ambler invited me to lovely Silverdale, told me much that I did not know and allowed me to take copies of Joachim correspondence and photographs. Her brother Paul was also helpful before his early death and I learnt so much from earlier conversations with their father, Jo, from whose book of memoirs I have liberally quoted in Chapter 3. Of Gertrude Russell's great-grandchildren, Anna and David Lloyd and Mary Cousins have kindly answered queries about Lloyd descendants and enabled the use of Gertrude's portrait. It was their stepmother who had become their father Rob's second wife after the death of their mother who helped in establishing this contact. Jellicoe cousins have also encouraged, especially Jacqueline Vivian. Her brother, Philip Wingfield, rescued letters from my mother to his mother, Norah. Susan Rose, an acclaimed author of books on maritime history and Nicholas Jellicoe have shared my interest in family history. Nigel Cayzer and Sir James Cayzer struggled for so long with family finances leading to an outcome which enabled many things. Jean Reader and Elizabeth Wilson helped with the Davies family information.

Finally heartfelt thanks to the surgeons, doctors and nurses at the Royal Hampshire County Hospital for all their help and kindness these past few years and also to Gail Baird and Dan Bernard at Tricorn Books who have been so much more than just publishers. Right from the start they have encouraged in every way, immensely patient with both my sometimes poor computer skills and times of doubt about the project. Their presentation and layout skills have led to a product which is far better than I thought possible with a small budget. Ann and I hope the book will be enjoyed by and useful to all Lionel and Myrtle's great-grandchildren, Tom, Sebastian and Hugo, Samuel and Rose and Alexander and Josephine already mentioned. Also Toby and Daisy Evans and Sam and Emma Knowles. Sadly Catherine King Ambler, Jenifer Phillips and Jacqueline Vivian have died before reading this.

Relatives killed 1914 - 1918

1. Alan Balfour, son of Great-grandfather James's brother, Sir Robert.
    1918 Tincourt New British Cemetery.
2. Percy Balfour, great-uncle, brother of grandfather, Maxwell.
    1917 Fins New British Cemetery, Sorel Le Grand.
3. Andrew Ogilvie, son of Great-grandmother Rachel's brother Andrew.
    1917 Tyne Cot memorial.
4. William Ogilvie, son of Great-grandmother Rachel's brother George.
    1915 Hangard Communal Cemetery Extension.
5. Sir (Henry) Guy Butlin, son of Ann's Great-uncle Sir Henry.
    1916 Thiepval Memorial.
6. Herbert Martyn Davies, Ann's uncle from Australia.
    1916 Crucifix Corner Cemetery, Villers Bretonnex.
7. Alan Davies, brother of Herbert Martyn.
    1918 Estaires Communal Cemetery.

Died after the War, partially a consequence of wounds

8. Alexander Balfour, son of Great-grandfather James's brother Sir Robert.
9. John Russell, son of Nina's sister, Great-aunt Gertrude.

Killed 1939 - 1945

1. Sir Nigel Cayzer, great-grandson of Great-grandfather Sir Charles.
    1943 Salerno War Cemetery, Italy.
2. Stephen Ogilvie, son of Sir Heneage, grandson of Great-grandmother Rachel's brother Willie.
    1943 St. Illtyd Churchyard, Pembry, South Wales.

Learning from Difference

'During the hundred years after Waterloo, Englishmen and Americans believed themselves moving on the great current of progress to the reign of universal peace and universal law. International war had been held to a minimum, economic and technical progress had exceeded that of the whole prior history of man. People, goods and ideas moved about with an unequal freedom and the lives of people everywhere were moulded by a gigantic worldwide scheme.'

Dean Acheson, 'Fifty Years After', *Yale Review*, Autumn 1961

'Burke was expressing a finite truth about the respect for and satisfaction with the governing institutions which the civilised English were quietly evolving — it really is a dreadful story, this business of killing the best of a generation and ruining the country's industrial development in wars for unconditional surrender — our problem in a nutshell is so to arrange the taxing and controlling system of the state that people are neither overloaded nor undernourished by their centralised schemes of welfare.'

Victor Montagu, *The Conservative Dilemma*, the Monday Club, March 1970

'England led the world in steam technology and was the home of the industrial revolution. But for some reason the thinking is that, because your grandfather worked with his hands, you shouldn't have to.'

Jay Leno, *Octane*, April 2012

'The most immediate danger is youth unemployment which in some countries is above 50%. This is a time bomb. Britain has a problem that will make itself felt in the next 15-20 years. In the 19th Century it was the most advanced engineering Nation in the world. Now it has more or less given up on engineering and replaced it with finance. That means you can be hurt.'

Helmut Schmidt ex-German Chancellor, *Guardian* interview 23 December, 2013

'These were the people who made a huge impact in Great Britain and around the world, bringing their education and knowledge to developing nations. They were also the people who fought and died for the free world.'

Rachel Ogilvie Godfrey writing to author of *Balfour and Ogilvie relations*, 2014
www.ogilviefamilytree.com

Other books by this author

Roads to Oblivion
Bay View books, 1996
ISBN 1 870979 82 6

(assisting Gerald Palmer)
Auto-Architect: the autobiography of Gerald Palmer
Magna Press, 1998
ISBN 0 9519423 6 0

Spithead Express
Magna Press, 1999
ISBN 0 9519423 8 7

Auto-Architect
(second edition, paperback), 2004
ISBN 0 9543121 12

Bristol Cars
Haynes Publishing, 2009
Reprinted 2010, 2011
ISBN 978 1 84425 4071

50th Wedding Anniversary at Blackland Farm

Contents

LEARNING FROM DIFFERENCE

Chapter 1

Why Write?

The experience of eighty years – denied for too many forebears, victims of battlefield, illness or other distress – engenders profound gratitude. There is the opportunity to reflect on disagreements, difficulties and mistakes, attempting to follow George Orwell's intimation:

> 'A man who gives a good account of himself is probably lying since any life when viewed from the inside is simply a series of defeats.'[1]

There is time to look again at papers relating to and written by family members. Their letters may sometimes disrupt the flow of the story but I hope that later generations will become more aware of these relatives, whom they did not meet. Other letters record the attitude of people involved with then current issues. Eric Hobsbawm wrote: 'It is the business of historians to remember what others forget.'[2] These are what forebears, politicians, civil servants, constituency officers and both employers and employees in industry and commerce actually said or wrote, not just recollections. Of course there is nobility in charging the enemy, in 'laying down life for friends', and emotion is boosted, but so much is lost when there is then no chance to listen to and talk with children, grandchildren and other younger people. Life demonstrates again and again how intentions and plans can be affected by the attitude and fate of others as well as personal failings. Each generation has to learn lessons anew. However, the experiences recounted – of living with physical difficulties, of trying to work for the British-owned motor industry, of the subsequent years in the Youth Employment Service, of tussles as a Parliamentary Candidate with the Conservative Party and then election as an Independent Councillor – have helped in trying to understand the human arena. The attempt at self-justification is admitted, but there is also the hope that these experiences may be of use to others. Much of education is subject-orientated, less about coping with living. The binding feature of all these happenings, and of dissent within the family, has been the struggle for employment and subsistence, for self and for others. In these conflicts there has been right and wrong on both sides. Difficult though it may be (and I wasn't much good at this) I now realise that it is better to try and understand each other's viewpoints, and learn from difference.

Though warfare may always be part of the human scenario, discussion, where possible, seems preferable.

The only grandparent I knew was the formidable grandmother. She can be christened FG, appropriately the initials of her forenames, Florence Gwendoline. My mother Myrtle died when I was eleven. There was then more contact with FG. She wanted me to follow in the footsteps of her family, no strangers to the world of power and position. She sent me books like Lord Beaverbrook's 'Men and Power' describing the actions of those in control from 1914 to 1918 when her late husband, John Jellicoe, had been a renowned Naval war leader. I was the only grandchild born before he died in 1935. Miss Scillitoe, FG's loyal and shrewd factotum, with whom helpful alliances were formed when staying, wrote in 1966: 'I always remember what joy you gave the late Admiral as his first grandchild at St. Lawrence Hall. I have a precious picture of you being nursed by him'.[3] At least my birth, with all its difficult consequences, had some purpose! FG's father, Sir Charles Cayzer, had prospered as a nineteenth-century ship owner and had become a Member of Parliament, as did one of his sons and a grandson. One of FG's repeated refrains was that she 'did not want me to be like my father'. Surviving letters suggest she was wary of Myrtle's marriage to Lionel Balfour, an earnest engineer and one who was willing to work with his hands. The name would not have helped, a reminder of A J Balfour's response as First Lord of the Admiralty after Jutland. In Beaverbrook's words: 'Balfour had acted in the conviction that the people must be told the unvarnished facts about the British ships which had been lost. Later news was to bring brighter tidings of the battle but in the meantime consternation and alarm spread throughout the nation'. Grandfather had to cope with the consequences of these words from a Balfour who was also a member of the War Cabinet which agreed to his dismissal from the Admiralty in December 1917. Fifteen years later FG was faced with the engagement of her daughter to a man of the same name. Whilst the connection with AJ, if any, was remote, Lionel had no parents still alive to sanction his lineage and there was no visible evidence of landed or titled gentry. Sir Robert Balfour, Lionel's great-uncle, had died just two years earlier, by which time his three sons were also dead. I have also been told of concern that one of Lionel's forenames related to European Jewry. As I grew older there was never any mention of these other grandparents, nothing of their achievements or the artistic and creative talents of which they had made good use. I was aware of Lionel's sister Rachel but not of other paternal relatives. It was as if these two had created themselves. Was there a door which could be unlocked, or a tunnel to crawl through, to find evidence of other family attitudes? I was ignorant of cousins who, I now realise, shared some of my thinking. In fact, as I was to discover, they certainly did exist and were going about their daily lives in the same country.

By the time I had more contact with FG after Myrtle's death, she still did not fully approve of Lionel, even though he had founded and managed an aviation company, had led what became the second largest employer in Portsmouth during the war years, and was then hoping to develop a subsidiary in India. Had she forgotten her own father's early struggles which had enabled her present standing? She wanted me to follow that path to power and position (no dirty hands – that was what chauffeurs were for!). I have always liked to draw and create, though at the time I was only making models, and thinking of a mechanical engineering and designing future. The appeal of the FG objectives is understood. What Max Hastings has called 'the intoxication of access', being in touch with decision making at high level is also understood, but, with absorbing interests and the pursuit of knowledge, life can be satisfactory outside the privileged circle. Position isn't necessary for fulfilment. After much experience and experiment I have also realised that a strong constitution is essential to cope with the pressures of power. It also helps to be able to readily digest the associated victuals, including alcohol with its lubricating appeal. This is especially true in politics. Whether as part of the hereditary makeup, or the consequence of youthful exposure to amoebic dysentery, I have come to understand that my digestion functions much better with simple food and a tiny amount of alcohol. The prima donnas often hint that it is unmanly to mention health problems (but not in later life when their bodies may be reacting to earlier abuse).

Derogatory parlance taunts those not at their best under pressure with lacking guts. The detractors who use the colloquial meaning, i.e. accusations of lack of stamina, tenacity, forcefulness, etc, fail to realise that, if a person has to live with an imperfect or damaged gut, it takes considerable tenacity to survive. As with some other ailments, it may be that the afflicted person rather than the medical profession can best work out how to live with this difficulty. Whatever others say, it seems best to try and optimise a situation. When pressured situations have become unavoidable, I have learnt to cope by not making any demands on the alimentary canal. Water is sufficient for survival at meetings, though discipline is needed when other participants in discussions and negotiations are uncomfortable with sobriety.

What seemed to be a personal inclination to creative activities, with increasing doubts about the climb up the greasy pole, was much better suited to my constitution. Of course it's no good if the result is insufficient funds for survival, but existence can be satisfactory without the quantity of wealth which some now seek for other reasons. Often it's the power of money – control, deference, inclusion, invitations, position, possessions, not just the cash – which appeals. Ownership means control over others, like rank in the armed services. Success is measured in press articles or company reports by the figures achieved. Those figures can become more important than inherent interest in the product and respect for those who make it happen. Throughout an enterprise, status in the workplace may be allied to measurement of salary and bonus. It is how the system has developed. When we sold a small family company, we were glad that employees retained their jobs, and the products would continue, but again the measurement of the sale was through the amount received. Wealth potentially benefits us all when taxes are paid. Expenditure and consumption nurtures employment. Historic buildings and other artefacts are restored. When asked what he did, it is reported that my cousin, Nicholas Cayzer, replied that his job was to make money.[4] I know that his aims were much wider than his own satisfaction. A country must always be grateful for the work of such individuals and the wealth they generate, but there are also different ways of making use of human existence. A recently encountered definition of the word 'bohemian' is appropriate: 'They don't make wealth their priority. Money is only a means of survival so they can live for their arts/craft/music/literature.' Pablo Picasso commented: 'Art is emotional and that doesn't blend well with the hoops that Society tells us to jump through to reach a certain goal.'[5] FG wanted me to persevere through all those hoops. Perhaps this would have been easier if I had had more of her genes and attitude. I had enough Cayzer genes to understand the importance of sufficient money, but for many generations, as I was to discover, paternal forebears had worked with their hands as creative artists, craftsmen and engineers.

There were aspects of FG's concerns which were valid. Lionel, with his creative activities, did not keep adequate financial reserves to cope with all potential difficulties and disasters. Reading his optimistic and far-reaching post-war plans, the sources of finance seemed so secure - therefore why worry about the overdraft at the Portsmouth bank? Did he believe the time would come when the loans could all be paid back? When the problems, including death, came one after the other, and the agreed backing was not forthcoming for political reasons, the company was in trouble. FG may have felt 'I told you so' but, with massive ingenuity, the company was rescued by others and Lionel still managed to survive the years that followed. FG's relatives have been and have remained financially successful. Many family shareholders are grateful. The Cayzer companies are investing in and maintaining employment. The 2012 Annual Report of Caledonia Investments ('47% of whose share capital is collectively owned by the Cayzer family') states under principal risks: 'regularly monitor forecast liquidity against a range of potential scenarios, include a significant element of highly liquid investments'. Lionel's scenarios did not consider the possible actions of the 1945 Labour Government and there was no liquidity. The downside of caution is that employment opportunities can be hindered. Lionel's efforts, whilst not increasing family wealth, initiated the company which still flourishes and provides employment as Portsmouth Aviation. Enterprise is vital to a country's future. I like to think that those who try and lose out, deserve some gratitude and respect. The lesson from all these family experiences is not to discourage future generations from entrepreneurial activity, but to constantly remind them to maintain reserves and not to incur debt which they may not be able to repay. It has often been written that engineers make poor businessmen because they are more concerned with the product rather than the profit. This is that bohemian aspect. A recent Jubilee-related commentary on Britain suggested 'we are fantastic inventors but contribute without razor sharp commercial instincts'. Making things means materials and tools, probably machinery and factory costs, and wages. They still have to be met if demand slackens. It is rather different in, say, the financial or property-dealing worlds where there is not the cost of manufacturing. But such dealing usually does not produce so much employment. Some play safe, some take risks, and above us all tower the twin edifices of fate and luck. Grandfather Jellicoe could so easily not have survived on the Victoria in 1893 or at Tientsin in 1900. Great-grandfather James, Myrtle, even Nina, might have lived for many more years with today's medical knowledge and treatment. As in other families, the story could have been very different.

I have ended up with a muddled existence, no great success, so far not too many disasters, but looking back there are those stupid decisions and mistakes. Lessons have been learnt and it has not been an easy time for my interests. No one has made a long-term success of British-owned volume car production. If I had withstood the wrath of relatives, and had the courage to become a dealer and restorer of those glorious thoroughbred machines of past years built by craftsmen, the demands of the balance sheet could have conspired against the pleasures of long-term ownership. As to expenditure, there would have been conflicts with the wish, through marriage, to replace the family unit lost in 1945. There is a relevant comment in Harry Bingham's book *Stuff Matters*: 'Most entrepreneurs told me that they were either single or had relationships that failed or a partner of extraordinary forbearance. Marriages are best formed after the entrepreneurial furnaces have burned back a little.'[6] There is an internet reply to one of Will Hutton's *Observer* articles which seems to correctly sum up the years since I was a child: 'After 1945 Britain failed to implement a coherent industrial strategy as adopted by France, Germany and others. The ensuing mess of industrial relations led to Thatcherism and the British economy's collapse into the seductive arms of the financial sector. Behind this lies a pseudo aristocratic ethos amongst the elite, sponsored by the unreformed and socially unintegrated (non-) public schools. This ethos undervalues technical training and productive work whether in the boardroom or at the work bench. We need to reach out, collaborate and integrate with other nations, not hide in the cosy mindset of a British, or more often English, national identity which is long past its 'sell-by date'. As to the schools, the word I do query is 'unreformed'. There has been reform in the schools but it has not led to 'social integration'.[7] There is now more hope with developments like Jaguar and Land Rover and BMW's Mini, and as I write there may even be prospects for Bristol Cars.[8] These companies may now be Indian- and German-owned but there is employment for British engineers and others. Our son, involved in recently developed methods of interaction between humans as were alternate forebears (his grandfather in aviation and great-great-grandfather with the railways), has now integrated the transaction processing firm he founded into a much larger global company. (See Chapter 17) These hopeful happenings confirm that there is a future for the country's skills if we reach out and collaborate with other nationals. And, as it happens, those (non-) public schools are also reaching out for other nationals as their pupils! Ironically this may be their route to survival having foregone the attempts at 'social integration' which many would have preferred.

The circumstances of my adolescence stimulated thought. The repeated admonitions to stop questioning, and the banishing of any discussion about my mother and her life, fuelled my enquiring mind. When, after experiencing life in other countries and on the factory floor in England, I reached the edge of the political arena, I perceived the dilemma which remains today. Which has priority? The needs and concerns of constituents, so evident to those who listen, or the demands of the Party? We must be grateful to those who are able to navigate this thorny path at whatever cost to their integrity. Older entrants, who may have built a business or have professional knowledge, and come in to offer what they have learnt as a service to their fellows, are especially valuable. I decided that it was not for me. It seemed better, after all the early deaths and being realistic about my own physical constitution, to try and establish a more stable platform from which future generations could advance. There were plenty of other dilemmas encountered within the industrial and educational arenas. Comments from the sidelines have only limited value. What matters is what can actually be achieved whilst in there coping with ever-changing events and the pressures from others. But I still hope the record of what I have experienced and observed may be helpful. It is part of my nature to continue trying to contribute. Despite the efforts of philosophers, scientists and other thinkers, humanity is still not clear about the origins of the Universe. St Augustine's 'out of nothing' is so hard to conceive and yet I believe we have to cope with 'nothing' after death. If the thoughts of a lifetime are to be written down, this must be done whilst this is still possible. Behaviour and attitudes have been accepted by tribal hierarchies and groups because they serve the aspirations of the leadership. Of course it's more comfortable to follow the crowd, but I still conclude there is value in asking questions. There is also regret that none of the family is involved in the remaining enterprises still including the Balfour name herein described. The difficulties encountered underline the achievement of the Cayzers and of other families like the Donaldsons and the Gaggeros which are also mentioned.

LEARNING FROM DIFFERENCE

Chapter 2

Balfour. Hutchison. Ogilvie. Maxwell

My father, Lionel Balfour,[1] never talked about his father or other relatives. But then this sort of conversation did not flow when I was staying at his second wife's houses. Born in December 1905, Lionel was eight years old when his father, Maxwell, died at Felixstowe in 1914. Any memories would have been of a sick man who was often away battling with tuberculosis at Berck Plage on France's Channel coast. He would have had little opportunity to talk about his Balfour, Hutchison, Maxwell and Ogilvie forebears. This is confirmed in a 1945 letter from his Great-aunt Minnie Ogilvie then aged 86, his grandmother Rachel's sister: 'I am shocked at your abysmal ignorance of your immediate family.' Minnie's book *A Scottish Childhood*, her other memoirs[2] and a cousin Nancy Balfour's correspondence with Lionel's sister, another Rachel, in 1988 were the keys to unlocking the door. Towards the end of her life this Rachel did refer to her father, having been made aware from her mother of his struggles with poor heath. FG was doing what she thought best, but instinct told me that I did not want to reject the Balfours and I knew nothing of these other relatives. It would have been preferable to have been able to grow up aware of all the genes possibly inherited than to have been, as it seemed, bombarded by the aura of the maternal family's achievements. The Royal Navy, like other forms of public service, has a proud tradition, but this has to be paid for by other activities. Researching the paternal family led me to discover determined engineers, merchants and traders who had coped with death and misfortune, often the companion of adventurous entrepreneurial activity. Others had been talented artists and musicians. They had not been employees seeking the relative safety of power and position within the Establishment hierarchy. Lionel's boxes contained more than the papers which helped in writing *Spithead Express*[3]. In keeping every letter and document it seems as if he was trying to make up for what he felt he could not discuss, perhaps also seeking to justify what others had questioned. There was then contact with a cousin, Charles Balfour, living in Italy. He is the grandson of one of my great-grandfather's brother's, another Charles, who went to America, and therefore Lionel's generation. He told me about the Ogilvie Godfrey family tree[4] on the internet compiled by Rachel Godfrey. I now know that we share a common heritage. Rachel Godfrey's great-grandparents John Ogilvie and Anne Maxwell are my great-great-grandparents. Other internet sites have also been helpful.

i) Ancestors and cousins

If you look at the Ordnance Survey map of Fife (OS No 59) you should find Middlefoodie west of Dairsie. We know that this was the dwelling of a John Balfour in the 17th century. This John is the top of the family tree at the back of the book. We do not know who he married but he had a son, John Patrick who married Margaret Lyall from St. Andrew's nearly three hundred and fifty years ago in 1666. They then lived at Leuchars. John and Margaret had three sons, James on the left of the tree, Alexander and Thomas. This James, who married Janet Farmer in 1722, was the ancestor of the Balfours who are the forebears and relatives of the author. Their lives are recorded in the pages to come.

The connection to other Balfours is not clear. Www.denmylne.co.uk/hist/balfour.html is recommended. This states that 'the name is derived from the lands of Balfour in the parish of Markinch. Bal-Orr is the original referring to the River Orr (now Ore) a tributary of the River Leven. The remains of Balfour Castle are just south of Milton of Begonie with Balfour mains further south nearer the river. Balbirnie, west of Markinch and many places in the northeast of Fife towards the shore of the River Tay have Balfour associations back to the 13th century. These include Fernie, Dunbog, Mountquhanie, Balmerino and Kirkton. These places are not far from Leuchars and Middlefoodie. Whilst there were very many Balfours in Fife, it seems probable that there was some relationship with known ancestors at the top of the tree. The Web also gives details of the Balfours at Westary and Trenabie in the Orkneys.

Before writing about the descendants of James and Janet Farmer I want to mention the descendants of James's brothers, Alexander and Thomas who were to have many connections with their distant Balfour cousins in the following years. This Alexander, who married Anne Lowe in 1723 lived at Bruckley, just south of Leuchars. His great-grandson was the first Lord Kinross. There are unknowns about his brother Thomas, but we do know that he married Christian Watt in 1722. Was he the same Thomas who had married Helen Bowman earlier in 1713? This Thomas and Christian Watt had a son James in 1723. This James married Margaret Ednie, daughter of the above Alexander and Anne Lowe. It was these cousins, James and Margaret Ednie who were the forebears of Henry Balfour (founder of Henry Balfour & Co.), and his son, another Alexander Balfour (co-founder of the trading company Balfour Williamson). The reason for writing about the origin of these two companies is that our direct forebears were to become involved in their later development.

James and Margaret Ednie's son, another Alexander (1765-1855) moved across the Tay at the age of fifteen to take up an apprenticeship with a merchant firm. The City of Dundee was the receiving port for jute shipped back from East Bengal (now Bangladesh). Local merchants had discovered that, when treated with whale oil, jute fibre could be spun as a strong and versatile material for mats, ropes and sacks. This led to the building of the jute mills. Engineering trades, railways and the increase in ship-building followed. Alexander eventually became leader of the Council as Provost from 1826 to 1828. Balfour Street near the University of Dundee remains to this day. In the corridors of the Dundee Hilton there are pictures of that era. There is no female presence. There are photographs of the docks with cargoes being unloaded. The impression is of a vibrant city playing its part in the developing world. Alexander's first marriage was to another cousin, Anne Balfour. (She died young and the connection has not been established). Their son, Henry, purchased the Durie Foundry at Leven in 1817 when he was only 21. The company's early products included stoves, kettles, cast-iron boilers and water pipes, often for Canada. In

1923 Henry married Agnes Bisset whose father had helped finance the foundry when established in 1810. The company was renamed Henry Balfour and Company. Their ironwork skills extended to many trades and by the 1840s they were building ships in their own yard at Methill. The company, as Pflaudler Balfour, is still at Leven today.[5] Henry and Agnes's younger son, Robert, worked with the Gourlay Brothers, sons of Henry's sister, another Margaret, who began building steam engines and locomotives at Dundee and also went on to build ships.

It was Henry and Agnes's elder son, another Alexander, born 1824, who initiated the Balfour Chilean connection. After working with his father at Leven, in 1844 he joined Stephen Williamson in Liverpool where they established a trading office. They had both been at Madras College, St Andrews. With David Duncan the three of them bought the 304 tonne barque 'The Gardner' to trade with South America. Balfour Williamson was established with an office in Valparaiso. The Company papers, now kept at University College, record their interests in 'most Chilean imports and exports including copper, nitrates and wool with some business in Peru'. There is a book written by L C Derrick-Jehu about the Anglo-Chilean community in the nineteenth century: 'There was no other country in the world, which was never part of the British Empire, where British associations and sympathies were so strong. Transactions are in sterling using the English language.' Balfour Williamson prospered. In 1856, twelve years later, Alexander and his partners commissioned his father, Henry, to build a bigger three-masted barque at Methill for the voyages round Cape Horn. The remains of this ship survive in South Australia today.[6] Other ships were built by the Gourlay cousins. When David Duncan left the partnership in 1863, the name of the Valparaiso branch was changed to Williamson Balfour. Now part of Inchcape, this name is still used for the enterprise which distributes BMW and Rolls Royce cars in Chile. In 1864 Alexander had married Jessie Roxburgh, daughter of the Reverend Dr. Roxburgh, whose family was known to both Ogilvies and Maxwells and mentioned in the letters they have left. Alexander is remembered as a concerned philanthropist in later life, putting the wealth from trade to good use both in Chile and back in England. His efforts are marked by a statue in the north-east corner of St John's gardens in Liverpool.[7]

Turning back to my own forebears, James and Janet Farmer on the left side of the family tree, we know that their son, John Balfour 1730-1811, my four times great-grandfather, imported timber from Scandinavia. Many trees had been cut down to build the navy's ships and there was a demand for wood. Charles Balfour has established that the timber was landed at Kirkcaldy and then transported to the Balfour saw-mill at Leven (Methill port was not developed until the end of the century). This John married Jean Wilson and they lived in a house on the saw-mill site. The family wanted to expand their activities but the local landowners did not sell their estates. Instead John leased Cameron and Wellsgreen Farms to the west of Methill. His son William (1767-1839), who married Alison Mitchell, continued with the saw-mill, John Balfour and Co, and also became tenant of the Bankhead Farm north-east of Leven. Of their sons John (1796-1867), who did not marry, worked on at the company in Leven and also built Elm Park, later Elmslea, a new house on Links Road. The second son, my great-great-grandfather James (1803-1876), married Isabella Hutchison, daughter of Alexander a flour miller in Kirkcaldy. Whilst Elmslea was still a base in Leven, James leased Milton Farm near Leuchars. Later more land became available near to Leven at Letham Farm, Pilmuir and Pratis all to the north of the town and still in the parish of Scoonie. It is not known when the family gave up the lease of Bankhead, but it is recorded in an 1861 Kirkcaldy census that James then farmed a total of 429 acres. The open fields are on the higher ground back from the coast. There's no shelter and the winds sweep in from the North Sea. Visiting in late April it was bitingly cold even though the sun was shining from pale blue skies. It must have been bleak in winter. James and Isabella's sons, Great-grandfather James and his brothers, looking out across the water seem likely to have been aware of the wider world and opportunities beyond what would have been available locally. By 1840 (when Provost Alexander would have been seventy-five years old) Dundee was the home port for over 300 ships.

ii) James Balfour and Rachel Ogilvie

The industrial revolution was well under way with the city's engineering skills much in demand. By 1859, when Great-grandfather James would have been sixteen, they were building steam engines and railway locomotives as well as the machinery for the jute mills. Did he decide that an engineering apprenticeship on the other side of the Tay would lead to good prospects? (There is no record, but as we know that Willie Ogilvie, see below, was at Gourlay Brothers and with the Balfour connection, it seems likely that this was also where he learnt his trade). By the time he had finished his training in 1865 he would surely have had many contacts with cousins and others in the city. Had he also met the then seventeen-year-old Rachel, daughter of solicitor John Ogilvie (son of James, grandson of John) and his wife Anne Maxwell? Alexander would then have been back from Chile as a partner based in the Liverpool office of Balfour Williamson. He would have had contact with Dundee where ships for the company were being built by both Henry Balfour and Gourlay Brothers. It was also at that time that James's one-year-younger brother, Robert, who would have been twenty years old in 1864, started in that Liverpool office, probably because he had met these other Balfours, Williamsons, and possibly Guthries at Madras College. Robert would have learnt of the development of the Chilean railway system. He may have talked to his older brother, James, about the opportunities in Chile for a trained engineer and it seems likely that there would have been other conversations with family and friends who all knew each other and moved in the same circles.

There is a photograph of James inscribed 'Dundee January 1866'. As Balfour Lyon was established that same year, 1866, following on from Lyon Hermanos, James must have gone to Chile after that photo was taken. The unanswered question is whether he travelled on the same boat as Alexander and his wife Jessie, whose voyage out is also confirmed as 1866. As Great-grandfather James's brother Robert was already working at Liverpool, it seems likely that they were travelling together. The date of that voyage tells us that Alexander was there in Valparaiso at the time of the start of Balfour Lyon.[10] Lyon was another prominent Dundee family. We know that George and William Lyon had set out for Valparaiso some forty years earlier to investigate business prospects. George married into a well-known Chilean family[9]. Carmen Santa Maria was his bride in 1830. Their son was another William. The two Lyon brothers prospered. Their enterprise became Lyon Hermanos, shipping agents, in 1846 (Hermanos means brother). Alexander may have helped with introductions and Williamson Balfour may have provided investment. We also know that George Lyon died in 1866 and his older brother, William, had gone back to England. So George's son, the younger William, was on his own at Lyon Hermanos. James seems to have arrived at a good time bringing valuable skills resulting from his engineering apprenticeship. William Lyon also had all the connections through his mother's Santa Maria family. Meanwhile James's five-years-younger brother Thomas, known as Thomas Cutlar, was also training as an engineer. He joined James and William Lyon before 1870. It was a period of growth. Those Chilean railways were being extended nearly three-quarters the length of that long country from Arica in the north to Puerto Mont in the south, some two thousand miles.

With Thomas in position with Balfour Lyon, James, after five years in Valparaiso, made a return visit to Scotland in 1871. If he and Rachel Ogilvie had met earlier, had she been waiting for him, or did they first meet that year? They were married in Dundee on 20th September, a union that both led to my existence through their second son and grandson and had a profound significance for the future of Balfour Lyon[11]. James and Rachel returned to Valparaiso. Balfour Lyon prospered as iron founders. Their engineering and metal work was much in demand for the railways and other machinery. During the next seven years three sons were born, Charles Frederick, known as Fred, in 1872; Maxwell, my grandfather, in 1874; and Percy in 1876. Then came the start of difficulties which had consequences for the family over the next hundred years. Rachel's younger sister, Minnie, takes up the tale both in the memoirs written in 1916 and 1943 and in her book written in 1952: 'In 1877 Rachel showed signs of consumption, a disease that had already proved fatal to two members of her family. She was advised to go to Arequipa, a Peruvian city 8,000 feet above sea level where the air is pure. The three boys joined her there with their two nurses in the spring of 1877. My mother (Minnie's father had died by then) decided to take my sister Mia and me, aged fourteen and eighteen, to be with Rachel. On August the 17th that year my brother Willie saw us off at Southampton on the Royal Mail steamer Tasmania.'[12]

Searching for the Tasmania, I could only find a ship of that name built in 1884 and eventually worked out that their ship was the Tasmanian (Minnie was writing over seventy years later) built on the Clyde in 1858. It was 2,250 tons and had been re-fitted with compound steam engines in 1871. Speed was 12 knots, which meant twenty-two days to Colon in Panama after calling at Barbados and Jamaica. Then it was across the Isthmus on the railway completed in 1855 at the cost of so many lives due to fever and construction difficulties. The Orroya took them down the coast of America to Callao. James met them there and, whilst they waited for the next ship, took them on the steam railway, opened in 1851, to visit the Peruvian capital, Lima. Then it was a voyage along the coast to Mollendo and another railway, opened in 1871, to take them up 8,000 feet to Arequipa. As Minnie wrote: 'Rachel was there to greet us and the next morning the eldest grandson, a little boy of six, i.e. Fred, joined us'. They all rode on horses to the house James and Rachel had rented at Savandia four miles out of the city, overlooked by the extinct volcano Misti. Minnie comments: 'The next six months were delightful, riding, swimming in the open air baths, and plenty of young men of sorts.' James still had to be in Valparaiso but joined them when he could, leaving his brother Thomas to look after the affairs of Balfour Lyon. For those interested in nineteenth-century transport, research suggests that he would have had two options. By sea it would have taken at least sixty hours direct to Mollendo, longer calling at ports en route. Being involved with the railways, did James go by train to Arica, say twenty-five hours for the one thousand miles averaging 40mph, then the much shorter sea trip from Arica to Mollendo? As the railway up to Arequipa would have been the same, it seems the journey could have been done in less then half the time if partly overland.[13] James must have been a kindly man. His visits to his sons and ailing wife would have been precious, but he still spared time to take Minnie and Mia to La Paz, the capital of Bolivia. The train took them to Puno (this line had only been completed a year earlier), then it was across Lake Titicaca by steamer and, in those days, a coach with two horses and six mules on to La Paz. Minnie comments: 'It was bitterly cold on the coach. Ice was thick on the ground and the wind was sharp. We noticed a woman ploughing with a wooden plough.' After this trip they left Savandia and James rented a town house in Arequipa.

Sadly Rachel's condition did not improve. She died in July 1878. Two months later they went back to Valparaiso where they all stayed in nearby Vino del Mar. Rachel's tomb, still in good order, is in the Cementerio de Disidentes. In March 1879 James seems to have decided that the three boys should be taken back to Scotland by their grandmother and aunts. At first they all stayed with son and brother George Ogilvie (married to Harriet Gordon) in their house at Broughty Ferry.[14] George had taken over the family solicitors after John Ogilvie's death. Mia, Minnie, and their mother then decided to settle in Clifton, partly looking ahead to the education of the three boys and partly because Willie (the Ogilvie brother who had seen them off from Southampton) had become a partner in a Bristol agricultural engineering business.[15] Summer holidays were spent with their Balfour grandmother, Isabella, at Letham Farm. After her death in 1885 they stayed with their aunt, another Isabella, Mrs Mclean, James's younger sister, at Haveney House, Leven. Minnie comments: 'Long summer days on the Links by the Firth of Forth returning ravenously hungry for glorious teas. Aunt Tibbie's home-made scones and strawberry jam were never forgotten.'

James stayed on in Chile with Thomas as their enterprise continued to thrive. A well-documented internet entry confirms that in the last quarter of the nineteenth century, Balfour Lyon had two well-appointed steam factories employing six hundred workmen and that they were the third or fourth largest producer of rolling-stock for the Chilean railways. Willie Ogilvie's partnership in Bristol wasn't working out. He had lost some of his capital and decided to accept a position as a draughtsman back in Scotland, where he would still have had contacts. As he himself wrote: 'I took a gloomy view of my prospects.' In another 1910 memoir just after her mother Anne's death, Minnie wrote: 'Willie was about to start another new job in Leith. I remember well that evening (this would then have been thirty years earlier) with his boxes all strapped in the hall. Something happened which made him leave for Leith with only a small bag. This was a letter from James Balfour offering him a good position with Balfour Lyon with the possibility of becoming a partner. Thus in a moment did the tide of fortune turn in his favour'. James wasn't just being kind to Rachel's family. He would have met her six-years-younger brother in the period before their wedding. He would have learnt that Willie had completed a tough and thorough six-year apprenticeship (6.00am - 6.00pm) at Gourlay Brothers[16]. Here was an engineer with the skills and experience needed in Valparaiso. James may also have thought that Willie could help Thomas to keep the family interest in Balfour Lyon if he was to spend more time back in England with his sons.

In a pleasing memoir Willie describes his arrival in the steamship Galicia in March 1882: 'James Balfour came on board to meet me and I went to stay with him and Tom at Vino del Mar.' Great-grandfather James did return to England in late 1883, worked in the Balfour Lyon office in London and lived in a flat in the recently built Queen Anne's Mansions in Westminster. This was a then state-of-the-art 14-storey building with hydraulic lift appropriate for an engineer. James visited his sons at Mia, Minnie and their mother's house in Clifton at the weekends, but he then also died in November 1884 at Guy's Hospital, only six years after Rachel and only forty-two years old. The death certificate records 'nephritis, enlarged and dilated heart' as cause of death. Nephritis affects the kidneys and the heart problem is self-explanatory. We do not know whether this was the result of so much hard work or whether he had picked up a particular infection. He was buried in Kensal Green Cemetery between the Harrow Road and the railway line into Paddington. Despite the loss of Rachel, he had, as confirmed in his Will, achieved so much in those 17 years in Chile. Brother John Balfour and brother-in-law George Ogilvie 'both based in Scotland, were amongst those to whom probate was granted with 'power being reserved' for bringing in William Ogilvie and two other brothers, Robert and Thomas, if required. Ten thousand pounds (the equivalent of over a million in 2012) was 'to be set aside and held for behoof of each of the three sons,' but 'his share and interest in Balfour Lyon and Company or any other firm in South America of which I may be a partner to remain in said firm or respective firms until the Executors consider it for the advantage of my estate that the same be uplifted and realised. They also to have full power to arrange with surviving partners as to the time and manner when my share should be withdrawn.' Willie Ogilvie became a full partner in 1886.

My great-grandparents, Rachel and James, were not to know that their three sons would all be dead by 1918. None of them had become involved in Balfour Lyon or Henry Balfour and Co. How much had they known about the source of their capital? Looking back it seems that Imperial Service was lauded as a paramount duty without sufficient discussion of where the money came from. Perhaps, and this may not have been helped by the lack of parental guidance, they may not have realised that the opportunities offered by the new industrial machinery in the nineteenth century were not going to be repeated. Why was the need to continue their father and uncle's efforts not seen as a priority? The enterprises and the wealth created needed to be carefully guarded. Charles Frederick became head of the school at Clifton and won a scholarship to Corpus Christi College, where he achieved a first in Classics, the study of the civilisations of Greece and Rome, an Oxford speciality over many centuries. He also became a rugby 'blue'. In her book *The Fishing Fleet* Anne De Courcy describes how the Indian Civil Service took the cream of Oxbridge graduates: 'In an average year two hundred graduates competed for around forty places.' Fred achieved second place in the examinations for his year. Standards were high and members of the ICS were nicknamed 'The Incorruptibles.' In 1895 Fred married Sybil Barker, sister of a friend at Oxford, and they had two sons, Philip and Ronald. In time Fred was appointed assistant magistrate for the area around Agra and Oudh, south east of Delhi. Minnie Ogilvie described what followed: 'With his fine sensitiveness Fred realised that he did not make Sybil happy and believed there was another who could satisfy her where he had failed. There was no break. Quietly and deliberately he took himself away, relinquishing career, children and life itself for her sake. Who will say that Fred's sacrifice was in vain?' Minnie asked a question which is still difficult to answer. Consider that divorce meant disgrace and that relationship with another whilst still married would have been difficult in that society. Despite his brilliance, he was caught by the taboos of that time. They could not just go their separate ways. Fred was steeped in the Classics, aware of the concept of a noble death, perhaps like many believing in some form of continuing existence - even reunion with James and Rachel – and there may have been further reasons why, again in Minnie's words, 'he died by his own hand' at Lucknow in August 1907. After consultation with cousins, including his grandchildren and great-grandchildren, we like to record his unselfish action as a contrast to today's often 'me first' society.

Fred's Will, dated November 1896, left the capital in trust with income to be paid to Sybil, but, if she were to have a second marriage, the trustees were to divide the capital between the children when they attained the age of 21. Probate was granted in 1908 with a net value of £21,415 (which equates to about £2 million in 2012). There is a Charles Frederick Balfour scholarship set up by Philip in his father's memory at Clifton. Sybil married James Craik the following year, and they are known to have been happy together. Both Balfour sons went into the armed services. Ronald served in the Navy and married Anne Smith. Their son, Hugh, married Sheila Weldon and retired as Rear Admiral after a distinguished career. He had served on the Royal Yacht Britannia from 1972 to 1974. In 1977 he commanded a small task force which helped to deter early Argentinian aggression against the Falklands and then in the 1982 campaign, when in command of Exeter, he directed the successful firing of the new 'Sea Dart' missile. From 1985 he commanded the Sultan of Oman's Navy for five years. Hugh and Sheila's son, Edward, now in Australia, has Charlie and two daughters, Catherine, and Louise, who has helped so much with and has given encouragement to this research. Both Ronald and Anne's daughters – Jenifer, married to Donald Phillips, and Ursula, married to John Mackenzie also a Rear Admiral - have sons.

Philip, Fred and Sybil's older son, born in 1898, was in France from 1916 to 1918 as a subaltern in the Royal Artillery. His 80-page handwritten memoir of those years comments on the sheer luck of survival. He admitted that 'the gunners had nothing like the continuous hardship and danger which was the lot of the infantry. Every gunner knows that.' But his words still record the deaths of many of his fellow officers and men, plus his own near-fatal experience:

'Just as I started to go (to give important new orders to the Battery) an infantry Captain advised me to wait to avoid fire from approaching enemy infantry. But I insisted and he told me to be quick. So I started to gallop as hard as I could. I heard a shot and then another very close and I could feel my horse had been hit as he staggered. However he went gallantly on. We galloped about 100 yards or so when he slowed and I had to get off. I found he had been shot in the throat. I stuffed his wound with my handkerchief but immediately a great gush of blood pushed it off. We walked on a bit then he fell dead by the side of the road. I owe my life to that horse who had refused to give up after such a bad wound. I then walked on to the village where a Brigadier stopped me and asked what had happened. It was not till then that I discovered that I was covered in blood.'

After 1918 Philip also survived 'Spanish flu', was posted to Egypt and during the next war became a Major General attached to the Indian army. In 1946 he was in Germany as director of civil affairs for the military government of the British Army of the Rhine. His last position before retirement in 1953, as Lieutenant General Sir Philip, was Commander in Chief of Northern Command. I was at Catterick in 1952 as a lowly National Service trooper. I regret that we did not meet then or later. He married Marjorie Rugge-Price, but there were no children.

Max, my grandfather, became an artist, his work interrupted by service – imperial duty again – in the Boer War. Quoting from Lionel Curtis's forward to Minnie's book: 'When he left Oxford, he went to the Slade and there made friends with Augustus John who told me that had Max lived he would have been in the front rank of modern artists. It was not to be, for he died of tuberculosis to which his mother had fallen victim'. Max's painting, *The Rape of the Sabine Women*, won first prize in a competition at the Slade. Minnie wrote that his work had an intimate charm, which corresponded with the charm of his character. We still have some of his paintings. In his earlier life there had been periods of what Minnie called 'overstrain' when Max had to be 'under medical care for a time'. In 1904 he married my grandmother, Nina Joachim, whose family are described in the next chapter. At first they lived at Max's studio, 118 Cheyne Walk, Chelsea, but then moved to Thurlow House, Golf Road, Felixstowe. They had two children, my father Lionel, and his sister Rachel. Max died in September 1914. His Will, signed at Berck Plage in 1910, left the capital in trust to be divided between them when they reached the age of 25. Probate was granted in 1915 with a net value of £12,795. Half that sum, with the increase in value, would have meant that Lionel would have received about £10,000 at the end of 1929 when he was 25. (£10,000 in 1929 is reckoned to be worth about half a million pounds in 2012.)

Rachel married Wilfrid Tatham, competitor in both the 1924 and 1928 Olympic Games and house-master at Eton. He served with the Coldstream Guards in both World Wars. Awarded the MC (after a recommendation for the VC) for his part in the battle of the Canal du Nord in 1918, a year after he left Eton, he was wounded and taken prisoner in 1942, escaped in Italy, was recaptured and taken to Germany. He later worked for the British Council in Athens and Brussels. Rachel also had some health problems and they had no children. In retirement they lived in St Helena, first at Woodcot then, after Wilfrid's death, Rachel moved to Longwood Farmhouse which had been refurbished for Napoleon's aide de camp, Count Bertrand. Rachel wrote nearly a hundred letters, some about St Helena life, others with appreciated insights into the family character: 'The Bishop and the ex-Governor are both keen churchmen but don't seem to hold it against me that I am not;' 'as there is no crematorium here, ashes can't be scattered to the winds in the sensible way;' 'I'm afraid I'm an up and down person, it's that Joachim blood, you may be much the same;' 'as family we are loners, not good at compromising when working with others.' It was helpful to read these and many other wise words though better still if they had been received years earlier! Rachel's portion from her two grandfathers' efforts was not all lost and what remained came to me and my sister Karen, who is married to Fabyan Evans. They have children – Nigel, Jessica and Alexander – and grandchildren. We have two daughters – Juliet, married to Jonathan Bench with three sons (Tom, Sebastian and Hugo) and Kate, married to Harry Morley with a son Samuel and a daughter Rose – and one son, another Max, married to Ay Rachawat with a daughter, Josephine, and a son – another Alexander Balfour.

James and Rachel's third son, Percy, joined the Army, leaving Sandhurst in 1895 when he went to India and was involved in the siege of the British Garrison at Malakand on the North West Frontier in 1897. After some years' further service in the Highland Light Infantry he left the Army and worked in the City. In 1907 he married Maude Browne whose family lived at Hoburne near Christchurch. Percy's Will, drawn up in June 1909, gives his address as Wisset Hall, Halesworth, Suffolk. This means that they would have bought or leased the house soon after their marriage and there are pictures of the two children, Betty and Ken, as babies and growing up. When war came Percy re-enlisted, survived the first years and returned to a training command in England. Towards the end of 1917 he volunteered for the front again. He was appointed to command a battalion of the Worcestershire Regiment. Willie Ogilvie's memoir tells us that early morning on 12th December Percy was checking positions before an attack. A German sniper was doing his duty and that was the end of the three Balfour brothers. He was buried at the Sorel Cemetery. Percy and his father James were the same age when they died. Probate for his Will, net value £11,303, was granted in April 1918 with benefit to the children when they were 21, and to the children of Charles Frederick and Maxwell if Ken and Betty did not survive to 21. The address given was 57 Hampstead Way, (off the Finchley Road and adjacent to Hampstead Heath), Middlesex, formerly of Wisset Hall. From the ages of Betty and Ken, it looks as if Wisset had been kept till the middle of the war, probably 1916 when they moved to London. As with so many, these children were to lose the benefit of nurture by both parents. Maude stayed on in Hampstead and became involved with the work of the church of St Jude-on-the-Hill. Parish magazines show that she was a member of the Parochial Council and leader of the Girls' Club. Percy's name is on the church's Roll of Honour unveiled on Easter Day 1918. The Stock Exchange War Memorial, unveiled in October 1922 (as it happened by the once Prime Minister A J Balfour, then City of London MP), also has the name of Percy Balfour, DSO Major, temporary Lieut Colonel. In 1933 Maude returned to Hoburne to live with her brother, Brigadier General Browne. He had served in France, Egypt and the Middle East from 1914 to 1918, subsequently commanding the 14th/20th King's Hussars in the early 1920s and then the Iraq Levies until retirement in 1933. He died in 1968 aged 90. Another brother was killed in the war and it was his son, Peter, who was second-in-command of the 14th/20th when I was at Sabratha (see Chapter 10). Maude was President of the Christchurch Division of the Red Cross from 1936-1957. She was also organiser of the Christchurch Women's Voluntary Service during the war. After her death in the 1963, a Maude Balfour Memorial Fund helped to build a medical loan depot in Waterford Road, Highcliffe.

Maude and Percy's daughter, Elizabeth Marian Maxwell Balfour, known as Betty, stayed in London. After training as a secretary, she became a teacher, played tennis to a high standard and worked with the Girl Guides. When war came she returned to Hampshire, joined her mother's division of the Red Cross and at first worked as a mobile member of the Voluntary Aid Detachment, known as the VAD. Later she used her training as secretary and personal assistant to the Branch President, then Lady Malmsbury. She also took charge of the headquarters stores and helping to train young recruits. In 1946 she was appointed County Director for Hampshire and remained in this position for 44 years. Under her direction the Hampshire branch organised camps for Hungarian refugees in 1956 and for Vietnamese refugees in 1979. Another achievement was annual first-aid cover at the Farnborough Air Show. She would have been present when the Aerocar was displayed at the 1948 Show, but she may not have been aware of the work of her first cousin, Lionel. Both activities were partially funded by James's efforts in Chile. She was awarded the OBE for her very many years of devoted toil and became a serving sister of the Order of St John. Winchester Cathedral was full for her memorial service in March 1998. The attendance list included 400 names including the Lord Lieutenant and the chair of the County Council. I found myself thinking of her grandparents 120 years earlier, Rachel at Arequipa struggling with tuberculosis in her lungs and with just four more months of life, James trying to cope, and with the three young boys, none of them with any inkling of the scene in the cathedral that afternoon. Percy and Maude would also have been proud. Field Marshal Sir John Stanier gave the address and commented: 'Betty was quite simply the most determined woman I ever met. She would never take No for an answer. She was a constant driving force at Headquarters and would never give up.' It's good if future generations can be aware of these powerful genes (Robert too) in the paternal family. It is not surprising that there were clashes with FG. Betty's younger brother, Ken, was another talented games player who had been racquets champion at Harrow. He went out to Kenya. There are accounts of his prowess at golf, and he was runner-up in the Rift Valley Championship at Njoro in 1931. He was then wounded in his right arm serving in the East African Armoured Car Regiment in 1940. He did not have Betty's driven personality, but seems to be one of those who gave pleasure to others by his presence. Denied a post-war sporting career by his injury, he became manager of the Mombasa Club for many years. A Google review of the Club in 2011 records 'wonderful ambience, very friendly staff, comfortable rooms sea facing.' Neither Betty or Ken had descendants, but many other children and young people were helped by their presence in the world. What remains from Betty's share of James's legacy is now the Balfour Historic Museum Trust, which supports charitable organisations, particularly education, heritage, conservation, arts and culture, in Hampshire.[25] A recent substantial donation has been to the refurbishment of the Old Learning Centre at Winchester Cathedral, now known as the Resource Centre. The work of repair and extension continues with much skill and care over the choice of materials. Whilst James might have preferred the money to return to Fife, I am glad to find myself thinking of my great-grandfather each time I walk in to Winchester. Some of these nineteenth-century merchants and traders returned to Britain and bought estates in England and Scotland. James and his sons were denied this option by early death. His grandchildren decided to use their inheritance in different ways, and as an example in this county, Hampshire, there has been a considerable paternal side contribution; Betty's efforts, the Museum Trust and Resource Centre, the employment provided by Portsmouth Aviation and the development of the Ryde Airport site, all stemming from those years of hard work in Chile. All in all this may have been a better contribution to humanity than concentration on one Estate.

iii) The other Balfour brothers and sisters
Great-great-grandfather James and three of his younger brothers Robert, John and Thomas (known as Thomas Cutlar) established or continued three manufacturing and trading companies in the 19th century. They also played a major part in the development and survival of Henry Balfour (now Pfaudler Balfour) and Balfour Williamson established by their distant cousins. In view of personal experience, it may be worth recording that all made their way by the 'University of Life' rather than extended study. Thomas returned to Scotland, not least because he learnt that Henry Balfour and Company was becoming short of Balfour family input. Henry, the developer of Durie foundry, had died in 1854. Of his three sons, Robert, the marine engineer who had also liaised with Gourlays, died in 1863 and Henry Thomas in 1891. Alexander of Balfour Williamson had died in 1886. His widow, Jessie, provided a loan to her father-in-law's company at a critical time with her late husband's partner, Stephen Williamson, watching over her position. In 1895 Henry Balfour and Co was dissolved and a new limited company was incorporated. Amongst other local businessmen, three of Great-grandfather James's brothers – John, Robert and Thomas Cutlar back from South America – became directors and remained on the board until their respective deaths. James's wife's nephew, Alexander Hutchison, was another investor, later a director, also an Archibald Bowman. He was presumably a relative of the Helen Bowman who may have been the first wife of Thomas Balfour at the beginning of

the 18th century. Robert Bisset Creeke, son of Agnes Bisset's sister, Isabella, was another director, but Henry Thomas's son and Alexander's nephew, Harry Robert, sold his stake in the new limited company. None of Alexander and Jessie's sons was involved. Frederick managed the Dawyck estate which Jessie purchased in 1897, the year in which second son, Ernest, died aged only twenty-three. Fred collected trees from around the world including the time he spent in North America with Balfour Guthrie. Dawyck Botanic Garden is now open to the public. The third son, Archibald Roxburgh, born only three years before Alexander died, remained working with Balfour Williamson. Alexander and Jessie also had three daughters.

Thomas Cutlar, with all his relevant ironwork experience, became chairman of Henry Balfour and Co. It was at this time that he built Carbery House and helped to finance the building of the Innerleven Golfing Society clubhouse. He died in 1900. John became secretary and was to serve the company for 30 years until his death in 1926. His son, another Thomas, became managing director in the 1920s. Robert had influence as a substantial shareholder and was even asked to be chairman in 1924. By then he would have been 80 and living in the south of England so that it can be understood why he declined the invitation. John, only then 78, became chairman. He was followed by Alexander Wilson. This Alexander died shortly after his appointment and my great-great-grandmother Isabella's nephew already mentioned, Alexander Hutchison, then became chairman in 1926. In 1933 Henry Balfour and Co, still led by Alexander Hutchison, negotiated a joint venture with the American Pfaudler Company to make glass-lined steel vessels in Leven. Throughout the 1930s the company expanded its products for the gas industry, for paper production, for sugar refining and many other aspects of chemical engineering. In the Second World War the company was contracted to make wings for Hurricane fighters. By 1941 they had three factories with a total output of around twelve pairs of wings each week. They also constructed landing craft and gun carriages. In 1962 they became Pfaudler Balfour and celebrated their '200 years of engineering excellence' in 2010.

Thomas Cutlar had obviously had faith in Willie Ogilvie, having left him to cope in Chile whilst he led Henry Balfour and Company, but he had also kept in touch with Balfour Lyon business, twice visiting Valparaiso before he died. Willie's memoir tells of life in Chile in the 1890s, the houses, expeditions on horseback in the surrounding countryside and social and sporting activities. It describes in detail the early twentieth-century journeys back to South and North America. His daughter Elsie's memoir tells of Chile's war with Peru and Bolivia in the 1890s, of the white house at Miramar on the top of a hill with wonderful views and then moving to Salto and riding up into the hills and along the beaches. She describes the ideal climate: 'eight months of sunshine with showers at night to keep things fresh then about four months mostly rain.'[17]. There was also hard work and responsibility. A turn-of-the-century Kelly's directory lists Balfour Lyon as merchants, manufacturers and shippers. Their activities included agricultural implements, hardware merchandise, iron founders, machinery imports, mechanical engineering and railway rolling-stock. In 1884 the State had taken over the railways and continued expansion. The Santiago Railway Museum has some of the locomotives used over those long distances. These include an example of 'those designed by the North British Locomotive Company and assembled in Chile by Balfour Lyon'.[18] In 1900 came horrible news. Willie writes: 'Tom's death caused me great grief as he had been a good friend also some anxiety as he had a large amount of money in the business and this would naturally have to be paid out. However I then received a telegram saying I had been appointed residual legatee. After transferring a comparatively small sum, the remainder of his share in the business was transferred to me'. Truly the Balfours had helped the Ogilvies.[19] Willie also wrote that he then went to England and took over the London agency of the business himself. He returned to Chile in 1905, and then again in 1911, taking the train across the continent from Buenos Aires. The Balfour Lyon factory was hardly affected by the 1906 Valparaiso earthquake. In 1926 Willie noted that Balfour Lyon still prospered and that a little boy named Ross, with whom he had played on the Galicia in 1884, was now, 42 years later, manager in Valparaiso.

Great-grandfather James's next-younger brother Robert (already mentioned in connection with Henry Balfour and Co), after six years in the Liverpool Balfour Williamson office, went to San Francisco with Alexander Guthrie, Stephen Williamson's brother-in-law, in 1869. In the book *Heirs of Great Adventure* Robert is described thus: 'In him Stephen had found some-one almost as progressive and determined as him-self. His self confidence and enthusiasm were to lead him into conflict with his seniors from time to time, but his industry and vigour made him an excellent choice.'[20] Alexander and Robert reached New York before the end of March. The overland route was not yet open so it was then down the east coast, across the isthmus then up the west coast, reaching San Francisco on 22nd April 1869 by which time his older brother, Great-grandfather James, had been working in Valparaiso for three years. For most of May, Alexander and Robert travelled inland by stagecoach, covered wagon or on horseback, to learn about local conditions and needs. On 1st June they opened their first office in San Francisco opposite the Merchant's Exchange. Their trading began by exporting wheat and extended to fruit, salmon and timber. Imports included cement, chemicals, iron and manufactured goods. Insurance agencies were taken on and the Pacific Loan and Investment Company established to provide loans to farmers. The second office was at Portland in Oregon with further offices later at Tacoma, Seattle, Los Angeles, Vancouver in Canada, where a large warehouse was built in the harbour area, and finally New York. Robert married Josephine Beazley in 1881 and returned to the Liverpool office in 1893 after twenty-four years in North America. In 1900 Balfour Guthrie were reckoned to be the largest grain buyers in the world. Stephen Williamson had a serious illness in 1900 (and died in 1903). Robert moved to the London office and shared the running of all the Balfour Williamson companies with Stephen's eldest son Archibald Williamson, later Lord Forres.[21] Meanwhile Balfour Guthrie prospered through their involvement in the Californian and Lobitos oilfields and, in 1911, they financed the building of a cement factory on the shore of Bellingham Bay between Seattle and Vancouver. The company also purchased land at Brentwood, east of San Francisco, which became Brentwood Irrigated Farms after 1910. Balfour Guthrie planted orchards in 1922 and also sold plots of land. They then organised the packing and shipping of vast quantities of apricots, peaches and vegetables until they disposed of their last holding in 1943. A Balfour Road and a Balfour Guthrie Park remain today.

In 1906, aged sixty-two, Robert was elected as Liberal MP for the Partick division of Glasgow. He was thought to have little chance in that constituency. It was very tough; whatever line he took he was bound to offend somebody. But he campaigned with boundless energy. 'He is the most active man, with the most prolific mind, I ever saw,' Stephen Williamson had written earlier. After the second 1910 Election, Robert was back in the House of Commons with a majority of just 345 votes, but this result still kept him at Westminster throughout the war years. In 1918, his last Election, by then aged 74 and standing as a coalition Liberal, his majority was 6,983 votes[22]. In 1911 he had been made a Baronet and in 1913 he had bought Langham Hall in Essex, retaining 7 Prince's Gate as their London house[23]. One of the Rolls Royce books records the purchase of a 'Twenty' with Hooper body in 1923 and then a Hooper Laundaulette in 1929, the year he died. Sir Robert's three sons had died before he retired from Balfour Williamson at the end of 1926 when he was 82. To quote from *Heirs of a Great Adventure*: 'the withdrawal of Sir Robert's immense capital, the largest ever accumulated by a Partner and the only six-figure sum to go out without a son to bring some of it back into the business, was an event which could only be viewed with apprehension.' (just one million pounds in 1926 would be the equivalent of 47 million in 2012.) His second son, another Robert, had died in San Francisco from typhoid at the age of two-and-a-half and the oldest, Alexander, at a nursing home in Lancaster Gate in 1923 from problems resulting from his war service. The third son, Alan, had been commissioned in the Royal Artillery in 1916 and then joined the Royal Flying Corps as a pilot. He was killed in action on 18th January 1918 aged 24 just over a month after Percy. He was buried in the cemetery at Tincort. His name is on the Langham Village War Memorial.[24] Alexander had two daughters. Margaret married Jay Ashbrook and also had two daughters. Susan with two sons is now living in America. Kate Ashbrook is now president of The Ramblers and general secretary of the Open Spaces Society. Alexander's other daughter, Nancy, wrote for *The Economist*, received the OBE like her cousin Betty, and became a noted collector of contemporary art. In her will, Nancy left her collection to the Contemporary Art Society. Her obituary in *The Independent*, 17th September, 1997, commented on her character 'Balfour loved a good argument. When fellow guests took each other to pieces at her parties, she basked in the verbal fireworks. Behind the scenes she was indefatigable. Her ferocious intelligence and frank, sometimes even hectoring conversation, were a combination that could be daunting. She was a support and inspiration throughout the art world and beyond.'

In December 1889 John Balfour (1846-1926 and the next brother after Robert), sold the timber business near to Henry Balfour and Co at Leven to James Donaldson from Tayport. The price was £600 (the equivalent of £54,000 in 2012). James Donaldson, still at the Leven site, is now a large nationwide group with 23 branches across the country. John Balfour and Company then concentrated on the production of animal feeds, an activity started by his unmarried Uncle John (1796-1867). As already described, John also worked as company secretary of Henry Balfour for 30 years. After 1900, he lived in Carberry House left to him by his brother Thomas Cutlar. John was Provost at Leven and both he and Thomas were at different times captain of the Innerleven Golfing Society. Both Thomas and the brother's father James were benefactors of Leven Parish church. This is still recorded on a plaque on the walls of the building. Carberry House, left to Robert, was given to Leven Town Council in memory of John. There is now a new development of apartments in part of the garden area. Balfour Street remains nearby. John's grandson, another John and his wife Pam live in the Borders, and their son Stuart is a Royal Air Force Officer currently based in Wiltshire. His daughter is at the same school as one of our granddaughters.

Charles stayed working in Dundee industries and then moved to the east coast of America settling in Newark, New Jersey. (It is his grandson Charles who has helped with the research for this book.) Charles's twin brother Douglas helped to run Letham and the adjoining farms whilst the leases were still held and then spent some ten years in California before returning to Fife for his last years. Alice, the elder sister, married a journalist called Lamont in America and then returned to London where she lived on into her 90s. Isabella, the youngest of the family, married a Minister of the Church of Scotland, the Rev Maclean, and lived at Leven. William Balfour, Great-grandfather James's older brother (1834-1911), travelled to Australia in the mid 1850s and married Mary Blackburn in Victoria. We have only recently learnt that they moved to New Zealand and an obituary in the *Timaru (South Island) Herald*, 1st February 1911, records some of his life:

> 'From 1876 he was manager of a meat preserving works at Washdyke owned by a Glasgow firm and also Chairman of the Timaru Milling Company. With an active interst in public matters he was for a time Chairman of Geraldine County Council and a member of the South Canterbury Hospitals Board. He also did a great deal for Washdyke School. After leaving Washdyke he went to live at Seadown where he had a good sized farm. A Scotchman, the type whose word was as good as his bond, he was respected by all.'

There is also a reference in *The Herald*, 2nd September 1882 that Mrs William Balfour gained first prized for a display of fancy butter. We know that Mary died in 1886. Seadown Farm was sold in 1895. William married Esther Luckman and they moved to Waverley on the south west coast of North Island. William's oldest son, James, married Charlotte Fowler and they had one daughter, Isabella Alma. James became manager of the 12,000 acre Heslerton Estate near Leeston south west of Christchurch 'with sheep, cattle, horses and green crops and ten men constantly employed.' Later they moved to a farm at Te Aroha in North Island and then retired to Wangnui on the coast, not far from Waverley.

Thomas was another son of William and Mary Blackburn. We have corresponded with one of his grandsons, Michael Balfour, who now lives at Hawkes Bay in North Island. Thomas's first wife, Isabelle Taylor, was killed in a horse and carriage accident. He then married Francis Bee. Their elder son, George, married Peggy Hall. Their three children are Jennifer, married to Mervyn Reynolds; Anthony (who lives in Lacombe south of Edmonton, Alberta Canada); and Michael himself, married to Helen Knauf. George's sister, Joan, married Alick McKenzie. They had a son, Robin, and daughter, Annette, married to Jim Hagan. Michael and Helen have three children. Wendy, married to Adrian Pritchard at Hastings; Jeffrey, married to Cindy Newton at Kaiwaka; and Judy, married to Neilson Anderson at Tauranga, all in North Island. Michael also refers to the Buchanans who are descendants of William and Mary's daughter, Mary, who married Henry Buchanan. In a letter from Nancy Balfour to Rachel Tatham there is a mention of a visit to England by Mary and Henry's daughters in the 1960s. Michael told me that he worked with metal and all the family had worked with their hands making use of those paternal genes. William and Mary are recorded as having five other children. We only have the mention at the end of William's obituary of a Mr C Balfour, accountant to the Timaru Milling company and Mr R Balfour, the well-known stock dealer. Are there other relatives, unknown to us in South Island? When research for this book began, William was just a name. We had no idea of what had become of him. Now there is this awareness of yet another brother who achieved so much. And Myrtle Jellicoe, at Government House Wellington, in the early 1920s never knew that some of her future husband's cousins were all around!

LEARNING FROM DIFFERENCE

Chapter 3

Figdor. Joachim. Smart. Wittgenstein

With James Balfour (1803-1876) and Isabella Hutchison (1811-1885) established as Lionel's paternal great-grandparents, one door is unlocked. Next comes the surprise behind FG's reference to European Jewry. Lionel's maternal great-grandmother was Fanny Figdor (1791-1867), daughter of 'one of the most successful wool merchants in Vienna' in the early years of the nineteenth century.[1] This was the period when Hungarian wool was the first choice of many English manufacturers. Two-thirds of UK wool imports were from that area. The Wittgenstein relationship is through the Figdor family. Fanny's brother Wilhelm had a daughter named after her, another Fanny, who married Herman Wittgenstein. The philosopher Ludwig, the one-armed pianist Paul[2] and their brothers and sisters were the grandchildren of this second Fanny and Herman. Their father was Karl. He is on record as believing that 'variety of experience was more important than formal education'. He had left home aged 18 and travelled to America to work as a waiter and musician. Yet he still became one of the richest men in Europe.[3] Thus Lionel's great-grandmother and Ludwig's great-grandfather were brother and sister. Lionel and Ludwig had the same great-great-grandparents, Isaac and Anna Figdor.

The first Fanny Figdor (1791-1867) married my great-great-grandfather Julius Joachim (1791-1865) who was also in the wool trade, based at Kittsee and part of the Kehilla Jewish community. Heinrich (1824-1897) and Joseph (1831-1907) were two younger sons with four older sisters and one older brother.[4] At that time in Hungary there were restrictions on the movement of Jews out of their acknowledged communities. In 1833, when Heinrich was nine and Joseph two, Julius and the first Fanny, probably aided by the influential Figdors, still managed to move to the capital city and settled on the eastern Pest side of the Danube.[5] This waterway had enabled trade and travel for centuries. The whole Joachim family would have been able to benefit from the early steam-powered boats then coming into use. Julius was able to develop his wool business. Five years later, on 15th March 1838, after a winter of heavy snowfall, large blocks of ice coming down the river piled up to form a dam. Soon the whole of the Pest side was under water. One hundred and fifty people drowned and fifty thousand were left homeless.[6] The Joachims managed to get across to the Buda side, but mud and debris flooded into the wool warehouses. Julius's business was badly affected. Prospects in the wool trade for fourteen-year-old

Heinrich and his younger brother had been derailed.

Joseph was already playing the violin. His talent seems to have been appreciated by his cousin, the second Fanny Figdor, then twenty-four years old. 1839 was the year of her marriage to Herman Wittgenstein. The nine-year-old Joseph stayed with them whilst studying with teachers at the Vienna Conservatory. It was Fanny whose confidence in Joseph was such that she wanted him to study at Felix Mendelssohn's Conservatory, opened at Leipzig in 1843.[7] Whilst Joseph was away, his parents and the rest of the family would have been getting re-established after the flood. Heinrich and Joseph's older sister Johanna married Georg Aranyi de Hunyadvar. Their son, Taksony, became chief of police in Budapest[8] and was the father of the violinists Jelli d'Aranyi and Adila, whose married name was Fachiri. They both came to England and there are later references in this story. (A third sister, Hortense, known as Titi, married the economist, Ralph Hawtrey. She died before he became Sir Ralph in 1956). Continuing with Joseph's story, it was Fanny who accompanied him to Germany. Herman had business connections and a house in Leipzig, so at first Joseph was again able to stay with them.[9] As with the Balfours in Chile, there may be interest in how they achieved these journeys. Did they use the river steamers, perhaps travelling west to Linz? From there it could have been a stagecoach or diligence to pick up another boat on the river Vitava north of Pisek, which could have taken them past Prague to meet up with a boat on the Elbe. Or did they travel all or more of the journey by the diligences which were now averaging ten miles an hour with teams of horses changed every eight miles?[10] For the last part of their journey they would have access to the first German railway from Dresden to Leipzig, opened in 1839. Joseph was now cut off from his own family; no weekends visits back to Pest along a motorway or autoroute.

There is a letter to Heinrich written in 1848 when he was 17: 'I long more than ever for the warm close intercourse with my nearest and dearest whom I have not seen for so long. How good it will be to see my dear parents and brothers and sisters again. I expect to be in Pesth (his spelling, histories and guides write Pest) by the middle of May, but I do not know what will have happened to Europe by that time. Perhaps we shall be hearing canons and not violins then'. It was not an easy life for young Joseph, but as Moser writes in his Joachim biography: 'Leipzig was the only place where Joseph's splendid talents could reach maturity and the sequel has proved how right she, i.e. Fanny Wittgenstein, was'. Amongst the many accomplishments of her own children and grandchildren, Fanny helped to give the world a much-appreciated violinist, personality and music teacher.[12]

By the time of Joseph's journey, Heinrich was nineteen His father's business may have been suffering but Heinrich already had the experience of handling wool. In an unfinished memoir, one of his granddaughters wrote 'he had very sensitive fingers, like Joseph, invaluable for recognising the quality of different kinds of wool.' Was it the Figdor influence again which also encouraged Heinrich to leave Pest? Did they reason that his future could be in London where they were marketing their fleeces? It was a time when many Jews from central and eastern Europe came to England.[13] Like Joseph it would have probably been a mixture of river boats and diligences to a port like Rotterdam and then across to Harwich. At the Great Exhibition at the Crystal Palace erected in Hyde Park in 1851, Messrs Figdor & Sons won the top medal for their fleeces.[14] What part did Heinrich, now Henry, play in this success? By the early 1860s Henry was sufficiently prosperous to marry, in the *Musical Quarterly*'s words 'the kind and amiable Ellen Smart, a member of one of Britain's most prominent musical families'. Ellen's father Henry designed organs and then became a fine organist and a composer. He was one of five organists at the Great Exhibition. Henry would surely been there in Hyde Park. If Ellen as a child had come to listen to her father, could they have met? She would have been seven years old in 1851. Later, after her marriage to Henry, Ellen recorded her father's compositions when he became blind in 1865 and helped him to continue his work until his death in 1879. Sir George Smart, a renowned conductor and later organist at St George's, Windsor, was Henry's uncle.[15] Among his many achievements it was Sir George who recognised the abilities of the young Arthur Sullivan so that he was admitted to the elite choir of boys who sang at the Chapel Royal of St James's Palace. This was the future Sir Arthur, partner to W S Gilbert.

The *Musical Quarterly* further records that 'the Joachims were an intelligent and highly cultivated family. Joseph (Jo or JJ to the family) was particularly close to his older brother'.[16] This is confirmed by extracts from Joseph's letters: 'Is Henry going to stay in London. Is there a chance to earn much in these times and in a land of merchants?' 'That the Jewish Bill fell through in the Lords is sad, little hope for the Jews anyhow.' (This was the Jewish Disabilities Bill to allow Jews to sit in the House of Commons without taking the Christian oath. This had been approved by the Commons but several times rejected by the House of Lords.) 'Friendly with Herman and Fanny (Wittgenstein). Played Paganini with Fanny. Looking forward to working hard in England. Will Henry help him with Shakespeare in English and with Virgil.' 'Would have written sooner but have been in Dublin, Liverpool and Manchester. Cambridge next week to play Mendelssohn Concerto in front of Queen and Prince Albert for £15.' 'Met Pauline and Adolf in Cologne (daughter of his mother's brother Eduard and married to Adolf Seligmann, a Cologne lawyer). Persuaded to go by boat to Koblenz, friendly acceptance by family Seligmann.' 'King wants him in Hanover because of a possible concert at Court. Death of Duchess of Kent. Can not go to Vienna because of delay of last concert owing to Court's mourning. Kaiser spoke a few friendly words. King very kind at performance of requiem.' 'Played in Hanover concert: The Eroica, 6th concert by Spohr, Schubert with choir, Mozart aria, and Cherubini overture. Cold audience in contrast to Vienna. Molique's death, a loss for music in London.'

These extracts, some from the 1850s, some undated, provide snapshots of his activities. In later years, when his own family were grown up, Joseph stayed with Henry and Ellen and their family when he came to England. In the words of the *Music in Nineteenth Century Britain* series,[16] 'as well as her brother-in-law Ellen welcomed many artists who provided music at their Airlie Gardens home in Kensington.' These visits continued after Henry's death in 1897 and we have Ellen's note describing his stay in 1905: '26th November 1905. J left this morning to travel straight to Berlin. On Tuesday he has his pupils and his concert. He had played at Englefield Green, three violin sonatas in the afternoon and in the evening Bach's double concerto with Mr Douglas Scott. He had lunch with Princess Christian (daughter of Queen Victoria) and tea with Lady De Vesci. On Saturday he went to see Nina and Max with me. Thank God for that beloved man who by his goodness and greatness lifts us to a better World.' We also have a copy of Ellen's long letter describing what was probably Jo's last visit to England. This was to 14 Albert Hall Mansions to which they had moved from 15 Airlie Gardens: '19th November 1906. JJ arrived with his daughter Lisel from Paris where he had played at three concerts with his quartet. Maud and Nina were at dinner. Jo was in very good health and spirits. Played 66 (I am told similar to racing demon) afterwards.' Ellen's comments are difficult to decipher but some of the activities of the following days are legible:

'Wednesday 21st. Concert in Queen's Hall. Very full.
22nd. To Bristol.
23rd. J returned about 3 with his quartet. They rehearsed here. Another concert (can not read). Jo's playing exquisite.
24th. Englefield Green concert afternoon. Princess Christian there after dinner. Mary Vesey recited several verses of Goethe and cast a laurel wreath at Jo's feet.
25th (still at Englefield Green) Great many people to tea and supper. Jo played, Norah Dawnay (an accomplished singer of that time) sang. Brahms songs with viola accompaniment played by Jo.
26th. Left Englefield early as J had rehearsal in Beckstein Hall (the earlier name for what is now the Wigmore Hall). Lovely concert.
27th. Tovey dined with us. Played Mendelssohn as no one else can, the slow movement of his Hungarian concerto.
28th. Lovely concert at Beckstein in afternoon. Played Brahms sonata. Jo said he enjoyed it. Max, Nina and the young Stanfords came in the evening.
29th. Jo and the girls went to Oxford. Dined quietly at home after. Played 66.
30th. Can not read, only that some-one was ill and JJ, Nina and Max went together and enjoyed it very much.'

This is all we have. We do not know when he and Lisel went back to Germany. We do learn that he was still very active in his last year and how close he was to the English family including my grandparents, Nina and Max.

Then in July 1907 Joseph, by now 76, became ill and Ellen travelled to Berlin. Here are some of the notes she subsequently wrote:

'Left Plymouth 2am 6th August on board ND (Nord Deutscher) Lloyd Kaiser Wilhelm der Grosse.
Bremen afternoon of 7th, at Berlin same evening and found Lisel and Hal, Ellen's son, at station.
8th August. Harold and Lisel fetched us at 10.30. JJ had had a better night but they told me I must expect to find him much changed. Dear Jo, he looked so grand, his beard much whiter. When near him one felt calmer with the influence of his magic personality. He said more than once 'I am so glad you have come dear' then he said how happy he was about Harold and Lisel. He asked after Gertrude and Rollo (her husband) and said Margie and Johnny were such dear children. He also asked about Maud, Max and Nina, and then about my voyage. I held his dear hand the whole time, that hand which will never again draw forth those magic sounds. He said it was a great disappointment not to go to England.
9th August. Found he was just getting over a bad heart attack. After injections he got better then had another bad attack in the night.
10th August. I was sitting in the outer room with Lisel. Jo asked Hal where I was. After sitting for a moment by Jo's side he opened his eyes and put out his hand saying 'Is that you dear Ellie' then 'Are you much with the children (i.e. Harold and Lisel)? Are you glad about them?' I said yes and he said that he had always wished it.

11th August. Jo had a peaceful night. He looked like a grand old lion at rest. Then he opened his eyes and said 'Is that you Ellie' and then about 'the children' again 'He thought they would be happy as they both had such good characters'. Presently he asked if we had been to the Museum. I replied that we were going for a drive as it was too hot for museums.

12th August. Hal came early to say that Jo had another attack in the night but afterwards slept. I sat a long time by the bed. After a while he opened his eyes and said 'Good morning Ellie. Are you well cared for?' and then after a pause ' How is Max?' (From Aunt Minnie we know that this was when Max was suffering from another period of what she called overstrain. It shows Jo's interest in and concern for the whole family).

13th and 14th August. Jo was under morphine all day and seemed to be sleeping.

15th August. I found Jo much changed. I sat some time by his bed but it was very painful. We left about 1 o'clock. At 2 Hal came to tell us it was all over. Quite quietly he just stopped breathing.

16th August. Jo looked beautiful to-day, noble, peaceful, surrounded by flowers. Many people came to see him.

17th August. Flowers overflowed into the next room. Telegrams were arriving every minute. His hands are folded in front of him in a natural attitude and one feels he might open his eyes and say something kind. In the dining room on two black pillows were all his orders, at least thirty of them.

18th August. He was taken to the Hochschule and we went too. There were crowds all along the route. A gentleman came from the English Embassy with a most sympathetic telegram from King Edward. He said the ambassador would have brought it but he was abroad.

19th August. Drove to Freidkop where dear Jo is to rest. He will be laid by the side of Amalia. It is on a high part of the cemetery, peaceful and not overcrowded.'

Ellen also described Jo's final year. 'His illness began in the autumn with a feverish attack at Bad Gastein. All through the winter he worked very hard though with sudden fatigue. After a time he would seem to be alright and kept on his strenuous life. In Vienna he had what they called influenza and he complained of pain in his right side. When he was well enough to leave Vienna, instead of going South as advised, he went back to Berlin to play at a concert. Soon after he had to rest. He went to Montreux for three weeks and from there to Bonn for the Festival. After Bonn, it was Munich, where he played most beautifully, and then Eisenach Festival where he conducted. There he caught a cold and was not well on his return. He had to give up England and took to his bed in June.' Ellen also wrote that 'he had actinomycoses which caused abcesses and that he had great relief for a time when these abcesses were lanced.'

The Times obituary, 16th August 1907, wrote 'the greatest violinist of our time but also a man of exceptional beauty of nature and character'. That may be, but family records hint that, like most humans, he was not without flaws which had led to difficulties with his wife and others. In his book of poems Rollo Russell wrote the following for Joachim. These verses point to one of the themes of this book. Art may be more attractive than industry or the creation of wealth but who pays the bills?

Master of music, whom immortal love
Gave the deep wisdom of melodious truth;
Child of pure harmony, full fraught with skill;
Heir to a treasure of the heart of worlds
Hidden from travellers whose tired eyes
Gaze on mere surfaces, or search in mines
Tricks of vain riches, glitters of the dust;
Thou hast well served, thy art was of a man
More than musician, more than interpreter;
Thy greatness touched us, patient, kind, reserved,
And in beholding thee we knew our strength
Flowing from regions where thou livest now.

I wish I had known more about Nina's father, Joseph's brother, my great-grandfather, Henry. He had prospered in England. Recently I found a list of 'top Jewish wealth holders in Britain 1809-1909'. Henry Joachim, wool broker, left £103,000, a considerable sum at that time.[17] He had indeed earned much in his younger brother's 'land of merchants'. The only momento we have is a set of pictures with a handwritten note: 'these pictures represent scenes in the Franco-Prussian war 1870. They were painted by a French artist and bought by HJ in 1871'. This looks to have been Ellen's writing.

In addition to helping her father, Ellen had nine children with Henry, but four daughters were still born or only survived a few months. As well as the London base they had a house on the hills above Haslemere called 'Highlands'. According to Nicholas Griffin, an American academic,[19] their son Harold Joachim, whilst still a bachelor, spent his summers at Highlands and had many discussions with the then younger Bertrand Russell on his visits to his Uncle Rollo who lived nearby. Gertrude, the eldest Joachim daughter, then married Rollo Russell after his first wife died. He was a younger son of Earl Russell, Prime Minister from 1846 to 1852. Jo Joachim had divorced his wife, the singer Amalia Schneeweiss, in 1884. It is known that Joseph wanted to be reconciled with his wife, but not how much they were together before Amalia's death in 1899[20]. Their daughter Elizabeth, known as Lisel, then lived with and helped Joseph acting as his secretary and accompanied him on his later travels. Family remembrance suggests that Lisel had long been keen on cousin Harold who, in his thirties, had been enjoying the life of a bachelor academic. During Joseph's last illness, Harold was in Berlin as recorded in Ellen's letters and notes. As Joseph had hoped, Harold and Lisel married in Germany and then returned to Oxford. Ellen seems to have kept Highlands for at least ten years after Henry's death. It remained a haven for the Joachims and their friends. We have pictures of the Sussex Weald by my grandfather Max Balfour which look to have been painted there or nearby. We know that Nina, the youngest daughter, and Max both studied at the Slade School of Art . It seems likely that is where they met. Then came the Boer War interlude with Max away in South Africa[21] He did not marry my grandmother until 1904. Max was thirty and Nina twenty-eight. As Max's parents were long dead, did Aunt Minnie talk to Ellen about the tubercular heritage and other problems? They went ahead with this all-too-brief marriage and my father Lionel was born at 118 Cheyne Walk on 11th December 1905 and sister Rachel in 1907.

In 1928 Nina, though the youngest, was the first of that generation to die. She was only fifty-two. There had been just ten years of marriage and Max had been struggling with ill health for half that time. She had been on her own for fourteen years. Had she lived she would have been fifty-eight when I was born, seventy when I was twelve. There would have been time to get to know each other. Instead she was never mentioned during my childhood. There were no pictures and I was too involved with my own concerns to enquire. Eighty years after her death I have read thirty letters written to her son Lionel. She is no longer an unknown. Her intelligence and good sense, her appreciation of art and music, her concern for others and obvious good company radiate from the pages. She had interests and ideas which differed to those of my maternal grandmother FG. Nina refers to her three sisters, Gertrude, Maud and Dorothy. Their nephew, another Jo, Harold and Lisel's son, has also written about them in his unpublished extensive and fascinating memoirs. Rollo and Gertrude Russell lived at Steep. An early memory is of falling into the fishpond at this house, Rozel, and the water closing over my head. A rescuer must have been nearby, or this book would not have been written. Rollo died in 1914. Gertrude continued with all her interests till her death in 1942. Jo records that Aunt G was a convinced vegetarian, socialist and pacifist and that 'she used to talk of the need for a new kind of history which glorified the great men of peace rather than the Generals and Field Marshals.' A particular concern was the Temperance Movement. She bought the Punchbowl Inn at Hindhead and arranged that only non-alcoholic drinks would be served. Jo remembers her as 'a loving, forthright, interesting and unusual woman: if she felt a course of action was right, nothing would prevent her carrying it out, even if it could lead to unpopularity in some quarters.'[21] Rollo and Gertrude had two children. Their daughter, Margaret married Edward Lloyd. They had three children, Frances, John and Robert. Their descendants with whom we have had contact while compiling this book are listed in the family tree. Their son John was another post-war casualty of 1914-1918. He married Alice Turner in 1928 but then died, aged 36, from the after-effects of war wounds and TB.

Maud (Aunt M), born after Harold, was an early student at Girton in Cambridge. After graduation she worked with the Women's Social & Political Union (WSPU) and was a committed Suffragette from 1908 to 1914. She has her place in history. When imprisoned, she was the first woman in Scotland to go on hunger strike. In 1910 a tree was planted in her honour in the Suffragette Arboretum in a field adjacent to Eagle House, Batheaston. In 1913 Maud joined with Sylvia Pankhurst and others to form the East London federation of Suffragettes (ELFS).[22] Keir Hardie and George Lansbury supported them and they worked closely with the Independent Labour Party.[23] In August 1914 when War was declared Maud was in Dublin with Sylvia. They returned to East London and Maud worked with the ELFS as manager of their toy factory and helping to find other work for the local unemployed. After the war her concern for the welfare of others continued but then, as she got older, her comment, recorded by Jo, was 'What more can I do?' It was the approach of a realist aware of the limits of individual action. When she was nearly 60, she opted for a more personal challenge. Every summer she travelled to the Dolomites and in the 1930s became known as a fine and skilful climber treated with awe and respect, as other family members were to learn when they later met guides who had climbed with her. 'Oh, Miss Joachim,' was their response. She had also bought Mouse Cottage at Steyning in Sussex. I now realise it was Maud. I was taken to meet, it must have been in 1946, but there was no reference to her earlier life[24]. I remember her tanned weatherbeaten face and the path next to the cottage up to Chanctonbury Down where I was told she walked to keep fit during the winter months. She died on 16th February 1947 aged seventy-eight.

Dorothy (variously Aunt D, Do, Dot or Dolly) was two years older than Nina. Dorothy was a nurse during the war and it then seems to have been her lot to assist her mother when she moved to Bournemouth, to a house called Durley Heath at the top of Durley Chine. Jo writes of holiday visits and how Granny Ellen in her bath chair was escorted down the Chine to watch them on the beach. Ellen died in 1925 and Dorothy was then able to make use of her share of interest from the Henry Joachim Trust. Two surviving letters written in 1932 from The Small House, Dover Road, Bournemouth, to which she must have moved, confirm her continuing enjoyment of life. She refers to Lionel's approaching wedding and subsequent plans: 'I was at the Italian Lakes in May last year. I rather liked Menaggio on Lake Como. There is a first class hotel the Victoria and a second class v. comfortable where I stayed. Venice may be too hot in June. I love it but you cannot do much in the middle of the day and remember you must wear a hat as it is very easy to get slight sunstroke for those not used to these hot suns').[25] Dorothy was at my parents' wedding on 11th June 1932, having given a writing desk, which we still have, and a cheque, but then succumbed to cancer and died on 15th March 1933. (Maud also sensibly sent a cheque).

Nina doesn't put the year on any of her letters to Lionel. After Cambridge he was a graduate apprentice with English Electric in Stafford. He would have been over twenty-one, which suggests the period 1926/1928. After work Lionel helped in Stafford Boys Clubs guided by some of the ideas from the Toc H movement[26] which was committed to building a fairer society.[25] 'Sugar is being stolen and we have locked it away,' he told his mother. Kind-hearted Nina responded: 'It seems a pity that to prevent the taking of sugar it should have to be done by making it impossible to get at it. I think I should have been inclined to try the other method first, i.e. to have it right out in the open and to trust to the boy's honour not to thieve it. Have it where every one can see it and make it a matter of shame if it is taken'. She later wrote: ' It must be difficult to fill up every minute of their time. I suppose starting crafts like raffia or toy making wouldn't be possible, but as I don't know the club or it's resources, these suggestions may be futile'. There were Toc H-supported discussions which encouraged Nina to write about her own views: 'I don't think the wealth of the country should be evenly distributed because it never could remain so. I think it should be in the hands of those who are well known to feel the responsibility they have for using it for the welfare of the community. But how is this to be achieved?' She also wrote: 'I believe evolution to be the meaning of life here and can only be wrought by the rough hard experiences of sorrow and disaster both in the individual and in the community'. Without any expressed religious comments she thus seemed to have coped with Max's death. Max was in her thoughts referring to the death of another artist: Nina added that 'he was at the Slade with Daddie'. She still pressed on trying to support the son and daughter they had produced together and enjoying the company of friends and relatives.

Jelli d'Aranyi, her great-niece, granddaughter of her father's sister, was based in London. 'I went to tea with Adela (see above Jelli's sister, another great-niece). Jelli was there rehearsing for a concert in Wales. As Adela had not yet come, Jelli asked if I would mind (underlined) sitting in the room while she rehearsed. I've never seen anything so beautiful as she looked playing, nor have I heard anything since Uncle Jo's death to touch it. Both she and Adela were most affectionate'. Then there were closer relatives: 'About Saturday's arrangements: we will meet Rachel somewhere. The plan then is to meet your cousins Kenneth and Betty (Uncle Percy's children) at the Zoo. Aunt Maude Balfour has asked us to go back and have tea with Aunt Alice. This afternoon I had tea with Mrs Alec Balfour'. Aunt Alice would have been Alice Lamont, born in 1838 and then nearly ninety. She was Max's aunt, older sister to James, John, Robert, Thomas and the other brothers. Maude Balfour would have been Percy's widow. Mrs Alec Balfour was Robert's daughter-in-law, mother of Nancy Balfour and Margaret Ashbrook. The contacts continued: 'I am going to dinner with Uncle Robert tonight'. Sir Robert was then eighty-five, coping with the loss of his own three sons and yet still concerned for the extended family. Nina was his nephew's widow. There are other mentions - of Aunt D 'coming to London, electric shock treatment for her back problem', of 'visits to Aunt Do at Bournemouth', of Aunt M, not yet with the house at Steyning, coming for theatre and concert outings. Aunt G was busy with her own interests in Hampshire but she is mentioned by Nina 're John's engagement to the widow. Poor Aunt G is making a great effort to make friends with her. I wrote to John hoping he would be very happy and got a very nice letter back from him.'[27]

Nina's life was more than her concern for Lionel and Rachel and her social activities. She was also continuing her work as an artist following her training at the Slade: ' I'm going to take a lovely studio almost next door here. This will save me going all the way down to Chelsea as working at big things is much more tiring than sitting down and working at small things. One stands all the time and has to walk up and down, backwards and forwards a lot'. Nina then further describes her work to Lionel: 'My big design is a tempera done for the reason of amusing myself by trying to produce something beautiful. It is based on doves in a mimosa tree, a sight I saw and sketched when I was at Pollensa (Pollensa, Mallorca,). I sent my drawing of Uncle Jo to the Director of the Fitzwilliam museum'. And in two other letters: 'next week I am putting in as a candidate for the International Women's Art Club and if elected, some of my pictures will be on exhibition at the Suffolk Street Galleries for a month'. Then: 'I took my works to the Galleries and a nice woman said 'I am on the committee and if I had my way they would all be hung'. In the afternoon I was told I had been elected'. There are references to sending small allowances to both Lionel and Rachel and how she had to be careful not to overdraw at the bank. Nina was not awash with money. The marriage settlement between Nina and Max, dated 31st May 1904, stated that Nina would only receive income on Max's death with the capital retained for the next generation after her death. There were the same conditions for the Maxwell Balfour Will Trust. Likewise the Henry Joachim Will Trust, dated 14th April 1896, was income only with the capital only to be released after the death of his son and all daughters. Without capital Nina had lived in lodgings as a paying guest, but from 1926 or 1927 she began to search for a house or flat: 'Rachel and I had a thorough house hunt last week. There is one of those De Vere cottages to be had. They are asking £4,000 freehold.' That obviously did not work out and in another letter: 'this morning our agent sent particulars of a flat which sounded suitable. I have asked Bob Witt to see if he can get it for us. It is in Prince's Gate.'[28] But then comes another letter: 'the trustees can not let me have the money to buy unless I indemnify them with my £400 of capital, which I can't do. So I shall not bother with a house for the moment.' Good for her. She wasn't going to be bullied.

There are several letters describing her plans for a trip to Persia in Autumn 1928. She wrote: 'I went to the lawyers and revoked my Will to-day, so you need not go looking for it. Everything will be naturally divided between you and Rachel in the money line straight from your father's and my father's possessions. The few things I have of my own I have left directions about. I haven't any money of my own.' The files confirm that the capital from some of the Trusts (but not 'Henry Joachim' whilst her brother and sisters were alive) would be transferred to Lionel and Rachel in the event of her death. In that same letter she continued: 'I go to Persia about the end of October. I think we are going in a tanker, one of the Company's boats that goes out empty with a few passengers and come back with cargo. It takes about a month at sea, Plymouth to Abadan, and then about 150 miles of land.' This ties up with what she had written when visiting Mallorca: 'I have made friends with the assistant Manager of the British Oil Company in Persia.' He seems to have told Nina about the cabins available on outward-bound tankers. On 23rd September, for once the letter is dated: 'I'm all in a flittery flutter because we may have to sail on the 15th (presumably October). At any rate we have to be quite ready by then. I wish you could see my room here. This is how it appears to me in a nightmare (a picture of boxes and trunks stacked). Well it is all great fun. 'All great fun.' These were the last words my grandmother Nina wrote to Lionel. She never made it to that tanker at Plymouth because she died on 5th October.[28] The death certificate gives cause of death as a) cerebral haemorrhage b) artery sclerosis. Nor did she have the chance of 'money of my own'. When Sir Robert died the following year, his will included a legacy of '£2,000 free of duty' for Nina. Harold and Lisel's daughter, another Nina, wrote: 'Aunt Nina was my delightful and much loved Godmother. Her death was a real blow. If I was ill, she always wrote charming illustrated letters.'

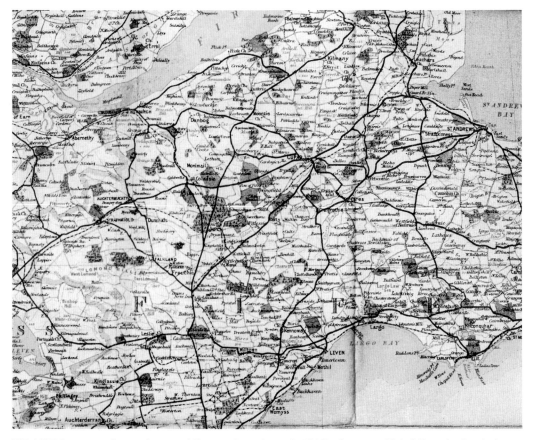

W&AK Johnston cycling and automobile map from the early 1900's. Leven and Methil on the South shore, Letham, Pilmuir & Pratis North of Leven, Bruckley, Middlefoodie & Milton South of Leuchars

Isabella Hutchison,
the matriarch
and five of her
seven sons
1812 - 1885

Thomas Cutlar and Douglas
(who helped with the farms
and also spent some time in
America) and 2 daughters,
Alice and Isabella, not
pictured

William
Chairman of Timaru Milling
Company and of Geraldine
County Council, South Island,
New Zealand
1834 - 1911

Great-grandfather James Balfour at
Dundee, January 1866, before
departure to Chile. Founder Balfour
Lyon later joined by Thomas Cutlar
1843 - 1878

Robert
Founding partner Balfour,
Guthrie; partner Balfour
Williamson & director Henry
Balfour & Co. Later Sir Robert
Balfour, MP Glasgow Partick
1844 - 1929

John
Secretary and director
of Henry Balfour & Co.
Provost of Leven
1846 - 1926

Charles
Skilled draughtsman. Moved
to America, worked with
Balfour Guthrie in Oregon,
then Newark, New Jersey
1849 - 1906

i

Landing craft for D-Day 1944, in production at Henry Balfour & Co, Leven

Fermenting tun constructed by Pfaudler Balfour on way to docks for shipping to Guinness brewery in Dublin 1949

The Balfour Guthrie office at Brentwood

Real Estate subdivisions and land sale marketing was increased to ensure Balfour Guthrie & Company's survival

Local children and transient families found summer employment in the packing sheds

'Carol A Jensen private collection' for those three Balfour Guthrie pictures

William's son
James was manager
of an estate near
Christchurch and later
farmed at Te Arohe

George Balfour

Four of William's grandchildren
in N.Z. From left: James, George
(see on right), Douglas & Joan, who
married Alick McKenzie

William

Granddaughter, Alma

Rachel Ogilvie

James married
Rachel Ogilvie

Rachel's sister, Minnie
in 1950

Rachel and Minnie's
father, James Ogilvie

Robert

Robert's third son, Alan, Royal Flying
Corps pilot. Killed France, January 1918.
Painting by Maxwell Balfour

iii

Charles   Son, Charles, doctor in America

John
Secretary and director
of Henry Balfour & Co.
and two of his three sons.
Provost of Leven
1846 - 1926

John Herbert, Argyll and   The second Thomas Cutlar, aircraft
Sutherland Highlanders   engineer, in RFC uniform

James and Rachel's 3 sons

Lionel's Uncle Fred, James & Rachel's oldest son, who died in India, 1907

Max, the author's grandfather, Boer War veteran and acclaimed artist. He died in 1914

Percy Balfour, Lionel's uncle. Killed in France, December 1917

Fred's sons from left to right: Phillip, later Lieutenant General Sir Philip. Ronald, later Commander RN

Lionel's cousin, Ken, son of Percy & Maude, taken when visiting England 1954

Ken in Kenya, right arm damaged by war wound

Elizabeth Balfour, daughter of Percy & Maude, Lionel's cousin as V.A.D in 1940

Betty as director of Hampshire Red Cross with Princess Royal. Presentation of Colours 1949

Maude Balfour, widow of Percy Balfour, unveiling the 1914-18 War Memorial at St Anne's, Soho

Grandfather
Max on left
with Lionel
Curtis and
Lionel
Hichens.
Cyclists'
Battalion,
Boer War

Rachel's grave Cementerio de Disidentes, Valparaiso

*'In holy memory of Rachel Ogilvie, wife of James R.
Balfour. This stone was placed by her husband and
children. Born at Dundee April 1st 1847. Died at
Arequipa July 23rd 1878. And buried here
September 11th 1878.'*

Statue of
Alexander
Balfour,
however
related,
founder
of Balfour
Williamson,
St John's
Gardens,
Liverpool

Letham Farm, 21st Century

Elmslea, Leven, Fifeshire

Thomas Cutlar's Carberry house   Nearby

Wedding group, Elmslea 1857. Some of the
family are identifiable. Photograph sent to James
in N.Z. in 1935 by Isabella Maclean, his aunt,
Great-grandfather James' youngest sister

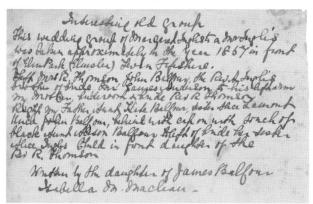

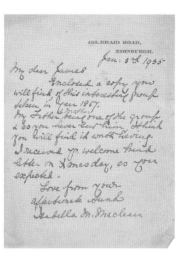

Innerleven Golf Club, partly financed by
Thomas Cutlar Balfour

Captains Board

L to r: Great-grandmother Ellen Joachim, née Smart, Grandmother Nina with Lionel and Rachel

Lionel and his mother, Nina

Grandfather Max Balfour on left, to his left, Lionel Curtis, his Godfather, initiator of Chatham house, who with Lionel Hichens served together in the Boer War. My Father Lionel wrote of Lionel Curtis, that 'He was like a good father to me.' Rachel at the front, on the left, Lionel on right, held by unidentified third man at Highlands, Haslemere

Lionel at Berck-Plage visiting father, Max, about 1912

Great-grandfather Henry's brother Joseph Joachim. Drawing by grandmother Nina Balfour, née Joachim

Joachim quartet, Joseph on left

Third from left: Joseph Joachim and Amalie Schneeweis's eldest son Johannes, on the left: Harold, later Head of Prints and drawings Chicago Art Gallery then Christa, daughter of Johannes' brother Hermann. On the right Christa's sister, Gaby her husband, and Johannes' wife, Emily

Right: Great-grandfather Henry Joachim's son, Professor Harold Joachim, at Oxford house with wife Lisel, daughter of Joseph Joachim

Suffragettes. Great-aunt Maud Joachim, on left with Evalina Haverfield. Mounted demonstration

Mouse Cottage where we visited Maud in 1946

Great-aunt Gertrude Joachim, later the Honourable Mrs Rollo Russell

Rachel (later Tatham) with her grandmother, Ellen Joachim née Smart

Ellen Joachim drawn by her daughter, Nina Balfour

On the left Great-aunt Dorothy Joachim, sister of Gertrude, Maud & Nina, as a nurse 1914 - 1918

THE LATE REV. WILLIAM H. BUTLIN.

A MUSICAL VICAR.

THE VICAR OF LEONARD STANLEY AND HIS SCHOOL CHOIR.

Adoniah Schuyler
1749 - 1814

Harriet
Rashleigh wife
of Rev Edward
Rodd

Grandfather of Billy, later Sir William Butlin,
holiday camp pioneer. The Reverend Butlin 'carried
on poultry farming and was a frequent prize
winner with his exhibits at shows , but to many of
our readers he will be remembered mainly for his
enthusiastic love of music, and his unflagging zeal in
popularising the art amongst young and old'

The Butlins, Susan and Edward
(Fox) with Frances and Claude in
front, and Dorothy and Schuyler
standing behind, at Trebartha Hall
north of Bodmin Moor, Cornwall

Ann's great-grandmother, Marianne Sutton with her four daughters. Clockwise from left: Gertrude, Marianne, Ann's grandmother Susan and Harriet

Ann's grandparents, Susan and Edward (Fox) Butlin with, from left to right Claude, Dorothy, Schuyler, and Frances

The Davies family in Australia. Alan, Morva, Greta, Harry, Winsome and Martyn

Morva and Claude Butlin with Ann and Christopher at Bishops Waltham 1947

Eagle Mont at Heidelberg then 8 miles from Melbourne

Charles Davies, Ann's grandfather

Lucy Davies, née Walker, Ann's grandmother

Morva with friends Teddy and Eve Jolly

Morva Davies, later Nankivell and then Butlin, Ann's mother

Muriwai Beach, New Zealand
L to r: Myrtle, George, John Doe, Prudy, Lucy, Norah

Myrtle, Agnes (Betty), FG
and Lucy

Back row: Grandfather
Jellicoe with staff; Sitting
front row Norah, Myrtle,
FG with George, Prudie
and Lucy

Prudie on the left, Myrtle's
youngest sister, Nan Frank
in centre, who stayed at
Peake during the war
(Lady Frank, later Lady
Coningham, twice widowed
& son, Sir Howard, killed
1944) see text, and on the
right Myrtle

Above & below: Myrtle at Grindelwald, Feb - Mar 1930, the year before she met Lionel. Her skiing partner that year was Ian McEwen

Myrtle with the Uptons 1931

Myrtle out with Royal Calpe Hunt, southern Spain, 1931. On the left General Godley, Commander of Anzac soldiers 1914-1918 later Governor of Gibraltar. On right, Admiral Chatfield, Admiral Beatty's Flag Captain at Jutland. Minister for Co-ordination of Defence 1939-1940

Lionel with BSA. Journey to Gibraltar whilst at Cambridge, 1926

Austin 7. Lionel on right

Lionel on left with Triumph motor cycle & side-car; Austin behind

Austin on road to Bourg Madame & mountains of Andorra behind

Photo captioned 'a team of nine for Granada'

Lionel helping at Boys Club camp when with English Electric at Stafford

First year with Lionel. His Austin 7 to right 1927

The next year with Talbot 65, 1928

St Lawrence

St Lawrence Hall, Ventnor Isle of Wight, destroyed by fire 1946. Now a housing estate

Back row: George, Lucy, Lady Bridport, Lionel, Lady Boyle, Prince Frederick of Prussia, Grandfather, Teddy Latham, Lady Spencer Churchill
Front Row: Author, Myrtle, FG, Queen Mary

King George V and Queen Mary at St Lawrence Hall

Lionel and Myrtle 11th June 1932
After the wedding at All Saints,
Langham Place

With button hole and monocle,
Sir Herbert Cayzer MP
(Uncle Bertie). Immediately
behind him, Nancy Balfour,
granddaughter of Sir
Robert. On her right, Great-
grandmother Rachel's youngest
sister, Minnie who went to Chile
and helped bring back Lionel's
father and his two uncles. On
Nancy's left Wilfred Tatham.
Note sailor mascot on Austin

At Heston (near to todays's M4 Heston Services). About to take off in **G-ABIY** for honeymoon, 1932

Christening tea at Cam Cottage Shedfield, July 1934
Left to r: Lionels' Sister Rachel, Molly Vesey Holt, Grandfather Jellicoe's sisters Great-aunt Edie, Great-aunt Grace, Mrs Buxton, Admiral Phillimore, Mr Buxton, George Jellicoe, Myrtle, FG, Grandfather Jellicoe, Mr Troup Surgeon, Gerard Wood, Lucy, Norah. The two Admirals together in a Hampshire garden (the Phillimores lived in Shedfield Place). 34 years after they had served in China during the Boxer rebellion (where grandfather Jellicoe was wounded), Admiral Phillimore was not at Jutland as he was then liaison officer to Imperial Russia

Windsor Castle and Eton, probably 1931. Lionel either piloting biplane above or taking photograph from another plane

Above & above right: With grandfather Jellicoe at St Lawrence, summer 1934

With Lionel, New Forest

With Myrtle, St Lawrence

4. Bagnoles-de-l'Orne. — La Cour des Thermes.

The thermal baths at Bagnoles (sign always noted on A28 north of Alencon en route to Andorra), where Myrtle was treated a year after my birth

G-ABIY with Lionel and godfather, Gerard Wood, probably 1931 before repaint in PSIOWA colour

Myrtle and Lionel at St Lawrence   Myrtle & Lionel, Davos, mid 1930s

Above: With Godmother Molly Vesey Holt and her daughter and son, Rosemary & Oliver, Orchard Bay

Above: With Humber which replaced Austin (sailor mascot transferred) *Right*: In the swimming pool of what is now Priory Bay Hotel

Above & right: With cousin Jacqueline Wingfield, later Vivian. The front of the Lines brothers' pedal car was modelled on the then current Chrysler 'Airflow'

Taken from the Agent's brochure for the sale of the much-loved Peake in 2004. The McPhail's had been there since 1948 after our departure

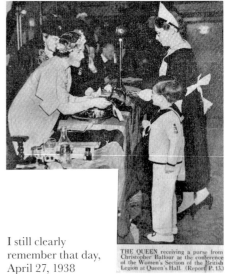

I still clearly remember that day, April 27, 1938

THE QUEEN receiving a purse from Christopher Balfour at the conference of the Women's Section of the British Legion at Queen's Hall. (Report P. 13.)

The pampered little boy, complete with 'Iron Duke' cap ribbon, who was meant to follow in the footsteps of his illustrious grandfather pictured behind. Not a hope!

Above & right: With Molly, who helped around the house and lived in Warnford. The Lines brothers' 'Rolls Royce' did not survive the post-war upheaval

The pony was called 'Tatters'. They tried to interest me but it did not have an engine

The left upper window was my room

From the lake

Above: Already affection for cars with arms outstretched round the Ford's bonnet *Left*: The Morris '12' and the new Ford '10' which provided transport through the war years

After Karen's christening
(born January 1944)

FG, Lionel and Myrtle at Peake

Near right: Probably
at Meonstoke House,
Myrtle's friend's
home
Far right: Myrtle's
friend leading the
parade (not carrying
a telegraph pole)

Right: With cousins
Annabella and
James Loudon at
Olantigh, Kent

Unknown patriotic
event. FG in centre

British Legion
service, July 1945.
In the centre from the
left: Myrtle, President
Southampton
Branch; Mrs Vincent,
the Sheriff's wife;
F.G., National
Vice-President of the
Women's Section; the
Mayoress, Mrs J.C.
Dyas; Mrs Chapman,
Branch Chair.
Those banners would
soon be at her funeral

Above: Open day Portsmouth Aviation summer 1945. Myrtle
crowning the winner. *Right*: Myrtle's gravestone in Warnford
church yard, this was the work of Joseph Induni (1893-1956)
a renowned sculptor and marble carver at that time

The fated trip to Davos in December 1946. Hotel Meierhof, Davos Dorf and just before I fell, tearing a knee ligament

Above: Buccaneer frame constructed during last holiday at Peake; sadly never completed *Right*: One of my model plane successes in flight above chimneys of Eton house

Salterbridge, Cappoquin Co Waterford, probably 1949

Above: the Wingfield Rolls Royce outside the front door. *Left*: My elastic-rubber-powered Sunbeam Talbot model

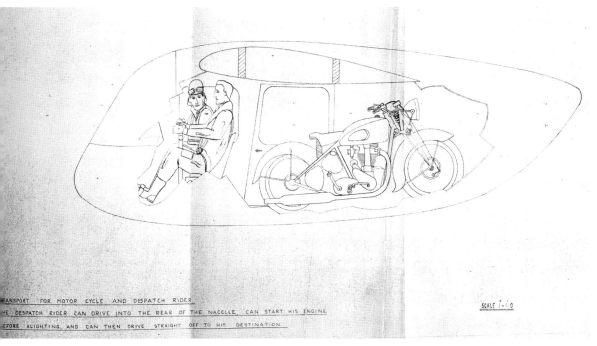

RANSPORT FOR MOTOR CYCLE AND DESPATCH RIDER.
HE DESPATCH RIDER CAN DRIVE INTO THE REAR OF THE NACELLE, CAN START HIS ENGINE
EFORE ALIGHTING AND CAN THEN DRIVE STRAIGHT OFF TO HIS DESTINATION.

SCALE 1·1·0

One of four drawings submitted with a design for a 'general purpose aeroplane for army requirements',
May 1943. The other three drawings were Ambulance, Staff Officer and sabotage party transport.
Was there provision for the motor cycle exhaust? This was the start of the Aerocar project

Visit of King George Vl to Portsmouth Aviation September 3 1942.
Left to r: Lord Mayor Sir Dennis Daley, Francis Luxmore, King George, Admiral Sir William James, Lady
Daley, Lionel, Jimmy Hawes, later founder with son, Ted, of Hants & Sussex, now H&S Aviation

Second left: Francis Luxmore, *centre*: Edgar Granville and then Lionel

THE COMPANY WILL APPRECIATE SUGGESTIONS FROM ITS PATRONS CONCERNING ITS SERVICE   1280

WESTERN UNION
CABLEGRAM

CLASS OF SERVICE
This is a full-rate Cablegram unless its deferred character is indicated by a suitable symbol preceding the address.

A. N. WILLIAMS
PRESIDENT

VPX

SYMBOLS

LC	Deferred Cablegram
NLT	Cable Night Letter
Ship	Radiogram

1946 APR 5   PM 9 25

Received at 40 Broad Street (Central Cable Office), New York, N.Y. ALWAYS OPEN

VIA W. U. CABLES

550 PORTSMOUTH 38 3

NLT L M J BALFOUR
CARE EDWARD BARBER BARBER STEAMSHIP LINE INC
17 BATTERYPLACE NEWYORK=

AIR SERVICE FLOATS LIMITED THE BINGHAM BUILDINGS ORILLIA
ONTARIO VERY INTERESTED IN AEROCAR FOR FEEDER LINE AND
CHARTER SERVICE ALSO CANADIAN DISTRIBUTION=

:GOULD.

THE QUICKEST, SUREST AND SAFEST WAY TO SEND MONEY IS BY TELEGRAPH OR CABLE

Portsmouth, Southsea and Isle of Wight Aviation Ltd (PSIOWA)

On the right Lionel and Francis Luxmoore with ferry pilots in front of Westland Wessex at Portsmouth early 1930's

Portsmouth Airport August Bank Holiday

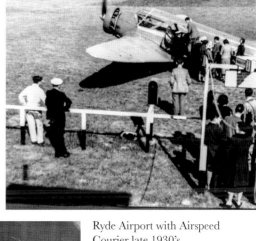

Ryde Airport with Airspeed Courier late 1930's

Lionel as one of the UK delegates to international conference on civil aviation November 1944

LEARNING FROM DIFFERENCE

Chapter 4

Butlin. Cayzer. Jellicoe

In the family chapters this book is primarily about paternal origins, of which I knew so little. However, Myrtle's parents, the Admiral and the redoubtable FG, have often been mentioned. As it is also intended as a work of reference for future family members, here is a short chapter with a few further facts about others whose attributes will have contributed to the gene make-up. Many Jellicoe forebears were of Hampshire or Isle of Wight origin. There were firm roots as with Balfours, Hutchisons and Ogilvies in Fife. The Solent, like the Firths of Forth and Tay, provided similar backgrounds to their upbringing. Ships and seafaring were all around. Grandfather Jellicoe's father became Commodore of the Royal Mail Line and was also Marine Superintendent in Southampton. His father, Samuel, had married Elizabeth Gardiner whose three times great-grandfather, Sir William Gardiner, had married Jane Brocas. This is the connection with the Brocas family from Gascony. Arnaud de Brocas was killed at Bannockburn in 1314. His father settled in England and his grandson, Bernard, was first 'Hereditary Master of the Royal Buckhounds', which was a political office with some royal duties. He acquired both the Beaurepaire and Roche Court estates in Hampshire.[1] His son, another Sir Bernard, was part of the conspiracy to put Richard the second, who had been a childhood friend, back on the throne. He was executed at Tyburn in 1400. The family still went on to provide Members of Parliament and High Sheriffs of Hampshire. Their names are on one of the walls of the Great Hall in Winchester, the only substantial surviving part of the castle.[2] Research has been difficult, but, as far as I can make out, the Commodore had a brother, the Reverend G S Jellicoe. It was his son, the Reverend T H L Jellicoe, rector of Chailey in Sussex, who was the father of the Reverend J B L Jellicoe who made his mark as a housing reformer. After his early death in 1935, *The Times* wrote:

> 'He will be remembered for his remarkable work as the chairman of the St Pancras House Improvement Society which has demonstrated that the improvement of slum areas by private enterprise is a sound financial proposition.'[3]

Grandfather Jellicoe's mother, Lucy Keele, was descended from Pattons and Rushworths. Lucy's maternal grandfather was Admiral Philip Patton who was Second Sea Lord at the time of the Battle of Trafalgar. Her paternal grandmother, Elizabeth, was the sister of Edward Rushworth, MP for the Isle of Wight, and it was his wife, Catherine, who built Farringford Hall, later the home of the poet, Alfred Lord Tennyson.[4] There is more about all these families in the appendix to Admiral Bacon's life of Jellicoe.[5] Grandfather's older brother was the Reverend F G G Jellicoe who was rector of Freemantle, Southampton from 1902 till 1915 and then of Alresford till 1922.[6] His two younger brothers, Herbert and Edmond, died young and it's the two sisters, known to us as Grace and Edie, who are in the picture of my christening at Shedfield in 1934. My maternal grandmother, FG, was the daughter of Sir Charles Cayzer, founder of the Clan Line and many other companies. Cayzer history is well covered in two books: *A Victorian Shipowner* and *Uncharted Waters*. The first book describes the Cayzer background near Lostwithiel in Cornwall.[7] I am sure FG meant well according to her own views on life priorities. They were just different to Balfour choices. We have only recently found her letter to my future mother-in-law, Morva Butlin, in which she wishes Ann and I much happiness in our married life. That wish has been granted.

Ann's father, Claude Butlin, was a Naval officer who served throughout the 1914-1918 War in a torpedo boat and then as first officer in Destroyers. He was awarded the DSC in 1917. For two years (1923-1925) he was a Term Officer at Dartmouth and was then posted to China. He returned to command the mine-sweeper FORRES, the tender to Dartmouth, and was then loaned to the Australian Navy as an executive officer on the cruiser Canberra. He met Morva after he had been posted to Australia. Morva's husband, Bill Nankivell, had died young and Morva had been left with twin boys, Bill and Peter. I have not traced the Butlins back to the fourteenth century like the Brocases. Instead we begin with the Reverend William Wright Butlin who was the much-respected Vicar of Holy Trinity, Penponds near Camborne in Cornwall for fifty years from 1846 to 1896. The family came from Rugby where they had established Butlin's Bank in 1791. This was sold to Lloyds Bank in 1868 by a cousin, Ann Butlin. Some of the funds seem to have gone to William Wright who married Julia Crowther Trentham from Northamptonshire. Of their sons, Henry was an eminent surgeon at St Bartholomew's hospital in London. He was a cancer specialist and a pioneer of surgery which completely removed a malignant growth. He became president of both the Royal College of Surgeons and the British Medical Association (BMA). He was created a Baronet in 1911 and died in 1912. His son, Captain (Sir Henry) Guy Butlin, was killed unmarried in 1916, joining the Balfours, Ogilvies and Morva's brothers as yet another casualty of that war. The first Sir Henry had two daughters: Olive, who married Percy Furnivall, another surgeon; and Violet who married Norman Morice.

Another son of William Wright and Julia became vicar of St Swithuns, Leonard Stanley, in Gloucestershire and grandfather of Billy Butlin, the future Sir William Butlin, who created Butlin's Holiday Camps and is recorded as giving £5 million to charities, mainly to underprivileged children, during his lifetime. Billy's inspiring life story is fully recorded on the internet[9]. His father, who had married Bertha, the daughter of a travelling showman, wanted to escape the confines of respectable Gloucestershire life and went to South Africa where Billy was born. The marriage did not last and Bertha was next in Canada with her second husband where Billy eventually joined them. As he was later to say: ' My education was intermittent but I learnt about people'. He returned to Europe and survived the war as a stretcher-bearer in France. One of his mother's family helped him set up 'hoopla' stalls at country fairs and this eventually led to his first amusement park at Skegness. He managed to become the European distributor for the dodgem cars which he had first seen in Canada. It was then more amusement parks, followed by the splendid idea of holiday camps.

William and Julia's daughter was Julia Frances, remembered for her missionary zeal in the Parish and also furthering the cause of Foreign Missions.[10] Another son was Edward Fox Butlin who became a mining engineer. There had been mining in the Camborne area since the start of the nineteenth century.[11] Edward married Susan Rodd, daughter of the Reverend Henry Tremayne Rodd, Vicar of Gwinear, and Marianne Sutton. The Rodd family owned Trebartha Hall.[12] Edward and Susan had four children: Claude; Ann's father, Edward Schuyler, who was sadly killed in 1922;[13] Frances; and Dorothy, who married Wilfrid Taylor. It is through her grandmother, Susan, that Ann is related to many well known Cornish families. Her great-great-grandfather, the Reverend Edward Rodd, Vicar of St Just-in-Roseland , Henry Tremayne Rodd's father and Susan's grandfather, was married to Harriet Rashleigh, eldest daughter of Charles Rashleigh and Grace Tremayne of Heligan. It was Charles Rashleigh who had founded the seaport of Charlestown in 1789. He lived at Duporth Manor and had an interest in the family estate of Menabilly where he had been born. Ann's great-grandmother, Marianne Sutton (married to Henry Tremayne Rodd), was the daughter of Robert Sutton, captain of a packet-boat which frequented these Cornish ports. Marianne's mother, wife of Robert Sutton, was Susanna Schuyler who was a daughter of Adoniah Schuyler, another sea captain. Ann's second name is Schuyler, remembering another interesting connection. Adoniah was the son of General Philip Schuyler whose family had helped to develop Albany, New York, and who had left Holland in the seventeenth century.[14]

Ann's mother, born Morva Davies, was one of the daughters of Charles Davies whose parents had emigrated from Wales. He had married Lucy Walker and they lived at Eaglemont, described in a 1906 letter written by one of Morva's sisters as 'a rambling old place with plenty of ground and trees around it. The house itself is fifty years old and we have been here fourteen years.' The house was in Heidelberg, then 'eight miles from Melbourne' and the family were involved in the Heidelberg school of painting. Lucy was a painter with considerable talent.[15] Charles and Lucy had three sons and four daughters. Martyn and Alan joined the list of relatives killed in France. We have a letter from Charles to John, probably a brother, in England dated 8th August 1916:

'I was looking forward with great pride to my two boys calling on you, but God has willed otherwise. I have just had news from the defence department that Martyn died from wounds on the 22nd July. I don't know yet but believe he is buried in France. My second boy, Alan, is wounded and is at Woolwich military hospital. He left here as a sergeant but when he arrived in Egypt there was a call for more men and he volunteered as a private. Had he not been wounded soon after he got to France he would soon have got a commission. My poor boy (i.e. Martyn) who has gone was at Gallipoli. After going back to Egypt he transferred to the Infantry where he was soon a sergeant and was promised the first vacancy in commissioned rank for his good work as an N.C.O.'

Alan recovered from his wounds and returned to France where he was killed in July 1918 shortly before the end of that cruel war. At least the third and youngest son, Harry, was not involved. Morva was the youngest of the four daughters and, as mentioned above, married Claude Butlin after the death of her first husband. Besides the Nankivell twins and Ann, Morva had another son, Christopher Butlin, who lives in New Zealand. There are now four Butlin grandsons, including a Henry, and one daughter.

LEARNING FROM DIFFERENCE

Chapter 5

Myrtle and Lionel

Nina's letters tell us about Lionel's graduate apprenticeship at English Electric in Stafford from 1926 to 1928 after an engineering degree at Cambridge. Before Cambridge he had been at school at Bradfield and during the later war years, from 1915, he had been at The Malt House near Swanage. Myrtle, second surviving Jellicoe daughter (an older sister, Agnes Betty, had died aged six) had been in New Zealand where her father was Governor General. We have her compulsory writings from school and also a few letters written earlier at St Lawrence Hall on the south coast of the Isle of Wight to her parents on their Empire tour aboard HMS New Zealand. These letters were written by Myrtle when she was eleven, interested in life and unaware of her fate in the years that would follow. Unlike Nina's efforts, they were dated. Granny was Agnes, after whom Agnes Betty was named, widow of Sir Charles Cayzer, who had died in 1915. Agnes, my Cayzer great-grandmother, lived more than forty years longer than Rachel in Chile.

On 9th March 1919 Myrtle wrote:

'We are having awful weather here. Yesterday morning the Aquitania passed by and came so close that we could see the people on board. Before lunch we saw two battleships so we all tried to see the names on them. The first we thought was either the Renown or the Queen Elizabeth, the other was the Princess Royal as it was the only one in Portsmouth harbour with three funnels. Granny has been in bed but hopes to get up soon.'

15th March: 'I went out riding yesterday afternoon up the path to the top of the cliff at the back of the house and came down by St Lawrence station then round by Old Park and home again. This afternoon we are going to cycle into the country to gather daffodils for the church to-morrow. I would have liked to have had a ride on a camel.'

30th May: 'They say that at extreme low tide it is all sand beyond the rocks and that it is delightful to have a swim then. It is not quite warm enough for us yet but we can bathe next week (Now Orchard Bay and deserted when we visited in 2012).

We have planted a lot more seeds in our gardens. Norah's and my sweet peas are coming up beautifully. I have nasturtiums, candy-tuff, verbena stocks, and, in my vegetable plot, I have French beans and mustard and cress and am going to plant radishes and lettuces. We are learning about Australia now and I know all the places you have been to.'

20th June: 'We went to the station (still then Ventnor) to fetch Granny who had been over to Southsea to open a bazaar. We read in the paper that you had been asked not to land at Sydney because the people have influenza so badly there. The Mauretania has just passed. She was going so quickly. We all wished it was the New Zealand with you and Daddy on board. Granny is going to have a garden party on the 11th July.'

Myrtle did not just stay at St Lawrence. There is one letter, written 18th September 1919, when she was visiting Gartmore, the Cayzer base described by its previous owner, Cunninghame Graham, as the most beautiful estate in Scotland, which Sir Charles had rebuilt and remodelled: 'Nick went back last night to school. We have put up a memory to our camp. Nick did it with four sticks and some strings. Heather wrote on a piece of wood to the memory of our old camp and we put flowers on it.' Both Nick and Heather's son, Peter, play a part in this story. I had a difficult encounter with Nick 38 years later.

Great-grandmother Agnes Cayzer seems to have remained active in her last year. The Jellicoe biography by Admiral Bacon tells of her death in November 1919 when HMS New Zealand had reached Vancouver. My grandmother, the FG, had to miss the visits to Washington, Key West and Havana. She returned across the Atlantic on board the liner Adriatic to take over the care of the family. My Jellicoe grandfather, now Admiral of the Fleet, was back at St Lawrence in February 1920. It was not to be a long stay. In August the whole family set off to New Zealand after the appointment as Governor General. They were to be away from England for four busy years in which FG, still young and active in her early forties, played a full part. Presumably there was concern about leaving St Lawrence Hall for so long (no flying visits) for there are sale particulars in the archives of Ventnor local history Society.[1] Fortunately they changed their mind or there were no takers and we grandchildren were able to enjoy Orchard Bay in those summers before 1939.

Some letters written in New Zealand, when Myrtle was at boarding school or her parents were away, have also survived. 3rd December 1922:

'I wish you could have come to the prize giving. We played a tennis match against Iona and we won.'

March 1923: 'We had a birthday party last night. After dinner we had a cabaret with the orchestra dressed up in white pyjamas with black spots. We had to pay to go which made it much more exciting. The birthday girls and the prefects always have to make a speech and we sing 'God save the King.'

11th November 1923: (sent just to her father) 'We have just come back from the most glorious bathe. The water is beautifully warm and I had a lesson in the crawl. Yesterday our second and third tennis teams played Iona and we won. Our first team played Napier. When is the next mail for China because I want to know when to write to Mummy and Lucy.'

9th August 1924: 'Miss Holland has thought of an awful plan whereby the whole school has to get 63% before they can have their extra week-end tacked onto the end of the holidays. I don't think mine ought to count considering I won't be coming back and I'm supposed to know all the work my new form did last term. Unfortunately I'm not blest with second sight. Rona Vaile (see later) is much better – thank goodness – but Mrs Vaile is staying down here until she's able to go to Auckland. Unfortunately as we are all quarantined we can't go and see her.'

The four years as Governor General were completed in November 1924 and the Jellicoe family sailed back to England. Myrtle did not know that, a few months earlier, Lionel had been near Gibraltar. He had ridden his BSA motorcycle across France and Spain in the company of other undergraduates with an Austin Seven and a Triumph motorcycle and sidecar. By the beginning of 1925 the Jellicoes were all back in the Isle of Wight. It is on record that Myrtle, now nearly eighteen, helped to manage St Lawrence Hall and looked after her father when he was ill. She also enrolled as a VAD (Voluntary Aid Detachment) nurse. There was still time for travel. Her album includes pictures of cruises to the Northern Capitals and to Egypt (with her photos of Aswan, Karnak, Luxor, etc) in 1925. Then in 1928 it was South Africa on the Arundel Castle with FG, Lucy and Norah (presumably Prudie and George and Grandfather, attending to his continuing duties, left behind). Sir Abe Bailey, Lord de Villiers and General Smuts were some of their hosts and they were all invited to the garden party at Admiralty House, Simonstown. In February 1929 it was Switzerland, staying at the Hotel Eiger in Wengen. In February and March 1930 Myrtle was at Grindelwald. On 17th February her father's letter from the steam yacht 'Jeanette' at Monte Carlo[2] is an echo from those years: 'I see from the papers that you have very little snow but I suppose you go up to Scheidegg to ski. Weather here is distinctly bad, on my way back from Nice it was snowing, but I manage golf most days. Bridge every evening and bed at 10pm I lunched with Baroness d'Orsey yesterday after church.'[3]

Meanwhile Lionel had completed his two-year apprenticeship with English Electric and started work as a junior assistant engineer with Merz and Mclellan in their Victoria Street office on Thursday 11th July 1929. Annual salary was £250, office hours 9.30am to 6pm weekdays and 9.30am to 1pm on Saturdays. Merz and Mclellan in Africa have now been taken over by Mott Macdonald. The rest of the company is now part of Parsons Brinckerhoff, a global consulting firm involved in power generation and distribution, mining, airports, highways, rail systems, engineering services for the construction industry, and much more. Parsons Brinckerhoff now employ 14,000 engineers and assistants throughout the world, but it seems that Lionel turned down the chance of remaining one of their employees. His mother, Nina, had died nine months earlier and the fruits of his grandfather James's efforts in Chile would soon be his. There were no parents or grandparents alive to advise caution. His first pilot's log records flying lessons just at weekends beginning on Saturday 2nd November 1929, liberation after the morning stint in the Victoria office. In February 1930 he bought a secondhand Avro Avian G-EBSD. That winter of 1930 he was skiing at Grindelwald with the Uptons and certainly met Myrtle.

In July Lionel had another Avian G-ABCD and at the beginning of 1931 he ordered a new De Havilland Moth biplane for delivery in the spring. By then a Puss Moth G-ABIY had been won in a raffle by Rachel, who then sold it to Lionel. Both planes (the Moth registered as G-ABJH) were kept at Hanworth and were later to earn their keep with many fare-paying passengers.[5] At the end of March 1931 he left Merz and McLellan, as he was later to write: 'because I could not stand sitting on an office stool and I refused to be always licking other people's boots.' The journey log book for G-ABIY confirms that on 2nd April Lionel flew from Le Bourget, Paris, to Lausanne. The entry for the next day states: 'Berne je ne puis pas trouver le place proper par ce que mon carte est mauvais.' He had to fly back to Lausanne, leave the Puss there, and then take the train to Interlaken and on to Grindelwald to meet up with the Uptons again.

There is a photograph which confirms that Myrtle was at Grindelwald in February 1931. Then there is a letter, dated 10th February on Baer Grand Hotel writing paper to her sister Norah in New Zealand about the Hawkes Bay earthquake on 3rd February, which devastated Napier and Hastings and killed 256 people; 'If you were at Omarunni, you must have had the full brunt of it.' (In fact Mummie had wired to say Norah was safe and well.) There are also references that could mean that Lionel was also there in February. In another letter to Norah, she wrote, 'You may not have heard me mention Lionel Balfour. He was with Uppy and Alleyne Upton last year. I didn't take much notice of him, he was out for such a short time.' Lionel himself wrote, in a November 1931 letter, 'Ever since you came with me to the Rendez-vous in Grindelwald, I have worshipped you.' There is no proof whether these references are to 1930 or to 1931 but what we do know is that Myrtle did not stay in Grindelwald until Lionel arrived again in early April 1931. Instead she had been invited to Government House in Gibraltar of which she writes in a vivacious letter to Norah, dated 30th March 1931:

'I hated Gib at first after Switzerland because it rained unceasingly for the first ten days, after that it cleared and we had marvellous fun. I of course did all the wrong things. Flipped my name card into Lady Godley's soup one day. My name was rather bad too after I'd lunched, teaed and dined in the same ship in the same day. I never once, in the three weeks I was there went to bed before twelve. There were thirteen females, most of them presumably fishing. I don't think any of them hooked anything! The only snag was that Government House was so frightfully formal. I've never seen anything like it - H.E. might have been the Viceroy of India. None of the ADCs had any sense of humour. There was a Gymkhana on horses. Five minutes before the Ladies Race, a man came up to me and said would I ride his horse rumoured to be the fastest on the Rock. His groom hung on to him all the way to the start. I did finish second and the owner was annoyed I hadn't won. But the race was so short. We should have won easily if it had been another 100 yards!'

Back at St Lawrence, after travelling to Southampton in the Anchor Lines SS *Tuscania*, the next letter to Norah dated 24th April, is in a different vein as it describes the turn of fate:

'I was most frightfully cut up about that awful skiing smash. It may not have got into the NZ papers. Lionel Balfour and Helen Stack going flat out down the Lauberhorn collided and she was killed. I had a most pathetic letter from Lionel. He said they had gone up the Lauberhorn together with two others. Coming down they'd crossed fairly close, both said sorry and then turned inwards together at the same identical moment about 15 yards apart. Before they could do anything about it their heads had met. Helen was killed instantly but Lionel only had as he said 'a slightly cracked skull'. Poor wretched Lionel, as he says, he wished he could have been killed too. Why Fate should have picked on Helen of all people. She was an only child and her father, Sir Lee Stack, then Sirdar (Governor), was murdered in Egypt in March. Lionel was taken to 'The Klinnick' as was Lady Stack and he could hear her weeping at night. We used to ski together, in fact Lionel was the only person Alleyne would let me do the Mannlichen (a steep run) without a third person.'

The tone of this letter also suggests they were both there that February. The slight skull fracture did not prevent Lionel from piloting himself back to Hanworth on 20th April. The need to concentrate (the log says fog and nasty weather across the Channel) may have provided slight relief, but it would still have been difficult to live with the grim thoughts that accompany these happenings. If only the clock could be put back, if only one of them had turned earlier or later. But no, it had happened and was not to be (perhaps never was) forgotten. Myrtle had written on 11th: 'Ever since I read in yesterday's papers about your ghastly accident, I've been trying to write to you to tell you how desperately sorry I am for you, but, Lionel, words don't work on these occasions. If there was any way in which I could help you, or anything I could do for you, I'd willingly do it. Would you care to come down here for a week-end. We'd love to have you. Don't bother to explain if you feel you'd rather not come because I shall understand. Lionel I just can't tell you how sorry I am for you.' There is also a letter to Lionel from Flora Stack written four years later from Chalet Alpenheim, Wengen: 'Thank you for your thoughts of remembrance of my darling child and the most beautiful wreath. It has troubled me in past years when I was told that other wreaths than mine were placed on her grave. If it were the same this year Miss Brunner said she would take the cards and keep them. I arrived yesterday and saw them to-day.'

Continuous activity may also have helped. Was this also a clue to his Herculean determination? He was alive. He must do all he could to justify his existence. After two days' use of G-ABJH, he was off again in G-ABIY to Avignon, Milan and Zagreb with a Mr Ramsey Green as co-pilot. Myrtle wrote again on 7th May: 'How are you? Is the head alright now? I hope the trip to Yugoslavia went off well. Would you care to come to a dance at the Turkish Embassy on the 21st?' The relationship was developing, but most days throughout that summer he was flying in one of the planes with more trips across the Channel to Europe. Later in May it was Nuremberg, Vienna, Venice and Cannes in G-ABIY with his sister, Rachel. On return, it was English destinations in G-ABJH, and then, at the beginning of June, G-ABIY to Vienna again with his Aunt, the once suffragette, Maud Joachim. This is likely to have been taking her for her annual climbing session. After a quick flight to Rotterdam it was down to Marseilles at the beginning of July with my godfather Gerard Wood and then preparation for the King's Cup Air Race. On 18th, 19th and 23rd of July, he flew over the whole King's Cup course in G-ABJH (over seven hours in the air each day) whilst G-ABIY was being tuned and tested. (On 24th, 15 minutes full throttle.) The race started on 25th. *The Aeroplane* magazine later reported:

'From the beginning of the race till the end the weather was of unmitigated foulness.

43

The competitors drove through deluges of rain and through low-lying clouds over the hill country for the whole distance. The Puss Moth won the Siddeley Trophy twice. That is to say Mr Jackaman won it officially, but Mr L.M.J. Balfour in another Puss Moth beat him by three places and about fifteen minutes, only his club at Hanworth forgot to send in his entry. Mr Balfour's average speed over the whole course was only a fraction less (127.36 against 127.54 mph) than the fastest pilot, Lieutenant Rodd RN in yet another Puss Moth.'

It was a magnificent achievement and once again I regret my failure to get Lionel to talk about those times. Clubs needed to send in entries for members of light aeroplane clubs confirming that the aircraft entered was the bona fide property of the pilot. Had the Hanworth club done their stuff, Lionel's name would now be on that magnificent trophy[7]. If earlier suggestions that serving officers should not be allowed to compete had been followed up, he would have won the 1931 King's Cup. That could have been a boost in later difficult years. Through August the same pattern of races, rallies and European trips continued except for one flight to the Island on 12th August when he landed at Somerton, just south of Cowes. It seems that, despite all these commitments, he and Myrtle had kept in touch. She had to cope with illness as described in her 20th September letter:

'The family's trip to Canada was absolutely disastrous. Lucy (her oldest sister) was taken desperately ill on board the ship going over. Ten days after arrival she had a very serious operation and afterwards she actually stopped breathing for five minutes. Mummie is still out there and so is my brother (George) who has had his tonsils hauled out at the same hospital. Daddie, although he had a bronchial cold, insisted on coming home as he has so much to do here. Result bronchitis and the Doctor has ordered complete rest in bed. I have got my work cut out. Besides looking after Daddy, I've the house to run and his room is stacked with letters, which I will have to deal with somehow. He is not allowed to look at a letter. When I went to Southampton yesterday, I got an awful shock, he looked so ill. Then of course the Mayor, etc, were there to receive him. However I managed to deal with them and also to keep the Press quiet. I am sorry to put you off at such short notice. Could you manage the first or second weekend in October. I went over to Shanklin Aerodrome (presumably Apse) the other day quaking in my shoes as I did not know what to say but it seems quite a decent landing ground and they say they often have had a Puss Moth down there. Do hope you can manage one of the week-ends. Apologies for the screed. P.S. Have just collected a nurse as I've come to the conclusion if anything went wrong the responsibility would be too much for my shoulders to carry.'

From the start this seems to have been a relationship grounded in life's realities. They found they were able to share their concerns and to support and comfort each other when faced with the horrors of accidental death and the travails of illness and business. With Lucy still in Canada, Norah returning from New Zealand and Prudie in Paris, Myrtle was in charge at St Lawrence and now had to cancel the October invitation to Lionel. Molly Vesey Holt came to help for a few days. Myrtle wrote on 5th:

'Daddy isn't much better. None of the Doctors seem to be able to make up their minds. I had Sir Thomas Horder down from London last Wednesday and he was no wiser than the local men. It's going to be a very long business and to start with I've cancelled all his engagements for the next two months. There are two nurses to look after him. Mummie has arrived back from Canada. I'm glad because attending to his correspondence, coping with the Press and looking after him was about as much as I could deal with. Amongst other things I have let 19, Prince's Gardens for a year. Mummie wasn't too pleased but in view of the fact of the last budget and Daddie being banned from London anyway this winter, when I got a very good offer I consulted the lawyer and an Uncle and they said you must try and get it accepted. You must (underlined) try and come in November. I have to go to Haslar for eight days nursing training from the 17th. On Thursday I'm coming to London to finish details of the house and drive down one of the cars which is sitting in the garage there. It is sickening you could not come down here now because the weather's heavenly.'

We also have Myrtle's comments in her letter to Norah, dated 9th November:

'Lionel proposed to me on Shanklin Aerodrome - of all outlandish places - and I said I might marry him. He is flying me to the Uptons (when he returns) and I suppose I shall have to make up my mind and you know how difficult I always find that. The thing I like best of all about him is his reliability and the fact that he's never tried to kiss me, etc, until after he proposed and then he asked my permission! He's so different that way to all other modern youths. Lionel's rather lucky in a way because he has no family to harass him.'

After further races and trips to Europe in both planes, Lionel did still land at Apse in G-ABIY on 10th, that second October weekend. It was then that he met up with Alexander Murray and his partners, the first sight of the sort of investment he was seeking. This seems to have been the start of Lionel's involvement with the Air Ferry ideas. He flew to the Island on 14th, this time with G-ABJH, and then again on 24th looking at possible sites for a better (and fog-free) Island terminal. He did not stay at St Lawrence, where there were still problems. Two days later Myrtle wrote that she was coming up to London for a wedding: could he be most frightfully kind and fly her back to the Island? 'I would not dream of asking you, but you did say in your letter to ask'. This was achieved and there was time for some further flights. Myrtle's thank you followed:

'Lionel, thank you a thousand times for being so kind to me. It was perfectly sweet of you to bring me back yesterday. Every time you take me up I love it more. Daddy's X-Ray showed definite trouble in his chest. Lucy is sailing to-day from Canada. There's an absolute mundalion (her word) of telegrams and letters from all over the world. Thank goodness I chucked Haslar. It was sweet of you to take George (her brother) up. He has done nothing but bombard me with questions ever since. He was flying in his sleep.'

This letter was signed 'love from Myrtle', not just 'yours Myrtle' as previously. By November they were becoming more committed. On 7th November 1931 Lionel was writing:

'You are an angel to say you love me a little, but there are all sorts of practical difficulties which you must think about before you decide.' He went on to explain his financial position: 'I am putting £5,000 (the equivalent of £250,000 in 2012)[8] into this Ferry Service which will reduce my annual investment income to £550. I ought to be paid about £400 as a pilot with some return on the capital. On the other hand I may lose all that and get no dividend on the £5,000. We shall have to wait for rather a long time so you will be able to change your mind if you want to, but with the knowledge that you might marry me if I succeed, I shall try ten times as hard and probably will.'

Lionel was already committed to escort Mr Ramsay Green again, now with his wife. This time it was round Germany in G-ABIY. He received Myrtle's response in Munich:

'The idea of ever promising to marry anyone has always scared me stiff, I couldn't bear to make a bosh shot of it, it would be so awful. I am hopeless at making up my own mind. I wobble and waver but this I promise you, if I do once say definitely I will marry you, there will be no wobbling over that. I rather fear Mummie (FG) would kick up a fuss. Could you stand that? She's such a mercenary kind of person. She thinks material things count so much more than others, on the other hand she's always nagging at us to get married. Anyway it's for you to decide whether you think I am worth squabbling for.'

Lionel replied on 13th November writing in the train back to Nuremberg on paper taken from the Regina Palast Hotel:[9]

'You have written me the sort of sensible letter I hoped you would. I would not dream of hurrying you into a decision, as you say its such a serious one and you want to be very sure. But I want to have your views on lots of things just in case you will marry me. I will face any amount of squabbling on your account however unpleasant it is.'

Lionel was back at Shanklin on 17th November. On 23rd Myrtle wrote to Norah, from the Upton's house at Balmaclennan.

'I hope you have received my cable announcing my engagement. Actually we got engaged last Tuesday at about 6pm on Shanklin Aerodrome. As we were flying here at crack of dawn the next day we said nothing about it to the family. We wanted a few days together so we could get plans fixed. I knew that if we just went to Mummie and calmly said we want to get married there would be a mundalion of questions and we wanted time to get the answers taped.'

With Myrtle's encouragement (additions to the draft kept are in her writing), they wrote a long letter to her father. Lionel described his education and apprenticeship and then how he had learnt to fly whilst working at Merz and Mclennan. It seemed, he wrote, that aviation was going to be the big thing of the future and it would be as well to get into it now. He had kept an eye open for a way of starting a career in flying and a month ago it had turned up. He thought it essential to explain but asked that it be treated confidentially. With the establishment of the aerodrome at Portsmouth, it would be possible to run an aerial ferry service to the Island. They were undertaking some rather delicate negotiations on the site for an aerodrome at Ryde. Once secured they would be in an unrivalled position but, until this was achieved, it must be kept secret or someone with more money might cut them out. The letter then repeated the details of his financial position as described in the letter to Myrtle and suggested that, if 'he would sanction their engagement,' they would wait till September 1932 to get married. By then they would know whether the Ferry was a success and, if not, he could get another job. As recorded in another letter to Norah, this led to:

'A deluge of letters saying on no account to announce it publicly until the family held a consultation over and with Lionel. Poor darling, won't he be put through the mill. He has a flying job which the family may kick at. If the family have refused to sanction our engagement we will just have to posses ourselves in patience. I don't want to marry without their consent but as we have no intention of giving each other up I suppose I shall have to. We want to buy a house - a very small one in Hampshire - as we want to keep Lionel's plane for trolling about in.'

In a p.s. Myrtle added:

'It's entirely due to your broken leg that I got engaged. If you hadn't, I should never have met the Upton's and have gone to Grindelwald with them, in which case Lionel and I would probably have never met.'

Their engagement was agreed and announced at the end of November. The rest of the family and friends took notice. They landed the Puss Moth in the fields next to Tylney Hall to have Sunday lunch with Uncle Bertie, FG's brother, and his wife Aunt Freda. They met Madden cousins in London. The Jellicoe aunts, my grandfather's sisters, came to St Lawrence. Another flight was planned to visit New Zealand school friend, Rona Vaile, now Baker Cresswell and living at West Meon. Myrtle's 3rd December letter recorded 98 letters and twelve telegrams:

'How am I going to deal with them, really dear, on second thoughts I don't think I will get engaged again!'

She wrote to Norah about Lionel in January 1932:

'He's just the sort of person I'd always hoped I'd marry, not (heavily underlined) one of Mummie's (FG) dreadful London Society types but a perfect gentleman in every sense of the word with very high ideals, reserved and rather shy, but with a terrific sense of humour. Also we both like the same things. Altogether he's a perfect darling and much too good for me. I am terribly lucky as I am sure you will agree when you meet him.'

In that same letter she wrote:

'I may learn to fly. I already twiddle the thing along in the air but I have not yet taken her off or landed her. Did I tell you that Lionel crashed whilst I was watching the other day. The engine cut out whilst he was taking off and he landed in a hedge. I thought he would be killed or the thing would catch fire and being alone on the aerodrome I wondered what I was going to find. However Lionel was not even scratched but the poor old Puss was badly smashed.'

He had survived again. Lionel gave up the flat in Elvaston Place and based himself at The Esplanade Hotel in Ryde whilst working to establish the Air Ferry. Myrtle wrote on 30th December:

'There is now a possibility of Ma and Pa going to Madeira sailing on 22nd January. Prudie may go which means Lucy and I will be left here. (Norah was still away) With you at Ryde it would be rather fun, wouldn't it, short of going to Switzerland the next best thing.'

Her father did regain his strength in Madeira. When he and FG returned in March, it was agreed that the wedding would take place that summer. The maternal Cayzer family advisors, sensibly aware of the potential financial perils of civil aviation, insisted that some of Lionel's capital should be tied up in a marriage settlement. Myrtle was concerned. She wrote to Lionel:

'Was my mother partly right when she said that being married to me might make it difficult for you financially. I don't want you to feel tied by the leg. It's so unnecessary. I'd hate to be a drag on you. I want to help not hinder.'

The wedding, amply described in press cuttings and photographs:

'Earl Jellicoe's daughter marries well known Aviator, four members of Royal family attend, the church a blaze of British Legion poppies and lilies'[10] took place at All Souls', Langham Place on 11th June 1932.'

There was time for a two-week honeymoon in G-ABIY: Geneva, Milan, Venice, Nice and Cannes and back for the first flight into Ryde on 27th June. Portsmouth Airport was officially opened on 2nd July and then the Air Ferry started with, as the pilot's log shows, Lionel often as pilot in a wide variety of planes besides coping with much of the administration. (E.g. on 19th August he flew G-ABJH three times and the Spartan G-ABLJ once across to the Island).

A recent discovery has been a cache of letters from Myrtle's father written in his own hand. I have commented earlier about the pressure from FG that I should attempt a similar or associated career regardless of my own personal interests. These letters show so clearly that this would not have been grandfather's way. He respected a young man's own choice, showed interest and wanted to help. In March 1934, when Myrtle was unwell after my birth, and the financial progress of the Air Ferry was not as Lionel had forecast, there was no criticism. Instead, in his own neat script, writing from the Golf Hotel at St Raphael, he made use of his contacts to try and enlist support. The results were handwritten replies from Lords Ebbisham and Rockley (which Lionel also kept) and useful contact with Sir John Thornycroft and Sir Herbert Walker, all involved or connected with railway management. The hoped-for investment from the Southern

Railway was not then achieved, but this would have been the prelude to the co-operation after 1945 agreed before the Labour Government intervened. A later letter that same year, addressed to 'My dear Lionel' (and signed 'yours affectionately, Jellicoe'), sympathises 'with the disappointing side of the balance sheet and also that the amalgamation with the British Air Navigation Company was not coming off.' He hoped that Lionel 'would manage to bring off an amalgamation with some good company so as to provide funds for the future.' This was not to be as described in *Spithead Express*. What matters is that these letters, and others to come in the next paragraphs, show the kindly persona, always concerned for the welfare of others, which, despite his eminence and renown, characterised my grandfather throughout his life.

I have already mentioned Myrtle's ill health, which continued for so long after my birth in February 1934. It was years later that I learnt more of the story which helped in understanding comments overheard in earlier years and sometimes feelings of guilt when I met Myrtle's sisters and other relatives.[11] It seems there were features of my mother's frame which made delivery by caesarian section preferable and that there were then problems with this operation. In the March 1934 letter to Lionel already mentioned, grandfather Jellicoe gives us some clues:

'Myrtle seems to be in a very nervous condition and to be suffering a great deal both from nerves and from pain due to the clots. I feel ever so much for you and for the anxiety through which you are passing. Certainly the winter of 1933-34 will live in your memory as a really bad time'.

There are pictures of Myrtle still lying in a reclining chair in the garden of Cam Cottage, Shedfield, in May. In April grandfather Jellicoe had written to her:

'It is so splendid to get such good reports on your progress. I hope that your 'sit up' today was a really pleasant change and that you enjoyed it. I am of course very anxious to see you and am thinking of coming next Friday on my way home from London. I would arrive at Winchester at 3 pm, come to see you about 4.30 p.m. and catch the 5.50 from Winchester to Southampton. Will you drop me a post card to say if this is alright. I enclose one addressed and stamped.'

Since finding this letter, when on the platform at the station I always think of him - probably on his own without today's aides, secretaries, or security, and with a cheery smile for the railway staff and others who recognised him. There is another letter to Myrtle written at the end of August 1934 from the Cayzer house, Gartmore in Perthshire, sent with a £20 cheque for her birthday:

'I hope that the next 12 months will make up for all that you have been through during the last 12 months.' He adds: 'The house is full here. We shot 130 brace yesterday.'

Myrtle was still not fully well in spring 1935 and she was sent off – protesting – for treatment by a Dr. Quiserne at Bagnoles de l'Orne in Normandy. The web entry states that the hydrotherapy baths are known for their healing powers for rheumatic, gynaecologic and circulatory problems. It was not where she wanted to be, but for us she is alive again in the twenty-two letters (again kept by Lionel) which seem to have been her life-line.

These are just a few extracts:

29th May: 'This is certainly a very pretty spot but it's going to be so dull. I am counting the hours till you come. We (FG was with her at first) drove right through Alencon but I could not see the aerodrome. The baths are an enormous building. The attendant appears after 20 minutes and enfolds me in piping hot towels. I tasted the water. It just seemed rather brackish and salty.'

30th May: 'I do miss you both (i.e. Lionel and me) and feel such a deserter doing nothing whilst you are working so hard. Mother and I duly had tea at the Casino. When I said to the gigolo that I could not dance, mother promptly appropriated him. I am afraid I still think the whole thing rather stupid. What lying in a bath can do I fail to see and, as for drinking special water and taking pills, one can do that perfectly easily at home. Ma told me yesterday that she had overheard Daddie saying that, if anyone in this World deserved to get on, it was you as you worked so hard.'

The problem seems to have been the circulation of blood through her veins. The daily letters to Lionel become more serious. She does not feel well. Quiserne wonders about a liver deficiency. She is suffering from hay fever.

Undated: 'I have had the most awful attacks of hay fever the last two days. It has been quite as bad as before, continuous stream and I have hardly slept for three nights. Its making me feel so rotten.'

On 11th June Lionel flew over to Normandy in another Puss, G-ABMC (see below), landing at Alencon.
Then she wrote on 14th June:

'It was such glorious heaven having you and I am missing you so much. Everyone in the Pension kept asking whether you got back safely.'

By then FG had returned for Charles Madden's funeral[12] and I was flown over to the Island 'to be a companion to Daddie.' He wrote to Myrtle on 17th June:

'You may like to hear news of Christopher. (I was then nearly one-and-a-half years old). He comes into my room every morning and has great fun with his tin toy motor car and playing hide and seek with grandpa. This evening he has been in the drawing room with me looking at illustrated papers. His one idea is to look at pictures of motor cars about which he is ever so keen. He just loves a drive in a car and takes every opportunity. This afternoon Mummy took him over to a wedding at Freshwater in the Ford.'

Proof of my life-long interest! If I had taken up the challenge of an apprenticeship in 1950 aged 16, and this grandfather had been still in action aged 90 (not entirely fanciful; until that fatal infection in November 1935, he had recovered his strength and kept fit with his golf), I think he would have encouraged me, but then he would also have had to witness another war. I like to think that we would have both realised the importance of the British-owned car industry in the post-war world!

The letter continued:

'I do hope that you are not very tired of your cure and that it is going to be of great benefit to you. Lionel was here for the weekend and played a lot of tennis. He played singles with Mummy (FG) and gave her 15. She was playing an A1 game and the second set was 5 all. Lionel was very busy with work but got a lot of fresh air and exercise too.'

Myrtle was fed up with the cure. On 19th June she wrote to Lionel:

'I am so miserable and depressed. I don't know what to do. I have been told that when I return I must do nothing for at least six weeks. Mrs L said I ought to go to a hotel where there is a lift because I ought not to walk up stairs. She said she felt like death the first year too, but have I really got to back pedal and go back to the life of a semi-invalid again? They say if one doesn't there's no sense in coming to Bagnoles and one's just heading straight for varicose veins. How I long to be of more use generally in the world. After all what do I do? Answer: Absolutely nothing. I really thought that after coming here I should be fitter. I really don't see why I shouldn't go to the RAF display.[13] If I have got to come here again, there may not be another chance or we shall probably be indulging in another war. Afraid this is a pig of a letter to send. It's wicked to trouble you the only person in the wide wide world who really cares a straw what happens to me.'

At last it was over and on 23rd June she wrote:

'I shall catch the 9.18 Autorail arriving Montparnasse 12.18 and then take a taxi straight to Le Bourget, lunch there and wait for the Envoy. If this trip is cancelled at the last moment, could Charles perhaps come or lend you his Leopard to fetch me?'[14]

This, I regret, was the distress that my arrival caused Myrtle, but the advantage now is that the Bagnoles stay was the catalyst for her writing which, added to all her other letters, gives us insights into her thoughts. This last letter also hints at other happenings. The Airspeed Envoy had been purchased to try and develop a direct Southampton- and Portsmouth-to-Paris route with connections to other internal British airlines. There were sometimes insufficient takers for the then just 90-minute journey. After four years unrelenting hard work carrying passengers every day, the faithful Puss Moth had been landed through some goalposts on a foggy night by one of the ferry pilots. In that last week G-ABIY had flown to Heston, Gatwick and Shoreham, some of the time on what were known as Army Co-operation contracts giving the gunners aiming practice. It was no longer capable of collecting Myrtle.

My grandfather's last letter to Myrtle was written from a house called Larkfield at Dunmury near Belfast. It was dated 21st September 1935, two months before his death. They were staying with daughter Norah, recently married to 'Fred' Wingfield[15], who was serving in the Rifle Corps. They had brought the car over (probably the Humber) and had expected a very rough passage but it was all right. There is a picture in the local Belfast paper of the two of them, grandfather and FG, with lovely smiles, shaking hands with the captain of the Lairdscastle in which they had crossed the Irish sea.[16] Daughter Lucy and her husband Teddy were dining that evening en route to Liverpool. Tuesday, they were going to stay with the Hawkes at North Berwick until 30th, then London on 2nd October and back to St Lawrence on 4th. And, as ever concerned for others, he hoped that Lionel's negotiations over the Air Services were proceeding satisfactorily. On 5th November he spoke in support of his brother-in-law, Sir Herbert Cayzer MP (Uncle Bertie) in Portsmouth [17], and then, on 11th, in London, he 'contracted a chill' whilst attending the Cenotaph Armistice service. He continued with other duties the next day, not wishing to let people down, but was then encouraged to rest. He was getting better but a lung was affected and he died unexpectedly on 20th November. One of the commentators who had seen him recently wrote: 'He still looked in vigorous middle age good enough for another dozen years of active life,' but we know from Myrtle's letters that he had had related illness three years earlier.

After the lying-in-state in the Henry VII chapel at Westminster Abbey, his body was taken to Horse Guards Parade on the morning of Monday 25th November before the State funeral. At 10.55am, the procession set out, down Northumberland Avenue, along the Embankment and up New Bridge Street and Ludgate Hill to arrive at St Paul's Cathedral at 11.45. Ten Admirals, including one French and one German, one Field Marshal and one Marshal of the Royal Air Force accompanied the gun carriage. Then came Myrtle's brother, George, and behind him the three sons-in-law, Major Latham and Lieutenant Wingfield in uniform and my father between them in civilian morning dress. Behind them came the Prince of Wales and the Duke of York. Then came no less than fifty-eight Admirals leading the rest of the participants. According to *The Times* report there were another one-hundred-and-thirty Admirals in the Abbey congregation.[18] It is only recently when looking at press photographs that I realised that Lionel had marched in this procession, such was the dark curtain that he seemed to have drawn over any memory of those years. Grandfather's tomb is in the crypt next door to Nelson.

Myrtle was to live just less than ten years after her father's funeral. She died on 10th November 1945 and, in the next chapter, how she did so much more than the 'absolutely nothing' she worried about at Bagnoles will be described. In 1938 they moved from Cam Cottage, Shedfield, to Peake House, Warnford, in the Meon Valley. I loved Peake, situated just below Old Winchester Hill. Years later, reading through all the paperwork showed that they had not owned the house. Despite Lionel's considerable inheritance, they had had no property investment as safeguard for difficult times. It was an old farmhouse rented from Lady Peel's Leydene Estate[19] reached by a minor road a mile through fields and woods from A32. Nearby were several cottages for those who worked for the farmer from near Petersfield who rented the surrounding land. I was then an only child. This was not my parent's wish as Myrtle's letters from that time make clear. Left alone, I was able to roam in the fields. It was not difficult to make contact with other children in those cottages.[20] The day came when these trysts were discovered and it was made clear that this was unacceptable. It was hinted that I was in some way different. This incident has never been forgotten and may have been the start of my continuing dislike of the English class system. Ever since I have disdained any notions of superiority through birth, rank or position. Another remembered incident was when I refused to have a metal sign denoting 'Admiral', inlaid in polished wood, attached to my bedroom door![21] When later elected, it was to try and serve rather than hold sway. I like to think that my grandfather would have understood.

From then on I was on my own discovering the pleasure of working with my hands. First it was those hard rubber 'Minibrix', but they could not be turned into machines. Then came the joy of Meccano and the ability to construct ever-more-complicated model cars powered by clockwork motors. Later rubber-powered aeroplane models were built both from kits and my own designs. These were flown in the surrounding fields with thoughts of a future helping Lionel build full-size aeroplanes in the factory at Portsmouth. There was also construction work building a causeway to an island on the pond adjacent to the farm's cowshed. Only later did I learn that over the years the carcasses of diseased animals had been thrown into the pond. Until the outbreak of war in September 1939, the maternal cousins assembled at St Lawrence Hall in August. Each year when we played on the secluded beach at Orchard Bay, a new baby appeared amongst the cousins, but there was no brother or sister for me. I learnt to become self-sufficient and to attempt my own decisions.

LEARNING FROM DIFFERENCE

Chapter 6

War and Death in the Meon Valley

It may have been lonely at Peake, but my protected and privileged room was paradise for a model-maker nearly six year old. It was full of light, one window looking over the lawn to Old Winchester Hill, the other towards the farm buildings and Beacon Hill beyond. Between the windows were large storage cupboards with a good working surface above. To the left of the window looking over the lawn was a wireless and, behind it, a map with large areas coloured red. It's now a shameful memory of gazing at that map, thinking that the British were a uniquely superior sort of people and how awful it would have been if born in another country. This may shock, but it's true. Probably because of what followed, early thoughts have remained crystal clear. The indoctrination was so powerful and those wall maps so cleverly presented: 'Island Britain' central, coloured in that dark brick-red, the dominions (the very word evoking domination) of the British Empire spread out below and to the side also in dark red. And, to cap the message, this sense of the global master race, all the other countries were printed in much lighter colours. I was just five-and-a-half years old when disarray began to encroach on all this pomp and display. One morning, 3rd September 1939, I was told to listen to that wireless and remember the words 'Herr Hitler' and 'at war'.[1] The end of a carefree existence had been signalled. The address book confirms that Molly Vesey Holt, one of my godmothers, whose distinguished husband had been killed in a most unfortunate flying accident in 1931[2], stayed for nine months, with her children also staying for shorter periods, presumably in school holidays. There were many other visitors, all no doubt appreciating the peace of that valley away from the turmoil of war. Of relatives, there were Joachims, Lathams, Loudons, Tathams, Wingfields and FG. Other names remembered included Coningham (ex-Frank), Edwards, Hallifax, Henderson, Maclean[3] and Powys Maurice.

Meanwhile Myrtle threw herself into the war effort, no more of the 'absolutely nothing' of Bagnoles when she had 'longed to be of more use generally in the World.' She had in the end managed some VAD training and there is a summary of all her activities, perhaps relating to expenses, petrol allowance or tax, amongst Lionel's papers.

1939 - 1942. Part time Meonstoke First Aid Post.

April 1941. One week refresher course, Winchester County Hospital.
May 1941 - June 1943. (Except for period of recuperation from surgery), two half days, one full day per week at Royal Naval Hospital, Beverley, Wickham.

1942. Sister-in-charge Warnford First Aid Post.

British Legion. Hampshire Branch. Vice-Chairman. Southampton Branch. President.
British Sailor's Society, Southampton. President of the Ladies Guild.

Meon Valley Civil Defence and Invasion Committees. Member.

We also have Myrtle's letters to Victoria Baldwyn who returned them to me many years later. She had helped look after me as Nannie at Cam Cottage and then for a short time at Peake. A letter dated Boxing Day 1940 was written at 'Whinshill', the house adjacent to Sunningdale golf course which FG bought at the beginning of the war when it was thought that the Germans might invade the Isle of Wight as they had the Channel Islands.[4] The grandchildren had been summoned for Christmas.

'All the children had the time of their lives yesterday. They still get on extremely well.'

I only have dim memories of that gathering. Myrtle's letter continued, mentioning more of her own work not in the above list:

'Daddie has been going backwards and forwards to Pompey[5]. Granny wants us to remain but I can't as I now work three days a week at Shedfield Cottage Hospital. It's hair-raising as there are between twenty and thirty patients and only the Matron and what VAD help she can get. The worst job by far though was when I had, with Mrs Colville's help, to lay out a little boy of six who had been killed by a bomb. He had his head bashed in and all one side badly burnt. It was a very grim and bloody job. Both Mrs Colville and I felt we could cope with anything afterwards. We have had crowds of refugees out our way too. As yet I have no-one as they say I am too isolated, however should Pompey receive similar treatment to Southampton, I shall take on some of Daddie's men's families. He now employs five hundred men and is extremely busy.'

Because of all these duties, there were sufficient petrol coupons combined with sharing transport. I went to a school organised by Fynvola Maclean's[3] mother in their house above Wickham. Sometimes I would be taken by Lionel on his way to Portsmouth, often it would be meeting up with others. There's a memory of adult conversation whilst we waited to transfer to another car in the forecourt of a large house in Shedfield, seventy years later the offices of an international organisation: 'He went down with the ship. He was recommended for a VC, but it's a posthumous DSC. I must attend the ceremony.' It is still so clear in my memory. The driver of the Vauxhall 'Ten' had just been widowed. The conversation was of her husband's bravery and the pride in the invitation to the forthcoming investiture. It was too often repeated in Naval Hampshire, particularly the Meon Valley. Handsome groom in Naval uniform, white-gowned bride escorted by flower-decked bridesmaids. Then away, perhaps to Cannes, Hendaye or Rapallo whilst the Dictators strengthened their armies. Then, after only ten or even less years of marriage, the valiant figure, perhaps trim in a St John's Uniform, with a future to be devoted to what children they had achieved (and later grandchildren), to duty, and the memory of a man whose face, never ageing, looked out from framed pictures on tables around the house. In a letter to Norah Myrtle wrote:

'We had a ghastly time when the Prince of Wales went down as there were so many wives round here.'

She also mentioned that, amongst others, Anthony Franklyn from that large Shedfield house had been killed.

To return to her letters to Nannie Baldwyn, this one undated:

'Hitler left us in peace last night but the night before we had anything but a quiet night though nothing to what Daddie had in Portsmouth. He was on guard at the Airport and spent from 9pm to 5.30am in the shelter. You will be sorry to hear that one of the Miss Medlicott's died of injuries after last week's raids. A bomb exploded in a tree in their garden.[6] She was outside watching (as one is expressly told not to). Isn't it tragic? Ivy Bishop[7] rang up to say her husband is prisoner of war which is more cheerful news.'

There was discussion whether a shelter should be built. Though still a peaceful spot, the German planes returned overhead after their raids on Coventry. Instead of a shelter, wooden screens were made and propped against the walls of the downstairs corridor. When these bombers were heard, we lay down between screen and wall. Was the idea protection from glass and splinters? I used to listen to the different engine notes. Sometimes unused bombs were jettisoned. We were not one of the houses in open country which were thus damaged, though it was thought that one bomb went into the pond. Myrtle was away in a nursing home in autumn 1941 and I was collected from the school at Wickham by other parents. In letters to Norah, only read in recent years, Myrtle described the investigations and her subsequent surgery. After an August consultation she had been told that 'her womb was six inches too high, stuck to my caesar scar, all out of shape and the tubes kinked and blocked.' This was the consequence of botched surgery at my birth nearly eight years earlier and it had been made clear that she could not have another child without a major operation. Then, in September, she had visited the surgeon, a Mr Gilliat, again. He had done 'another blow out of the tubes without anaesthetic, somewhat painful but highly successful.' With that achieved it was felt, she then wrote, 'that it would be easier to put my womb back in its proper place. The operation is on 9th October, in bed for three weeks then three months going carefully, no nursing at Beverley, etc. However I feel its worth it but of course its damned expensive.'

On 20th she wrote to Norah:

'For the first time I am really feeling fit. Pain not so much from the actual op as from a nicked blood vessel which has formed a sort of clot. Thank goodness it has at last decided to disperse. The operation was a great success. The womb was freed, also some adhesions, and cysts removed from one ovary. I could not sleep for the first nine nights but now all is well.'

It seems that all really was well and it is only now with hindsight that we wonder about the significance of that clot. Before returning to Peake she spent a few combative days with FG at Sunningdale. We have her 5th November letter to Lionel:

'I am longing to come to my nice warm home. I asked Scillitoe for one of mother's fur capes. Was there a row, she was furious because I was wearing it. If I had not known I'd get pneumonia if I took it off, I'd have thrown it at her. You must come for me on Friday. I must come home and be warm. I am sorry the Ford has been giving trouble. You will have to drive slowly because the Ford isn't as comfortable as the Morris and I shan't like bumps.' (It is not known why the Morris was not available.)

By the spring of 1942 she was fully in action again and writing to Victoria Baldwyn in March, 'Is there any chance of you meeting us in Southampton on the 14th? It's the opening day of their Warship week. Both Lady Jellicoe and I are patrons and we have got to attend the opening lunch at The Polygon[8]. I can't take Christopher. Would you be able to give him lunch (at my expense) in the ordinary part of the hotel? I know he would love to see you again (as I would too) and you could then witness the parade. I am frantically busy as we have our own Warship week immediately after Southampton and I am Chairman. Warnford with 130 people has been given a target of £750, which seems fantastic to me. The Bishop's Waltham area has to raise £62,000.' There is another letter that same month with the first mention of boarding school for me: 'I took him to see his school on Saturday. He is trying to get me to postpone his going. I would love to but feel its for his own good.' This was Highfield School near Liphook on the Hampshire/Surrey border.[9] I do remember something of that tussle. I lived in this adored house in a lovely position, not some City flat. I had my room. I had my interests. Why be away for two thirds of the year when I could attend a local school and be in my own room every night and at weekends? Why did my parents who had produced me (with more difficulty than I then realised) not want me at home? They would not listen. As it happened, it did not work out as planned. We do not control events. Myrtle wrote in August 1942: 'Christopher had a disappointing term as he spent most of it in the Sanatorium with whooping cough. I was completely fed up. It seemed so infuriating to send him there and pay large fees for him to be ill. Naturally I felt I might as well as have kept him at home till September.' Yes, Myrtle, if you had listened to my pleas!

Boredom remains the prevailing memory of that still well-known school. The lessons seemed interminable, so long, with so little of interest. I was constantly admonished for drawing cars and other machines. Then there were what seemed to me to be pointless ball games. I much preferred constructive physical work which provided exercise at the same time. We were made aware of the war by the chapel roll-calls of old boys who had died on the battlefields and the accompanying hints that we too must be prepared to lay down our lives for our country. Memorable was the day when the headmaster, tears streaming down his face, got up after lunch to announce to the whole school that his son, Hugh, had been killed. In total sixty-nine Highfield boys were killed in the two World Wars.

With just one half term exeat, and no access to telephones or emails, letters were the only source of contact with home. Letters confirm that Myrtle continued consultations with Mr Gilliat and in March 1943 she was given the 'all clear' for further possible conception. In July 1943 she wrote to Victoria Baldwyn: 'Prepare yourself for a grand surprise. Incredible and unbelievable as it may seem, I am at long last going to have another baby. Daddie and I are simply thrilled about it.' That summer I was told that the longed for second baby was on its way. My sister, Karen, was born also caesarian but without complications in January 1944 just before I was ten. In her letter to Lionel, Myrtle was ecstatic: 'I am so utterly thrilled with Karen and just did not think it was possible to be so happy. How can I begin to thank you.' It has been a source of regret that as children we saw so little of each other.

I remember all the soldiers and their equipment during the Easter holidays 1944, but I do not think I fully appreciated why they were there. The A32 had been widened. Bedford and Austin trucks, Morris 'utilities' and Ford V8 powered 'bren gun' tracked carriers were parked along the verges of the straight stretches south towards Exton and then past the old kennels after Corhampton. When I cycled through Warnford Park, groups of soldiers relaxing outside their tents called me over. Many of them would soon be lying dead or wounded on the beaches or in the fields of Normandy. The conversations are forgotten but there is still this strong memory of how somehow they still managed to be cheerful when they must have been aware that this could have been their last beautiful English summer. Nearly seventy years later I like to go back to the Park and see that grassy stretch on the right before the road curves left to the bridge over the River Meon. I think of those men. I can still picture some of them in my mind. Though there have been some hesitant attempts at service and speaking out, I would have liked to have done more to justify their sacrifice. Some Officers came to Peake for baths and refreshment and the family was invited back to the big mansion, then still standing in the Park.[10] Up the curving staircase, busy with uniformed soldiers and scurrying clerks, we came to one of the large-windowed, well-proportioned rooms looking out towards the lake. Against the back wall, the large map clearly showed the outline of Normandy and the Cherbourg peninsula. Myrtle catches some of the atmosphere in a note this time to Lionel whilst staying with her younger sister, Prudie Loudon: 'We had a much disturbed night as convoys came past our windows from 2.30am, but finally one convoy came to roost outside.'

For some reason I was there at Peake before the invasion. Excercise 'Dreme', practising for D-Day, took place on the night of 4th April 1944. There was poor weather in the Petersfield area and one Horsa-towing Stirling, flying low below cloud, brushed trees on the crest of the hills above Peake. What followed will never be known. The Stirling tug crashed south west of Romsey and the crew of six were all killed. Either the tug pilot, desperate to regain height, pulled the release mechanism or the glider pilot thought he had more chance on his own. There is a steep slope down from the crest, it can be seen in the photograph of the author on 'Tatters'. The Horsa would momentarily have gained height above the ground. Did the pilot see the gleam of the lake just over a mile ahead in Warnford Park, that might have been about 50 seconds at the Hora's 80-90mph gliding speed? Water was always an option for a safer landing but the glider did not make it. The wing-span was 88 feet and, in the darkness, one of the long wings may have hit the surrounding trees, spinning into the ground to an abrupt halt rather than flopping on to a lake surface or a controlled landing ground. There were no survivors from the two NCO pilots, twenty-six soldiers of the King's own Scottish Borderers and one RMAC attendant. I remember being told by the villagers how they had taken the bodies away and the remains of that glider became firewood, not one of the 106 Horsas which Lionel's company repaired on site in addition to the 34 rebuilt at Portsmouth. The names of those who were killed are recorded on the wall towards the back of the church, to the right of the font. There is also an archive report on the Web referring to HorsaLG999-Aircrew remembered, Leslie Eastman.

Nan Coningham was another of Myrtle's friends who was glad to rest at the sanctuary of Peake in the middle of that war. She was the widow of Sir Howard Frank, one of the founders of the estate agency which is now Knight Frank.[11] After his death she married 'Maori' Coningham who became a distinguished Air Marshal in the Middle East, but was then killed in post-war civil aviation[12]. I remember her there with her daughter Jane during those 1944 summer holidays. Her son, also Sir Howard, who had succeeded to his father's baronetcy when eight years old, had landed in Normandy with the Guards Armoured Division and now had a few days' leave to visit his mother. He spent some of his precious time in the downland fields helping me fly my model aeroplanes. Still crystal clear is the image of sitting in the back of the Ford 'Ten' as Myrtle spurred the little side-valve engine up the hill from Meon Hut to get Howard back to his regiment on time. We were late and they calculated that they had a better chance of catching the last available Meon Valley train at Tisted than diverting off the main road and up the lane to West Meon station. The train was just about to depart as we turned into the Tisted yard and waited when it was seen that a uniformed Officer was running from the car. Howard was part of the Guards advance which liberated Brussels on 3rd September, but was then killed on 10th September aged 21. He is buried in the Leopoldsburg Cemetery[13].

Safe at Highfield during the winter of 1945, we were told nothing about the horrors in Germany as the Russians advanced towards Berlin. Except for hunger one day per week when lunch was just small squares of cheese and dates, we were ignorant of realities in the wider world. That spring I was even able to initiate a model aeroplane club. In August, after peace in Europe, some of the grandchildren managed to reassemble at St Lawrence Hall.[14] The tyres were nearly bald on all the cars and replacements were often unobtainable. I remember being commissioned by Lionel to go round all the wheels trying to remove the flints and stones with a spike. I think we took the Ford across on the ferry to Fishbourne. You could climb down the stairs and see the engine below. Back at Highfield, with the war in Japan also over after the controversial and horrific dropping of the atomic bombs, I came home for half-term at the beginning of November 1945. My sister, Karen, then nearly two, was left at Peake whilst the three of us, Lionel, Myrtle and me, were together on Corhampton golf course. I so clearly remember Myrtle saying how much she enjoyed our 'grown up' conversation and she looked forward to all the things we could do together now the war was over.

The following Saturday there was a summons to the headmaster's study. The Canon, as he now was,[15] had assumed that I had received a letter from my father and that I therefore already knew what had happened. So he told me how sorry he was about my mother's death and that FG was on her way to take me to Myrtle's sister, Norah's house at Tilford. I was to stay there until the funeral at Warnford the following week. But I had not received any letter. It may never have been written, Lionel having had other more immediate concerns. As with other matters, there was no consultation. 'They' knew best. I have often thought back to that afternoon looking out over the Highfield playing fields. I remember clearly that I felt no emotion. I probably did not take in the full implications of Myrtle's death. It had not been a constant relationship then. I feel I know her better now after reading so many of her letters. She was so busy with her duties. I was cared for by Victoria Baldwyn and then packed off to school. What concerned me was that, if I was not going to stay at school, why could I not go back to my own room at Peake and be with my father and sister rather than in a strange house where there was nothing to do? I was told to go up to the dormitory and pack some things. I returned with my case to the hall of the headmaster's house and soon saw FG driving herself in the pale green Rover[16], swinging onto the circular gravel area below the steps. I remember it so well - going to the door for the front passenger seat and requesting that we went to Peake. The response was that it would be better if we were altogether before we all went to the funeral the following week.

The cousins were kind. Then, on the day of the funeral, Norah announced that it had been decided that I should not come with them to the church at Warnford. Such instances are not forgotten. As I write, it's as if I am still in that room at Tilford and I remember protesting: Why had I been taken away from school? I had prepared myself to put on a brave face. Norah was adamant. With others who may have supported her, they presumably thought this was the sensible decision, that perhaps I might not behave and my presence might be disturbing to all the important adults who were coming to the funeral. They can not be blamed for this, they were coping with an unwanted situation, but the sense of rejection, that I was somehow inferior or not up to the mark, lingered, perhaps later fortified by other events to come. It may be one of the reasons why I have always rejected the 'do it, don't ask questions' approach and tried in my later work to find out what people, particularly younger people, were thinking. They returned from the funeral and took me back to Highfield without telling me anything about the day.

It was years later that I found the relevant press reports amongst Lionel's papers. Perhaps he just could not talk about these events but kept all he had so that I could eventually learn about it all. *The Times* for Tuesday 13th November has the death announcement. 'On 10th November suddenly after an operation --- beloved wife of Lionel --- daughter of Admiral of the Fleet, etc., ---- funeral at Warnford Thursday, 15th November 3 p.m. ---- Cars will meet 12.45 p.m. Waterloo to Petersfield train (change at Haslemere).' It's interesting to me now to see that there was no mention of us two children. Does it show the mindset? This was for the great and the good. For those who did not know, there may not have been any children. I have been told that it was FG's wish to hold the service in Winchester Cathedral. Perhaps Lionel was able to fight this. I thought of this at Betty's service, another Balfour and this time in the cathedral. The County still came to Warnford as described in the report in the *Hampshire Chronicle and General Advertiser* (as it was then called) of 17th November 1945, which was also found many years later: 'Lady Myrtle had won for herself in Hampshire, Portsmouth and Southampton a position of extremely high regard by her delightful nature and her unstinted work for good causes. All kinds of organisations in the Meon Valley enjoyed her personal help. The funeral service took place on Thursday when the high esteem in which Lady Myrtle was held was clearly displayed. The little Church in Warnford Park was decorated from the altar to the end of the nave with beautiful flowers and wreaths while outside in the churchyard poppy wreaths and floral displays of all kinds covered the ground from the grave to the church door. No less than twenty-four standards of the British Legion formed a guard of honour. Representatives from all the many organisations with which Lady Myrtle had been connected, many personal friends, and the large numbers of villagers who were anxious to pay tribute to one who had won their love during her life among them, made a congregation which overflowed from the Church leaving many standing in the Churchyard throughout the service.'

Besides all the dignitaries, her mother, sisters, brother and a few Cayzers were listed in the report. Mrs Percy Balfour was there, 28 years after Great-uncle Percy was killed, though no record of daughter Betty. There were fourteen representatives from Portsmouth Aviation and many of the Meon Valley names remembered from those childhood days: Chester, Chrystal, Christian, Dreyer, Edwards, Gaselee, Green, Haines, Hulbert, Mack, McLean, Samways, Seward, Tigwell and Veale. Canon and Mrs Mills from Highfield also attended. Was the Canon surprised at not seeing his pupil? I would have liked to have been there and seen it all and I am glad to have found this description of the day for the grandchildren and great-grandchildren she never knew. There is such an understanding letter to Lionel from Hedley Burrows, a distant cousin, then Archdeacon of Winchester and in 1947 Dean of Hereford. Whatever personal belief, it is the Church and its comfort at its best:

> 'God be thanked that the last service for Myrtle was felt to be in harmony with the loving thought and deep sorrow which filled the Church. I have thought of you every day since and agonised at times for the awful loss and strain which those days must have placed on you. How you bore the strain of the gathering at the house afterwards I don't know. We all mean so well but we can not grasp quite what the loneliness is for you. The sense of sorrow in your neighbourhood is very great.'

Myrtle had achieved so much more than 'absolutely nothing.' We know that internal pain led to this operation. There is evidence that she had first sought assistance from Mr Gilliat. He wrote by hand on 12th November:

> 'I was horrified to read of your wife's death. Please accept my deepest sympathy. I had already dictated a letter saying how sorry I was that I had been unable to obtain a room for her in London. I have destroyed it.'

Instead she went into Sarum Road Nursing Home, Winchester. The death certificate gives intestinal obstruction of the small bowel caused by adhesions resulting from former abdominal operation as cause of death. In one accompanying letter, written on Sunday 11th, the day after her death, Dr. Robertson wrote to Lionel:

> 'I was so happy and so thankful when I saw you after the operation. It seemed that, despite enormous diagnostic and operative difficulties, your wife would get well, indeed there seemed no reason whatsoever why she should not get well. When I saw her at half past six, she seemed content and so thankful that the operation had been safely completed. It was my great honour to have had a quiet talk with her on Saturday morning. When I left her before noon, it seemed to me that we had achieved our aim, that she would await the operation with confidence feeling that it would end the pain and set in motion the process of recovery. She smiled at me before she went into the theatre.'

Myrtle's granddaughter, Dr. Juliet Balfour, has studied this letter and another letter we have from the surgeon and written the following:

> 'These letters shed some light on the possible causes of Myrtle's unexpected death. It was clearly a very difficult case diagnostically but there seemed to be no cause for concern when Dr. Robertson reviewed her after the operation. Why did she die only a few hours later? In his first letter on 11th November, the surgeon indicates that

they thought they had found the source of the problem during the surgery as their 'examination of that organ reveals exactly the condition which would justify those very symptoms' but then admits 'the seat of the trouble was elsewhere, and in such dire and threatening form'. Dr. Robertson's second letter on 22nd November lists the possible causes for her pain that had been considered pre-operatively. These were: gall bladder trouble, appendix trouble, kidney trouble and intra-abdominal adhesions, the last possibility being considered as she had had three abdominal operations."

Juliet comments that:

'A previous operation performed by Mr. Gilliat in October 1941 revealed these adhesions and the distortions they had caused. Dr. Robertson states that at operation the gallbladder was normal and a right kidney abnormality was found that would have produced her symptoms exactly, making the other possible diagnoses unlikely. He doesn't say if he then operated on the kidney or not but it seems he didn't look any further for other pathology. Sadly, it appears from the death certificate that the real culprit was intra-abdominal adhesions leading to small bowel obstruction which, undiagnosed and untreated, could have led to her rapid deterioration and death. Bowel adhesions could have caused the worsening pain that led to her having the exploratory operation and, if the obstruction was not discovered, could have led to perforation of her bowel and then peritonitis. However it is not known whether the obstruction was confirmed by a post-mortem or whether it was deduced from her symptoms just before death. Neither of the letters mentions any post-mortem or indeed her symptoms post-operatively, so some doubt remains. Another possible cause could have been sudden and massive pulmonary embolism (blood clot in the lungs). We know from Myrtle's letters that she had had problems with her legs since her first Caesarian Section and these were being 'treated' when she went to Bagnoles de l'Orne in 1935 (p.49). She could have been suffering from recurrent and untreated deep vein thrombosis in her calves. The advice then was to rest as much as possible, which would have made her prone to further clots. Nowadays sufferers are given blood-thinning medication to reduce the clot and then long-term drugs such as warfarin or other anticoagulants to prevent further episodes. These clots in the deep veins of the legs can break away and travel to the lungs where they can block arteries and, depending on position and size, these blockages can cause sudden collapse and death. We now know that one of Myrtle's granddaughters has been diagnosed with Factor 5 Leiden mutation, an inherited blood abnormality. This significantly increases the risk of deep vein thrombosis in the legs and pelvis during and after pregnancy and after major surgery. It is possible that Myrtle had this too.'

Myrtle was saved the later difficulties at Portsmouth, but equally her counsel, her presence, all her contacts, and her probable wish that Lionel maintained control in England, could have led to a different outcome to what follows. After Lionel's death, there was a letter from Molly Vesey Holt: 'I have been vividly reminded of the long friendship with your mother and particularly the time I spent at Peake when you were about seven. The really sad part was that Karen, who was so desperately desired, never had any of her own family life. Karen's birth was safely achieved though yours wasn't.' Myrtle's friend also then wrote: 'I may be a silly old thing but I can't help feeling glad at the idea of those two being reunited again. Your father will be coming home to the last resting place which is the one he should share with his beloved Myrtle's earthly body. I am sure their spiritual bodies will be in peace and happiness together.' Of course there is sadness, but it is only part of the story. Fate cannot be avoided. Many other families had to cope with loss during those war years. For those still alive there is always much to learn from all experiences. Having brought us into the world with some difficulty I like to think Myrtle would have wanted her grandchildren and now her great-grandchildren to be helped in making full use of this precious gift of life. This may be a good reason for giving more priority to family life than personal ambition. I hesitated over including the many details of Myrtle's life. But then the address at Jenifer Phillip's Memorial Service suggested that 'eternal life' could be considered as what succeeding generations hold in their memory. We can remember Myrtle through her letters.

AVIATION AND INDUSTRIAL TRUST LIMITED.

SUMMARY OF PLANS FOR POST WAR DEVELOPMENT.

1. SUBSIDIARY COMPANIES. A Holding Company under the above title at present with Nominal Capital, has been registered to take control of the various Subsidiary Companies which themselves will take over the various activities as described in this Brochure in detail under their appropriate sections.

The Subsidiaries and their activities are:-

PORTSMOUTH AVIATION LIMITED.	The Design and Construction of Aircraft commencing with the Aerocar Series at present under development.
ISLE OF WIGHT AIRWAYS LTD.	The re-opening of the Isle of Wight Airways commenced in 1932.
VECTIS AIRPORTS LTD.	The Extension and the Development of the Ryde Airport.
AERO REPAIRS LTD.	The Overhaul, Repair, Maintenance and modification of Service, Air Line, Club, Private and other aircraft.
AIR TRANSPORT COLLEGE LTD.	The development of the Air Transport College, which is a Correspondence College to provide specialised training in all branches of the Air Transport Industry and to further a world wide knowledge and understanding of the Art of Air Transport.

Confident in the future, Lionel wrote up plans for the Aviation and Industrial Trust. The 118-page folder is dated 27th August 1945.

LEARNING FROM DIFFERENCE

Chapter 7

Family disintegration. Canada. Near miss in India

Consider Lionel's situation after Myrtle's death. All the letters (many intimacies not included here) confirm how close they were sharing all their thoughts. He was going on for both of them. He seems to have had an inner strength incubated by the loss of parents and coping with other events like Helen Stack's death. He wrote to Norah in December:

> 'I have wanted to write to you and each member of the family and thank you for your kind letters, but firstly I have not had the heart to write and secondly I have felt I must first write to Myrtle's local friends so that they will continue to ask the children out and also to reply to the letters from the British Sailor's Society and British Legion people as she would have wished. This I have managed to do but I have seventy letters left. I know how fond of you Myrtle was. When I first asked her to marry me she said 'Oh, but you have not yet seen Norah, she is much nicer than me.' Please don't refrain from talking to me about Myrtle because you think that will make me sad. I want to talk about her and remember all the happy times we had together.'

Much else can be gleaned from other correspondence that he kept. There is the transfer of the lease of Peake from Myrtle's name to his name confirming that, despite those original legacies, he owned no property. For my and my sister's future survival, the Cayzer attitude to money and settlements proved its worth. The Balfour-Jellicoe marriage settlement meant that some funds had to be kept for our maintenance and for our education, with a consequent reduction of Lionel's personal spending income. At least there were the means, if care for us two children could be arranged. Lionel was still chairman and joint managing director (with Francis Luxmoore) of an organisation which, at its peak in the war, had employed over 2,000 people, had large factories at Portsmouth and Christchurch and workshops at Bognor, Cosham, Felpham and Southsea. It was now a different story. In Lionel's own later words, 'sudden cancellation of war work led to a drastic reduction of the organisation followed by substantial losses incurred between 1946 and 1948'. The figures that are available show that, despite profits throughout the war years which were as high as £23,000 in 1942, the bank overdraft in 1945 was still around £60,000. It had been reduced from the top figure of £79,000 in 1944. I wish there had been more communication between us and I had known these figures. But I doubt if I would have had the understanding to have asked why overdraft reduction had not been a priority. Total wartime profit of £88,505 could have cleared that overdraft and left them in a stronger position to cope with the losses to come. In part the answer may have been the need to pay the wartime Excess Profits Tax. In a letter dated 24th October 1946, accountant Percy Cansdale, who was a most loyal helper until Lionel's death, wrote:

'The Company was not earning profits in the standard base years 1935 to 1937 used for comparison so for Excess Profits Tax purposes the Company was in a very disadvantageous position.'

I like to think that a Cayzer company would not have got into this situation, though they might not have been sufficiently adventurous to attempt the solution, which may not have been too far from succeeding. This is the difference which is the theme of this book, and again I hope the account of different decisions taken will be helpful to future generations. In that same letter Percy Cansdale also wrote:

'There is a very substantial carry forward of loss against future profits for income tax purposes. The amount involved is at least £25,000. This will improve the Company's financial position very appreciably.'

Perhaps this hope decreased concern about the overdraft but, and this is so important, there still had to be profits for implementation of this carry forward.

What is so clear is that Lionel did not slacken his efforts and did not allow them to be diminished by the loss of Myrtle. We survived the Christmas holidays with a housekeeper. Myrtle's friends did help. David Green's parents, William and Winifred, were particularly kind, frequently asking me to their lovely house near Swanmore with its views to the Island. The memory of their affection and compassion is rekindled and treasured when we visit and enjoy the gardens which David, as well as his many public duties, has diligently developed over the years. Lionel also had to deal with all the paperwork concerning Myrtle's estate. John Miller, a Portsmouth solicitor, was, like Percy Cansdale, another lifelong supporter. There is Lionel's letter to Mr Miller, 27th January 1946, which confirms his own difficult financial situation but also shows that he is still optimistic for the future. He just had this admirable ability not to be defeated.

'I wonder if you are making good progress with Lady Myrtle's affairs. I am anxious to get these matters including the payment of Doctors settled as soon as possible. I know that Myrtle would not have liked me keeping these people waiting for their accounts yet I find my-self a little hard up running the whole of the house and the children from my income instead of from our joint incomes as before. (Financial reserves are helpful when coping with death, medical bills still have to be paid after an unfavourable outcome, settlements need to have their paperwork sorted). I am now established with a housekeeper and her daughter of four who makes a good companion for Karen, and I have hopes that the arrangement will work well. We have just accepted fixed price contracts for Aircraft repair with the probability of being able to make considerable sums out of them which I hope will generally strengthen our financial position. We hope also to get a decision from the Government soon as to whether they intend to purchase Ryde Airport. (In both cases this optimism was not justified. See my book *Spithead Express*.)[1] Our most exciting project is the small twin engined aeroplane which we are designing for the export market. It is being most favourably received by all who have seen the mock-up and I expect before long we shall build up a good order book. The prototype is likely to fly in June (1946) and we hope for production by the end of the year.'[2]

This was what became the Aerocar. A design for a 'general purpose aeroplane for Army requirements' had been submitted in March 1943. The idea was to transport specialist personnel or act as an ambulance. Another possibility was to carry a motor cycle in the central nacelle. The rider could then start his machine whilst landing and then ride out through the opening rear hatch. (Were exhaust fumes to be endured in war time or perhaps a tube to the outside air would have been fitted?) A Government contract would have helped costs, but the submission was ignored by Whitehall. Lionel and Francis Luxmoore then decided to refine the design for the post-war private owner/aerial taxi/ feeder liner market. From our viewpoint nearly seventy years later, the confidence seems staggering. With the benefit of hindsight, one asks 'did he really not see the precipice ahead?' Yet it's that sort of confidence which enables some (but only some) entrepreneurs to succeed. He had already achieved so much against the odds, though many will rightly question an achievement which has entailed loss of capital. He obviously really did believe that £60,000 overdraft was not something to worry about. Money would flow in from worldwide Aerocar sales, then that £60K would be paid off and his own shares in the company would soon equal and surpass the value of that capital from his grandparents which he had put in. Because he was so confident, he shrugged off the loss of the investment from the pre-nationalisation Southern Railway[3] and was able to look at the national plans dispassionately. He continued to Mr Miller: 'I think in many ways the present Government's Policy for Air Transport is right in view of the huge capital now required although it is bad luck on small pre-war operators like our-selves. Its success will depend on how far the dead hand of State administration can be kept out of the set-up.' Written in January 1946, these were far-seeing comments. He could write thus because he saw the future in manufacturing a product with so much potential and this was what the company was going to do.

Two months after this letter Lionel and Walter Jenks, the ever helpful and loyal company secretary, were travelling to implement their plans. Another recently found letter to Mr Miller, dated 14th March 1946, refers to this trip: 'Mr Jenks and I are off to Canada in the Mauretania and will go on to Kansas City. I have booked an air passage back from New York. We have found Mr Edgar Granville MP, who is joining us, (see below) a tower of strength as he knows the leading members of the Government and goes straight to them on our behalf.' The Canadian Car and Foundry Company was interested in making the Aerocar and we still have Lionel's long report on discussions with a Colonel Mulock and a Mr Lloyd (in charge of aircraft production) at that company on 23rd March. Here are a few extracts:

'They regard any production, aeroplane, pot or pan or railway car (like Lionel's grandfather!) as just another engineering job to be taken on in their whole floor space. Every square foot of floor space must be kept busy and it is quite in order to mix in a few aircraft. The man hour content of the Norseman (which they had taken over from Norduyn who sold over a thousand during the war) was 5,600 and they seemed to think our estimate of 4,000 man hours for the Aerocar was reasonable. Their policy was not the sale of a plush airliner but rather the 'bush truck'.

'They had the Burnelli and the Norseman for this purpose and would now like to add the Aerocar as an executive aircraft. Colonel Mulock thought our price of $22,000 was reasonable but would hope to produce for $17,000. He said it was important to maintain all-the-year-round use therefore skis and floats were essential.

'We would have it over the Republic Seabee and Grumman Widgeon amphibians which could not fit skis, and they liked our proposal to de-snag the nose ski in Switzerland. He thought we could get floats from Edo in New York. A conservative estimate of the Canadian market was twenty Aerocars a year and they were prepared to manufacture in these small numbers. Canadian Car was in a paramount position as they had a nationwide sales organisation in existence and a wide diversity of manufacturing activities to keep their overheads down. They were establishing a chain of service stations for aircraft and had the resources of their magnificent machine shop to keep aircraft in the air carving parts out of the solid if necessary. With regard to South and Central America, Canadian Car have an agency in Mexico which handles South American business. It should be possible to sell Aerocars there.'

In New York there was discussion about making Commonwealth Aircraft's Trimmer Amphibian at Portsmouth. Lionel's pilot's log-book records that he flew a Trimmer on 2nd April. At the Edo Aircraft Corporation, College Point, New York, on 3rd April the Aerocar seaplane version was discussed. After general observations on Edo's current work projects and the planes to which they were fitted, Lionel reported on their suggestions for the design of the fittings, estimated weights and the positioning of the floats. Edo 'depreciated the idea of bracing the floats only to the wing spars because the floats would have to be below the engines which would make it difficult to use them as boarding platforms and it would be difficult to achieve sufficient side bracing.' They also looked at the design of an advanced small helicopter and were offered sole rights of manufacture in Britain. 'The Hunting Group are also biting but, if we follow up, we shall undoubtedly get first preference.' On 11th April Lionel and Walter Jenks went back to Canadian Car. They submitted a draft agreement for manufacture of the Aerocar in Canada and possibly later in Mexico. Colonel Mulock thought that Continental engines should be fitted, either the 125hp or 185hp units, and it was agreed that the development work on their installation should be done at Portsmouth. Canadian Car would not require a sample aircraft or set of pattern parts for production but would work from the drawings. However they might want an Aerocar for 'winterisation' tests before their own production commenced. Lionel and Walter would send Mr Lloyd copies of all Canadian enquiries received so that Canadian Car could assess the demand and follow up.

Meanwhile in England, chief accountant Sid Smith sent a seven-page report to Percy Cansdale that same 11th April. He was sounding a warning:

'Costs for work in hand and anticipated £286,000, estimated income £241,000 and this, he wrote, without taking the Aerocar expenditure into consideration. But, if the Christchurch factory was closed, costs could be reduced to £221,000 and income would still be £241,000. If Aerocar plans were put to one side, there was sufficient space at Portsmouth.'

So Lionel returned to some difficult decisions. They could make a profit but at the expense of the product on which he was building his plans for the company. The downside to his confidence and optimism may have been a reluctance to accept that other organisations and other people might not react in the ways which he envisaged. This was also true on the domestic scene. A letter from one of Myrtle's friends dated March 1946 awaited him at Peake when he returned:

'I hate to think I might be hurting you in any way especially after all you have been through lately and I must seem terribly grateful and unkind but I do feel it best if I tell you now: That I honestly do not want to get married. I can't express all my reasons and feelings because I am bad at any form of self-expression. The war years have not been kind, severe illness, hard work and overwhelming sorrow. All I want to do is live in this house which I love dearly and run it for Daddy. To please him I would like to have a crack at the Bar. He is so keen on me doing this. All his hopes and ambitions for Patrick were shattered in 1944. If I could pass even some of the preliminary exams, he would be so proud and happy. Although I must say no to being your wife, will you please let me help you as a friend in any way possible with the children or your household. Christopher I do not know so well but I do love my goddaughter (Karen) and for your sake as well as Myrtle's I would like to help. I am sure you would be a wonderfully kind husband but, although I am fond of you, I don't want to think about marriage. If, after some months, I change my mind, please can I let you know if you have not changed your mind by then.'

This friend's father had been a merchant in Calcutta and lived in a lovely Hampshire house with lawns going down to the River Meon. His son Patrick, her brother, had survived North Africa (where awarded the Military Cross and Bar) and had got over halfway up Italy. Then in July 1944 he had been killed by a mine when attempting to clear a path so that his soldiers could bathe in lake Trasimeno near Perugia.[4] Unlike Howard Frank's father, who never knew the fate of his elder son, Patrick's father lived on well into his nineties (I talked with him the week he died) and I don't expect a day ever passed when he did not think of his son and what might have been. The media tackle the war against Hitler with a broad brush, but there is less published of individual family tragedies and the pain suffered by parents and relatives. The dead do not write their memoirs. As Lionel tussled with weightier problems, this proposal must have seemed the answer to domestic matters, a house and a home for Karen and myself, but the prospective partner had her own differing thoughts. She was not a machine to be adjusted to his specification.

Back at Portsmouth, he was still in command. His employees did what he said. If he had paid heed to Sid Smith's warning, if he had perhaps suggested that the Aerocar prototype was mothballed for a while whilst finances were stabilised, he might have remained as managing director or at least a director for the rest of his life. (Sid Smith was still there in the 1975 company photograph some years after Lionel's death). He did accept that the Christchurch works would have to be given up, that it could not be the factory in which to build the Aerocar. Now we come to the part of the tale which a talented novelist might find hard to imagine and I still do not know all the facts. Somehow Lionel had made contact with an Indian Maharajah, the Jam Sahib of Nawanager, who had further increased his wealth through profitable war contracts and wanted to initiate industrial development in his State. He was particularly interested in aviation.[5] This may have come about through Edgar Granville, later Lord Granville of Eye, mentioned earlier. He was then Liberal MP for Eye in Suffolk and knowledgeable on aviation matters.[6] His sensible contributions to the 1946 Civil Aviation Bill can be read in Hansard for 6th May that year. He had become interested in the work of Portsmouth Aviation and Lionel had seen the value of a parliamentary contact. In 1942 Edgar Granville had resigned the Liberal whip because of disagreement with war policy and sat as an independent. That same year a maverick entrepreneur, Denis Kendall[7], who had worked with Andre Citroen in France and then returned to England to become manager of arms manufacturing companies in Grantham, stood against the national candidate in a by-election and just managed to become Independent MP for the Grantham constituency.[8] These two MPs, together as independents, are likely to have had some discourse so Edgar G would surely have been aware of Denis K's plans to provide post-war employment by making a 'people's car' in the Grantham factories. Some of the finance was coming from India and there was a picture in the Grantham Guardian of Denis (who owned the newspaper) escorting the Jam Sahib on a visit to look at the car prototypes. We know that Denis Kendall was soon to encounter supply difficulties from component manufacturers who gave preference to established customers. Then there is another press cutting which states that Denis 'had high hopes of getting a million pounds of capital from a Maharajah, but that money found its way into a short-lived aviation company.'[9] That's not exactly true as the parent Portsmouth Aviation Company still flourishes, but it's not too difficult to suppose that Edgar Granville observed what was happening. He may have managed to interest the Jam Sahib directly in a different investment opportunity or he may have done this through Geoffrey Foster, who as an English cricketer had befriended the Jam Sahib's uncle, 'Ranjitsinghi', and then gone to Jamnager as adviser to the State.[10]

In July 1946 Lionel was back in America and his pilot's log-book shows that he again flew a Trimmer. (The previous day he had also flown that other amphibian, the Republic Seabee, for which they may have been considering an agency for Europe). In Lionel's files there is a copy of an eight-page contract with Commonwealth Aircraft for the manufacture of the Trimmer Amphibian in Great Britain. 'Portsmouth Aviation will take immediate steps to manufacture to British Airworthiness Requirements ------ Commonwealth at their own expense will supply one production model 'Trimmer' insurance and freightage paid to Southampton ------ Commonwealth will order a minimum order of at least 500 Trimmer amphibians to be supplied by the end of December 1947.' Whether this contract was ever signed is not known. It may have reinforced the 'not to worry about the overdraft now' thinking, but Google tells us that only two Trimmers were ever made in America. There is a YouTube film recording a flight in one of them.[11]

In England again, there was another letter from Myrtle's friend: 'I am having the pleasure of Miss Balfour's company longer than expected. Nurse could not come back because she had the flu. She is being so good and sweet. We go for expeditions in the pram in the morning, what intrigues her most are the frogs in the pond.' Nurse was Norland-trained and Myrtle's friend now commented:

'I am sure you will be delighted to see the back of the housekeeper (of whom Lionel had high hopes in his letter to John Miller). I've always had a bad opinion of her but hoped she might improve. Nurse Pamela is so conscientious herself and was so appalled at the housekeeper's slackness.'

She then thanked Lionel for sorting out the car:

'I ought to be able to tow a succession of horseboxes by the time you have finished with it.'[12]

She was attending Captain Tony Collings's riding school with her horse 'Remus'[13] and staying at The Gables Hotel, Porlock. That summer 1946, when I was back from Highfield, Lionel's sister Rachel replaced the housekeeper at Peake. This did not work either. Ann spent time with Rachel during her final years. On one visit she explained that 'she could not stay at Peake because I was so difficult'.

Looking back, it seems that I was a disaster-area, falling out with all family members —and more to come! But now I wonder. Rachel liked epicurean food. Was I already suffering from food intolerance? Rachel was of the generation that you ate whatever was given to you. It probably never occurred to her that some foods might be causing me digestive problems and therefore ill-temper. I was packed off to a hotel near the beach at Shanklin with nurse Pamela and sister Karen. Lionel joined us for the odd day.

I returned to school and we have a written record of what followed. Lionel flew out to Nawanager at the end of August 1946. It seems that he had a warm welcome from the Jam Sahib and his staff including Geoffrey Foster. There must have been an agreement there and then, for two weeks later he was in Bombay (since 1996 Mumbai) and appointing architects for the construction of a new factory. His initial summary of what had been agreed and the plans for implementation were written up in Bombay and airmailed back to Portsmouth.[14] They are confirmed in subsequent correspondence. The clearest summary is in extracts from two letters sent to a potential joint managing director at the beginning of 1947:

'A very satisfactory arrangement for the set-up of Portsmouth Aviation (Nawanager) Ltd has been agreed with His Highness the Jam Sahib. Preliminary plans for the factory to be established at Port Sika, 25 miles from Jamnager, have been completed and sent to our Bombay architects for the preparation of the drawings.[15] It is hoped to have the plant operating in 18 months to two years time (i.e. towards the end of 1948) for the manufacture of the Aerocar and other engineering products. The capital for the Indian Company (other reports suggest over one million pounds) is being entirely found through the Jam Sahib and this Company is appointed as sole advisers and consultants for twenty years. We are to provide the services of a British joint managing director and other key British staff to work with an Indian joint managing director. Whoever is appointed would have to go out to Nawanager in the late summer of 1947 to supervise the construction of the factory and other kindred matters.'

Another memo confirms that 'early in 1947 £150,000 of Indian capital was invested in Portsmouth Aviation in England and Mr G.N. Foster joined the Board in Portsmouth representing this Indian interest.' This was now a serious commitment involving much work over the following months. It is all fully described in files which have recently been found. Lionel's summary from Bombay in September had many details. Here are just a few extracts:

1. The site of the factory at Sika is unlimited in extent and will border on an airfield to be constructed by Nawanager State with 2,000 yard runways.

2. It is adjacent to a new deep water port to be completed within two years on a reef connected to the shore by a railway. Raw materials and finished products will come into and leave the factory through this port.

3. Electricity will be provided from a new 12,000 kilowatt generating station being erected at Sika.

4. Water will be available by the time the factory commences. There will be no gas.

5. £230,000 is available for the construction of factory buildings, offices and housing accommodation. I propose to provide housing for about 1,000 operatives at the outset. It is desirable to keep sales staff and departments not essential at the factory in Jamnager where no housing problems exist. The money allocated should amount to about 142,000 square feet e.g. main hangar, 25,000, sq ft, main factory and stores, 70,000 sq ft.

6. £80,000 is available for plant shipped, installed and working. This has to cover hand and machine tools, vehicles, air compressors, lifting gear, salt baths, work benches, typewriters and office equipment and furniture, etc. Much might be bought second-hand and some items could be manufactured in the works by trainees. As dollars will be available it should be possible to purchase items of U.S.A. origin if advantageous.

7. The following products are envisaged, but subject to review on my return to Portsmouth. Quantities for first year of operation: 20,000 Voss washing machines, 10,000 refrigerators, 10,000 electric heaters, 100,000 aerosol DDT bombs and 100 metal Aerocars.

8. It is also proposed to run a service station for Aerocars and do general maintenance and repair work on Dakotas, Vikings, Freighters, etc, and probably an engine shop for overhauls.

9. It will be necessary that planning for Aerocar production and products in England does not suffer because of preparation for the Indian factory.'

The faithful staff at Portsmouth had replied with their reactions in October (1946). There were four pages of foolscap notes and queries for Lionel to study before they all met to discuss the project. These included comments on equipment supply, factory layout, assembly times, training of Indian staff, employment conditions and contracts. The initial thinking was that the following key personnel would be required under the direction of the joint managing director: chief engineer/works manager, chief inspector, chief accountant, assistant works manager, production engineer, chief draughtsman, personnel officer, maintenance engineer, transport superintendent, tool room manager, machine shop manager, assembly shop manager, material controller, chief process planner, chief storekeeper, buyer, sales department. Many of these people could be engaged initially for Aerocar production in England and subsequently transferred to India, their duties being delegated to their second-in-commands. These notes were accompanied by an internal memo direct to Lionel: 'We are making enquiries in regard to matters relating to key staff. I have a list with prices of plant, tools and equipment now available. There are other matters I would like to debate when the general policy is decided. It is felt, in view of the magnitude of this task, combined with the work in progress on the Aerocar project in this country, that to avoid delay by the constant referring to yourself for a decision, that if you could see your way to delegating the making of decisions other than those of major importance, that we shall have more opportunity of achieving the desired result in relation to the building programme and eventual initial production date.'

Lionel must have felt enormous relief and that his confidence and optimism was justified. There was a future for the Aerocar, about which they had many enquiries and expressions of interest. Besides India there was the possibility of manufacture in Canada. The Indian money would soon be with them so there was no need to worry about the overdraft. There was going to be employment for existing staff and others to come. There were no worries about planning and not too many bureaucratic obstacles. Nawanager was still one of the block of unfettered 'princely states' surrounded by British India, one of those patches of red at which I had gazed at Peake. In time there would be a return for the money from Balfour Lyon in Chile. Though it seems he knew little about the work of relatives, there was the potential in India to match the achievements of Great-uncle Robert in North America and the Balfour brothers at Leven. Was he even aware of the fate of Uncle Fred forty years earlier at Lucknow? It had been a long hard road since 1932, and he had coped with the loss of Myrtle, but it seemed that they had got there in the end. The next major query concerned production in England if they were not going to continue with the costly rented factory at Christchurch. A Percival 'Procter' G-AHCT was part of the post-war charter fleet (see *Spithead Express*). Lionel's log-book records that he flew this Proctor to Blackburn Aircraft at Brough at the end of October and to Short Brothers at Rochester on 9th December 1946. On this flight Francis Luxmoore and Walter Jenks were with him and it was 'a very rough 35 minutes.' In his recent book about post-war British aircraft Arthur Ord-Hume writes: 'The Board of Trade allocated 80,000 square feet comprising the former erection bays at the east end of Rochester airport. The intention was to employ four hundred people, mainly sheet metal workers. But this offer was not backed by finance.' Reading about those years it seems that both Blackburn and Shorts did have room in their factories, but costs would be high, UK finance was not forthcoming and there was also increasing concern about supplies of steel. India seemed more hopeful and thoughts seemed to be turning towards concentration on the Sika site. From there they could achieve worldwide deliveries, backed up by Canadian Car's production in Canada and possibly Mexico.

I now played another part in this story because of my impetuous stupidity. FG had invited Lionel and me to join her for Christmas 1946 at the Fluela Hotel in Davos Dorf. The two of us, side by side in the cockpit, started from Portsmouth in G-AHCT, but fog was soon rolling in from the channel and we only just made it into Lympne where, in those days, it was necessary to clear customs. Lionel returned from the control office with discouraging news. Thick fog was expected to continue over Northern France for the next few days. The Procter did not have sufficient instruments to cope with such conditions. The plan to fly over the Alps had to be abandoned. Instead it was a night at Folkestone and continuing by train to Davos. After a few days of lessons on the nursery slopes, I was impatient to master my skis. I set off on my own to climb above the others. I pointed downhill, loving the thrill of speed, but I could not stop. For three whole days I was laid up with the injured knee increasingly swollen. Those days were going to make a difference to several lives. When I hobbled downstairs to the sitting area of the Fluela there was another lady at the table with her brother, Lionel and FG. I didn't think too much about this newcomer at the time. We were soon back in England and I was still hobbling when I returned to Highfield. In the Easter holidays this lady appeared at Peake. She was separated, though not divorced, from her Midland manufacturer husband. Like Myrtle's friend she was the daughter of another wealthy merchant who had made his fortune in Calcutta between the wars at a time when Churchill had said in the House of Commons: 'The loss of India would be final and fatal to us. It could not fail to be part of a process that would reduce us to the scab of a minor power.'[16] This merchant was separated from the lady's mother, lived in a large manor house with another lady and was master of the local hunt. Lionel's new lady was also a keen horsewoman. We will call her PC after her maiden name. I was not too worried about her presence. Lionel had kindly provided me with my own workshop and I was busy making models and other things.

Had those at Portsmouth, and Lionel too, realised the future significance of another event which had taken place whilst we were at Davos? On 1st January (1947) Lord Mountbatten had been summoned to Downing Street by Prime Minister Clement Attlee and given the task, despite the Churchillian misgivings, of dismembering the Indian Raj. At that stage it was not thought that this would affect the Princely States so Lionel and Portsmouth Aviation did not yet have cause for concern. They were busy with the charter planes, repairing bus bodies in the workshops and any other work that came to hand. It had taken longer than originally planned but on 18th June (1947) Francis Luxmoore began taxi-ing trials with the Aerocar prototype. *Flight* magazine commented:

'The aircraft was wheeled out of its hangar at 4pm. The pilot was so satisfied and confident with the way everything felt that he took the aircraft off at 7pm. So short an exploratory period before first flight is very likely something of a modern record. In the short amount of flying that has been done, the prototype has behaved well and comes fully up to all expected of it. A tremendous amount of interest has been shown in the Aerocar by concerns all over the world and orders have been received to the value of £2 million. In the light of Britain's uncomfortable financial position, it is greatly to be hoped that production will be inaugurated at the earliest opportunity.' (See *Flight* magazine 3rd July 1947 also more of this in *Spithead Express*).

Lionel kindly sent a telegram about this initial flight, which I remember receiving during lunch at Highfield. I was already impatient to leave as others of my age had already gone on to their next schools including Eton and much of the work was repetition of the previous year. Because of the family situation it had been decided that I should be held back and stay that further year at Highfield. Now I found it even more difficult waiting till the end of term. In early August 1947 I was at Portsmouth airport taking my 'Box

Brownie' photos of the Aerocar's take-off and landing trials. Somehow I still had to cope with another five years at school, but afterwards the factory would be there and it seemed there was now an assured future for this appealing little aeroplane. I regret that, despite repeated pleading, they would not let me fly in that prototype. What a memory that would have been, but it remained a time of hope and looking forward to a manufacturing future. Mountbatten's activities accelerating the arrangements for the partition of India had not yet become a cause for concern. Back at Peake there was anther bombshell which I should have anticipated. Lionel came into to my room one morning and announced that he was going to marry PC and hoped that I would approve. I should have held my tongue but all my vibes were telling me that this would not work out and this I indicated.[4] I should have realised that whatever the marital happenings between them, PC was also prepared to use the money and organising abilities to act as a housekeeper to Lionel, Karen and me. Here was a solution to pressing current problems. The wise response (I was too young for this) was to let the future look after itself. I was fond of Myrtle's friend, but her mother had died some years before and her father, unlike PC's father, did not have another lady to help run that lovely house.

Proposals for the development of Portsmouth and Ryde airports after 1945

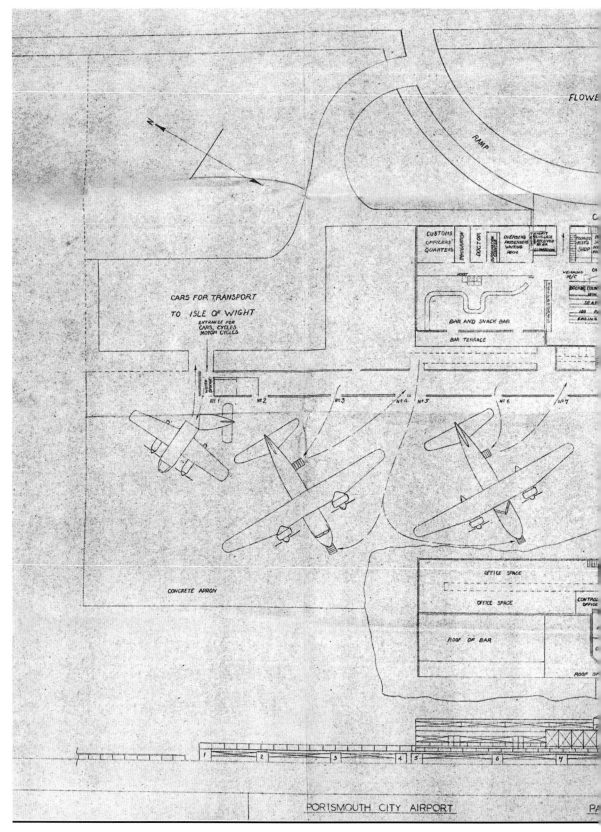

On the left Bristol Wayfarers for the ferry, then Aerocars for charter/air taxi use. Note Lionel's initial bottom right

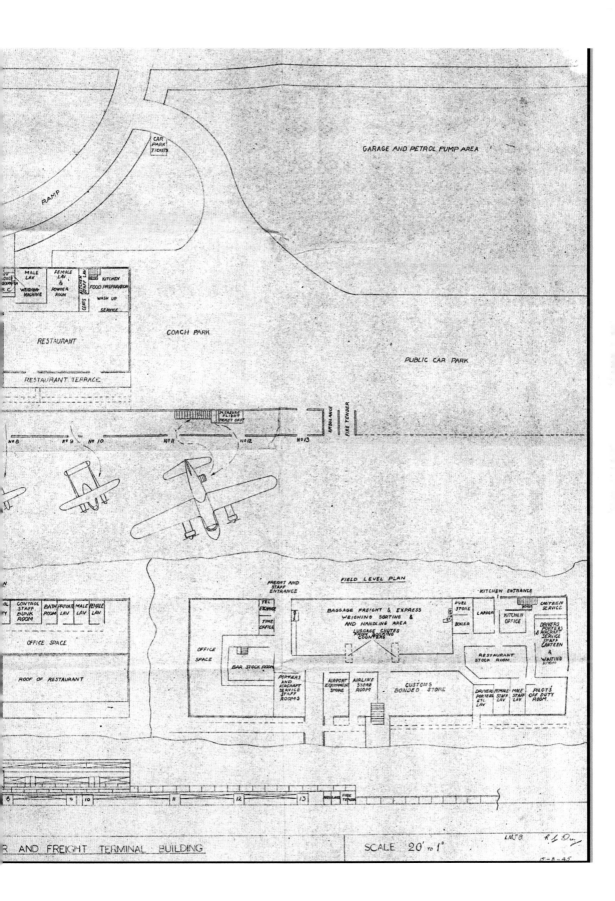

GARAGE AND PETROL PUMP AREA

CAR PARK TICKETS

RAMP

MALE LAV.

FEMALE LAV. & POWDER ROOM

WEIGHING MACHINE

KITCHEN FOOD PREPARATION

WASH UP

SERVICE

RESTAURANT

COACH PARK

PUBLIC CAR PARK

RESTAURANT TERRACE

PLEASURE FLIGHT TICKET OFFICE

AMBULANCE

FIRE TENDER

Nº8   Nº9   Nº10   Nº11   Nº12   Nº13

FIELD LEVEL PLAN

FREIGHT AND STAFF ENTRANCE

KITCHEN ENTRANCE

CONTROL STAFF BUNK ROOM

BATH ROOM

PRIVATE LAV

MALE LAV

FEMALE LAV

TEL EXCHANGE

TIME OFFICE

BAGGAGE FREIGHT & EXPRESS WEIGHING SORTING & AND HANDLING AREA LUGGAGE CHUTES WEIGHING COUNTERS

FUEL STORE

BOILER

LARDER

KITCHEN OFFICE

CANTEEN SERVICE

DRIVERS PORTERS & AIRCRAFT SERVICE STAFF CANTEEN & WAITING ROOM

OFFICE SPACE

OFFICE SPACE

BAR STOCK ROOM

RESTAURANT STOCK ROOM

ROOF OF RESTAURANT

PORTERS AND AIRCRAFT SERVICE STAFF ROOMS

AIRPORT EQUIPMENT STORE

AIRLINE STORE ROOM

CUSTOMS BONDED STORE

DRIVERS PORTERS ETC. LAV.

FEMALE STAFF LAV

MALE STAFF LAV

PILOTS OFF DUTY ROOM.

8   9   10   11   12   13   FIRE TENDER

R AND FREIGHT TERMINAL BUILDING

SCALE 20' to 1"

LMJB

15-8-45

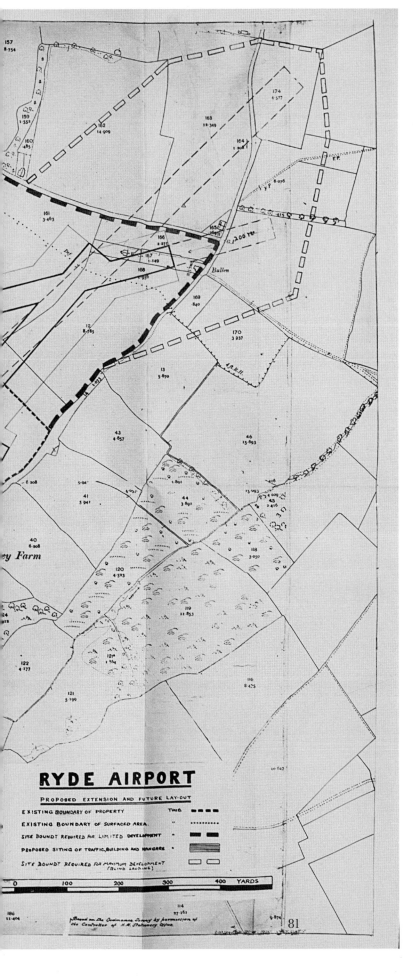

Ryde proposals submitted to the council which included moving the A 3055 Brading and Sandown road to the west

RYDE AIRPORT

PROPOSED EXTENSION AND FUTURE LAY-OUT

EXISTING BOUNDARY OF PROPERTY

EXISTING BOUNDARY OF SURFACED AREA.

SITE BOUNDY REQUIRED FOR LIMITED DEVELOPMENT

PROPOSED SITING OF TRAFFIC, BUILDING AND HANGARS

SITE BOUNDY REQUIRED FOR MAXIMUM DEVELOPMENT
(BLIND LANDING)

0   100   200   300   400 YARDS

Based on the Ordnance Survey by permission of the Controller of H.M. Stationery Office.

81

LEARNING FROM DIFFERENCE

Chapter 8

Approach to Eton. Indian conclusion

After the horrors of the war years in which, as at Highfield, many of Eton's former pupils had been killed,[1] aspirations, for those who did not have family estates, farms and companies, seemed to be swayed towards the more secure occupations. There appeared to be preference for administrative and institutional work which provided a service to others. This might be through the professions, finance, law, medicine, etc., perhaps the church or politics, or in the Civil Service or the Armed Services. Common to all these activities are defined relationships: soldiers have to sign up to 'Queen's regulations' and then obey commands; accountants and solicitors ask for signatures on detailed client agreements; the Civil Service and Local Government have established rules and customs. All such work is important in a civilised society. The expertise and experience of British service industries, particularly in finance and law, are increasingly appreciated by other countries and valuable fees are received. There is a difference in gaining the wealth which can come from making and trading things. All the potential uncertainties of working with employees, subordinates, those on the factory floor and union representatives have to be faced. The relationships are nothing like so clearly defined. There are also all the other manifold difficulties with which Lionel was struggling - finding capital funding, sourcing materials and manufacturing space and then selling products in the open markets of the world. The Eton of my time did not seem to welcome construction, innovation and working with the hands. I did not understand at the time, but now - looking back - the aim seemed to have been to promote abilities and qualities for helping in the running of the country. Reference was not then made to the 'Establishment' concept, but, as I look back now, the school ethos seems to have been about future participation in this elite. Who paid for it all was not discussed. Group loyalty, keenness and team spirit were fostered through playing games. The appetite for position and recognition was encouraged. 'Getting on with it' was praised, questioning was not. It is now many years since I left the school and attitudes do seem to have changed. Much to be welcomed is the now 'fully functioning Design and Technology Department recently moved into new accommodation.' Entrepreneurial activity is now encouraged.[2] Appendix 2 describes some of the other more recent heartening developments at the school.

Lionel and PC, the new Mrs Balfour, drove me to this Eton in September 1947. A parking space on the hill below Windsor Castle allowed me to slip into WH Smith's to buy the then current copy of *Flight*, 11th September. By the time I had got back to the car, I had already read the following paragraph headed INDIAN AEROCAR:

'With a capital of £1,125,000 a company has been formed in India to produce the Portsmouth Aerocar. The Company plans to construct a works and plant at Port Sika, but immediate production will be commenced at Jamnager. Mr E.L. Granville, who is chairman and managing director of the Portsmouth Aviation Company at Portsmouth, will also be chairman of the Indian Company. Mr G. Foster has been invited to become deputy chairman at Portsmouth, and Mr L.M.J. Balfour is expected to go to India as resident joint managing director of the Indian company. Mr W.H. Jenks, secretary and director, has already gone to India. Mr J.R.C. Miller is to become a director at Portsmouth and Major F.L.Luxmoore is to become the director in charge of the development of the Aerocar and technical adviser to both companies. It is understood that the provisional orders now number 288 representing £1,750,000.'

'Is this really true?' I asked, pointing to the paragraph when back in the car. 'Oh! We were going to write,' they replied. There was just time as we drove over the road bridge to Eton, then still open to traffic, to learn that they were off to Nawanager in November and that Peake would be given up. I now wonder why there was still so much confidence when Partition between India and Pakistan had already come about, on 15th August. The answer may be that the Princes still then had their money and Geoffrey Foster was on hand at Portsmouth to confirm the Jam Sahib's continuing commitment to the planned Aerocar enterprise. Presumably they had not been able to find a suitable joint MD and at that stage the new board members had confidence in Lionel and all he had achieved since 1932. From his viewpoint, he did not own a house in England, Karen was young enough without school worries, and I could be parked at school and sent to aunts for school holidays. I was later to learn that PC had found acceptance difficult in Hampshire and so was glad of a new start, escaping – as it were – from Myrtle's shadow. As with much else, there had been no discussion about my schooling. In fact there was no alternative. With no UK home I could not have attended a day school. An April 1947 letter from Mr Miller explained that income from trust the marriage settlement 'could be expended for the maintenance, education and benefit of children.' It was available for Eton. A typical bill was £116 12s 3d (summer 1951). Lionel's sister Rachel had secured a place for me with her friend, John Herbert, at the 'The Hopgarden'.[3] It was not the best start to those schooldays. I was thinking of other things when introduced to other new members of the House. It had just never crossed my mind that the family did not own Peake, which I had thought of as a home for life. What would happen to my new workshop? What would happen to my models? Where would I go in the holidays?

It was therefore necessity, not choice, which had taken me to the school. I had probably seen too much of the realities of life and death to be concerned about Eton's traditions and Etonian foibles. Having other worries I was not much interested in learning about the different House colours, and other coloured caps and scarves awarded to those with sporting prowess. It was explained that we should aim to achieve as many as possible for the honour of the House. Was another idea of these awards to incubate the desire to appear in future Honours lists? I have been aware of Douglas (now Lord) Hurd both as a radiant Eton scholar and when we were both prospective parliamentary candidates. He writes of the period after school in his agreeably readable memoirs: 'Friendships remained when rivalry faded, or rather became a very English game. We continued to measure each other's social standing by awards gained or even invitations received.' Of course the sentiments are understood, but there are some of us for whom these things are of less concern. Anyway I wasn't fully English. My insufficient enthusiasm for kicking a ball on muddy fields became a source of contention. One senior in the House (later a much respected Eton housemaster) could not understand my attitude exemplified by reluctance to play as a substitute in some wretched match when I had already arranged special tuition with Mick in the school of mechanics. He just could not accept that my priorities were the satisfaction of creative work, plus the wish to learn skills that would earn money. His knighted diplomatic service family knew Aunt Rachel and reports of my intransigence were filtered back to add to her previous disquiet about my behaviour at Peake. Lionel went to India in November (1947). The Christmas holidays were still at Peake with PC and Karen present. I think they had delayed their departure. It could not have been easy for PC, who had been caring for another stepson of my age, the son of her previous husband from an earlier marriage. Whatever our subsequent disagreements (we were miles apart in character and temperament) PC gave me one of the best presents I have ever received, a weekly subscription to *The Motor* magazine. I was told to pack up my things and allowed to include some of my models. It was good of them to be prepared to pay storage charges. Some have survived to this day.

The lease of Peake must then have been terminated, though I still hadn't understood. (In a May letter I asked: 'What is happening to Peake?' I still thought it was our house and this was only a temporary absence!) PC and Karen's departure for India followed, accompanied by a kind lady taken on to assist in looking after Karen. One of my letters to Jamnager described the Easter holidays (1948):

'Caught 6.59 a.m. Green Line bus. Bull's[4] family kindly gave me breakfast and an excellent one too, grapefruit, fried eggs, bacon and tomatoes. They live on the river at Hammersmith. Met Aunt Lucy (Myrtle's oldest sister) and caught another Green Line to Sunningdale. Just before Heathrow[5] there was fearful clatter and the driver got out. There had been minor clattering and we had been going very slowly and bumpily. A tyre had punctured, come right off the rim and was red hot. The next day at 3.45 p.m. the awful journey began carrying heavy suitcases in the rain to the station. I met the cousins (they would have been Aunt Norah's son and daughter) and here we are at last (in Southern Ireland) after a journey which I thought would never end. I was sick on the boat, the only one of us. They have gone to get a small 1932 Ford as the Rolls[6] is having something done to it in Cork.

These cousins kindly welcomed and put up with me for further holidays, with Aunt Lucy collecting me from Eton. Whilst it was not the much loved Meon Valley, I appreciated the sense of space and panorama from the Knockmealdown Mountains behind their house, Salterbridge, near Cappoquin. There was a sense of mystery, of marked difference, when we set out to towns like Fermoy and Mallow. A particular memory comes from catching mackerel at Youghal and hanging the fish from strings secured to nails banged into the wood coachwork of the Rolls.

There was not much news from India. Another of Lionel's notes states that at the end of 1947 it had been agreed that the Jam Sahib would acquire the Aerocar prototype. Another recent discovery has been the report in the *Courier-Mail Brisbane* dated 2nd April 1948:[7]

'G.N. Foster was here on his way to visit his daughter in New Zealand. Forty years ago he was one of five brothers who all played cricket for Worcestershire. He played with Ranjitsinghi and, when Ranji returned to rule as Jam Sahib, Foster went with him. He is adviser to the present Prince who is interested in aviation having bought up the Portsmouth Aviation Company of Portsmouth England. This firm planned and then produced the prototype of the 5-seat Aerocar that might solve a lot of problems in the World's feeder airlines. This aircraft was demonstrated last year at the SBAC Show. Powered with two Cirrus engines it is not powerful enough for Australian operations in hot weather conditions. Portsmouth intend trying it with Blackburn 'Bombardier' 180 hp engines. The prototype will be fitted with these and probably come out to Australia on show this year. A factory is being built in Jamnager and the Aerocar will be produced for the world there. There is no shortage of labour. The Indian Government is enthusiastic. All very nice - the point is however that with any support here Mr Foster would be happy to produce Aerocars in this country. I hope he gets that support.'

Geoffrey Foster was both a director of the company and aware of what was happening in India, so it seems that he thought there were still prospects for Portsmouth Aviation Nawanager after Partition and the accession of the Princely States. That summer (1948) I flew out to Karachi in the 'Schools Special' Solent flying boat. We were only in the air during the day and for most of the journey we were low enough to see the land and buildings over which we flew. First night was at Augusta in Sicily where, the next morning we were told to swim out to the waiting machine whilst our cases were taken by launch. The second day we flew across the Mediterranean and then along the coast of North Africa, which I came to know a few years later. That night we landed on the Nile and stayed in houseboats. Then it was low over the Arabian peninsula. There's still this mental picture of looking down and suddenly, with no other sign of life, seeing one solitary horseman, robes flowing out behind, galloping over the desert. The third night was at Bahrain and then along the coast of Baluchistan skirting the Arabian Sea to Karachi. Lionel and PC were there to meet me and we flew in a Jamair Dakota to land at Nawanagar Aerodrome. Jamair had been set up by a character called J B Muff, in partnership with the Jam Sahib. Pictures via Google bring back memories of talking to Mr Muff.[8] It was an aviation-minded State and there would have been plenty of maintenance work for Portsmouth Aviation. We went to Bedi Port and I was shown the packing cases which, I was told, contained the components of the second Aerocar prototype G-AGNJ in the big sheds, which can still be seen in photographs of Bedi.[9] We visited the nearly completed power station at Sika. There was no sign of a factory being built, but for the moment the Princes still had what were known as their Privy Purses[10] and the Jam Sahib had become leader, known as Rajpramuk, of the United State of Surastha, also called Kathiawar.[11]

It was an odd summer. Lionel wasn't the commanding figure walking round the factory at Portsmouth. PC just wasn't my type. My sister was only four and a half. There was a feeling of inertia, but surely they would not have stayed if there was no hope and when there were still other possibilities like Australia and Canada. My salvation came from the Jam Sahib's vehicle superintendent. This kind man allowed me to roam around the Motor Garage. Ranjitsinghi had befriended Frank Lanchester, had mostly bought his cars and then, later, had Daimlers fitted with Lanchester radiators. There are pictures of Frank visiting Jamnagar. Some twenty years later I wrote the following for a magazine article:

'Imagine, if you will, a large white building, from the outside a cross between an aircraft hanger and a pre-war cinema. The face is ornate. In the middle there is the main doorway with decorated arch, above an oval window and above that an intricate coat of arms. I walked under the arch and through the inner doors into a quiet, cool and scrupulously clean cathedral like hall. On either side of the main aisle, as if in silent prayer, were two rows of identical Lanchester radiators peering out between P100 headlights and supporting bonnets of pale blue. The cars had bodies from the leading English coachbuilders, saloons, limousines, laundaulettes, cabriolets and tourers, all the names from my childhood books, which must have provided employment for many craftsmen. One of these was later sent to Portsmouth. I tried but failed to get my hands on it.[12] Beyond, as it were in the choir stalls, were the lesser vehicles, the Ford V8s, the Hudsons and the Packards together with some post-war Lanchester Tens and Hillman Minxes. Behind the main building lay the Old Motor House with all the old cars still there in the stalls which must have originally been built for the horses and their carriages. I have a mental picture of sitting high up on a buttoned leather seat holding a wooden rimmed steering wheel and looking down on a smaller tiller steered car with tiny coal scuttle bonnet. Either side stretched twenty or more vehicles of similar age.'[13]

They also had a miniature tourer fitted with an electric motor and a Lanchester-style radiator, which I was allowed to drive on the local roads and tracks. I could not travel far on one charge, but this was a splendid introduction to the freedom of the road. I do not know the machine's origins. It may have been a Rytecraft adaptation or perhaps specially built by Lanchester. Lionel at first had the Hindustan version of the Morris Ten and then a Lanchester Ten (LD 10) for his own use. A Mercury Utility was provided for cross-country trips.

I flew back to England in a Lockheed Constellation, which was much quicker than the flying boat. I clearly remember thinking that all I had seen, the teeming masses, not the privileged few in our curious clothes, was the reality of life. Where parents or relatives were abroad, we were encouraged to write letters and Lionel kept what I sent during their next ten months in India. Re-reading them now, I spent much of the time when not in the classroom still making models. Having my own room took the place of what I had had at Peake and was some substitute for the lack of holiday base. Looking back, I spent too much time on these interests though I still managed acceptable results in school. Enough exercise was taken to mostly escape the stricture of the House Seniors. These little individual initiatives absorbed some of the longing to get on with life. Here are two letters sent to India from that time:

'The meeting of the aeromodelling club went off successfully. We are going to be provided with a test bed for engines and a good set of tools. It was held in an aeronautically minded beak's (master's) school room. The walls are plastered with magazine cuttings including one of the Aerocar. We had a rally to demonstrate our capabilities to the Lower Master. Of course it all went wrong. He arrived late and by that time planes were getting battered. Then it started to rain.'

'Yesterday was taken up with the first club competition. I started building my 'Petrel' (the name of the model) the weekend before and then, after getting up almost before the crack of dawn on the day of the contest, it was tested before lunch. In the afternoon, after some adjustments, it flew extremely well. We then had a hundred or so jeering spectators. After the crowd had dispersed I gave the 'Petrel' a lot of turns (to the rubber bands which turned the propellor). She went up to about three hundred feet and then began a long glide down. We tried to follow and then presumed that she hit a tree. After a half hour search, it was given up for lost. Although search parties have been out, the 'Petrel' still has not been found. I am a bit fed up as it both cost a lot (there was a small allowance from the settlement) and showed signs of being a good performer.'

We had to put up with that jeering crowd. This was another of the lessons which I was beginning to absorb. I understand now that they weren't interested in creative activity; rather this was a chance for gang solidarity all laughing together at us oddballs. Whenever near Eton, I look up to those tall trees. The brass bearing for the propellor shaft may still be there. It wasn't such a good place as those open fields around Peake.

Later there was my letter about another Eton reality:

'I was beaten by the Library (the house prefects) last night. Three of us were accused of lying, a statement which I hotly denied as we did nothing of the sort. I think it was the fault of one of the boy's maids. The beating hurt exceedingly and the bruises are still sore.'

This was then the Eton system. Members of the Library could decide on corporal punishment. They did not have to ask for authority. They did not have to listen to victims. It was probably much the same in other Houses. They thought we had done something wrong and anyway, in my case they didn't like my attitude to games etc: 'he's being awkward.' Then there were the individual Library members. They had to support the proposed action to prove their own worth. It all helped in understanding that life isn't and can't be fair. Alan Clark's comments in his diaries: 'Eton taught him about deceit and cruelty, the essential components of adult life' and 'enjoyment of the pain of others, that's a very familiar element in Politics' are harsh, but have aspects of truth.[14] Looking back now, I reflect that I did not even think of turning the tables. With a swift movement I could have turned round and - they would have not expected this - grabbed the cane and struck out. At that time such an action would probably have been branded as cowardly rather than heroic. Authority was not to be challenged. Eton helped with the subsequent better understanding of difference. There was a choice. If the pastimes, social aspects and disciplines were agreeable, a move towards those 'establishment' positions, with hard work balanced by its clubs and ceremonies, could lead to a comforting feeling of acceptance and involvement. For these future activities the school taught pupils to cope with conflicting demands from events and other people in pressured situations. Looking back, the less publicised value of the Eton experience, at least at that time, was that one learnt early that there might be a degree of ostracism if other paths (not one of us) were chosen.

One Saturday, I think it was early spring 1949, Lionel suddenly appeared alone at Eton. I do remember mention of serious problems at Portsmouth which had led to him hurriedly flying back to England. Was this the time when the bank called for action on the overdraft and his own influence and authority was curtailed? It was kind of him to come to visit me in the midst of difficulties. I wish we had been able to discuss the whole situation, though I do not think I would then have sufficiently understood to be of much assistance. A few months later they all came back from India and stayed in PC's mother's basement flat in Eaton Square. This was a difficult time. During the summer holidays I walked the streets to escape. PC insisted that I always had a hat ('a gentleman's attire') and there was fury when she passed me in the car and saw the wretched item stuffed in my pocket. Gradually it sunk in that there would be no Aerocar factory in India. Whilst the Princes retained their Privy Purses for a few more years, their States and their revenues were taken over by the Indian authorities. The hope that Geoffrey Foster had expressed in Brisbane for Indian Government support had not been fulfilled. Lionel wrote in a later note:

'Owing to the political conditions in the Indian States following on the British withdrawal it became impossible to secure in India the finance for the Indian Company and no progress could be made with the proposed factory and arrangements for the manufacture of the Aerocar. The non-fulfilment of the Indian agreements led to protracted negotiations for a settlement. Whilst 260 provisional orders (his figure, Flight had said 288) had been received for the Aerocar, due to lack of finance it was not possible to 'productionise'[15] the prototype.'

Back at Portsmouth other directors had taken control of the company whilst Lionel was away. He helped with the negotiations at Ryde and took on other tasks, but he was no longer managing director. (see *Spithead Express*). Letterheads show he was still a director in December 1950, but not after that. Later, he started other companies as described in Chapter Eighteen. Ten years later he wrote to me about 'trying to get back on the Board of the Company he had spent so much time and effort creating, that some Directors were willing but others not.' Lionel had made the mistake which I have since seen repeated by both aspiring entrepreneurs and experienced directors. They are so keen to advance their products, so confident that in the end huge returns will result, that they do not think about the downside of finance or assistance offered. I have known venture capitalists give high praise to a new product, offer to provide finance and then at the first opportunity dismiss the original directors from the board. I have been close to an elderly manager and owner who welcomed a younger man who, it was thought, would preserve the future, and then found himself chucked out. The lesson may be to advance more slowly and keep 51% control of the company, unless you have reason to be so certain about the future or can live with losing it all. It is understandable that new directors will want to take different decisions and work in different ways. If you want to stay, retrench and keep that 51%. The Cayzer cousins have wisely always been determined to maintain financial control and are careful about wills and settlements.

The Government had determined that taxpayer's money could be routed to the established aircraft firms (Avro, Bristol, de Havilland, Handley Page, Vickers, amongst others) for fighters, bombers and large civilian projects. They were not in the business of supporting a relatively unknown upstart like Portsmouth Aviation. Canadian Car was a prospect for the future but did not bring money into the company and they would only receive a small slice of each completed plane's sale price. The Jam Sahib's potential finance must have been a much-welcomed lifeline; prospects for the future and a settlement with the bank at Portsmouth. What will never be known is Myrtle's attitude to bringing in the Indian money. I do not think she would have wanted Lionel and the family to live in India. She had all her interests and connections in Hampshire and would probably not have wanted to leave her son in England. She is likely to have underlined the value of Lionel keeping his position at Portsmouth whilst making short visits to Jamnager to oversee an employed manager. Would she have asked her uncles and cousins to support her husband's plans and what would have been their reaction? The Cayzers financed the building of ships for their profit-producing routes. They were air transport operators, though not without difficulties. They still invest in engineering companies which make components. Financing a completely new machine for a new sector of the market is a different matter. It would have been understandable if they had refused. Or could they have used their muscle? Could they have achieved planning agreement on the land then owned at Ryde? There are factories there today. Could they then have financed the development and construction of the plane on that land? There might still have been a question mark over the supply of steel and other materials. There would still have been risk, a questionable investment for a family which was determined to preserve its wealth for the benefit of many other family members. But if they or others had come in, there would have been sufficient money to 'productionise', that word of his, the Aerocar at Portsmouth. This meant working to recreate the wooden framework of the prototype in metal for series production at Sika (as depicted in the drawings of the factory) and elsewhere. There could then have been production at Canadian Car, if they were still interested, and even in Mexico and Australia. This was not a defence project funded by the taxpayer. There could have been a long-term future in the civilian marketplace for a plane which was meticulously designed for reliable use all over the world. We have the assembly, pilot instruction and maintenance manuals, including thirty-three separate drawings depicting flying controls, hydraulic, servo and electrical systems, inspection panels, jacking points etc. We have the flight test reports and suggestions: 'after six hours the twenty one point inspection' and, after a bad landing, 'check for elongation of (nut and bolt) holes': all this careful detail and the versatility of float and ski versions. Fifteen years later the Islander and its later derivatives were designed for the same market. Britten Norman had their share of problems but eventually achieved production at Bembridge and elsewhere.[16] Now well over a thousand of these planes have been built, the longest production run of any post-war British aircraft. It has been used by fifty-six operators in twenty-six different countries. Today when I look up at the Trislander flying in from Alderney, I reflect that it might have been an Aerocar development.

Many have criticised the Mountbatten actions. Surfing the internet produces comments like 'the shameful treatment of the Princes'[17] or 'the Princes expected justice and fair play, not lies and half-truths to beguile them into a snare'[18]. Sir Conrad Corfield, political secretary to Mountbatten and in charge of negotiations with the Princely States, argued strongly that they should be allowed to remain independent as a valuable 'Third Force' if they so chose. He was overruled.[19] Charles Chenevix Trench also wrote:

> 'The Princes would have gathered tremendous bargaining power and their position would have been unassailable. Their support would have been sought by most of the stable elements in India.'

Geoffrey Foster must have still supported Lionel and the Sika plans when the Jam Sahib seems to have been caught in that snare, none of them fully realising what might follow. Then it all collapsed. The money was not available. At Portsmouth, the now-controlling directors concentrated on work which would produce profit as soon as possible in order to save the company. Understandably they did not see the search for more funds to still 'productionise' the Aerocar prototype as a priority. They were surely right, even though this cut out the Canadian Car option[20]. There was subsequently an air of failure surrounding Lionel's effort. FG and others voiced their criticisms. We praise those who play safe, we praise those who succeed. But we still need risk-takers for some to succeed and provide the money for the country's many tax-financed services. I hope we are becoming more tolerant and supportive of the 'near-misses,' the term which I believe describes Lionel's effort. Portsmouth Aviation still prospers and is becoming a global company with branches now in Arabia, Canada, the Emirates and soon in Mumbai. It has a well-regarded reputation for its engineering and design skills and thus takes on valuable work for which there is profit. Employment is provided. It did not have to start from nothing and thus benefits from the base of skill and reputation built up by Lionel and his colleagues. Would H and S Aviation, successor to Hants and Sussex, now one of the world's leading aero engine repair organisations, have come about if Lionel had not employed Jimmy Hawes in 1933? We cherish Jimmy's son Ted's last Christmas card sent shortly before his death: 'Now 85, having survived the war and enjoyed many good things, I have no complaints. It has been a great privilege to have known your father and your good self.' Ted understood, even if FG did not! The fruit of Great-grandfather James's and his brother's hard work in Dundee and then in Chile has not been wasted. As a postscript, Nawanager, now known as Jamnager, also prospers. The all-weather offshore terminal has been built at Sika handling up to eight hundred ships a year[21], the State Electricity Corporation flourishes and a large petroleum storage area has been built near the site which might have been the Aerocar factory. The present Jam Sahib no longer has power and lives in Muff bungalow built originally for the Jamair pilot.[22]

Athur Ord-Hume has commented in his recent books about British private aircraft 1946-1970 with the Aerocar on the cover of volume two:[23]

'As peace loomed, the Directors (of Portsmouth Aviation) embarked on the design and construction of a really practical twin-engined aeroplane. It performed perfectly. Every-one who flew it spoke glowingly of its handling and performance. The orders started rolling in but the Company had no money to make that leap into aircraft production. No-body wanted to help. An outstanding design was thus crippled by National political failure to provide any aid whatsoever to a small but established firm that happened to be onto a winner and holding a full order book. Had but a fraction of the aid given elsewhere been available to Luxmoore and Balfour, the Aerocar would have returned its investment by way of rich earnings. Abandoned UK projects such as the V-1000, TSR-2 and others are well remembered. While the Aerocar was at least as serious a loss to aviation, it is regrettably forgotten today.'

This is an appropriate commentary on the painstaking efforts of Francis Luxmoore (supported by Lionel) to ameliorate all the details of that superb British aeroplane. The evidence is that it would have served owners without the trying defects in the products of the car industry (see Chapter 19). Whilst I only have memories of that August day at Portsmouth Airport in 1947, one of my most cherished possessions is that copy of the maintenance handbook.

Hidden talent among school leavers

THERE WAS a hidden wealth of talent among school leavers which was not being used, said Merton's Careers Officer, Mr Christopher Balfour.

And society was losing out by not developing it, he told the Wimbledon Guild of Social Welfare's annual meeting.

"A hidden wealth of talent lies among those who leave school early without any qualifications or the basic attributes to earn a living.

"Many of them are unable to cope with basic maths and spelling and lack the capacity to be punctual and reliable.

"They are the young people for whom the prospect of a job is getting less, and in other parts of the country they are not getting jobs at all."

Mr Balfour said it was difficult to solve the problem for nobody knew what the youngsters would be capable of if the circumstances were different.

"It may be if school classes were smaller, they would have responded to more individual attention.

"Perhaps employers should lower their standards and take a greater part in training or pay higher taxes so that schools can do more.

"There is so much talent there, much of which is hidden, and such people need help and encouragement."

He said the job of the careers service was to awaken

CAREERS AND YOUTH EMPLOYMENT OFFICERS are available to help young people and their parents with problems concerning careers and further education. They can also assist in finding suitable employment.

If you would like an interview with an Officer, please telephone your nearest Careers and Youth Employment Office to make an appointment.

Interviews with pupils in school time must be arranged through school.

ED 157

LONDON BOROUGH OF MERTON
Education Committee
Chief Education Officer
R. GREENWOOD, M.A., F.R.S.A.

CAREERS ADVISORY SERVICE

MR. C. J. J. BALFOUR
Principal Careers Officer
Careers Office
Merton Technical College
Morden Park
London Road, Morden
Tel. 01-640 4191/2

Office Hours— Mon. to Fri. 9 - 12.30 p.m.
1.15 - 5 p.m.
& Tuesday evenings 5.30 - 7.30 p.m.

MR. D. H. GODDARD
Deputy Principal Careers Officer
Careers Office
Mitcham Court
Cricket Green, Mitcham, CR4 4XT
Tel. 01-648 9361/2

Office Hours— Mon. to Fri. 9 - 12.30 p.m.
1.15 - 5 p.m.
& Wednesday evenings 5.30 - 7.30 p.m.

June 26, 1

Newsman's Diary

CHOOSING THE RIGHT JOB

AN ex-Parliamentary candidate, merchant se factory worker is the man who will be helpin youth to find the right job. **Mr. Christopher Ba** 36), is Merton's new Youth Employment Offic brings to the job experience in many branches of and commerce.

He joined the Youth Employment Service only five years ago when business commitments allowed him to do the job he wanted. He felt he could be of most use in youth employment and expects his varied background to be a big help.

He said he is very aware that he is being paid by the taxpayer and hopes to continue what has been running well and provide what young people want.

"It is essential to get into the schools and find out exactly what is wanted. When I first joined I realised that in many places the service was falling short of its aims.

"I think things have improved a bit over the last few years and I shall be doing my best to carry on the improvement. There is such a vast scope for increasing what we do."

Although he stood as Conservative candidate for Gloucester in the last election, he has no thoughts at the moment of standing again.

"There is too much important work in Merton to do before I think of a political career again," he said.

Mr. Balfour, Raymond Road, Wimbledon, is married with three young children.

Youth Employment Service
Training Board
and
Institute of
Careers Officers

A CAREER AS A CAREERS OFFICER

The buff Y1 on which were recorded a school leaver's employment progress plus national insurance details

Jan	Feb	Mar	April	May	June	July	Aug	Sept	Oct	Nov	Dec	**BOY**

Surname (caps)	Date of Birth	D/B verified (inits)	MLH No.	Occ Classn
Other names	S/leaving date	NI no.		
Address	EMPLOYMENT/FURTHER EDUCATION/TRAINING RECOMMENDED		
....	General		
....	Specific (now)		
....	Later (and when)		
School................................	EMPLOYMENT/FURTHER EDUCATION DESIRED (if different)		

EMPLOYMENT RECORD (including part-time and holiday employment)

Employer	Department/Occupation	From	To	Reason for leaving and other notes, e.g. wages, hours, job details

NI CARD ⎰ For part-time or holiday employment (UI 691 (S/L date) to RB.............(inits) ⎱ Included in EDS 80 for....................19......
(inits)................................

BOUNDLESS OPPORTUNITIES AT DOWTY

CRAFT APPRENTICE

The Craft Apprenticeship is designed primarily to produce the skilled craftsmen to meet the demands of the Dowty Group. The high standard of products produced by the Dowty Group requires a constant supply of skilled turners, millers, grinders, borers etc.

QUALIFICATIONS
No academic qualifications are laid down but we prefer applicants to be sitting at least some C.S.E. or G.C.E. examinations. These examinations help to determine the subsequent technical education.

AGE LIMITS
Candidates should normally be within the age range of 16-17 years at the start of training. Applicants are advised to apply in the December prior to leaving school.

TECHNICAL EDUCATION
Technical education is an essential part of the apprenticeship. The course studied will be determined by the Technical college staff in conjunction with our training staff. The education

An automatic machining process being described to junior operatives

Directors:
L. MAYS, M.C.I.T.
G. T. DAY, M.I.M.H., M.I.T.A.
M.C.I.T., A.M.B.I.M.
S. D. MITTEN
Secretary:
F. MAYS

Telephone:
01-542 2484

MABODYS LTD

LYON ROAD
MERTON, S.W.19

COMMERCIAL VEHICLE BODY BUILDING : VEHICLE PAINTING
COMMERCIAL VEHICLE REPAIRS

Our Ref: GTD/SF

Youth Employment Officer,
Careers Office,
Wimbledon, Merton & Morden,
Merton Technical College,
Morden Park,
London Road,
Morden,
Surrey.

30th August 1972

31 AUG 1972

Dear Sir,

We would appreciate your assistance to fill vacancies for Apprentice Bodybuilders to undergo training for the construction and repair of commercial vehicle bodies.

If you have any suitable candidates who may currently be seeking employment, we would welcome an opportunity of arranging interviews.

We trust that these vacancies may appeal to school leavers with a practical and mechanical aptitude who may be seeking a suitable opening in the Motor Trade.

Yours faithfully,
for MABODYS LIMITED.

G.T. DAY
Executive Director.

SUBSIDIARY OF L. V. MAYS TRANSPORT LTD., MERTON, S.W.19

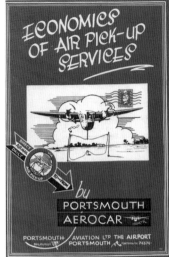

Painting of second Aerocar G-AGNJ. Are any components still in the sheds at Bedi Port?

The authors own effort with his Box Brownie at Portsmouth Aerodrome August 1947

Drawings of float and ski versions in the Aerocar brochure

Lionel as chairman and joint Managing Director at Portsmouth in 1940s.
He did not realise that a few years later he would have neither office nor job.

Above: Electric car I was allowed to use
Left: Motor house

Above: Entrance to Manvillas Palace with Hindustan '10'
Right: Pratap Palace

Karen at 'Saifi Manzil' bungalow with Effie
Antipas, daughter of Greek engineer building
power station at Sika

Mercury 'station wagon' allocated for cross-country
journeys on unsurfaced roads

INDIAN AEROCAR

WITH a capital of £1,125,000 a company has been formed in Inda to produce the Portsmouth Aerocar. The company plans to construct a works and plant at Port Sika, but immediate production will be commenced at Jamnagar. Mr. E. L. Granville, who is the chairman and managing director of the Portsmouth Aviation Company at Portsmouth, will also be chairman of the Indian company. Mr. G. Foster has been invited to become deputy chairman of the company at Portsmouth, and Mr. L. M. J. Balfour is expected to go to India as resident joint managing director of the Indian company. Mr. W. H. Jenks, secretary and director has already gone to India on the Board of that company. Mr. J. R. C. Miller is to become a director in Portsmouth and Major F. L. Luxmoore is to become the director in charge of the development of the Aerocar and technical adviser to both companies. It is understood that the provisional orders now number 288 representing £1,750,000.

Above: The Jam Sahib garlanded on his return to Jamnager

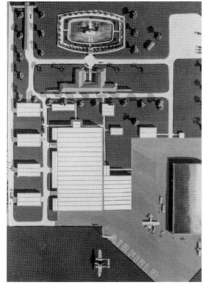

Above & left: Factory and office plans drawn by Bombay architects, Pabritain and Salonki

How could it all go wrong?

Aerocar

Two of a set of drawings for publicity

First flight 18th June 1947 G-AGTG

All those who built the Aerocar

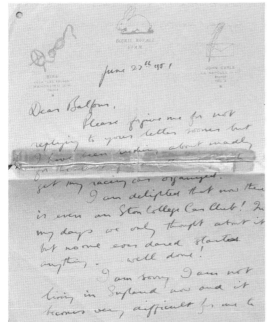

THE ETON COLLEGE
AUTOMOBILE SOCIETY.

Will meet on

.... At 8. 50. P. M.

n.. To Hear.............

On...

Please be punctual.

Secretary.

Left: It helped to have this encouraging letter from
Prince Bira, successful E.R.A. driver in pre-war
years. There is a monument in his memory at the
Pattaya circuit in Thailand

Right: Visit to Rootes
Ryton on Dunsmore,
March 7 1952
only Anthony Bullen,
at the back of the
Sunbeam Talbot in
dark suit , went on to
work in the car
industry

Right: Rootes factory
and offices

The Singer '9' from which Peter Stoddart was evicted the following autumn. Pen-y-Gwnyd Hotel in Snowdonia the last holiday from Eton with Jonathan Henty and Robin Hooper, Easter 1952

PC's 'Super 12' outside her basement flat in Eaton Square. An attractive Singer car before they lost out in a competitive market and were bought by Rootes

The Morgan 3-wheeler, in which the test was passed at 16, at Petersfield

The garages and coach houses of England were full of magnificent vehicles. This Cabriolet body Rolls Phantom 2 was offered at £100 in 1956. But neither bank nor relatives would loan money and where could they be kept? Where is this car now?

National Service, Catterick Camp, autumn 1952

Victory for the regimental team, Suez 1953

With 'Centurion' in Sahara

Fiat Millecento outside Regimental HQ, Sabratha

Another officer's 'Speed Six' outside the officers' mess

Territorial camp. Wiltshire

Austria

Salzburg. Michael Young, author, Adrian Moyes

Bearing problems reported on earlier SAs. But here is this 1939 car at INDICATED 90mph, 4,700 rpm, four up on German autobahn, north of Nurnberg

Hispano-Suiza 37.2

Above & right: For sale at £120 in a small Cotswold garage. Shared ownership with Kit Power, probably 1921 but fitted with a later body. It was sold to America. Like the Rolls, have found no trace of this car, in spite of enquiries of Hispano Owners' Clubs

This shows the commanding driving position from which one looked out on those formidable headlamps and the stork mascot

Restoration started. At Carol Wethered's house in Marlow. Letter to *The Autocar* 1934: 'I discovered a 1923 Hispano. It possesses wonderful road holding at 60mph without effort. Nothing has given me greater pleasure to drive. I am taking the car by sea to Gibraltar for a tour of Spain and France. An ideal vehicle for long distance traveling.'

Frost's garage, Cambridge. Mr Frost and his son were constantly helpful and understanding

FG's Triumph '1800' at Whinshill, the
Sunningdale house now demolished and replaced
by blocks of luxury flats

FG and Armstrong Siddeley Saphire, still with sailor
mascot, Scotland September 1956

Uncle Bertie, on left, ushers his shooting party guests into the back of his design choice
for coach-built Rolls Royce Silver Wraith

Lanfine gardens and entrance with Tony Cayzer's MK6 Bentley

Cambridge Expedition to Afghanistan 1955

BP Austria

Purfina, Greece

Herat main street

Typical bridge on the main road to Badakshan

Repairing a broken bridge on the route
back from Badakshan to Kataghan

The Boharak plain in 1955 was still exactly as described by Marco Polo in the 13th Century

Buddha at Bamian, later destroyed by Taliban

Above: Swimming in the
river Kokcha
Left: Tea break

Grape seller

Local Shura

The road to Jurm. The
furthest east we were
permitted to travel

Taken from Hunting Clan DC3 looking down on the construction of the Kariba Dam

Unloading British built locomotives from Lanarkshire at Durban

British cars for export, Birkenhead docks spring 1958. More interesting than wondering what I was meant to be doing! Note from left: Riley 1.5, Morris Minor Travellers, Hillman Minx, Land Rovers

Lanarkshire in Southern Atlantic, December 1958. It was in my nature to talk with all the crew!

Umtali, Saturday 17th January 1959. Hillman Minx, Austin A40 and Morris on forecourt of Volkswagen and Rover garage across the street. Mr Cohen's green Chevrolet in foreground, alongside Vauxhall Velox

General Election, March 1966. So much not then understood!

Mrs Balfour in the centre, who opened the Gloucester Conservative Association annual Christmas fair held at the Technical College on Saturday, pictured with her husband and Mr John Priday the Association's President and Mrs TF Lawson chair of the Conservative ladies section

Lone male at tea party

Tory short list

MR. R. J. MORELAND   MR. C. BALFOUR

TWO of the potential prospective Conservative candidates for Gloucester are pictured here. They are Mr. Robert J. Moreland (23), son o Mr. S. J. Moreland, managing director of the Glou-

pher Balfour (31) of Compton House, Redmarley.

The third member of the short list is Mr. M. F. Turner-Bridger, a Berkshire County Councillor. Selection will be

OOKING round at the garden party of the Gloucestershire Conservative Central lies' Tea Club at Highnam Rectory is Mr. Christopher four, prospective Conservative candidate for Gloucester e was introduced by Mrs. L. Pencey (on the left) and irman of the Tea Club, and nked by Mrs. T. Lawson, the sident.

Mr. Balfour, who was accomlied by his wife and two ng children, congratulated ladies on organising the at.

was, he said, such meeti and organisations that le the foundations of a tical party.

rs. Lawson thanked Mrs. H. Hammond for loaning club the garden of her se in which to hold the ty.

Her Sincerity

COMPLETELY RAW TO THE HURLY-BURLY OF THE POLITICAL ARENA, AGAINST AN OPPONENT OF THE STATURE AND EXPERIENCE OF MR. DIAMOND, AND AGAINST A COUNTRY-WIDE SWING TO LABOUR, HE HELD THE GLOUCESTER TORY VOTE STEADY AND EVEN POLLED 150 MORE VOTES THAN MR. JOHN STOKES DID IN 1964.

Right: l to r: Jack Diamond (Labour), author, City High Sheriff, Councillor Frape and Stina Robson (Liberal) handing in nomination papers March 1966

Mr. Balfour's success in the election must have astounded even himself

After our marriage at St Peter's Church, Bishop Waltham, 9th July 1960

| Karen | Elizabeth Mack | FG | Author and Ann | Lionel | Morva and Claude Butlin | PC | Jill Nettlefold Rosamond Scott |
| | | | | | Rosamond Nankivell | George Jellicoe | |

Above: Hugh Boustead
Right: Kit Power as best man

Below: A lovely house and potential base for restoration of historic vehicles. But planning regulations then still prevented such 'change of use' and it was a potential financial 'black hole'

'Olympic' after collection from Rochdale

The 400, now with Maximilien Gagnebin in Switzerland and Ann's Mini at Wheathill Close, Leamington

All those journeys in the Austin which Max and Juliet cheerfully survived, the weekend trek from Leamington to Redmarley and holidays in France

Looking towards
Mont Ventoux

The Twynings, Redmarley

Extension whilst we were at Leamington

After collecting furniture from Ann's aunt's house in Devon

The Austin earned its keep as load carrier and tractor in the fields

Delahaye 135

Another £100 wreck, this time a Delahaye 135. Roughly refurbished to running order

Though later re-bodied, at least engine and chassis have survived

Juliet, Kate and 'Motto' rescued when Ann's brother went to New Zealand

Water replenishment from drainage ditch alongside M5

With Juliet after collecting from Cheltenham Ladies College

Outside Cheltenham Careers Office with Ann's half brother, Peter Nankivell

Prescott hill climb

Forest of Dean District Council 1980. Author at right, rear row. Some of the older councillors in their younger days had crawled on their hands and knees along the tunnels of local mines. It was a privilege to work with them

Visit of Sir James Scott-Hopkins, local MEP to the Bridge Project.
He helped many by his always cheerful and encouraging attitude

Attending
local
events

Picking apples at Redmarley

Workshops

A 1955 Lancia Aurelia half way through restoration by Christopher Balfour's Bridge Project

Bridging the gap

Those of you who can remember the long-defunct *Veteran & Vintage* magazine will perhaps recall the occasional erudite and interesting articles submitted by Christopher Balfour. You will also know of his personal addiction to Hispano-Suizas and Delahayes, and although anno domini has now dictated a switch of allegiance to Bristols ("those heavy 1939 controls were defeating me"), you might be surprised to learn that his current interests also embrace the restoration of post-war Humber Super Snipes, Daimler Conquests and Lancia Aurelias. If this might seem to indicate some kind of *volte face*, let us hasten to explain the nature of Christopher's interest.

Because this column believes wholeheartedly in what Chistopher is doing, we are delighted to give space here to details of his Forest of Dean Bridge Project, a residential base where those who cannot get jobs can find occupation and companionship, learn new skills and perhaps find the path back to employment or self-employment.

Located at Broadwell Lane End Old School, Nr Coleford, Glos, the Bridge Project also provides a base for local community organisations, and receives support from various Government departments, trades unions, local employers, and Parish and District Councils, but that aspect of its work which concerns us here is the restoration and renovation of classic cars.

Working under the supervision of skilled volunteers, as an educational activity, a group of enthusiastic youngsters have already completely refurbished a 1955 Lancia Aurelia which would otherwise have been scrapped, and are now turning their attention to the Daimler Conquest and the Humber Super Snipe.

The Lancia has passed its MoT and has attended a number of shows during the past 12 months, but perhaps more importantly several young people, for whom the outlook was bleak, have found a new interest and something in which they can personally take a pride.

The publicity thus generated has been good for the Bridge Project as a whole, and has also resulted in further vehicles being donated to the group for restoration. They hope to participate in the Government's newly announced Community Programme for the 'longer term unemployed' and in addition to vehicle restoration are also tackling furniture renovation and toy repair, for the benefit of local schools and community groups, an arts workshop is teaching drawing and painting and screen printing, and generally the whole place is a hive of activity.

It all takes cash, however, so anyone with old but still serviceable tools, equipment, motor cars – you name it – which they would be willing to donate should telephone Chris Balfour on 0594 35016. More power to his elbow.

Members of the Forest of Dean Bridge Project tackling a Humber and two Daimlers

One council achievement was to gain support for local flood prevention schemes.
These have been beneficial in more recent years

WINTER SPORTS BY CAR HEADLIGHTS

Piquancy In Detail

Addressing fellow members of Gosport Rotary Club on "Sugar and Spices," Mr. J. Hern (who has been associated with the grocery trade since 1929) said there were more than 50 different types of spice, and in pre-war days he handled 14 varieties of sugar.

He explained the difference between black and white pepper and spoke about some of the rarer spices.

Cloves were obtained, he said, from the unopened buds of carnations, while saffron was obtained from the autumnal crocus.

To get 1lb. of that commodity, 60,000 blooms would be required. Strongly denying the allegation that grocery mixed sand with sugar, Mr. Hern said many people in the past were burned at the stake for diluting saffron.

Vanilla flavouring could be obtained from the orchid.

Dealing with sugar, he said it was possible at the present time to get 12 varieties.

In the manufacture of icing sugar, special precautions had to be taken, because with particles becoming suspended in mid-air, there was the risk of an explosion.

Mr. Hern passed round for examination, samples of spices and sugars, and especially admired by Rotarians were pre-war coffee crystals and sugar candy.

THANKS FOR BUS SERVICE

Gosport Borough Labour Party, at their annual meeting, asked the Secretary (Mr. A. K. Abraham) to write to the Provincial Bus Company conveying the members' thanks to the drivers, conductors, and maintenance staff for keeping a service running in Gosport and district during the wintry spell.

SCOUT "ENVOYS" SHARED FUN

Petersfield Heath as Testing-ground for "Auto-Sledge"

PETERSFIELD Heath became a miniature St. Moritz yesterday.

Scores of people were out sliding, skating and enjoying toboggan rides.

Ice hockey matches were played on the 22-acre Heath Lake, which was frozen over completely.

In the early evening the winter sports continued by the lights of cars, parked by the lakeside.

Out on the ice for the first time on Saturday afternoon was a 4 m.p.h. "auto-sledge" invented by Mr. L. M. J. Balfour, a mechanical engineer, of Heath Lodge, Petersfield.

The sledge, designed to travel on both hard snow and ice, was driven by a large worm screw engaging on the ice and powered by a 1 h.p. two-stroke engine.

An 8 h.p. edition of the sledge, capable of 12 m.p.h. and designed to pull a Nansen sledge with 1,100lb. of equipment, is now being experimented with by the British North Greenland expedition.

Slight falls of snow occurred throughout the Petersfield district, yesterday, and the highest temperature for the day was 30 degrees.

Ice-bound roads continued to make conditions for traffic extremely dangerous. A single-decker Rogate to Petersfield bus, on Saturday afternoon, skidded into the roadside at West Mark, Sheet. The crew and the two passengers were uninjured.

On Sunday afternoon an articulated British Road Services lorry skidded and crashed into a hedge on the main London - Portsmouth road at Sheet.

Mr. M. J. Balfour riding his auto-sledge on the Heath Pond at Petersfield.

Patrolman Tribe Got the Meat Through

BUT for the prompt action of an Automobile Association radio patrolman on Butser Hill yesterday, a large consignment of meat for Portsmouth may have been held up.

Just after 4.30 p.m., Patrolman Eric Tribe discovered two ... In order to avoid further trouble, he interrupted the ...

Icy Inclines at Gosport

BECAUSE of the icy conditions on the inclines in Fareham Road, Gosport, between Cams Alders and Wych Lane, buses had to run a ...

Autosledge prototype. British North Greenland Expedition 1953

Auto-ski and auto sledge development 1952 - 1953. All built with his own hands

The car roof seat which did result in
a small profit

Examples of Portair products

The concertina ladder folded into a
small space

Workshops at LMJ Balfour and Co. Patent development and consulting engineers at Petersfield

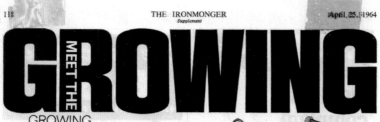

MEET THE GROWING

GROWING DEMAND FOR PORTAIR PRODUCTS

THE LIMPET AND NEW LIMPET MAJOR

Adhere's to any flat non-porous surface, yet can be released at the flick of a finger. Designed especially for the everyday wash. Precision built with STRONG METAL FRAME and high quality rubber rollers, Polythene drip tray. Stove enamel finish in red, white, blue or yellow.

RETAIL PRICES —
Limpet
(7" x 1¼" rollers)   42/5
or less Drip Tray   39/11
Limpet Major
(10" x 1¼" rollers)   69/11
or less Drip Tray   65/6

GENEROUS DISCOUNTS
Obtainable from leading factors.
Write to us for full information.

PORTAIR PRODUCTS LTD.
CHURCHES MILL, WOODCHESTER, Nr. STROUD, GLOS.

THE NEW CARRYWELL TRAY

The nearest approach to a non-spill tray ever produced—it must be seen to be believed. Manufactured in fibreglass with stove enamel and steel finish.

THE NEW WRINGSTER

with 10" x 1¼" rollers is a lightweight clamp-on type Wringer for attachment to sinks, tables, garage doors, etc. Unique feature enables Wringer to be inclined over sink avoiding need for Drip Tray. Stove enamel finish, white

QUICK TURNOVER

The tough little Portair Limpet has proved invaluable in tens of thousands of homes.

Will adhere to any flat non-porous surface yet may be released at the flick of a finger. Adaptor now available for other surfaces such as Walls, Fluted Drain Boards, etc. Greatly extends its usefulness.

GENEROUS DISCOUNTS

Obtainable from leading factors. Write to us for full information and particulars of interesting new Portair products.

PORTAIR "LIMPET"

★ Precision built
★ Strong metal Frame
★ 7" high quality rubber rollers
★ Polythene drip tray
★ Stove enamel finish in attractive shades: red, white, blue and yellow.

RETAIL PRICE
or less drip tray 39/11
Adaptors 3/6

42/5

PORTAIR PRODUCTS LTD.,
CHURCHES MILL, WOODCHESTER, NR. STROUD. GLOS.
Tel: Amberley 2224

METAVANTE ACQUIRES NOMAD PAYMENTS LTD., ESTABLISHING EUROPEAN PRESENCE IN PREPAID PROCESSING

Leading provider of prepaid and debit card processing and licensed software in U.K. and Europe to join Metavante International Group

MILWAUKEE, Jan. 10, 2008 – Metavante Technologies, Inc. (NYSE: MV), a leading provider of banking and payments technology, today announced the acquisition of London-based Nomad Payments Limited, a leading provider of prepaid and debit card processing and licensed software. Nomad will now operate as Metavante Technologies Limited, part of the Metavante International Group.

The acquisition is expected to add approximately one percent to Metavante's 2008 revenue and have no significant impact on the company's profitability in 2008. The purchase price was approximately $58 million.

Nomad is an early leader and innovator in the European prepaid payments market, providing processing services for many different types of payment providers, including gift cards, money share cards, which enable individuals to provide cash to relatives living, studying or traveling abroad, and general purpose prepaid cards that can be used as an alternative to a bank account.

"Acquiring Nomad presents Metavante International Group with the opportunity to establish a European center of operations, with a blue-chip client base, multi-currency capabilities, high volume processing platform, proven business model and an established European sales channel," said Frank R. Martire, Metavante president and chief executive officer.

Significant market opportunities include financial institutions, retailers, government agencies, program managers, open loop gift cards, professional organizations and affinity groups.

"Metavante's extensive experience in prepaid processing is complementary and easily transferable to the United Kingdom market," said Donald W. Layden, Jr., president of the Metavante International Group. "It also offers a rich opportunity to expand the prepaid processing value chain by offering synergistic Metavante services such as closed loop and loyalty programs, and fraud monitoring to U.K. and European markets."

"Prepaid cards as a direct substitute for today's cash and checks give Europe's banks an ideal mechanism to achieve efficiencies after Single Euro Payments Area is in effect," said Gareth Lodge, senior analyst with TowerGroup, the global research and advisory firm. "TowerGroup estimates that by 2010, prepaid card usage will be EUR75 billion, a 600 percent increase over 2005, and 375 million cards will be in circulation, a 1,000 percent increase," he added.

Nomad was established in 1991 as a card payments software provider, establishing its payment division on 2005. Debit and prepaid card processing clients include the Bank of Ireland, Clydesdale Bank, Newcastle Building Society, IDT Financial Services, and Tuxedo Money Solutions. Licensed software clients include Bank Zachodni WBK, the fourth largest bank in Poland, and ING Ukraine and Romania, BRD - Groupe Société Générale, and EFG Eurobank, which operates in Poland, Romania, Serbia and Ukraine.

About Nomad
Nomad has a well-deserved reputation for delivering innovation in card payments to its clients. Nomad continues this trend by being a leader with a fit-for-purpose prepaid capability for issuers, which meets the requirements of international scheme open-loop prepaid cards, featuring cardholder web service capability. The service manages all of the complexities surrounding card processing on behalf of members, including card and PIN production, customer service facilities, fulfillment and transaction authorization.

LEARNING FROM DIFFERENCE

Chapter 9

Eton queries? Preparing for work

Following on from the comments at the beginning of the last chapter, David Young (later Lord Young and Minister in the Thatcher era) in his autobiography *The Enterprise Years*[1,] after referring to innovators like Brunel and Stevenson and the speed of growth in Britain in the first part of the nineteenth century, wrote:

'Administrators are anything but entrepreneurs. Gradually the antithesis of enterprise, a strong contempt for trade, was growing. The children of industrialists and inventors were absorbed into the land-owning gentry. Even Brunel sent his sons to Harrow. The urge for enterprise was submerged in a search for stability. Numbers in the main professions increased and their very spirit was antagonistic to enterprise. They claimed expertise and integrity in an attempt to rise above the market place. Public schools resisted teaching science which was seen as inferior to classics. If taught at all, it was pure rather than applied for science was seen as having association with vulgar industry and commercial utility. Vocational preparation carried with it the stigma of industry. The world of business was openly disparaged. Tom Brown's schooldays describes business as 'mere money making'. The military, politics, the civil service and the professions were exalted. Oxbridge reflected a similar set of values.

Not everyone agrees with Lord Young who is still (in 2013) a successful practising now-octogenarian entrepreneur (there have been clashes with Downing Street), but these words mirror personal experience, particularly those costly attempts to minimise risk 'niceties' proffered by the professionals. When setting up a company, we rejected the costly inessential extra 'safeguarding' contractual arrangements proffered by solicitors. Risk is the savour of the entrepreneurial life. Lord Young's words confirm the reasons why James's sons (my grandfather and his two brothers), educated in their case at Clifton, did not carry on their father's pioneering industrial efforts in South America. Such was the Eton in which I found myself in 1950 having achieved School Certificate 'Very Goods' in Latin, French and History, with credits in Scripture Knowledge, Greek, Elementary Maths, Additional Maths and General Science. I did not attempt Physics or Chemistry.

There was also the growing awareness that, after the Indian venture, there would not be a place for me in the Aviation company at Portsmouth which Lionel had founded; also that he now had little money. Looking back now, it seems questionable whether circumstances and this education had equipped me with the skills needed to take that company forward. I had the idea of making motor caravans, using the skills employed in building bus bodies, and the company would have been one of the first in the field, but by the time I put this to Lionel he was already on his way out. Did I have sufficient understanding of 'commercial utility?' This is where the directors who took over have succeeded. I reflect that my priority could have been the creation of products with too much quality rather than concentrating on 'making money'. Again it's the vital difference; on the one hand the love of good machinery, on the other what will sell at a profit in the marketplaces of the world.

It isn't possible to accurately represent one's thoughts as a schoolboy sixty-three years ago. I had not yet started to write diaries. However, letters and material kept show that, after the demise of that aviation opportunity, I started to think seriously about my earlier interest in cars and connected work. The introduction to 'The Times Survey of the British Motor Industry' published in October 1950, which I purchased at the time of choosing specialist subjects for the next two years, reads:

> 'The figures for the first six months of the year illustrate the extent of Britain's lead in motor-car exports. In that time the British Industry exported 203,626 cars (77.6 percent of output), the United States 67,749 (2.2 per cent), France 44,495 (36.2 percent) and Germany 26,749 (28.9 percent). British manufacturers are entitled to claim that their success largely results from their determined endeavour to make the modern British car thoroughly acceptable all over the world, whatever the local conditions. The products have sometimes been condemned as a whole because individual vehicles have given trouble and there is concern that, when there is more freedom of choice, they will no longer be in demand. It is clear that Companies will have to exert every effort to maintain their lead. They are also concerned that the total amount of taxation at home may prevent them from continuing with those larger types of car which the world requires in addition to the smaller car.'

Comments are remembered about how different types of cars would be needed in countries with just tracks rather than constructed roads. But I also then subscribed to magazines about road development. It seemed to me that more roads would be built and that cars which Britain should be able to build would be used all over the world. It therefore seemed important that British companies maintained their lead. I wanted to see how I could contribute. Mechanical and constructional work had always appealed, not the pure science mentioned by Lord Young. It took me years to realise that I could have left the school. It was not till working in the State system years later that I understood that there had been no law to keep me there. I could have left and gained the skills still missed – touch typing, basic accountancy and more thorough (rather than self-taught) practical mechanics and engine knowledge. If the settlement could have been used for accommodation, there were many colleges offering appropriate courses, better still if combined with an apprenticeship, but none of these thoughts crossed my mind at the time. The prevailing view was that Eton was only left early if in disgrace for some heinous behaviour or crime. If I had left, there would have been roars of disapproval from FG, PC and others, what a disappointment I was etc.

As reading and writing appealed, the choice was made to become a history specialist.

There was some enjoyment, but what of the future and with no money? Then it came to me that Eton did not have a Car Club like other schools. There were some others interested (Robin Benson was a particular support) and it fell to me to approach Robert Birley, who had become headmaster in 1949. His permission was needed for such a venture. A highly intelligent and well-meaning man, he was concerned that we were interested in the reckless, ego-boosting, speed-merchant kind of motoring. This is understood. In some quarters car-interest was regarded as a form of depravity and, anyway, administrators had drivers. It's true that, if the mind has been completely occupied with hard study of intellectual or political matters etc, the thought processes may find it difficult to concentrate on car controls and other traffic. If chauffeurs are available, it is sensible to let them cope. None of the biographies say whether Robert Birley drove a car himself. The discussion is still so clear in my mind. I countered his concerns by talking of my interest in design and the future of the British industry. (I failed to suggest that there might not be a British-owned industry one day if well-educated people did not participate!) A compromise was achieved. We could not have a Car Club – that smacked of getting hands dirty with old wrecks. We could have an Eton Automobile Society dedicated to the serious study of the subject, but it had to be limited to twenty-five members and, yes, we could invite speakers. We also had in mind a clubroom where we could learn about contemporary components.

I soon realised that we had hit a goldmine. No-one refused an invitation. The difficulty was that they were going to expect an audience of more than twenty-five. We had to check attendance before each event, transferring memberships and inviting guests. One evening, probably Stirling Moss complete with fixed-head XK 120, we had over fifty. It was rumoured that Robert Birley was coming and we prepared for a showdown. He was a very busy man and often cross-booked his appointments. Or did he take a look and decide not to intervene?[2] Everyone was kind. Prince Bira, writing 27th June 1951 on Ecurie Royale, Siam paper, agreed to support: 'I am delighted that now there is even an Eton College Club (not Society!). In my day we only thought about it but no-one ever dared start anything.'[3] I still have letters from Sidney Allard[4], Mike Couper (Monte Carlo Rally), Eason Gibson (*Country Life*) 'it is indeed kind of your President, Mr St Aubyn, to ask me to dine with him', Goldie Gardner (MG Records) and Alan Hess (Austin Public Relations). There were others. The Duke of Richmond and Gordon came specially when George Monkhouse, a friend and associate, showed some racing films. Later he sent us Members' complimentary passes for Goodwood. The Duke (the present Lord March's grandfather) is gratefully remembered for his encouragement of our interests. There had to be one Master involved and Giles St Aubyn was always helpful. He owned a Bristol 401, an early introduction to the marque.[5]

Next came contact with the Rootes Group in Coventry, then regarded as one of the 'Big Six' British manufacturers[6]. I had written asking both about support for the Automobile Society and possible work after leaving Eton. Their reply to the latter question led to a considerable hiatus: 'Yes, they had a technician apprenticeship for entrants aged eighteen. School Certificates in Chemistry, Physics and Maths were required. The then compulsory two-year National Service would be better deferred till after apprenticeship. There could then be more useful experience in Engineering or Service regiments i.e. REME or RASC.'[7]. This was a practical alternative to the hindsight leaving-at-sixteen suggestion. Eton was not then organised for this situation. The vocational aspect had hardly been considered before School Certificate. I had not done Science. However these new needs were treated as a challenge. Although it didn't work out for different reasons, gratitude remains for the school's response in arranging a personal syllabus. The reports sent to Lionel only seen in recent years (that's how it was, he had other concerns) hint at the mismatch between education and industry (as recorded by Lord Young) in a school for administrators. Typical of the Eton spirit, they still tried and encouraged. My History tutor was generous showing genuine concern (I wish I had read this at the time): 'Part with regret though much better that work should be directly related to future. An all round brain without prominence in any one subject. I hope he does well.' My House tutor, John Herbert, wrote in a long letter: 'His unusual need to pass in Physics and Chemistry has led to a very strange programme of work, but his very real determination to achieve a definite objective makes sense of the scheme. I certainly wish all luck with his new ventures, automobile society included.' The scheme included English and, to fill a gap, thinking of export markets, Spanish. English was fine. 'He reads aloud with real understanding and can express himself competently in speech and writing', Spanish much less so with reports from two different masters: 'He is distressingly bad in all oral work', 'the less said about his pronunciation the better, he reminded me of an Arab attempting classical Greek', and ' he must try to train his ear to the sounds of Spanish.' However one kind report did say: ' He was struggling. He started late and then absent (because of the strange programme) for two out of five schools each week.' The Science reports were mixed: 'He started off superbly, top of the division'. That wasn't a surprise, for this was mechanics, but then came chemistry: 'He has not found it at all easy to get results. He does not think chemically.' And Chemistry again: 'He has tried desperately hard to obtain a sounder grip but he is still by no means able to tackle simple problems with much confidence.' I just wasn't attracted to pure science, which was far removed from mechanics. John Herbert came to my rescue in his next letter to Lionel which again I wish I had seen at the time:

> 'I will not bore you with lengthy descriptions of Christopher's contests with the elements of (pure) science. He has taken immense trouble. It would be rash for me to prophesy success. He can so easily take a firm grasp of the wrong end of the stick. My slender experience of practical engineering (his Maths had helped with the design of the D-Day harbours!) makes me wonder considerably why Messrs Rootes should consider certificate science an asset. The actual information in the certificate course can be of little use to an automobile engineer. Certainly Christopher has done his utmost to think in an idiom which does not come naturally to him. Curiously enough I do not think he would experience the same difficulties over motor engineering technicalities. I do wish him the best of luck and hope that I may be permitted to see much more of him.'

Alas I never did. There were no J S Herbert House dinners. He died quite young. But then, having never seen these letters, I would not have been able to thank him for the immense trouble that he had taken. They are recorded now. These are only some of his many kind words: Eton at its best. All the assessments by those conscientious masters have proved correct. I still enjoy writing. Now, in a country adjacent to Spain, I still find it very difficult to 'train my ear to the sounds of the language'. I still love mechanics. Pure science has no appeal. Years later, when I had finally forsaken motor industry attempts in order to work (see Chapter 15) in the State schools (before returning to write about the industry using those English skills), I realised again and again how many of the school leavers I encountered might have benefited from the care and personal attention which I had received at Eton. 'Might' because of the practical difficulties found by the Fleming Committee (with which Robert Birley had been involved) in admitting state scholars[9] and concerns about the consequences of exposure to a different culture. We are still struggling as a society with the cost of achieving something of Eton-style nurture for many more in our schools. Many dissent from any such ambition and, anyway, it isn't realistic without the vast change in current national priorities, which I would welcome.

The other Rootes enquiry was more successful: 'I have written to Mr St Aubyn about your proposed visit. I do hope that it will be possible to arrange and I have also mentioned the question of equipment and instructional material for your proposed workshop. I do assure you we shall be pleased to help as far as we can.' This was from a Mr Lloyd Dixon, export sales director, followed on 5th February 1952 by: 'delighted to know you have obtained permission to come to Coventry. Arrangements will be put in hand to collect you at 10am and we note you must be back before 8 p.m.' There was no progress on a room, so no equipment. On Friday 7th March seventeen of us were swept the seventy-odd miles to Ryton on Dunsmore in Humber Pullmans and taken round the huge assembly plant. Taken over by Chrysler in 1967, bought by Peugeot in 1978 for one dollar, the factory was closed in 2006 and is now being redeveloped. There are distribution centres already in operation though no British lorries will be on site. There may be housing developments. Would this troubled history, repeated in other British-owned car companies, have been avoided if some of those seventeen, so carefully and expensively educated at Eton, had worked long-term in the company? Even if some of them had, or had the wish, to struggle to a position of power, and were possessed of great stamina, patience and saintly conciliating skills, it could have taken decades to alter the combative attitudes between management and those who made the cars. They would also have needed to make a profit. There have been immense difficulties throughout the history of the industry in Britain. This question, so relevant to the lack of employment now, is discussed in Chapter 19. Some of these difficulties have been avoided in other countries, partially by different attitudes and a different structure of education. There are now great improvements in Britain but with ownership, and some management, from other countries. One of the seventeen, Anthony Bullen, more determined than the rest of us, bravely started Tornado Cars with Bill Wodehouse in 1957 but left when he married in 1960. Tornado produced around six hundred cars until they were forced into liquidation in 1964.[10] Another Etonian, Kit Power, not one of the seventeen on the Ryton visit, did survive the Rootes graduate training course and stayed for three significant jobs. First he was assistant to Geoffrey Rootes when he was managing director. Next he worked in the Export offices in London. Then he became Number 2 -- vice-direttore-- at Rootes Italia representing Rootes interests in Italy. Carrozeria Touring assembled the Super Minx and the Alpine to reduce import duty. They then suggested a touring body on the Alpine underframe and running gear, which became the Venezia. His last position was managing the shipping department handling the shipment of cars, trucks, CKD and parts. Then American Chrysler bought into the company and subsequently took control in the mid-1960s. He moved on to many years of marked achievement in worldwide management consultancy and recruitment. If Rootes had remained a British firm, this is one Etonian who might have had some beneficent influence on the future of the industry. It can only be 'might' because of the problems which he would have encountered. A few others were involved in different ways but none of them in a position to influence the fate of the company[11] (and see Chapter 19).

All these activities, the 'strange programme of work' and now making model cars instead of aeroplanes[12], meant that I was not much concerned about the tribal aspects of Eton; acceptance, chapel, conformity, networking, popularity etc., well described in many books. Nick Fraser writes that 'the best thing in Eton, indeed in life, is to have been elected to Pop, coloured waistcoats and all – near-grown boys pine for the honour'. I can't decide whether he is serious about this or whether this is a continuation of Eton banter. He also writes: 'never being too serious is at the core of the school style, become adept at banter.'[13] There is no recollection of any wish to be elected to Pop, not that there would have been any chance with my attitude and performance at team games. It would have taken time away from creative activities and banter had no appeal.

I was far more concerned about the future and coping with the family situation, probably also too serious. The river was always a consolation. A specific number of points for exercise had to be recorded each week with a certain beating if you cheated and were found out. I discovered that a large bonus was awarded if Henley and back by river was achieved on a whole holiday during the Regatta week. Additionally this bonus could be carried over for several weeks. It's about twenty miles each way 'as the crow flies', considerably more than forty in total with all the bends in the Thames. There was a small group of us (I can't remember who) in our separate single sliding-seat riggers. It was lovely weather. Curiously, when the 2.2 litre Bristol is on top form, windows open, seeming, without vibration, to skim the surface of a good clear road I have found myself reminded of that June day, probably 1950. On the open straight stretches below Cliveden, body muscles warmed up, slide rhythmically clicking backwards and forwards, the sculls pushed against the smooth water propelling us forward. As with the Bristol, man and machine so smoothly skimmed the surface. Both experiences are the same sensation, gliding with minimal contact, but in a car not so magically serene with later harsher wide tyres. We hardly lingered at Henley, but were still above the last lock when the time for calling holiday absence was approaching. It was a punishable offence not to be present. There was no time to go through Boveney Lock. We helped each other carry the boats along the side paths and then it was into the water again and hard for rafts. Alf Claret,[14] aware of our effort, was still by the sheds and helped to put the craft away quickly. Then it was a run back to the house. John Herbert was there – I think I was the only one from his House – full of smiles: 'don't worry about absence, I'll fix that, come and have a hot drink.' When out of school dress, you still needed a cap if without sporting recognition. This was a particularly pernicious Eton rule. It meant that even fully grown in your last year you still had to wear the ordinary blue and black school cap known as a 'scug', meaning a person of no account. Wherever you went (and you still had to gain exercise points) you were immediately recognised as a failure. One escape from potential derision was to only go for runs, where a cap was unnecessary. This fate was avoided by my selection as stroke for one of the novice eights. It just happened that we had a good crew and cox. Coming down towards rafts and the finishing line, we really got the boat moving, a powerful performance by all. It seems to have been an automatic award of the 'lower boats' cap for the winning stroke. So there were no more worries on that score. There were no awards for someone who, as it sometimes seemed, was trying to drag the school into the world of industry.

Away from Eton, PC had bought an old house near the lake at Petersfield. To the side there was a large barn-like room in which Lionel set up a workshop with machine tools. Despite money shortage, he still wasn't going to become an employee and start 'licking other people's boots'. Putting the difficulties aside, there is much to admire in this decision and we now know, as described in Chapters 2 and 3, that all his direct forebears on both sides, maternal and paternal, had been their own bosses. He had become chairman and managing director by his own tremendous efforts before the age of forty. Of course he did not want to change if he could somehow retain company director status. This he managed for the rest of his life as described in Chapter 17. It's just unfortunate that I was told again and again what a good thing it was to work for other organisations and enjoy life-long security, Lord Young's 'search for stability'. It really was not surprising that I too always found employee status difficult. It probably has to be endured at the beginning, even Lionel did it for nearly twenty months, but I have seemed to get on better when using my own initiative. Apart from the Automobile Society, an earlier effort had been to discover that the driving test could be taken before the age of seventeen with a three-wheeled car. Eventually I managed to find and purchase a Matchless-engined Morgan with most of my savings from childhood. The test was passed at the second attempt.[15] On the first, we were bowling along a street in the middle of Portsmouth when the hood detached itself from the windscreen and enfolded the test official and driver. It was decided that another test should be arranged. This simple machine, so easily maintained, gave much pleasure. It gave me the freedom to decide between staying with FG or with PC and Lionel during holidays from Eton. It was also my own private space, a relationship with cars which has continued. These relationships may also have been a sort of mother substitute. FG disapproved of the Morgan and, when I often arrived with dirty hands after some mechanical mishap, she kept on about that was what her chauffeur was for. Money was always short. Small hand-outs were gratefully accepted. I was fed and provided with accommodation at both these houses, paid for by PC when at Petersfield. Sixty years later, I have realised the mistake I made. In accepting their largesse, I had surrendered part of my freedom. Why did I not find work, any work, during the holidays and try to build up my position? It seems to always come back to this. Would it have been better to have left the school and got stuck in? That's what Great-grandfather James and many others did in the nineteenth century, and there's the example of Herman Wittgenstein. I do remember, at Petersfield, looking out of the top floor window towards Butser Hill and wondering whether there was a way of getting right away from an increasingly difficult situation. If not as an apprentice, could I find some other working position, hopefully with accommodation, until I could be my own boss? Courage was lacking. I hope that students today will not come to regret their long-delayed start in the money-earning world.

Nick Fraser mentioned above, and first published as recently as 2006 (reprinted 2008), quotes Simon Barrington-Ward. (When Simon, as a new Bishop, had been in front of the Queen, he had found an Etonian school-friend by her side holding the oath): 'It's almost dream-like. There is an incongruous sense that we are all play-acting and that we will go back and find that we are just starting again.' Nick Fraser writes that this observation was about so many Etonians sharing membership of the Establishment. There are comments in the book from the successful clothing entrepreneur Johnnie Boden: 'Etonians like to say they make entrepreneurs, but they are in fact terrible. Business can be boring, they would rather do cool things. There's the need to belong to an establishment so they do safe things like law or media. To really succeed in business, you have to be prepared to make a fool of yourself. I don't see that as a very Etonian thing.' This apes Lord Young. Nick Fraser also points out that Johnnie Boden draws attention to the oldest paradox of the school: 'whilst claiming to develop individuality, it nonetheless sustains its own style and conformism.' These assertions need to be countered. They may still be true of some Etonians. Because they are often based in London near the centre of events, they are the ones who seem to be written about. But it's a large school and its pupils have had differing backgrounds which influence their decisions. Some have no wish to be members of the Establishment. There are those who have made use of that superb tutorial system to develop their creative talents or fashion questioning lives. Absorbed in their work, perhaps coping with inevitable business problems including debt (a sure remedy for feelings of play-acting), caring for employees, pioneering new developments, they are not interested in position within the system. I cite Anthony Bullen and Desmond Norman, both already mentioned as examples. They both recovered in different ways from problems and pressed on. There are many others. I hope there will be many more as the new Design and Technology section makes progress following on from the excellent 'School of Mechanics', where I spent many hours. 'Making a fool of yourself' could mean the aftermath of failure, which is better considered as a learning opportunity. The quest for commercial control may have to be different to the merits of 'team spirit.' There are other aspects of human nature. I have touched on all this in other chapters. Because I believe it is so important, I believe it can bear repetition as well as apology. Experience suggests that the budding entrepreneur should be wary of trusting partners they bring into the business. It is advisable to retain 51% of the capital at least in the early stages. Too swift an expansion may later be regretted. Borrowing needs to be watched. Worst-case political outcomes need to be considered. Sometimes only personal and painful experience rams home these lessons. None of this was taught in my time sixty five years ago. There is evidence that these difficulties are now discussed and there is now contact with those who have succeeded after leaving Eton. (See Appendix 2) The school tried to help but was not set up for what I thought I wanted. My interest, some might say obsession, got in the way of other considerations and the school was just a memory by the time I realised that the obsession was unattainable. Talking now with our son and daughter's generation, there seems to be more concentration on making money. The post-war spirit of service, of using the privileged education to help those less fortunate, is still around, but at the present time, seems less pronounced. Were those ideals, which all had to be funded, ever sufficiently realistic? The National Health Service comes to mind. Nicholas Cayzer, two generations earlier, understood the dilemma. Wealth creation is the foundation stone for private and public enterprise. There is a difference, too, between those who make money, recharging themselves with traditional pastimes, and those who gain fulfilment from their perhaps craft-based daily toil and for whom wealth beyond the needs of survival may not be the priority. The House intake in September 1947 included three potential lawyers and two who took over family estates, one in New Zealand, one in Scotland, and then there was my muddle. Whatever the merits of different attitudes and occupations, the common Eton experience was about relationships, about how to be with other humans, getting to understand their motivations, their attitudes to power and position and learning how to live with one's own failings and weakness. It was also about coping when under pressure which may come in all sorts of ways, including from the media or fellow-travellers. Some of my Eton contemporaries, and their sons, have reached what are regarded as high positions in the hierarchy.[16] The time at the school helps in understanding the circumstances, constraints and plots which can limit their authority. That humanity is subject to these limitations sustains the appreciation of other aspects of existence beyond the pursuit of power and wealth. It's hardly sensible that we deride those Etonians that have achieved power when they are often the ones who have learnt to function with those pressures for the potential benefit of us all.

LEARNING FROM DIFFERENCE

Chapter 10

Eton. War and faith. National Service in Libya

So much has been written about war, its misery, its pain, its glory. I hope to contribute something else: the aroma of war at Eton in those post-war years in a victorious but depleted country. My forebears, as I was only to learn many years later, represented different viewpoints. There was the Jellicoe aura (and I was the grandson he had known), this heroic figure caught in the maelstrom of world events but also subject to criticism. Now there is more agreement that he made wise decisions whilst under enormous pressure, that his self-disciplined life was devoted to the service of his fellow men. Just as important we read in those letters (Chapter Five) of an attractive humility and concern for family and for others. I think I realised the importance of island defence, that the war had been won, but wasn't personally attracted to the military life. Shooting, guns, uniforms and the like had no appeal. Creation seemed preferable to destruction. I now know that other family members had gone further and spoken out against war. Jo Joachim (see Chapter Three) was the same relationship to me as Nicholas Cayzer and Philip Balfour (Chapter Two). Jo was grandmother Nina's nephew, Nicholas was FG's nephew, Philip was grandfather Max's nephew. I am glad to have had the conversations with Jo. He had been represented to me as strange. Not so. His father was Henry Joachim's son. His mother was Joseph Joachim's daughter. He did not want to be fighting his many German cousins and he was also a Quaker.[1] He therefore went through the interrogation processes to be accepted as a conscientious objector. This was the action of a brave and thoughtful man. The voices of his aunts, Gertrude Russell and Maud Joachim, (also Chapter 3) were also heard supporting the cause of peace. It was a mixed gene pool appropriate to the thoughts that follow.

Emanating from indifferent performance at ball games, (John Herbert wrote 'a little too clumsy to hold a place in the house side'), suspicions as to whether I pushed hard enough in games of 'passage football'[2] and my solitary model activities; from such behaviour came the little hints that I might not be sound, might be one of those who let down their comrades in the face of the enemy. It was all the testing process. Would this one be loyal, put himself last? As at Highfield, with the reading out of the fallen, for me, and I know some others because this was discussed, self-examination was in the background of one's thoughts: 'How would we cope in battle?' At Eton the connection with war was unavoidable. The walk to College Chapel went past the memorials to all the Etonians killed. Recently there has been a new plaque listing those who have won the George Cross and the Victoria Cross. Eton and other schools, have in part, been pre-military training grounds for centuries. Whatever future historians write about twentieth century wars, and lost opportunities for peace, the training and experience on those playing fields (as has often been suggested) did contribute to the result. We do not know what Europe would be like without their sacrifices, which were often buttressed by religion. My classical tutor was a clergyman who had won fame and medals for gallantry during the war.[3] I remember him with affection, but he was an ardent supporter of the life to come. Spiritual dedication, bravery and selfless behaviour were part of the deal. Death in battle had the compensation of earlier entry to this better existence and meeting friends and relatives, so it wasn't really too bad. (In my case, as he pointed out, should I find myself in this situation in another war, it would also mean reunion with Myrtle.)

Many like the life of soldiering (and the other armed services), particularly the comradeship. If there are not artistic, creative or constructional interests, which can become full-time paid occupations, this life, particularly with the regimental ethos, can be much better than some of the alternatives. War, buttressed by that faith, is the peak of the professional activity. The memoirs of survivors testify. I dwell on the words of one who was known to me, which I read and re-read to imbibe an ethos different to my own. It's that difference again and what can be learned from both viewpoints. This is Ann's godfather, Hugh Boustead, writing about 1916 in his book based on his letters to his parents at that time before he was commissioned.[4] His words are singularly interesting because they show the reactions of a literate twenty-one-year-old in the thick of it day after day, night after night, no return to Officers's quarters. Many of that war's memoirs were written by Officers with more comforts and, it seems, a readier access to recognition, via citations and decorations. Here are two extracts:

'We disembarked one morning in a country of folded hills and rivers, the plains of Picardy. The farms, where we slept in the hay, held everything we wanted; the peasants were kind and hospitable and only too ready to sell us eggs, milk and chickens in abundance, and wine. We knew that this idyllic life in a beautiful un-marked countryside had to be savoured for the enchanting interlude that it was. We were tied inextricably to one another by our training and shared experience.'

'Coughing and spitting and weeping and blinded by the tear gas, we could hear those of our comrades who were wounded moaning under the debris. Six of the section, three on either side of us, were utterly destroyed, torn to pieces. We could hear the continual crack of rifles but could see nothing. We moved through an orchard. The Second Lieutenant got through but the next seven were dead in a circle of a few yards picked off by clean shooting without a murmur. I was not an N.C.O.[5] but to follow these seven seemed madness. I led the remainder round the edge of the orchard. I was blown across the road with a hole through my kilt and thigh. My main relief was the chance to get some sleep'.

This was one of several wounds, one later much more serious. The more one reads, the more one understands that other attitudes, other choices and other decisions could have prevented the start of that war in 1914. Christopher Clark's diligent research has resulted in *The Sleepwalkers*, published in 2012[6]. The following are only some of his words. All of his concluding chapter is valuable:

> 'The crisis that brought war was the fruit of a shared political culture. One thing is clear: none of the prizes for which the politicians contended was worth the cataclysm that followed. Asquith wrote of 'Armageddon', French and German generals of 'a war of extermination' and the 'extinction of civilisation'. They knew it but did they really feel it? The protagonists were sleepwalkers, watchful but unseeing, haunted by dreams, yet blind to the reality of the horror they were about to bring into the world.'

Despite the experience of both Boer and Balkan wars, neither politicians nor participants seemed at first to fully understand the awful consequences of unleashing the new weapons. For willing participants, from Eton and other schools, this was to be an extension of the playing field, though - as they were to discover - with stiffer penalties. Others were cajoled or dragged into the country's service. Many, but perhaps not all, experienced what Vera Brittain described as 'the compelling power of enlarged vitality.'[7] In another book Wickham Steed provided insight into how human beings worked: 'The whole region seemed to vibrate with magnetism; and I began to realise that, dreadful and horrible though war might be, the atmosphere of it could and did give men power to endure and do things of which they would have felt incapable in the surroundings of their ordinary lives. Later, when on further visits to the British and French lines, I thought I divined the deeper meaning of this atmosphere of war. Many of the officers and men were under the spell of 'something in the air' that seemed to transfigure them. Their words and, more eloquently, their bearing and behaviour, bore witness to it. This atmosphere was that of a no-man's-land between life and death, between this world and the next, an intermediate region in which men scarcely paused to think whether they were dead or alive. If they were alive one day they might be dead on the morrow. Thus, to them, the chief realities were discipline and duty and obedience to higher commands. It was more than a mood, it was a way of being. It was not exaltation. Rather it was a sober fact. In it danger appeared to be so much a matter of course that to face it was as natural as to eat or sleep.'[8]

For Hugh Boustead and many others, both those who survived and those who did not, the halo of war was an unrivalled opportunity to prove character and selfless service. The aim was survival, or death and remembrance with honour. And, with another life to come, was death so fearful? This is what my grandfather wrote in the Appendix to *The Grand Fleet*, a sentence I have always found difficult: 'They fell doing their duty nobly, a death which they would have been the first to desire.'[9] Yes, maybe, but the dead do not write their memoirs. As one who, after much consideration, is now an atheist, I so value this - to me - sole existence, the opportunity to create, write, think and talk with daughters, son and grandchildren. Wickham Steed's sentences above were written in the certain belief of 'the next world.' Hugh wrote at the end of his book after a life of service in different countries:

> 'The experience was indelible. The war stands like a great peak on the horizon of one's life. To be still alive at the end was almost unbelievable and the fact of survival gave me an even greater zest for life. Honour, courage, unselfishness and a good heart stamp the true man. I still found these qualities when fortune led me from soldiering to administration.'

There is one word missing from Hugh's list. That word is 'profit', understood by Great-grandfather James, by Nicholas Cayzer and Dudley Escott, not so fully understood by Lionel. For, without profit, where are the taxes to pay for wars, administration and so much else? Hugh came to stay with us in Gloucestershire (where we were then storing some of his furniture) some fifty years after those war experiences. Then, as now, I would be spending some time working on the cars. Hugh also wrote about his time as a naval cadet before he 'escaped' to the Army: 'the smell of oil was a torment and made me increasingly dislike the engineering side of the Navy'. Here was the chap, he may have thought, who had snaffled his beloved god-daughter, evidently enjoying attention to a typical Bristol oil leak. He was a kind and generous man, but, in awe of all he had achieved and mindful of previous worries at school, I remember wondering if I was rated as a 'true man'! Some days later I was deputed to drive him right across the country. I hoped, though with some trepidation, this was the very man who had exhibited such bravery, that we could have some discussion. Soon after we set off, he was asleep. All I got was the occasional murmur 'this is the most comfortable car I have ever been in' and then back to sleep. I did not have the chance to suggest that the comfort was the result of good British engineering, already a matter of special interest and concern to me. I do not think I had then sufficiently realised the importance of manufacturing industry and I would not at that stage have talked cogently about the importance of profit.

Now the point I want to make is this: it's not critical of Eton's illustrious military connection. I find myself thinking of Alan Clark's description of Harold Macmillan's memorial service in 1987:[10]

> 'The Grenadiers' Return was played and I thought of the fife music and the decimated battalion marching back from Hulloch on 26 September 1915 past the wounded, laid out in rows, groaning from their injuries. And the young classical scholar, less than a year out of Eton, pale and shaken but heroic nonetheless.'

It's magnificent and this spirit continues. I have only recently read that according to Alan Mallinson, writing in 2009: 'The army remains smart enough to attract quality Officers. It is the largest single employer of Etonians.'[11] That's all right but I would like to have seen more of a stab at encouraging equivalent numbers of entrepreneurs and manufacturers and traders in the years since I left the school (and before). I would like there to have been more understanding and support of the harsh world of business success and failure. Money has to be made through profit to support the administrators, the military and the rest. I'd also like to see more recognition of those Etonians who tried in the vital aviation and motor industries, the likes of Anthony Bullen and Desmond Norman already mentioned, the future Duke of Richmond and Gordon at Bentley and later Kevill-Davies & March, Lionel Martin at Bamford and Martin later Aston Martin, Charles Mullens at Nuffield, George Wansbrough at Jowett and Gordon Keble[12], Prince Bira, Sir Henry Segrave[13], Francis Luxmoore, Lionel's partner, and many more. They do not have a plaque, but they also contributed. What if the Royal Princes had completed an engineering apprenticeship? But it was not in their genes and they do well where they are.

Thus I come to my own experience. It's all connected with the difference between the potential glory and honour of the battlefield and the less glamorous factory or workshop floor. I had the invitation to join the Rootes Group when I left Eton. They did not seem to be insisting on success in School Certificate Science, accepting that I had worked at the subjects. It must have been the Easter holidays 1952 when I went to PC's house at Petersfield. I explained that I was delaying National Service and would hope to join REME, or a similar Service Regiment, in a few years' time. Many others, who wanted to press on with their training for work or profession first, also did this. It was an accepted decision. Desmond Norman went straight to the de Havilland technical school. Bill Nankivell, Ann's half-brother, trained as an architect before joining an infantry regiment. He was appreciated as an older Officer with more experience of life. Looking back, the response, orchestrated by PC, was abnormal. It was understandable at the time because of the background. Was I really going to let them down, they said, by shirking National Service directly after school? Even thinking of not going into a frontline regiment showed what a coward I was. What would other people think? I was stuck, once again beholden because no money and I had not got started two years earlier, and the 'coward not front line' tag chimed with those earlier school worries about conduct in the face of the enemy. So far as FG was concerned, I had already disgraced myself. Earlier, after her intense pressure to serve the two years in the Navy, I had joined the sea cadets and done a short training period in the Indefatigable in Weymouth Bay. I hated every moment; seasick, too tall, kept hitting my head, couldn't sleep in the hammock, could not come to terms with ordinary seaman attire. It was horrid. There was no way I would do National Service in the Navy whatever the Jellicoe heritage. Anyway Grandfather was much shorter and stockier. (I think he would have understood). Now, after that, I was proposing to delay and not go into a proper Regiment. Years later I found a letter from Rachel to Lionel written at that time: 'I have been told that Christopher has been offered a job in Rootes. I gather that he is car mad. This sounds a little old fashioned nowadays. I should have thought the modern young man would have been atomic mad at least.' It's a little disparaging. Was it really old fashioned to see the value of retaining a British-owned car industry? The point is that she was reflecting her experience as a pre-war Eton Housemaster's wife, confirmation again of the anti-workshop mantra. Yet again it is the different viewpoint. One thing is certain and for that I will always defend her. She had resolutely determined not to sell capital (in stark contrast to Lionel) and some of this in time came to Ann[14].

Weakling that I was, I gave way. That summer, Regimental Colonels from the Armoured Corps (ex-cavalry and certainly front line) came to Eton. I was ignorant; there were no Cavalry predecessors. Philip Balfour had been a gunner, Percy infantry, though I did not know that then. These Colonels were at separate tables, may have been separate classrooms, with boards in front of them saying where they would be stationed in a year's time. That's when we should have coped with basic training, passed WOSB (the War Office Selection Board) and completed Officer Training at Mons. One board said Libya. I knocked on the door. A weather-beaten, firm but so welcoming and smiling face looked up. Did I like riding? Did I have my own horses? I tried to smile back: 'No, but I had seen North Africa from the flying boat en route to India, read about that coastline and would really love to come to Libya.' I don't now know if those were the exact words, but something like that. I may also have mentioned that I liked engines and machinery. This was now a tank regiment. The Colonel smiled that irresistible smile again: 'Does not matter about the riding. We need someone to cope with all the other things.' The long and the short of it was that I was accepted provided I passed the training to get my commission as an Officer. But PC wasn't satisfied: 'You can't join a Cavalry Regiment if you can't ride properly'. 'The Colonel said it wasn't necessary,' I countered. Why didn't I stand up to her? Not wishing to make a fuss, I suppose. Horses were one of her pleasures

107

and she would pay for some of the lessons. Churchill's words come to mind: 'No-one comes to grief, except honourable grief, by riding horses.' There was this feeling that the car interest was less honourable. I understood, but I should have been firm about my different interest. Instead I agreed to be taken round to the local tailor. As he measured me for breeches I said 'make them loose, I hate tight clothing'. That was the next mistake. She saw me trying them on and was immediately critical. I was then away and on return found that she'd gone and blasted off at the poor tailor. Didn't he know his job? etc. That time I did remonstrate, saying it was all my fault, but she still insisted that I could not go near her riding pals unless they were remade. So once a week I set out chafed by this over-tight garment to Chawton near Alton. Now I like looking, even talking, to horses, but I wasn't much good at sitting on them. Then this particular animal shied or something. The next I knew was waking up in Alton hospital with Lionel looking anxiously down at me. I had come off and hit my head on some stone or rock. No more riding. Recently we came across the offending hardly worn breeches. They were gladly accepted by some people who did 'wardrobe hire'.

September 1952 saw me going by train (rail warrant provided) to Catterick Camp in Yorkshire, not to Rootes in Coventry. (To this day I do not know the result of those Science School Certificates. Presumably they were sent to Lionel). He did keep the 7th October letter from 22716789 Trooper Balfour CJJ, A Squadron Serial 52/18, 65th Training Regiment.

'On Sunday we went to Church. Before one of the 'chaps' (oh dear, sounds a bit class conscious) came in and asked if he could come as he wanted to see this Lord he had heard so much about. I saw Nigel[15] afterwards, he is up at the 68th, but still have not been able to contact David.[16] We managed to break into the bathhouses last night and had a really good wash without being caught. We had a really frightful morning drilling and I very nearly got put on detention for incompetent halting. However all was well despite the fact that I then got shouted at for almost every movement I did. I find it rather difficult to get everything exactly in the military manner and am unfortunately rather conspicuous (because of height) if I make a mistake. Meals are a bit haywire as one of the dining rooms is out of action and there is hardly ever enough food for every-one. An officer comes round and asks if we have any complaints. He was rather surprised when we did actually complain about the situation to-day.'

We 'passed out' on 23rd October and the next day I accepted a fellow recruit's lift down to London in his newish Ford Prefect. It got later and later and I rushed to Waterloo. I could have used my warrant. It would have been quicker from Yorkshire. I had missed the last train to Petersfield, caught the last one to Guildford, and tried to work out what to do. I had very little money and anyway there were neither trains nor buses. I talked to a friendly taxi driver and he agreed to take me up to the A3 roundabout for most of my remaining cash. Easy to get a lift, I thought, after all I am in uniform, but no. It was around midnight and the very few cars around would not stop. After a few miles I could see some old huts in Coldharbour Wood. They were locked, but against the walls there was some shelter. When I was too cold I walked on up to Hindhead where I found a house with a back porch which provided shelter from rain. After an hour or two of fitful sleep, as dawn was breaking, I was back on the road. Soon a naval officer on his way to

Portsmouth stopped and took me to Petersfield. I often think of that night. It is one of the experiences which makes me sympathetic to those who have nothing and no place to go. It all comes back when we drive past those woods. There was a rebuke for causing worry, but we did not have mobiles. Earlier I had replaced the Morgan with a Singer 9 Coupe. (Money must have come from somewhere, but the balance was small). I decided to drive back to Catterick on Sunday evening especially as a fellow trooper had asked me to pick him up if I did return with a car. We met north of London. The passenger seat folded down with a mattress so that the passenger could lie flat. He was soon asleep. It's a good thing he was. About 2am, around Boroughbridge the car suddenly spun - it must have been ice. He was thrown against the door, which opened, and then out onto the road. Another never-forgotten moment of horror. I managed to stop the car and went back. He appeared unhurt, perhaps because he was relaxed, but over the next few days his back became heavily bruised. He was generously understanding and did not reproach me. That was kind. It is reassuring to see reference on Google to some of his many subsequent sporting achievements. This is why the old cars, which we still own, all have extra bolts on the passenger door. And we take every precaution in Andorra and elsewhere when faced with slippery roads; chains, spikes and socks for the tyres, preferably cars with good traction.

The War Office Selection Board was nearly a personal disaster. We were all sitting outside the assessment room. The door was ajar and I happened to hear discussion of my performance organising the crossing of an imaginary river (planks, ropes and things). One of the assessors was adamant that I had made a bit of a hash of things, not a strong enough lead, and this was true. However the others pointed to my other results and all was well. I don't think I would have actually minded staying in the ranks, but would have had to put up with the rebukes from PC and FG. Soon we were at Mons Officer Cadet School at Aldershot.[17] Typically much of the one letter which Lionel kept, dated 15th March 1953, was related to my continuing fascination with the car industry and its products. After 'it is really glorious here with the sun streaming down day after day. We have finished our classroom wireless and will spend the next week doing exercises over the South Warnborough and Froyle area. I hope to get a Standard '14' with a truck body. Thank you for the loan of DAD (they were away). She seemed to be going very well.' (DAD was a Singer Super 12, a well engineered car but more expensive than rivals, excellence versus the market again.)[18] Those wireless sets were almost the cause of another disaster. I had the same relationship as with today's computers when they malfunction. Impatience. During the closing exercise on Salisbury Plain, one wireless broke down completely and I ended up with one of my troop's tanks right bang in the 'enemy's' sites. At the subsequent inquest I was blamed again, insufficient leadership: why hadn't I sent a runner or done something, anything, to retrieve the situation? At the closing interview it was emphasised that my effort on the Plain was a very black mark, but, as I had done well in other things, I would receive my commission and not have to do the course again. They then let slip that I had been in the running for top cadet before this regrettable incident. This surprised me. Looking back over the many years I don't think I ever had that vaunted leadership make-up. It's always seemed better to work with people in common endeavour rather than ordering them about. That's what I have done in other small enterprises. You shape the metal, I will pay the bill and co-ordinate things, but we are of equal worth. My apparent problem, in other people's eyes, was borne out three years later, again on Salisbury Plain, during the territorial session which we had to complete before being free of the National Service commitment. With my troop we were discussing how best to tackle an assignment. What were their thoughts? Then suddenly from behind a hedge a senior officer jumps up: 'What on earth do you think you are doing? As an officer you work it out and then give orders.' Of course he was really right. If you must have wars, then there is no time for listening. All of which has made me conclude that I would have been better suited to a Service Regiment peddling knowledge rather than that leadership concept. Cynically, I sometimes think that 'leadership' can become the art of getting people to do what they may not want to do.

There was some time before I flew to Tripoli. FG was pleased with my commission when I visited, so I plucked up courage. Why was I in awe of her? She was brave. She was opinionated. But also with a kind heart. She could have been a battlefield leader, but less good at common endeavour, at reconciliation between differing viewpoints. I explained that the regiment was based nearly fifty miles west of Tripoli and life would be more enjoyable with a car. Also I had heard that some money might eventually come my way. Would it be possible to have a small advance? I received a cheque for £600 and there was a little in hand from the sale of the Singer 9. I had already scoured the catalogues. Still wanting to learn about the industry and particularly assess competition from other countries, I lighted on the new Fiat 'Millecento' which had been announced in April. I wrote direct to Turin. The money was transferred. When I arrived in Tripoli after an adventurous flight via Malta landing at Idris Airport[19] the first call was Libya Motors, where the Millecento awaited me. After obtaining a Libyan driving licence and driving round that beautiful city, the white buildings, the palm trees, the shimmering blue Mediterranean, (now better known to the world in less happy circumstances – Ghadaffi had not then arrived on the scene), it was out on the road to the regiment at Sabratha, the road which went on to Tunis and along the coast. There was none of the building which now borders the road all the way to Zavia and beyond. To one side was the esparta grass with desert scrub beyond, to the other sandhills with occasional glimpses of the sea. Sabratha itself was an Italian colonial-style settlement, a village square with houses around. In the near distance the still largely intact remains of the Roman theatre soared to the usually cloudless sky. As you got near, the golden stone contrasted with the often turquoise blue Mediterranean beyond. It was awe-inspiring to stand in the auditorium, reflecting that the building had been there for nearly two thousand years and on all that had happened in the world during that time.[20] The entrance to the ex-Italian Army barracks was at the edge of the village and I was to find that my room looked straight out to the theatre, my first sight each morning. The beaches nearby were sandy and deserted, the water warm for much of the year. It was good to have such an interesting experience, but the alternative viewpoint is that those after-school years are better used for learning so as to achieve income. As I did not have any horse expenditure, the pay, with care, was just sufficient.

Unlike a service regiment where technical knowledge and skill was needed to provide, maintain and repair, there was no particular vocational task for a potential 'front line' Officer in peacetime. Everything related to what would happen in war. The idea seemed to be that the sergeant, corporal and troopers in your troop would get to know you and when the time came would follow your lead, but the hours passed slowly with little to do except look at battle tactics and tank and gun maintenance. I expect I discussed when I should have ordered. From time to time the tanks were taken to practise firing on the range and, during my first summer, there was one exercise out in the desert, the regiment split into opposing forces. That was glorious, the stillness and the sense of space, waking early having slept with the rest of the troop alongside the tanks. I then had good hearing, and, with my awareness of machinery, I distinctly heard the whoop of tank starters away to the south and seemingly moving east. The others did not seem to hear so clearly, but we had been preparing for attack from the south in discussions the previous evening. I plucked up courage and went round to the headquarters truck. Diffidently I explained my thinking that our opponents were doing a circle round our position to attack us from the other direction. That smiling Colonel listened carefully to his very Junior Officer. It was agreed that we would spread our defences in both directions. They did come in from the north east. It was all so exhilarating, as Hugh Boustead wrote, and I began to see why participants did not think of death. It was indeed the playing field writ large. But in other ways, when sitting around and not on exercise, it all seemed a bit pointless unless there was a war to make use of the training and prove the bravery. Certainly some Officers talked like this and they had to wait quite a few years till Margaret Thatcher and Tony Blair provided their opportunities. For all National Service Officers not practising a technical skill, and having left before there was a battle opportunity, it was a questionable use of two years. Some made use of regimental kudos to assist in their ascent through the tribal establishment. At Mons, the thought amongst some cadets (this was put to me) was: 'Volunteer anywhere for active service, see if you can get to Malaya and then you will have a medal when you attend one of the village memorials near your estate.'

For me there was less questioning because of that Colonel who was so kind to me. I spent even less time getting to know my troop. The words of that interview at Eton came true. There were other things to be done. A couple of months after arriving at Sabratha, I was summoned to headquarters. With another slightly older officer, we were to take a party of soldiers to join a combined operations exercise in the eastern Mediterranean. Beach assaults from landing craft were practised in the Greek Islands. Mountbatten was there. Our Regimental party was duly inspected. Even if I had understood what had happened in India, it would not have been acceptable to say, when saluting: 'Do you realise that you have changed my father's life?' From there it was up through the Dardanelles in an aircraft carrier. Never forgotten was sleeping out just below the flight deck, probably in a gun position, and watching the water slide by as we passed the Turkish coast. After a few days in Istanbul, it was back to Tripoli. Then came the next summons: 'We want you to take the Regimental motorcycle team down to Suez to compete in the area championships.' The first plan was to take our machines, but this was vetoed, due to cost I suppose. It was my task to organise something when we arrived. I was not going to ride: we had some accomplished trials experts. I was to use my Officer rank to smooth the way and here at last I was a bit of use. The machines supplied were tatty. By working on the REME Officers (where perhaps I should have been?) and actually making use of my experience with the Morgan etc., we managed to put together three acceptable motorcycles. Out in the desert with them, they kindly taught me to master steep ascents and descents. They accepted this then callow nineteen-year-old. The Sergeant, I can see his good-natured face now, was an experienced professional and he led the team to victory. Then there was yet another summons, this time to be told of my appointment as Assistant Adjutant. Perhaps they had observed my deficiencies as a troop leader, too discursive, not enough ordering etc, or was it just that I had been so much away? It was lovely for me to have a proper job made more interesting when the Colonel and the Adjutant were away from time to time. One of their activities was playing polo in the Malta tournament. In the next-door office was the second-in-command, well known for his wartime bravery, still bearing wound scars and with many medals. It was years later that I realised that he was related to Percy's widow and her father, the Brigadier General who had commanded the Regiment in the 1920s (see Chapter 3). It now seems extraordinary that I did not know this at the time. I do just remember that 'Bodge' Browne as he was known, always a kind and genial man, did once make a passing reference to a possible connection, but I did not know what he was talking about. This is yet another example of the value of family discussion and why I have wanted to write this book. Did he have memories of Percy and even of grandfather Max?

Life in the Officer's Mess was a bit of a problem. The food was superb with masses of the best drink. It has taken me many years to realise that my system just wasn't built to take in more than small quantities of alcohol and the same applied to both rich and some ordinary food, which most consume without difficulty. But this, it seems to me, was, perhaps still is, the bargain of the frontline regimental experience. You must be brave and loyal in war. When not fighting, life will be made as agreeable as possible. Drinking together is part of the bonding experience. You learn to help each other when in your cups. Not necessarily with drink (though of course it can help), but because of the bonding, you will selflessly go to help a wounded comrade, or those under your command, and thus you will also cope with the death of a brother officer and your men. Alcohol plays its part in war. Hugh Boustead also wrote, and it makes one think: 'I was told to bring in what was on the wire (i.e. bodies). The German raiding party, all very young, smelt strongly of rum and had evidently been over-primed before they left their trenches.' A particular difficulty was the band night in the Mess when Officers put on their best blue uniform and the band played some of those blood-stirring tunes which had so often taken the Regiment into battle. One of the trophies was the Emperor's silver chamberpot captured at the battle of Vitoria in 1813. This had been given to Joseph Bonaparte by his brother, the Emperor Napoleon. Referring to band nights, the Mess rules state: 'The P.M.C. (President of the Mess Committee) may then call for the Emperor. Each individual drinking the Emperor's health (usually champagne) shall precede it by saying 'The Emperor'. The Senior dining member or the P.M.C. will select an officer to finish the drink.' Some managed to drink it all whilst the drum beat. For others it was more difficult. I already knew that amount of alcohol would mean a difficult few days ahead. Fortunately it had been explained that alternative responses were acceptable, though this meant subsequent attention to the uniform. You just did not go to that kind Colonel and say 'look I have a problem, can I be excused the Emperor's chamberpot?' That was not the way. Such customs were important in building up the traditions and camaraderie of the Regiment. You had this physical connection with all the other Officers, some incredibly brave, who had sipped from the same pot throughout the centuries. And it is this spirit which has helped the country to survive.

The other Officers were all kind to someone who did not entirely fit. I hope I would not have let them down in war, though in a way I let them down at the end. In Tripoli one weekend, certainly not in my cups, I fell over, landed on some projecting marble and how my right elbow hurt! I had been talking to the Volkswagen agents about exchanging the Millecento for a (thought to be) longer-life Volkswagen (Beetle). The plan had been to drive back along the North African Coast and up through Spain at the end of September. Still conscious of the cash problem, the hope was that the VW would provide transport in England for many years. I was in uniform and called in at the British Military Hospital.

They took a quick look and agreed my arm needed to be x-rayed. Agreeing to return, the Millecento was driven, just using my left arm, to the VW people and left there. That was my last Libyan drive. At BMH it was found that the end of my elbow had broken off. They would strap it together, but it needed to be screwed, in order to keep the full use of my right arm. The superb treatment at the taxpayers' expense still amazes. This was not war, just a stupid slip. The VW garage bought that Millecento for a fair price (which helped to keep me going in England). I was flown, strapped up, to Malta, where it was a rather painful wait. Eventually another plane to Northolt, a car to the military hospital at Millbank, and soon into the operating theatre.[21] I woke to find Lionel there. It must have been two years after the hospital at Alton. I never saw the Sabratha camp with its white airy buildings again. Nor will anyone else now. That lovely camp was pulverised by NATO Missiles in August 2011.[22] The words of William Butler Yeats come forcefully to mind:

> Things fall apart; the centre cannot hold
> Mere anarchy is loosed upon the world.

As it was so near the end of the two years, the authorities agreed that it was not necessary to go back. It was an inglorious end to what may have been the wrong direction, but still time spent with good people in what was then a delightful country. And it has to be said that this all came about because of PC. Different genes, different beliefs and attitudes. She had other intentions for me, but the actual consequence was beneficial. Another Officer kindly sent back my trunk.

LEARNING FROM DIFFERENCE

Chapter 11

Cambridge mistakes. Afghanistan

This is partially an attempt to justify what is now seen as weakness. A reader may prefer to skip these early paragraphs and move on to the references to the journey to Afghanistan, an attempt to remember a period of peace amongst welcoming people in that beautiful country. However the initial contents could be of value to any who are debating whether to attend university or start working and earning. They also have relevance to discussions about vocational and academic education. After National Service, when I could have been halfway through the Rootes apprenticeship, I had no qualification, no job and about £500 remaining from the sale of the Fiat. Lionel had written that a place had been booked at Cambridge, but, sitting in the Assistant Adjutant's Office at Sabratha with a job to do and with pay, I was not concentrating on the future. Now, back in England, I learnt that, if I accepted this place, board and tuition fees would be paid from the funds in the marriage settlement. The possibility of some income in February when I was twenty-one was mentioned. There was no interview, no discussion about subjects to be studied or how three years at university would be mutually beneficial to self and to society. It was privilege gone mad. Acceptance was, I suppose, because of Eton, commissioned service in a 'frontline' regiment, and maybe a little because of the success of a brilliant uncle who had also been at Trinity. I was to be allocated to the same tutor, H O Evennett. Talking to anyone who would listen, they all said: 'take the place, get any degree and you will find there will be many job opportunities.' But the aim was to save the British motor industry, not any opportunity! If FG was observing, she may have been pleased that I was apparently being weaned away from my mechanical interest.

The elbow had been screwed up, I was sent to Headley Court for remedial physiotherapy.[1] All this treatment, plus board and lodging, was at the taxpayers' expense. A roadworthy Citroen 'Light Fifteen' was bought for £300, leaving £200 for survival till the lodgings in Cambridge were reached. Ridiculous though it now seems, it was only after arrival that there was discussion about what to study! At least in this area student awareness has progressed. I hope this experience was later put to good use when advising others about further education after school (see Chapter 14). I learnt that there was no way I could study engineering. The Cambridge course was theoretical, needing an aptitude for applied mathematics. (The Science School Certificate results were still not known, but my faculty for maths was inadequate anyway). There was no basic mechanics or business studies course. I should have backed away, turned down the offer from the settlement and somehow found paying work, selling the lifeline Citroen if necessary.

There was no knowledge of the Youth Employment Service which was meant to be available to all (see Chapter 14.) What I should have done is easy to write with hindsight. The only excuse is that it did not seem so easy at the time. Mr Evennet suggested that I started by reading Law. He explained that, if I did not want a career as lawyer or solicitor, the knowledge gained and a good degree would be valuable in administrative or managerial positions within the system. There were a few weeks of struggle. It was all about past judgements, obviously important but tedious for someone who wanted to create for the future. Thinking this would have some relevance to the motor industry, the change was made to Economics. This was mainly theory and then at the end of the first term I was asked to write an essay describing a British car manufacturer's thinking prior to building a new factory. Working hard on this project, I concluded that, because of all the shop floor disputes and stoppages in the Midlands and at Oxford, it might be sensible to start again (i.e. on what is now known as a 'green field' site). I researched future road plans and possible housing projects and reckoned that a site outside Swindon might prove suitable. Besides the future M4, there was good rail connection via Didcot and access to the docks at Avonmouth and Southampton. Population growth was forecast. The tutor, Professor Maxcy, later co-author of one of the standard books about the industry, did not like this at all. Had I not listened to what he had been saying, especially that supply lines had to be as short as possible, with factories near to component makers? Though it may well not have been suitable for a British company, I smile to myself every time we pass the Honda factory at Swindon. In the book George Maxcy and his co-author wrote: 'There is no reason to believe that the British industry is inferior to its competitors.'[2] Is learning best from books or practical experience? By 1959, the date of their book's publication, practical experience of both British vehicles and the products of other countries (particularly in Libya and on the Afghan trip) suggested that this sentence was incorrect. The industry was and would become more inferior. Somehow the tussles with economics continued but then, in January (1955), came the time when such study no longer seemed to matter. I start the story by quoting from a lecture given a year later at the Royal Central Asian Society on Wednesday 18th January 1956, Admiral Sir Cecil Harcourt in the chair:

> 'Mr De Baer and some friends of his at the University of Cambridge at the beginning of 1955 asked if we could give moral support for an expedition they were planning into Afghanistan. He has now returned to tell us of the expedition and to show some of the slides taken by expedition members'.

I was one of those friends. I had met Oliver De Baer that first term, learnt of his plans and that the expedition needed someone who knew something about the insides of motor vehicles. Instead of buckling down to economics (or still escaping and finding work somehow), I leapt at the opportunity. It was motor industry contact once again, a way of surviving the long summer vacation without money and travelling for nearly four months in countries which had some similarity to the delights of the North African coast. There was also a bit of wishing to prove oneself, remembering the concerns about behaviour in battle. Oliver explained the objectives in his lecture:

'Our expedition started because the Long Vacation gave us a gap which we had to fill and we wanted to fill it by travel. We chose Afghanistan because it was within easy reach of Cambridge in the time available, because one of us spoke Persian[3], because the country is remote and little visited. Our aims could be summarised as follows: firstly to compile a regional survey of a given area, agriculture, religion, industries, customs, geology, including as much photography as possible; secondly, a survey of the nomads of the area; and thirdly, the collection of botanical and entomological specimens for the British Museum.'

I was asked to be treasurer and it also became my task to organise transport and some of the supplies. In addition I was advised to write to the British Museum. I had collected moths and butterflies (hordes of 'blues' then on the chalk) on the South Downs when at Peake. There's a nice letter, dated 26th January 1955, from ND Riley, Keeper of Entomology: 'I am decidedly interested in obtaining collections of insects from that area.' It is discomforting now to read the brash letters written by this then twenty-year-old. We were unrestrainedly using the Cambridge name for our own ends. I wrote to Mr Baldwin, public relations officer at Rover, using our headed notepaper, on 26th January 1955:

'A geographical and scientific expedition will be leaving this June to spend eight weeks on research in North East Afghanistan. The most suitable vehicle for our purpose would undoubtedly be the Land Rover and therefore ask if the Rover Company would lend us two of their products. We realise that you must be bombarded with many requests of this kind, but feel that further examination of this particular expedition may convince you that it is worthy of your support.'

I laid it on about 'following in the footsteps of Marco Polo on his way to visit the Great Khan at the end of the fourteenth century, an area since seen by only a handful of Europeans', and that the expedition was supported by the Geographical department of the university and learned societies in London. I concluded:

'We know there is not a large market for vehicles of any kind in Afghanistan. However we will be passing through many Middle East countries and by the very nature of the expedition will achieve considerable publicity, which may be of some value to your Company. In view of the fact that this will be the first attempt ever made to reach 'the roof of the World' by motor vehicle,[4] we are making every possible effort to ensure that our support comes only from British owned firms. Should you be able to help us, I shall be pleased to come to Solihull or London at any time.'

Looking back, it was risible ('at any time'!) but I had the action I craved and dry textbooks and essays, the reasons why I was at Cambridge, were no longer priority. The Rover letter did not result in two vehicles, but we were offered OUE 271, a long wheelbase truck with a roof over the load bed and two basic rear seats. There was a window in the back panel of the cab. Communication was possible, not access. This machine had been reconditioned after a 23,000 mile journey round Africa with a Colonel LeBlanc. There are a dozen or so letters, all individually compiled for different recipients, still in the files. Mr McCandless of Fina Petroleum wrote back: 'As explained when we talked on the telephone, we were originally prepared to pass the request (for free petrol in return for publicity) to our headquarters. However as we have received, by successive posts, four applications, two from Cambridge, two from Oxford, we decided that we could not approach the Group. Whether the publicity return from the support of one was commensurate with the work involved might have been a risk we were willing to take, but, in the light of hard commerce, to take the risk frequently would be rather inexpedient.' He then suggested that associate companies might be locally interested whilst travelling over their terrain and attached the names of those marketing Fina petrol along our route. We wrote to Purfina Francaise in Paris and they kindly arranged the gift of 110 litres at Calais, 70 litres at Vitry le Francois and 80 litres at Strasbourg. Oliver wrote a skilful letter in French to Purfina Hellenique in Athens. The response provided free fuel up to Istanbul. Then there's a note from Oliver: 'write all your usual stuff and try and get fifty gallons from BP Austria to get us through to Greece.' I must have succeeded because I remember taking off the Fina advertising stickers, replacing them with BP and putting Fina back at the Greek frontier. Turkey was solved by an introduction to Hugh Wilson at BP Aegean from Kit Power (see Chapter 9 and this chapter later). After Turkey we had to pay for our own fuel. My diary for the journey East (1st July, Tehran) notes: 'No more free petrol but not a burden at a price below two shillings per gallon.' Examples of other letters in the file are from clothing firms who all gave us their garments, from Dunlop, who provided two sets of tyres along the way, and Air Charter who took us across the Channel in return for publicity photographs. It was another goldmine like the Automobile Society.

In February 1955 I had my 21st birthday. There are many files about the marriage settlement and associated children's trusts. They show there was discussion about the interpretation of Myrtle's Will. I do remember that some income then came to me and I became aware that capital would be distributed on marriage. With carefully controlled expenditure, I could cope. As treasurer I approached the local branch of Lloyds in April 1955, explained that in the long term I would be in receipt of funds from the marriage settlement and could we have overdraft facilities for one year? They agreed and we soon had our own Expedition Account. The three statements are in front of me. The highest overdraft figure was £351 soon after our return. This was then steadily reduced by receipts from broadcast talks, magazine articles and lectures. There is an agreement signed by all of us at a meeting on 9th October: 'Ten per cent is to be paid to the member or members, the remainder to the Expedition's account. All literary contributions to be submitted through the Expedition's Literary Agent.'[5] I think there was also the odd well-wisher who approved of our effort. When we came to close the account in April 1956 the final debt was £67 3s 5d, which worked out at a payment of £16 15s 10d by each of the four of us. It was the cheapest three-and-a-half months of my life and the precious trust income was not being used. Every night was spent in the open lying beside the Land Rover on those simple roll-up camp beds with sprung metal supports (that's except when we were guests at embassies thanks to Oliver's contacts). I can't remember any rain. Despite one outcome, it was a never-to-be forgotten experience. Rather than try and describe the whole journey in this book, copies of Oliver's spirited effort *Afghan Interlude* published in 1958 are still around.[6] At the time of writing Amazon have one copy at $185. The full text can be downloaded from the web and the book has also been translated into French.[7] The other crew members were John Stayt and Dickie Thompson. Their contributions and all the incidents before departure are in the book. Even the big 1930s MG saloon, replacement for the Citroen and a suitably British product which had

'Westlands', the house at Broughty Ferry built by George Ogilvie, great grandmother Rachel's brother (married to Harriet Gordon) in the later half of the 19ᵗʰC. For years we did not realise the significance of this painting by Grandfather Max Balfour. This was the house, their brother's home, to which Mia and Minnie Ogilvie brought the three young Balfours on return from Chile. Max would have often visited. His painting looks west towards the skyline of Dundee with the Tay Bridge to the left and the Sidlaw hills to the right

The Rape of the Sabine Women Maxwell Balfour. Date painted: 1897 Oil on canvas, 80 x 139.7 cm
Collection: UCL Art Museum. Won first prize in a competition at the Slade

Studies for Queen Victoria's Diamond Jubilee. Sadly tuberculosis took over and he was unable to complete

Mr Clisset chair maker at Bosbury in
Herefordshire 1898

Old Pensioner at Trinity Almshouses

Rachel and Minnie's mother, always known as Granny Olgilvie

Max's visit to Kashmir in 1896 when he met up with Fred and Percy also then serving in India. This was the last time the three brothers were together

Sunrise Srinager

Sunrise form SS Aristo, Feb 2 1900

Native of Kashmir

The authors grandmother Nina, née Joachim, painted by her husband Max

Looking over the Sussex Weald from the Joachim house, Highlands, Haslemere

Studies for portraits

Probably Scotland, possibly Islay

Afghanistan
En route to Boharak

Faizabad

Climbing above the plain. Glimpse of distant Hindu Kush

The Boharak Plain

Kuchi people, Afghan Pashtun nomads, migration from the mountains to the Indus Valley

taken me around the country visiting factories and collecting equipment, is featured at the beginning:

> 'It rapidly grew to a mighty roar as a black car of formidable vintage drew to a halt beside us. We've got the jerry cans (vital to store any surplus free petrol), a passenger shouted, and with a merry chatter of valve gear the black car reversed.'

There are other sections of Oliver's lecture which are included for the information which they provide. He referred to the outward journey:

> 'Instead of via Beirut, Damascus and Baghdad, we headed East across Anatolia reaching Tehran via Tabriz. Thinking back and comparing the lush green of the countryside and the coolness of the nights with the Syrian desert, which we crossed on our return journey, it seems one of the most pleasant parts of the trip.'

Later he described some of the bureaucratic difficulties he coped with in Kabul whilst I attended to maintenance: 'We learnt that permits to enter the Wakhan[8] would not be given. After a further refusal for Nuristan, we were offered Badakshan.'[9]

All of us were staying in one of the houses in the compound surrounding the green lawns of the magnificent original British Embassy building. This had been built on the instructions of Lord Curzon: 'The British Minister in Kabul should be the best housed man in Asia.' From 1947 the building was owned by Pakistan after partition in India, but still used by the British until the 1980s. In 1995, when empty, the building was gutted by an anti-Pakistan mob. There are now discussions about buying back the site.[10] I made myself known to the British chief mechanic at the Embassy garage. He kindly looked over the Land Rover during our first stay and introduced us to the local representatives of FAO. They strongly advised fitting heavy-duty springs and had a spare set available (see report to Rover page 122). I visited the Embassy garage again before our return journey. Mercifully the broken left-hand mounting of the transfer box was discovered. It was in two pieces. After suitable welding, and replacing the rear shock absorbers and related bushes with spares brought with us, I was beckoned over to another part of the Embassy garage. There was King Zahir Shah's Phantom 3 with drophead body in polished aluminium made by Park Ward. It had been a present to Zahir from the British King (George VI) for his 25th birthday.[11] It had been brought in for service. This Rolls and other Royal cars survived the Russian invasion helped by special sheds built by UNESCO. Then, when the Taliban plundered the royal palaces, this beautiful creation by British craftsmen was destroyed. According to internet sources, all the aluminium was melted down to make cutlery and the cylinder head served as an anvil. Its W B Yeats again, as at Sabratha, 'Mere anarchy is loosed upon the world'. There was a further Rolls Royce connection. One morning we woke to the crisp roar of a Kestrel engine. The two remaining silver Hawker Hind biplanes of the Afghan Air Force were stunting against the backdrop of mountains and deep blue sky.[12]

Oliver continued in his lecture: 'The Governor of Faisabad explained that our permits were only valid for 'non-prohibited areas'. That was the Kokcha valley as far east as Jurm. We established camp by the river in the plain known as Boharak. We were given complete freedom to do what and speak to whom we liked. The official attitude was co-operative and the people were invariably kind and helpful. We were not allowed to visit Shiva, the

12,000 foot high lake where the local herds and the nomads spend the summer months.'[13] The abiding memory is of sparkling fresh air, blue skies, the mountain backdrop, rivers teeming with fish, the fertility of the valley, orchards laden with fruit and smiling children in their colourful clothes. Their parents were cultivating the land with wooden tools or looking after their animals much as they had done for centuries past. They encouraged me when I set out with net to gather specimens for the British Museum. As Oliver said, they were so welcoming and he could speak enough of the language to talk with them. One got the impression that, whilst they were happy to see our small party, they did not want any more interference from other countries. This was right in the middle of Zahir Shah's peaceful 40-year rule from 1933 to 1973. Afghanistan has not always been a country of conflict.[14] In 1964 Sir Olaf Caroe, who had been governor of the North West Frontier Province of India from 1946 until partition in 1947, wrote:

'Afghanistan is a country of great natural beauty which might become the Switzerland of Asia attracting tourists in thousands. The rulers and people possess a political sagacity which will enable them to avoid, as the Swiss have, a too close identification with any external power influence.'

We now know that Sir Olaf's hopes have not been fulfilled. We travelled the major routes where the surfaces were all in appalling condition. This was some while before the Russians started their road building. In the north we went via Maimana to Mazar-e-Sharif. Three times we crossed over the Hindukush by the Shiba Pass (before the Salang Tunnel was excavated), on the outward journey to Kabul and then to and back from the Boharak valley. We gazed at those incredible Buddhas (now tragically destroyed by the Taliban) in the fertile Bamiyan valley.[15] Then, when we finally set course for England, it was across the southern deserts to Kandahar. We drove north past Farrah overnight. This is part of my diary entry scribbled in the middle of the night of Sunday 28th August 1955.

'Oliver is driving. I have just woken from a fitful sleep. Am I in an aeroplane? Memories of exhausts in the Sahara. Is that one of those diesel lorries? No. Our exhaust system has fractured. I look at my watch. In twenty minutes it will be my turn to control the machine. The brakes go on. Thank goodness one can hear the squeal. I must brace myself, feet against the division, hands to one side - that's better. Through the window in the division I can see the speedometer in the lights of the instrument panel. 30-35, change up, 40-45. Now she is gliding over the hardened ripples of sand. I glance at John in the other seat. He is awake now. That last bump caught him. Oh! The brakes again. Bang. Up come the beds and hit the back of the seats. How does the car hold together? It will soon be in my hands. Twenty past one. What will happen during my two hours? Burst tyre? Another broken spring? Or I will not see a broken down bridge? Still that's fifteen minutes away. I gaze out at the stars. The moon has gone but its still possible to look out and see the absolute nothingness which spreads on and on. And here we are in this man made collection of pieces of metal. Ah! The brakes are going on for the last time in the present driver's hands. It's up to me now.'

I remember thinking, as the four-hundred-year-old minarets of Herat came into view in the morning light, how much we had done since we had entered the country past those same impressive pillars only three months before, far too short a time to properly appreciate all we had seen.[16] We had caught a glimpse of life in earlier centuries still then viable without the intrusion of industrial goods and services. Would I ever get back? If I had been told what was going to happen to those people and that countryside over the following fifty years, the response would have been disbelief and emotional concern. Every turn of the wheel would now take us further away from this attractive place and nearer to all the problems to be faced in England. We had to press on to be back in time for the Cambridge term. The exhaust finally broke off a few inches away from the manifold before we reached Meshed and had to be taken off. 'Noise similar to an open cockpit light aeroplane,' the diary recorded. A garage in Meshed fabricated an exhaust and attended to our other welding needs as listed below for 31st August. I see I put 'HELP!' against this list in the diary. (It was a good thing that I was already used to lying under cars and carefully examining structures. This continues today with the Bristols.) More work was necessary at Tehran. On 5th September it was Hamadan, 6th Baghdad and then across the desert to Damascus. The diary says we left at 5.30pm soon after the Nairn bus and, after border delays, arrived the next night at 9pm. At least we saw Iraq and Syria without war. I was also more aware of the markets available to the British car industry. Then it was across to Ankara and Istanbul and home through Europe, but via Oliver's parents in their lovely house at Auribeau above Cannes. More details of the journey can be found in Oliver's book.

There certainly were problems to be faced. There had been a letter from Mr Evennett, the Cambridge tutor, awaiting me at the Tehran Embassy. I had not done well in the Economics examination. Would I come and see him directly we got back to England? I was not surprised, I had hardly had time to go to the examination hall! He could not have been nicer when we met. He realised the pressure I had been under and had heard good reports of what the Expedition had achieved in Cambridge's name. I could not now get an honours degree and many left the University after such results. However, he hoped I would stay. He had worked out that if I did a year's history, a language for another year, and got reasonable results, Cambridge would probably award me an Ordinary degree which would stand me in good stead in the future. It may have been the time when I should have again faced up to my situation and left. I knew that I preferred action and enterprise. I liked to read and learn but not as a full-time occupation. But there was still the question what to do with no qualification, not even an ordinary degree. The other consideration, which I may have fastened onto as an excuse, was that there was so much sorting out to be done after the Expedition. Letters of thanks and suitable pictures went to suppliers. After I had delivered the specimens, the Department of Entomology at Cromwell Road wrote: 'No shattering novelties, but most of them are welcome. I have marked those I am particularly glad to have because we had no representatives of the species concerned from Afghanistan.' These were mainly from the Lycaenidae group. I prepared an article which according to the letter I still have from the agent, John Johnson, was accepted by the *Autocar* at the end of the year. (This was my first published writing. I had no thought that I would have become one of their employees forty years later!). My effort had to be watered down. The editor considered that it could be damaging to Rover's reputation. Here are a few extracts:

'In the plains to the North-West the only possible route was following the two deep ruts made by the heavy lorries. But the ruts proved too deep. We could only slowly move forward with one wheel in a rut and the other on the ridge between for the worst stretches. It was rather like sailing a dinghy with two of us hanging on to the high side to prevent overturning. We spent whole days with the speedometer between four and six miles an hour.'

'In the south, if one forgets about the appalling surface, it is possible to cruise at 50, but now and again comes a small but treacherous unmarked wadi for which it is essential to slow down and it is often difficult to see them till too late.'

'The hard springing did not provide a comfortable ride in the back, but it is unusual to take passengers in the truck version over long distances. This kind of spring paid dividends in other respects. On the few occasions when we broke a leaf, it was easy to make a new one out of odd metal.'

I did not include other diary notes about the British car industry. This is Tehran, 4th July:

'Talked to Dunlop Rep. He had sold his old Humber (wartime staff car based). Impressed by new Pontiac. Mowlems (contractors) disgusted with new Super Snipes (o.h.v. Mk IV). Cooling, back axle, gear change problems: If they had not already paid cash, they would have thrown them away.'

And Kabul, 24th July:

'Ford Pilot well-liked, but has not been reliable. American diplomat uses 1927 Bentley. He told me it was tough simple and reliable, that he could not find a more suitable vehicle.'

The report that I gave to Rover when I returned OUE 271 pulled no punches. Leaf breakage was on more than 'a few occasions.' It has been a life-long interest to detect vehicle faults. This was my first written report which others might read. It is in front of me now. These are just the major items:

Tehran, 3rd July. Split bonnet cross-member welded. Broken leaves both front springs, one rear spring replaced.
North Afghanistan, 13th July. Main leaf right rear spring replaced.
Kabul, 29th July. New heavy duty springs all round. This was a kind provision by Mr Le Riche of the F.A.O.[17]
Bahrek, 13th August. Grease nipple lost from front universal. Plugged with cork. Noise front of engine.
Faisabad, 21st August. Right rear shock absorber. Bottom collar broken off.
Kabul, 23rd August. (as mentioned in text) Transfer box mounting and new rear shock absorbers. Noise was weak spring tensioner in timing chain. Replaced.
Farrah, 25th August. (also in text) Exhaust silencer removed after welding split.
Persian border, 29th August. Exhaust pipe fractured near manifold. Whole system had to be removed.
Meshed, 31st August. Exhaust system re-made. Chassis crack below left door welded. Right rear spring anchorage broken and welded. Two broken front leaves replaced.

Tehran, 1st September. Bolt tightening. 'Tractor' joints leaking badly. New washers to seals.

Beirut, 10th September. New propellor shaft.

Italy, 18th September. Exhaust again welded.

Cambridge, 23rd September. New starter motor fitted.

TOTAL MILEAGE: 15,500 miles.

I added some comments on the problems encountered, emphasising that OUE had never left us immobile. The engine never faltered, the radiator header-tank never needed more fluid and oil consumption (with regular changes) was minimal. Whilst spring breakage was a recurring hazard, repair was easy. There was a sense of achievement that my area of responsibility had not let us down. This then furnished me with more confidence, less need to fret about courage in battle! Rover were not so positive. I had hoped they would appreciate how we had found weaknesses which could be rectified. Their attitude was that they had not expected OUE to be returned in that condition. I replied that there was a market for the Land Rover where we had travelled, but if potential problems were not sorted, they would increasingly turn to vehicles like Toyota's Land Cruiser, which had first been marketed with that name in 1954.[18] I said that people we met liked our vehicle, appreciating that it was less bulky and probably less thirsty, but it had to be reliable. We left it at that, another encounter with the British car industry.

The successful conclusion of the Expedition resulted in some national publicity, which pleased FG. She kindly organised a reception at Sunningdale. Expedition members were paraded before the local nobility and gentry. The general view seemed to be that this was a good example of British pluck. FG, shrewd as ever, took me to one side saying this was all very well but where was it going to get me and what plans did I have for the future? I probably mumbled that I was working on this. She replied that this was not to be repeated the following summer when she wanted me to escort her to Scotland. Back at Cambridge I did what I could with the history syllabus, but my interests were elsewhere. With Kit Power, who for sixty years has been a constant support in different endeavours, a Hispano-Suiza in poor condition had been rescued from a Cotswold garage before leaving for Afghanistan. I think it cost us £120. Renovation was an antidote to study, but that is a story which has been told elsewhere[19]. At the back of my mind I was wondering whether there could be a future, if I could obtain the initial finance, in buying, reconditioning, and then selling on some of the high-quality cars which were then available so cheaply. Whilst I still did not have training as a mechanic, I was learning all the time. This would mean contact with the machinery I liked though not helping to save the British industry. Weakly though, I funked the tussle with FG, PC and the rest. Instead I contacted the University Appointments Board. They replied: 'The only motor firms that have graduate training schemes are Fords, Rootes and Vauxhalls. BMC, Rovers and AEC[20] do not reckon to take arts graduates.' Having already missed out on Rootes once, and less keen on their products after the driver experience in the Fiat Millecento, I preferred to consider alternatives. Ford and Vauxhall were American owned. Was there any other way into BMC? I preferred the feel of their cars, particularly the Minor and some of the Rileys, all originally from the Nuffield rather than the Austin stable.

I didn't then progress these enquiries about the future. Instead I concentrated on Cambridge life. There was a growing relationship, we will call her X, and her kind parents invited me to their house. I had all I could wish for that summer, including a return to some rowing, and managed to pass the History exams. In the middle of July four of us, the other three being Simon Preston, Adrian Moyes and Michael Young, took the black MG across the Channel as far as Salzburg and then up the Eastern side of Germany through Nurnberg. Those big SA saloons had a reputation for bearing problems. BRX never missed a beat and there's a photograph of the speedo needle nudging 90mph. Instruments often read fast then. I expect the true speed was nearer 75. The diary records that on Wednesday 15th August I arrived at the offices of the Velvet Crepe Paper Company in north London. I had seen an advertisement seeking an undergraduate assistant for the managing director for three weeks during the summer. I don't think he had worked out what I should do (one of the staff said he just wants to tell his friends about you), but I reaped the benefit. They made all sorts of paper products, tissues and the like, and I was given odd jobs around the factory. I was also handed the keys of the company Ford Zephyr[21] and made various collections and deliveries. I started to change my opinion of Ford products. That Zephyr felt all of a piece, with none of the harshness and vibration of some other cars of that period. The engine was smoothly responsive and the controls satisfactory. I realised that the Ford training scheme should not be disregarded. Those weeks also meant that I was saving the precious Trust income. I reported for duty with FG at Sunningdale on Thursday 13th September 1956.

The plan was that I should drive her to Scotland in her Armstrong Siddeley Sapphire 346 to visit Cayzer relatives. Why she had such a big and heavy car, which she sometimes drove herself, I do not know. On this occasion she would not have wanted her chauffeur with her for the whole ten days, nor would she have wanted to drive the whole way on her own. She would then have been in her 79th year. We first visited James Cayzer and his mother (who had been a close friend of Myrtle) at Kinpurnie.[22] Then we drove across to Lanfine, the estate near Newmilns some fifteen miles South of Glasgow, belonging to her brother, my great-uncle Bertie Rotherwick. We stayed four nights. There are still clear memories of those days; the interior of the house, the efficiency, the willing retainers all at the beck and call of this always-smiling monocled chieftain of small stature. He had somehow survived the battlefields of 1914-1918. At the battle of Loos in September 1915 his horse had been shot and he had been knocked unconscious.[23] He had built up his father's business. He had been elected to Parliament and was now a Peer. FG did not discuss. Uncle Bertie, four years younger, was different. He seemed to radiate goodwill and encouraged conversation. His first question the day after we arrived was 'did I shoot?' I replied positively that the opportunity to shoot had never come my way and did not much appeal, but I greatly enjoyed walking on moors and mountains. The factor was summoned.[24] Could Christopher join the beaters the next day and at what time should he report? It was invigorating walking across Auchmannoch Moor looking over towards the Firth of Clyde, and chatting with the other beaters, all doing the job together. That evening Uncle Bertie remarked that the Factor had been pleased how I had apparently fitted in. He then told me about his plans for British and Commonwealth now that Union Castle was part of the Group.[25] He had high hopes for the future of the Commonwealth as an agency to bring benefit to participating countries. This enlarged company would service some of its needs. B and C ships would sail the world's seas. The following evening we talked again and he asked me about my future plans. I replied that I had long been interested in the British car industry and hoped to find a way to contribute to its future. Quick as a flash he referred to the difficulties with the unions and that it would be difficult to reach a position of influence. He then said - and I have never forgotten - 'If you were to achieve authority in another sphere, people might listen to you.' Nothing more was said and FG made no relevant comments as I drove her south again. I can't remember, but I don't think

I twigged that the future might include some involvement with Uncle Bertie's shipping and transport companies. My own thinking still related to working in the car industry.

At Cambridge for the third and last year I worked away at French, the language chosen. After the Zephyr experience, I asked the appointments board about Ford's training scheme for Arts graduates. Their hand-out dated 31st October 1956 described 'eight months general training moving round the most important departments. The graduate then goes into the department of his choice.' Salary, if National Service had been completed, would be £600. A representative would be visiting Cambridge on Tuesday 12th February 1957. On that day I met the genial Mr G S Campbell. We seemed to be on the same wavelength and what's more he was aware of the Afghanistan Expedition. It was a company with an American parent and it was not BMC, but Mr Campbell was so encouraging that I agreed to attend the interview panel in the summer term. Had I been able to follow through this plan, hindsight suggests that it could also have been the route to BMC. Just ten years later in 1967, when all the complicated negotiations between the holding company BMH and Leyland were taking place, the BMC component was recruiting managers from Ford (see Chapter 19). I would have had those ten years' experience, but this does not mean that I would have made a contribution which might have helped to preserve the British car industry. It was not to be. I have already mentioned suggested digestive difficulties when I was a child. There had only been the occasional problem whilst at Eton and Sabratha and I had learnt that alcohol intake had to be restricted. By the early summer of 1957, the whole system seemed to be playing up. I sought the help of Dr. Bevan (later I discovered he had helped my distant Wittgenstein cousin).[26] He listened to my tale of problems, knew I had done the Afghanistan trip, and recommended a trip to Addenbroke's hospital for tests.

It was found that I had the amoebae which caused dysentery lodged in my gut. Unless they were obliterated, I was going to have more and more trouble for the rest of my life. This was the one less happy outcome of the Expedition. There had been some stomach troubles whilst in Afghanistan, but they seemed to be sorted by the time of the return journey. Addenbrooke's had to seek advice from London and eventually I was hauled into the hospital. I was given the course of drugs. The Cambridge nurses had no experience of the side effects. They made me feel very odd indeed. Then I had to wait and be tested again. Some while later it was found that those drugs had not worked. I was to become an in-patient at the Hospital for Tropical Diseases in London when a place was available. By this time I had missed the interview panel at Ford. I apologised to Mr Campbell and sent him a copy of 'Afghan Interlude'. I don't think I managed all the French exams, but the university kindly awarded an Ordinary Degree after consultation with the French tutor. Friends were helpful. Kit Power organised the sale of the Hispano. X was continuously supportive and coped with the odd behaviour. Eventually, after the end of the Cambridge term, I found myself in the London hospital amongst expatriates from all over the world. For some there was no hope. Each day they were more yellow and often died. Bilharzia was mentioned as a particularly nasty parasitic worm. I was more fortunate. After another vicious course of drugs and more tests I was eventually pronounced as free of the amoebae. There is an appropriate paragraph in Graham Turner's *The Leyland Papers*, a book to which I shall refer again in Chapter 19.[27] Graham is writing of Sir Henry Spurrier of Leyland: 'Had caught dysentery which ruined his digestion. He seldom enjoyed formal dinners and usually ate scrambled eggs. Sometimes moody because of his variable health.' This has been my situation. The amoebae were no more but they had left a damaged gut. I got myself into some inappropriate situations till I eventually realised that I needed to stick to simple fresh food and further restrict alcohol intake.

LEARNING FROM DIFFERENCE

Chapter 12

No Portsmouth. Africa. Other jobs and happenings

Out of hospital and still without paid work, two difficult years followed. There was no job opportunity for me at Portsmouth and I had lacked the courage to stand up to those who opposed my wish to delay National Service and start the apprenticeship with Rootes at 18. A possible lesson for those who follow is that, if you disagree with your elders, and can see another way which will provide means of survival (which may mean living cheaply), it may be wise to back your own judgement. As recorded, I did not stand up and every decision taken then compounded my original weakness. Once the wrong path is taken, in mountains or in life, it may become increasingly difficult to regain the preferred route. On the other hand, acceding to others led to consequences that neither they, nor I, foresaw. What might have happened if I had gone to Rootes directly after Eton will never be known. Instead I learnt about people and power, which has been helpful when writing the books. In the end, knowledge and the attempt at understanding human limitations may be as important as position and increasing wealth. We have, at least so far, had sufficient money for the family's needs. It has been possible to learn to live with the physical side of the Afghanistan outcome and other problems. It is a constantly remembered privilege to have experienced life in that peaceful valley, also to have had a little contact with the Kuchi nomads. Whilst their way of life has been interrupted by war, commentators report that a million Kuchis are still supplying well over half the sheep and goats in the country's livestock markets. There are alternatives to Western consumerism.[1]

Now came some unexpected happenings. The good Mr Campbell wrote to say how sorry he was that 'all places on the 1957-1958 Trainee Scheme had been filled.' Ford's comparative success at that time when other companies were floundering surely stems from the work of people like Mr Campbell. The company had a well-thought-out training scheme and were prepared to travel the country seeking suitable trainees. Then in October came a letter from Sir Nicholas Cayzer, son of another of FG's brothers, who was taking over the reins of British and Commonwealth from Uncle Bertie:

'We had a family discussion yesterday and we are prepared to offer you a job. Uncle Bertie would like to see you in due course, but I think it would be a good thing if you and I had a talk first. I am so anxious if you join us that it is really the thing for you. There are always lots of troubles and difficulties in one's career but to get off to a good start makes a difference.'

When I went to see him at St Mary Axe, he explained that the family wanted to bring in some younger members to work in the company. It will never be known how much pressure there had been from FG, his father's sister, his aunt. Because at that moment I had no other prospect, and maybe the conversations with Uncle Bertie came to mind, I replied that shipping had not been a primary interest, but I was aware of future transport opportunities. I also knew they were investors in engineering companies and said I would be glad to work in that area. (Again thinking of Uncle B, I do remember it crossed my mind about buying into motor industry related firms at some future time.) Cousin Nicholas replied that there would be many things I could help with on the engineering side but that he would want me to start at Birkenhead and Liverpool to get to know the company's core business. This seemed a reasonable proposition and Nicholas's comments in his letter were encouraging. The invitation was accepted. The salary was modest but sufficient. It was agreed that I should go to Birkenhead at the end of the year. I learnt that FG and Uncle Bertie were both pleased by my acceptance. Then a letter came from Mr Campbell:

> He was 'sorry about the Trainee Scheme however there was a vacancy on the permanent staff of the Export Division in London'. Would I attend for interview? He then continued: I look forward to seeing you again and personally expressing my appreciation of the book 'Afghan Interlude' which I have just finished reading. It was for the most part excellent reading and quite one of the best travel books I have read for a long time.'

That time is burned into my memory. Export, after all the travelling, was a niche into which I felt I could fit. Other positions might follow. It looked as if there was a good chance that I would be accepted by Ford, and it would be through my own efforts. There was no one to consult. Lionel had his own problems then (though he might have counselled caution with the maternal family after his experiences). Any rational person would have said there was no comparison between export assistant and the potential in a family company. X yet again was helpful, but did not have enough knowledge to make a judgement. I knew what a rumpus there would be if I told FG that I was going to Ford. In the end, I opted for the primacy of family loyalty, a decision later regretted. I set out for Birkenhead where a room had been booked in a small private hotel. Alderman Carroll, who was in charge of the office in the Liver Building in Liverpool, was affable.[2] He led me to one of those high desks and gave me a stack of 'bills of lading' to look at. After a few days I started to record load details and was given other clerical tasks. This carried on for four months. At least the reality of boring work was experienced. I was then told to report to Captain Banbury, marine superintendent, at Victoria Dock, Birkenhead at 9am on Monday 10th March 1958. The suggestions were to observe how the loading pattern was worked out in the offices and watch the actual loading. I was not allowed to operate any of the cranes, but I could go anywhere including boarding the ships as they came in. The trouble was, there was no specific job - I was just a spectator. It was difficult, having previously thrived on work and purpose. It was a very different situation to Sabratha four years earlier, or to the organisation of the Expedition. To this day I wonder what else I could have done or what Cousin Nicholas meant me to do. Certainly he had many other infinitely more important concerns than how I was occupying my days. Then I learnt that Uncle Bertie had died and I had never got to see him. A message came that I need not come to the funeral, better to stay on the docks. This was odd. Out of respect for Uncle Bertie, I should have defied the intimated instruction and had the contact with other family members. I pressed on and, as in the army, engaged in the spirit of 'common endeavour'. I got to know some of the dockers, listened to their problems and even came in early on a cold snowy Sunday to assist manually on a rush job. One weekend Kit Power kindly came up from Coventry where he had joined the Rootes Graduate Trainee scheme. I kept in touch with X as best I could and we met up on the occasional weekend. There were others learning the trade with different companies. There are records in the diary of playing squash and tennis. Life was looking up. I finished at the Docks and went back to the Liver Building. Gina Barbour, who had a lovely house near Chester and had known Nicholas when he was based at Liverpool, had heard about me and invited me to stay with her as a paying guest. This was an improvement on Birkenhead.

I was summoned to the London St Mary Axe office on Wednesday 16th July 1958 there to be told by Cousin Nicholas that my services were no longer required in the company. I was not the sort of person they wanted, but, if I returned to Liverpool, there would be payment for four weeks. This took me so much by surprise that I was speechless. What would have happened if I had responded robustly and questioned his statements? Looking back I realise I was in awe of this man in the same way that I had been in awe of the seniors at Eton when the beating was not resisted. It was the system developed over the centuries to promote authority on the battlefield, part fear, part respect. Cousin Nicholas was now in command and was developing his own future strategy. He may not have wanted me in the first place but, when number two, he had to respond to family pressures. Uncle Bertie, who may have been my supporter, was now dead. On 28th July Cousin Nicholas wrote: 'I am sorry that things did not work out as they might have done, but I am quite sure you should follow your own instinct and make your own way at something that appeals to you. Ships are just not on.' Looking back this letter reflects the contradictions of that time. I had continually been discouraged from 'something that appeals', and had seen the acceptance of the offer to go to Liverpool as family duty. The reward, besides some financial security, would be working loyally for a family team (and Uncle Bertie's hopes) instead of the lonely road after Myrtle's death. Not so many years later, ships were 'not on' for the family company either! The huge container carriers seen in the Solent have 'Maersk', not 'British and Commonwealth,' in large letters along their sides! Owing to previous discord, there was no discussion with FG. This may have been my mistake, but it could also have led to further dissension within the family. It was probably better that I kept quiet and made use of the episode as a valuable lesson of life. This was when I realised the importance of financial independence, and the potential difficulties when working for others, which Lionel had always resisted. If independence could be achieved, it was vital to maintain reserves and control expenditure to cope with the unforeseen. I also saw that no situation, even with family, should be taken on without a written contract. Later, when working in the employment services (Chapter 14), I was always wary of companies which did not have thought-out training schemes. It must have been forty years later that Cousin Nicholas was staying with his daughter, Nichola Colvin, at Tangley. We went over for lunch. Afterwards, whilst her father was resting, Nichola and her husband, Michael, told me that the sacking had been discussed the previous evening. Cousin Nicholas, now Lord Cayzer, had said that I would have made a good shop steward. Michael (then an MP) kindly remarked that this seemed to him a commendable attribute. This helpful thought has remained in my mind. We much regretted their fate a year later.[3]

The reality may be that my 'common endeavour' attitudes could have been helpful in a global transport company. A good relationship between management and employees in such a business does help. Only recently I have heard how, at current Clan Line reunions, Bernard Cayzer's concern for the crews is not forgotten (Bernard was Nicholas's younger brother). This was not the chosen future and we on the Jellicoe side need to remember that because the inheritance was divided between four daughters and one son no of us had the voting power to affect decisions. Over the following years, the company moved out of shipping and concentrated on financial services and investment. The tough world of winners and losers would not have been my preferred habitat. I thought more about production, about work efficiency and conditions. I was probably insufficiently focussed on the priority need for profit. This may have been apparent from my attitudes. The point is that Cousin Nicholas found that I did not fit with what he had in mind and he was determined to succeed after coping with other personal difficulties.[4] He was bearing the whole weight of the whole family's future. He needed people with whom he felt in tune and therefore my dismissal was the right decision. Other relatives with more suitable aptitudes joined the family company. We shall never know what might have happened if Uncle Bertie's plans had been continued. There would have been no certainty of continuing success in a difficult world. It was a courageous and visionary decision to change course. There were still some near misses, but the wider family has reason to be thankful for Cousin Nicholas's actions, which also pointed the way for successors like Peter Buckley and all that they achieved. It took a bit of time, but what happened is now better understood. Men of business have to act in different ways to kind regimental Colonels, like those I had met during National Service, and it is the work of the former which make the lives of the latter possible. Much was learnt from the experience, particularly the need to probe and question the intentions of others. I am particularly glad now to have this background knowledge of life on the docks and the ships and getting to know some of the crews, also of the difficult decisions leading to the creation of the family wealth today.

Over the years I have also noted the history and progress of other nineteenth-century trading families. They have also changed course, but in different ways. Some ten years after Great-grandfather Charles Cayzer started work with William Nicol and company, agents for McKinnon and McKenzie in Bombay, James McKay joined McKinnon and McKenzie (MMC) in Calcutta. By 1914 James McKay was sole senior partner in MMC. By 1929 he was the Earl of Inchcape and this name was adopted by the company. Amongst many other activities (they are the world's leading shipping services provider) they bought into car distribution by the purchase of Mann Egerton in 1973. By 1989 this was two-thirds of their group turnover and they now distribute cars in twenty-six different countries including, as already mentioned, Rolls-Royce in Chile through Williamson Balfour. William Jardine and James Matheson were two other Scotsmen who founded a Far Eastern Trading Company in 1832. In 1975 Jardines bought Zung Fu Motors, distributors for Mercedes, in Hong Kong. Jardine Motors now distribute twenty-one brands in UK and have eighty-three sales and service locations. Wikipedia reports that Jardine Motor's worldwide profits for 2011- 2012 were sixty-one million dollars. I think back to my mention of the British car industry to Uncle Bertie and his response about achieving authority in another sphere. Distributors can have some influence with manufacturers. This could have been an avenue akin to my interests. But, even if I had not been sacked, would I have seen the opportunity at that time and could the family have been persuaded to take this route? Looking back still has value in recognising what might have been.

Once again there was the handicap of no qualification. It was not only that I had taken the wrong path, but as if I had now slipped off the path down a narrow gully. Was it possible to climb back and then still find the right route? The reader will be spared every detail of the next seven years but some happenings may be of interest. I could not face up to contacting kind Mr Campbell. Pride got in the way. That was not going to be my foothold. I then learnt from former contacts that there were likely to be vacancies in the next graduate training scheme at Rootes. I still didn't rate their products highly, but it was becoming a matter of self-preservation. I had to get back on the path. The interview was not until February 1959. Looking back, this was the time when I should have found a way of achieving a bank loan and started trading in the now valuable historic cars which were then so cheap. Instead I wrote to the Cayzers asking if I could spend the next two months or so on one of the ships I had got to know when at Birkenhead. I can't remember how the envelope was addressed, but it was read by Uncle Bertie's son, then the second Lord Rotherwick. Another kind man, he at once agreed to this plan. Cousin Nicholas had been away and later made it clear that he would not have agreed! I was just thinking of survival. I needed board and lodging till February and had achieved this on a family ship![5] X had done her best to encourage but I was still pretty despondent. The prospect of reasonable remuneration in a year or two had disappeared. I was the one who had got it wrong, but I think we both realised that our long-term hopes were receding. I was so pleased when she married a hard-working man of business who progressed to a high position far above anything I ever achieved. It was good to sometimes see her picture looking elegant. We did have an evening together before we both married. I think and hope there was understanding. Sadly she died some years ago, before her biblical span.

I joined the Lanarkshire at Birkenhead on Wednesday 10th December 1958. The ship was crewed by twenty-three Officers (Captain RB Linsley) and sixty-one Asian crew members. My diary for Friday 12th December reads: 'vessel rolling and pitching very heavily. Shipping water over decks and hatches fore and aft.' It was not pleasant but, after a few days, the sickness stopped. For Tuesday 16th December: 'All very lovely with the sun setting behind the Tenerife mountains and then the lights twinkling on the slopes of the hills as we passed in the dusk.' Thursday 18th: 'Boiler tube fractured'. I remember trying to show solidarity (common endeavour again) receiving the old tube and then passing the new one through the small boiler door to the engineer working inside. That's been the stuff of nightmares, climbing through and getting stuck because of my size! Entries for Friday 19th and Saturday 20th December, Dakar, had more serious content:

'Inspection of boiler tubes revealed four more broken. One had split. With no water, the metal had crystallised, probable temperature reached 3000 degrees. It was decided to use outside contractors to fit four new tubes which were carried as spares. The four Arabs who did the work then found that other tubes had cracked and needed to be changed. Cost of these repairs was the equivalent of £300. The Ship's engineer explained that it was better on an old ship to repair when things went wrong than have costly overhauls. The work took five hours and then two hours to raise pressure in the tubes before testing by the Lloyds Surveyor.'

Then came the fifteen-day voyage from Dakar round the Cape to Durban. I learnt about shipboard life. Here are some further extracts form the diary. The diary tells of: 'Boat and fire drill, the boats are arranged so that they are easy to swing out and difficult to raise i.e. 'single-cranked'. A more modern ship will have electric motors.' 1: 'Blowing the tubes whereby excess carbon is blown out of the boiler with steam. Carbon spreads over the operator.' 2: 'Visiting the Asian crew's quarters situated either side of the steering flat. The new insecticides deal with the cockroaches but, until their introduction three years ago, these insects bred all over the ship in the Tropics.' 3: 'A morning down No 2 hatch. 20 ton electric motor bogies had shifted probably while we were rolling at the start of the voyage. The dockers had put the wire securing ropes round the protective wood instead of the metal of the steel pillars in the hold. We tightened all the bottle screws we could reach and the carpenter wedged the bogies with wood. Jaguar 2.4 examined (always this interest). Noted poor finish beneath dash.' 4: 'Cleaning out the fuel system of a Morris marine engine (8 h.p. Series E) in a lifeboat.' 5: 'Talking with Nazir Hossain who cleans my cabin. He has a boy and a girl and returns home for three months leave next spring. He does not like flying as the plane caught fire at Baghdad on his last flight to London.' I hope I contributed and was not resented. One of the cadets had bad toothache. I asked whether he could be put ashore at Cape Town. It was explained that cargo and costs must have priority so 'he had another 72 hours of agony ahead of him. He does not complain and accepts the position.' These were the years when British exports were flourishing. I noted the following cargo:

> On deck: Two English Electric Locomotives (Bodies; underframes and bogies in hold), two powered railway coaches, two trailer coaches.
> Below: Atkinson lorry, Austin Gypsies and vans, Land Rovers, Jaguar. Hudswell - Clarke diesel locomotive. Lister engines. Blast furnace pipes.
> Spare parts: Albion, Foden, Leyland. Boilers. Sugar Rollers. Tyres. Batteries. Oil. Grease. Then the lighter goods: Beer and Whiskey, china, wall-paper, chemicals, carpets and general hardware.

The diary then records Durban 6th January, Beira 12th January. It had not been my intention to trade on the family relationship (with two months wait before the Rootes interview and no money, I was just seeking a way to travel at minimum expense) but I did receive invitations as a Cayzer cousin. At dinner with local managers: 'The garden is full of lovely flowers and looks onto the nature reserve. It's like a large edition of the Meon Valley. Apartheid and other matters were discussed.' The FAO (see Afghanistan) representative said: 'I know of no place in the World where so much is being done by so few for the advancement of a native population.' I learnt that a company called 'Motor Assemblies' were producing Standard and Nuffield cars from CKD (completely knocked down) parts in Durban and there was a similar Rootes plant at Cape Town. At Beira the Cayzer relative business got out of hand.

I was entertained by local traders and managers at the Beira Club. It would have fuelled Cousin Nicholas's concern if he had heard about this. I was parading under false colours as a future manager rather than a sacked employee! It wasn't my intention to deceive. I was just grateful to Uncle Bertie's son for his kindness. It was then time to think about getting back for that interview. I had been given some introductions in Southern Rhodesia, now Zimbabwe, which included an invitation to visit a combined farm and tobacco plantation. Having said goodbye to the Officers and crew of the Lanarkshire who had all been so kind to me, I met up with a Mr Cohen, manager of the Manica Trading Company. We left Beira railway station at 6.30pm on Friday 16th January. Instead of an early morning activity watching out for animals either side of the track, the single-berth sleeping compartment was so comfortable that I did not wake till we reached our destination at Umtali. There was just time to take a picture of the Volkswagen and Rover garage across the street (Hillman Minx, Austin A40 and Morris on the forecourt) before joining Mr Cohen for the drive to their Salisbury office (now Harari) in the company's green Chevrolet. The diary records:

'We left at 7.45am and were in Salisbury at 10.35. 160 miles. The road winds up over a pass with Umtali nestling in the valley below. It's a pleasant climate and many service officers retire there. A long stretch of sparsely populated scrub land then continues till the outskirts of the Capital. The road is a single strip not quite twice the width of the Chevrolet. Passing procedure when each car puts its outside wheels on the dirt border is at first alarming.'

On Sunday I joined an excursion flight in a Hunting Clan DC 3 to visit the Kariba project. The dam was then half completed, with British and French consulting engineers, Italian contractors and British and American machinery. We were told that twenty-four European lives had been lost, also many African deaths. On Monday, I was given a tour of Manica's Export and Import departments, then in the evening travelled out to the Lone Cow Estate (pictures on the Web) in a Morris Minor. The next day my kind hosts (through a contact in England) showed me their tobacco planting. The Dodge tourer, reputed to be the first car which had driven through from Kenya in the 1920s, was in a corner of the drying sheds. The cattle herds were in other fields and could only be seen in the distance. That night I returned to my room at Meikle's hotel in Salisbury. On Wednesday, thanks again to Manica (the web confirms they are still a major trading company), I visited the Seddon lorry factory in the morning. This was a small English company which had sold sixty vehicles adapted for Rhodesian conditions and backed by an efficient service department. That afternoon I boarded a Bristol Britannia. One of these contacts had helped again. I found I had been upgraded to first class. The diary records: 'Kilimanjaro just visible. Nairobi 6.30 p.m. Khartoum 10.30. Rome 6.0 a.m. Lovely views of Mont Blanc and the Alps. Am impressed by Britannia travel. Tourist class probably not so good but I had three seats and slept well. London Airport 9.30 a.m. Raining.'

It was then back to reality in England. Not aware of Cousin Nicholas's displeasure, I wrote my thanks. I remember that letter because of all the thought that went into it. I acknowledged that I was not wanted in Liverpool, but asked if there were any job vacancies in other offices or perhaps connected with trading. I mentioned the kindness shown by everyone I had met. Understandably in the circumstances, Cousin Nicholas replied that I was not wanted anywhere in the company and that was that! I now realised that I had to make my way as myself on my own terms. Whatever my opinion of the products, I had to attend that Rootes interview. I accepted their offer: it was the only lifeline I had. On the first day, the training officer saw the old MG saloon, which I had managed to keep, having sold the second Fiat before leaving England.[6] He immediately said, again so clearly remembered: 'We don't want enthusiasts here. Making these cars is just like making pots and pans.' I now understand what he meant, but the fact remains that there are no Hillmans and Humbers now and the car makes that have survived are more than pots and pans. I carried on observing and - where possible - actually working in the different departments. As on the docks, if, as a trainee, one asked to do a job, there was the difficulty of working too slowly and affecting production and wages. I do remember managing to assemble most of a Minx engine quite quickly. I was ever more aware that the products lagged behind their competitors. When attached to sales I tried to talk about the Mowlem experience with Super Snipes in Tehran and what I had observed during other travels. The response seemed to be that some faults were unavoidable. Production was the priority - let the customer sort out problems. Looking back now, the zigzag course I pursued was madness and all because I had not concentrated on a qualification at 16 or 18. I had no status, not even a false one as in Africa! Six years earlier I had had responsibility as assistant adjutant. All I had done since then was to take paths which led to dead ends, found devious ways of accessing the marriage settlement and damaged the gut! When I asked about prospects with Rootes after training, there seemed little hope of influence. And what had I to offer? Six years in which I could have become a qualified accountant, engineer or mechanic. I had been better placed for communication with directors while at Eton and Cambridge! Hopefully young people today will not get themselves into a similar stupid situation. For some, a practical apprenticeship with pay will be a better route than a university degree. The web has plenty of information, as an example under 'engineering apprenticeships', I still regret the demise of the Youth Employment Service - see Chapter 14. It must have been at that time that I, at last, came to my senses. It was reprehensible to think of abandoning Rootes after all they had done for the Automobile Society, and after they had given me a lifeline, but I realised that I had to change course, forget about the car industry for the moment and still somehow obtain a professional qualification. I noticed a training course for personnel management (now human resources) at Hendon Technical College, for those who already had some industrial experience. The Birkenhead saga seemed to suggest that there was some empathy with those who did the work. Concern for the future of Rootes as a British company was validated when the American Chrysler Company took complete control ten years later. Those months were still experience for which I remained grateful. The knowledge of work and conditions on the production line and in other departments, together with all that I had picked up whilst travelling, was helpful background when I came to write about the industry. Those six years may have been misdirected but they were not without value.

I am grateful to the lecturers at Hendon who taught me many of the things which should have been learnt years earlier attending a Business Studies Course. At last I was on the way to a qualification. Based in London, it was easier to accept weekend invitations from friends in Hampshire. While staying with Christian Ross Stewart, a much-valued confidante from years past, and her parents at Droxford, there was a dinner party with Philip House. I found myself sitting next to Ann Butlin, who had only been included at the last minute. She well remembers my post-food sleepiness, then not understood, but she managed to communicate that she was about to drive to Ireland with three Australian girls who she had not yet met. I jotted down the address of my Aunt Norah Wingfield,

Myrtle's sister, in County Waterford. They found themselves driving through the village, so ventured up the long drive where they were warmly welcomed and asked to stay the night. Ann then wrote reporting on their visit and asked if I would like to spend a weekend with her family at Ashton Farm, Bishops Waltham. It did not take long to realise that here was someone who shared much of my thinking. She accepted my proposal shortly before leaving for a trip to visit relations in Australia. She returned and we were married in July 1960. Somehow she has put up with my moody times and other ill health, till we have together managed to work out what foods can be properly digested. It is great joy to now have more constant good health. She has supported both the difficult 'working for others' years and the self-employed enterprises. Her skills and laborious efforts in property maintenance, her work in field and garden, have been greatly appreciated by many. Besides being a loving, ever-loyal, patient, selfless and wise companion, she has been a good mentor to the next generation, (making up for my deficiencies) and has given many days to caring for the generation senior to us in their old age. Through three generations, the family owe her so much.

The next milestone was a communication from a Cambridge acquaintance who had heard through other contacts about my recent studies. He worked for an engineering employer's association in Birmingham and they wanted another assistant who would learn to put the employer's case in negotiations with the trades unions, just the sort of thing I had been learning about at Hendon. This appealed. Contact with the car industry from a different angle. So Ann and I moved to a flat in Harborne and I began a probationary period working in Edgbaston. This branch of the Association was run by a retired Brigadier and we were his subalterns. Unfortunately for me, one of the perks of the job was a delicious lunch (the Association had its own kitchen etc) with rich and tasty food. I was stymied again. If I joined the others, as it were in the 'Officer's Mess' where current negotiations and other matters were discussed, I was pretty well out of action for the following few hours. It was not acceptable to miss that lunch (when not on a negotiation) and bring in a sandwich. It was interesting to have this view of the problems in the factories, but there were several instances when I thought the employees had a better case than the employer. The Brigadier was another kindly army man and understood. By then we had also learnt that there was more money than we had expected coming our way from the Settlement after marriage. I explained to the Brigadier that we now had to sort out our family position. He responded by asking whether I would become a liaison officer for the Duke of Edinburgh's Award Scheme with responsibility for the Birmingham and West Midlands area. Reasonable expenses would be paid. I was pleased to accept. It seemed that a possible path was in view.

The next step was to establish a base. We did not find anything we liked in Warwickshire or Worcestershire and started to look further to the south west. Eventually near the border of Herefordshire and Gloucestershire, and close to a junction for M50, we found Compton House with many outbuildings and fifty acres. In some ways it was stupid, the house was too large; but for me it was like getting back to Peake after all the discord and disruption of the fifteen years since Myrtle's death. We employed contractors to work the fields, we took some of the fruit to the local market and we worked to improve the fabric of the house. I had now bought the first Bristol for £370 and started on the now fifty-four year association with the good people at Bristol Cars in Filton.[8] Several times a week I took the 400 up to the West Midlands, petrol paid, to explain or talk about the Award Scheme to training and personnel managers or company directors in the

Midlands. These were the days before limits and there was no holding back on the empty M50. (M5 not yet built so the rest of the journey was not so good). I revelled in that superb British product, best of all I remember a late night journey up to Snowdonia, again no other traffic, to gain experience of Award Scheme expeditions. This was a rewarding time involved in different activities. As at Eton and Cambridge, there was participation at manager or director level. There was even the task of organising an Award Scheme conference in Birmingham. Sir John Hunt of Everest[9] came up to talk to the industry representatives who had been gathered together at one of the hotels. In the afternoon Prince Philip visited Scheme activities. I muffed my introduction to royalty. Too late I thought of a much better answer to his well-meaning questioning. He spoke of that day in a talk to the Institute of Directors (November 1962):

> 'Only last week I was able to see the Scheme in operation in a number of large works in Birmingham. From meeting the training officers, the youth organisations and the education authorities involved, I got the impression that the Scheme has given a lot of satisfaction and enjoyment to the younger generation and that the organisers were pleased with their results.'

We also thought of using the Compton outbuildings to offer assistance in assembly to purchasers of what we considered the most promising kit car of that period. This was the Rochdale 'Olympic' created entirely from glass fibre without any supporting steel chassis. We financed the build of an example which was displayed at the Racing Car Show in London in January 1962. A fire at the factory hampered further production. We were saved from further expenditure which we could not really afford. I was still dithering about on the edges of the car industry following the instincts, as Cousin Nicholas had suggested, but there were also the doubts about the industry and realisation of the large amount of money needed to make an impact, the reasons why I had accepted the offer from the Cayzers! Looking back, the muddle of my thinking then has been echoed by the subsequent muddles in the British-owned companies. If I had realised what, fifty years later, I now understand: if I had been tough in my bargaining, and if I had had the gumption to withstand the comments of older relatives the historic car trading route could have been the best way to proceed. Ann was marvellously supportive (there were still some difficult sessions when I got the food wrong), and she produced Max and Juliet in good order. Life was at last making some sense, but the foundations were insubstantial. We had thought there were sufficient holdings in the Trust funds to sell some of the shares in the family companies. After the Birkenhead experience I was not overburdened with loyalty! Then we discovered that the canny head office advisers had worked out a way of valuing the shares at well below their potential value. This was good financial management. It was our ignorance not to have understood. Those share sales stopped. I was learning so much from Award Scheme contacts, meeting many different people in Midlands factories, schools and colleges. At last I became aware of the Youth Employment Service, which I had not discovered at Eton or Cambridge. It was then mostly run by Education Authorities. In a few years I was to join this Service, paid work in which I felt I could contribute. The family money could then be more carefully guarded. This is all described in Chapter 14. Also at this time Lionel had started again taking over (aged 56) a Portsmouth Aviation subsidiary, Portair Products. He was determined to manage this company his own way, not brooking discussion. However he did want our investment. This was one of those intractable situations when there was merit on both sides. I think Lionel felt that, as he had contributed to the marriage settlement, we would willingly now provide cash even though there was no such Will provision. We knew that this cash could only come from the further sale of potentially undervalued shares. After some heart-searching, we decided that we should only make a small investment. This also pushed us along the road to accepting paid employment and strengthening our total resources. This was an example of not agreeing with an elder, of Ann and I backing our own judgement (as suggested at the beginning of the chapter). Previous hard-won experience about the importance of maintaining reserves was now proving beneficial. We still think that this was the right decision not least because we were then able to assist Lionel financially in his last years. These difficult issues are further discussed in Chapter 18.

Politics was another growing interest at that time. Compton was one of the larger houses in the area and, instead of car trading, we were drawn into local activities. Before long I found myself vice-chairman of the Newent Conservative branch. I was then swiftly elected to both executive and finance and general purposes committees of the West Gloucestershire Conservative and Unionist Association. The Party often enthusiastically embraces younger people who show interest. Providing the captive is willing and loyal and rations controversy, he or she will be showered with praise. It was a heady experience for someone who had known criticism and rejection. I was sucked in. This led to interesting occasions. The family all went to the 1963 Blackpool Conference, as it happened in the Bristol 406 prototype which the factory had sold to us.[10] This was the year when Harold Macmillan resigned and Alec Douglas-Home eventually took over the leadership. Ann and I were in the room when Lord Hailsham announced that he would disclaim his peerage. Joyce Mann, then near retirement, was the helpful and encouraging deputy central office area agent[11]. In 1964 she asked me to join the area panel of speakers. The honeyed letters arrived: 'your great kindness in undertaking to address a joint meeting', 'it was very kind of you to have been put to so much trouble'. It's the lubrication which oils democracy. Hopefully, previous happenings countered any tendency towards self-exaltation. The files also show that by 1964 I was the sole West Gloucestershire representative for the whole West Midlands area, covering fifty-one constituencies and also, with one other, representative for the area Conservative Political Centre committee. It was rather different to working on the Rootes production line, but that experience (and the docks) helped in understanding something of the lives of all those hard-working Midland people. It was also valuable, if considering progress in politics, to be seen by all those representatives. It was Angela Darricotte, the kind and helpful West Gloucestershire Agent, who kept on urging me to ask to join the approved list of Parliamentary Candidates. I was still naive thinking just in terms of service to my fellows and I confess that, despite my disinterest in school awards and caps, there was an attraction in the MP status. It boosts the ego to come into a room and find that there is a demand for one's opinion. Later came the realisation that, like the Award Scheme, Eton or Officer label, this approval and interest in my thoughts was only because of the Party label. Many years later, having written books, I found there was the same demand, but this was because of self-directed toil rather than an adopted association.

In the next chapter I will try and explain how I later came to accept that the House of Commons and gut deficiency would not be good bed-fellows, also that the nasty side of fighting elections, unappealing to those who prefer quiet reasoned discussion, has to be coped with before 'service to fellows' can begin. As suggested in the first chapter, it is still essential for democracy that candidates come forward who are prepared to attempt the balancing act. Some do still manage this, combining sound argument, good humour and a smile and at the same time trying to avoid provocation. It is not easy, especially when supporters are baying for more vitriol.

LAND OF KIND PEOPLE WHO FEAR RUSSIANS

By OLIVER DE BAER,
Leader of the Cambridge Expedition to Afghanistan, 1955

AFTER travelling for two days across the featureless desert of Eastern Persia, we drew up at a barrier across the road. As there was no one to open it for us, we opened it ourselves, and so entered Afghanistan. From Herat, we decided to travel along the Soviet frontier to Mazar-e-Sharif, and then to turn south across the Hindu Kush. Everywhere we were greeted with extreme kindness by the local people, who had no hesitation in telling us of their fear of Russia.

However, even in the smallest hamlets we also found someone who would hold forth on the evils of Pakistan, and on the supposed suppression of Pathans in that country. Many of the more irresponsible elements declare they are ready to go to war.

Crossing the mountains named Paropamisus by Alexander the Great over 2,000 years ago, we entered the Oxus plain, a desert where midday temperatures reached 125 degrees in the shade. We began to notice peasants with portable telephones tapping the wires, and this, coupled with the feeling of being expected when we stopped in villages, convinced us that everything we did was watched. We received confirmation of this in Kabul, where we were told that not only the route we had followed, but even where we had camped had been reported. Other foreigners in Kabul had similar experiences to recount.

Kabul "a Village"

The main impression given by Kabul was that of a large village. Donkeys are far more common in the streets than motor-cars, many of which belong to foreigners; water is supplied by gutters running down the sides of the streets; the women all wear dark *chadris* (veils), which descend to their ankles.

Now that trade with Pakistan is on a very reduced scale, and the Iranian frontier very little used—as much because of the lack of roads as because Afghanistan is in dispute with Iran over the waters of the Helmand River—it would be easy to imagine that Afghanistan has become another Soviet satellite. Nothing could be further from the truth. If the petrol comes from Russia, nearly all the lorries that use it are American; if it is the Russians who are surfacing the streets of Kabul, it is the Germans who are building a hydro-electric station on the Kabul River. In spite of apparently cutthroat Russian tenders, the contract for carrying out preliminary drillings for oil has gone to a Swedish firm. Few contracts are given to Britain, which is greatly mistrusted for the part which she is supposed to be playing in supporting Pakistan in the present dispute.

Banned Areas

Where Britain and Russia are mistrusted, where Americans are accepted provided that they are *dona ferentes*, Germans are sure of a welcome. A knowledge of German is almost as useful as a knowledge of English, and in countless out-of-the-way places it is possible to find German and Austrian technicians sometimes ex-Nazis—running electricity stations, cotton mills or sugar factories.

The United Nations Technical Assistance Mission, which trains Afghans for the improvement of agriculture, health, industry and a host of other underdeveloped aspects of the nation's economy appears to be universally admired. Much of its popularity may be ascribed to its being entirely non-national and non-political.

Our applications to enter several areas were refused, but eventually we heard that we would be permitted to visit the little-known and isolated province of Badakhshan, in the north-east of the country.

We left Kabul at the end of July, and headed north through the magnificent scenery of the Hindu Kush. Jagged scenery of the Hindu Kush. object was to survey the area

towards which we were now heading, and we set up a camp at Barak, some thirty miles to the west of the Soviet frontier. We were able to explore and photograph a number of valleys which were unmarked and which no European had ever penetrated before.

We stayed in Barak until the middle of August, as we intended to watch and photograph the yearly migration of the nomads as they came down from Lake Shiwa. We had been refused permission to visit these tribesmen in the 12,000-foot high pastures where they spend the three summer months, but we received news just in time that the lake had frozen over and that the migration to the Oxus plain was beginning.

Colourful People

These people were by far the most colourful that we had seen; they are Pashto-speaking Pathans whose way of life is doomed by the plans which the Afghan Government has for settling them. They still wear their tribal costumes and set up their famous black tents as they have done for centuries. The haughty-looking women scorn to wear veils, whilst the men all carry rifles of an ancient pattern and wear great bandoliers. Their horses and camels are among the best in a land renowned for both.

Our movements were severely restricted for security reasons. To the north lay the forbidden Lake Shiwa, whilst to the south, tantalisingly visible but equally forbidden, lay the snow-covered peaks of Nuristan. As one of our objects had been the measuring of one of these—said to be over 22,000 feet high—it was a very great disappointment that we were not to be allowed outside the very limited area in which we were working. We had security officers attached to us night and day, and all our movements were watched most carefully.

After leaving Barak, we headed for the town of Kishm, near which lies the 12,000-foot high Hezarat-e-Mohammad mountain—the highest peak in the area that we were allowed to climb. The unbelievably sure-footed Badakhshan ponies —whose fame had reached the Grand Khan Kublai seven centuries ago—took us with uncanny ease to within a thousand feet of the summit. We had at least climbed a mountain which no European had climbed before.

[WORLD COPYRIGHT]

The expedition was widely reported. We also have cuttings from *The Yorkshire Post, Cyprus Mail* and *Tanganyika Standard*

Mr. Balfour was one of a four-man scientific expedition which boarded an air charter plane on June 16 for the beginning of a 5,500 mile trek to their research area which was centred at Bahrek, a village near Faisabad, in the province of Badakhshan.

"While obtaining our permits on arrival in Afghanistan, I was amazed to see, in their files, copies of the Portsmouth Evening News and the Hampshire Telegraph and Post containing stories of our proposed expedition," said Mr. Balfour. They crossed the mountain

Portsmouth Evening News
24th September 1955

In a room piled with [...]
equipment and lined wit[...]
of remote oriental [...]
Oliver de Baer outlined [...]
the difficulties and haza[...]
ing the expedition. The [...]
brochure states that [...]
ghanistan "research [...]
tions are welcome," b[...]
members of this part[...]
spent the last four [...]
filling in thirty-two for[...]
providing 240 passport [...]
graphs of themselves [...]
effort to gain the r[...]
visas, and even so th[...]
pect to meet considera[...]
lays in Kabul, the cap[...]
Afghanistan. They hav[...]
told that they will [...]
allowed within thirty m[...]
the Russian frontiers, ar[...]
will be provided with in[...]
ters to guard their activ[...]

All the equipment f[...]
expedition has been p[...]
by various firms approac[...]
the party. One of the [...]
acquisitions was a bo[...]
thousand aspirins and a [...]
and codeine tablets. A [...]
vention which will hel[...]
is an electric shaving [...]
which runs off torch batteries.

Cambridge Varsity
4th June 1955

---

ranges of Hindu Kush at two points before reaching Bahrek, where they encamped to carry out two weeks' intensive study of the village — their religion, their customs, what the people eat and wear and how they live.

From Bahrek could be seen the most beautiful and northern-most ranges of the Hindu Kush—" so tantalizingly wonderful, but we were, unfortunately, not allowed to explore them because of the danger involved," said Mr. Balfour.

The party continued their research, journeying from village to village — filming, photographing and collecting soil specimens, insects and butterflies.

MOST GENEROUS

"Everywhere we went we were treated with hospitality and kindness — the villagers were the most simple and generous people I have ever met," Mr. Balfour told a reporter.

He went on: "We did not meet ferocious tribesmen, though late one night we woke suddenly to find 15 men surrounding us. To our relief it turned out to be the headman of the nearest village, who, fearing for our safety, had brought 14 of his men to guard us throughout the night."

The Sphere
25th June 1955

BY LAND-ROVER TO AFGHANISTAN : Three members of the Cambridge expedition to an uncharted region of Afghanistan are seen at Southend before leaving on their 5,500-mile drive across Europe and Asia. They will make a complete geological-botanical survey in Kaffiristan, an uncharted region, and will also try to locate a 24,000-ft. mountain.

LEARNING FROM DIFFERENCE

Chapter 13

Tussling with the Tories. Parliamentary candidate

In February 1967 I received a letter from the Chairman of Gloucester Conservative Association, a solicitor and businessman. Here are some extracts:

'I can not help feeling that you should have discussed the relevant parts of your speech with me. Whilst clearly you are entitled to exercise an independent judgement you do represent a large Association so that not only must you consider your position and whether you are able to carry on as prospective candidate but I must also consider the effect your remarks had on the Association members. A condition precedent to any final decision is that you must decide whether you are able to support the fundamental policies of our Party. If you have any doubts about this, clearly you can not put yourself forward as a representative. On the other hand if you are quite sure in your own mind that you can give the Party your full support then I must clearly discuss matters with my Officers, indeed possibly with the members generally as to whether the undoubted damage of your remarks can be overlooked.'

How was it that this letter came to be written when the previous Association Chairman, a teacher in one of the Gloucester schools, had written on 17th May 1965:

'I am looking forward immensely to working with you and I, personally, feel refreshed by your forward looking ideas.'

I still have Angela Darricotte's letter from the previous year in which she explained about 'the business of becoming a Prospective Candidate' and that 'practically all Conservative Associations are bound by their rules only to adopt Candidates on the approved list.' Angela also referred to the Gloucester City Association and 'that they had financial problems and have had no agent for the last twelve months.' (I did not then realise the significance of this remark!) After an interview with Paul Bryan, member for Howden and responsible for candidates, at Conservative Central Office on the 8th February (1965), I was accepted on this list. The following month I attended the interviews for the

Labour-held West Gloucestershire constituency but did not even make the short list for final selection. Afterwards I wrote:

> 'I had put it around that I would be happy to continue as candidate for many years in the Constituency where we had made our home so it was with high spirits that I drove down through the Forest in the old Bristol to the Victoria Hotel, Newnham-on-Severn. I had had encouragement from several sources including Angela - 'the sort of person the Party needs', she had kindly written. This encouraged me to think that I had a good chance of getting onto the short list. But I sensed a hostile atmosphere from the moment I walked into that dreary room with its dark brown paintwork to meet the Selection Committee. I found my-self facing questions which bore no relation to all the problems which I was so eager to discuss. With experience I might have been able to turn this to my advantage. Instead I floundered and even committed the great sin of admitting that I did not know the answer to one particular query. It was not much consolation to be told later that many had wanted me (and all the good work which Ann would have done in the Constituency) but that the 'wrong' people were on the Selection Committee. My rejection was an example of what can happen if superficially well known. Relatively knew to the area, we had already been active and perhaps too vociferous on local committees. Some may have regarded us as upstarts. It wasn't Hampshire or Fife where the family had had long associations. It is probably better to arrive either as a stranger or really well known - tried and tested.'

In fact I now realise that those down-to-earth 'wrong' people were right, though it was to be many years and much tortuous experience (including the words of the Gloucester Chairman quoted at the beginning of this chapter) before I realised that the initial steps towards Westminster politics were not about 'all the problems I was so eager to discuss'. There are other arenas for such discussions. Conclusions can then be fed to those in power. Those West Gloucestershire activists were seeking a seat winner who, at least in their early years in the Commons, would serve as loyalist lobby fodder. Realism about the pursuit of power was more important than utopian questioning ideas about a fairer society. I was only partially 'the sort of person the Party needs.' As I write in May 2013 there are references to grassroots Conservative activists as 'mad, swivel-eyed loons'. This is not a fair judgement on activists known to us. Those who serve in constituency associations will always be subject to conflicting pressures. Their efforts are a valuable contribution to democracy, particularly now when many MPs are young and with scant working experience. Association Chairmen, Chairwomen and other office holders are an important reservoir of knowledge and opinion. Critics of present governance may come to better understand by becoming involved and playing a part in tasks like choosing a candidate. There is so much experience from the generations which have served the Conservative Party. It still needs participants who will help in its evolution.

In April a letter came from the Gloucester Conservative Association: 'Your name has been submitted to this Association by the West Midlands Area office as a potential parliamentary candidate.' The city's Labour Member of Parliament was Jack Diamond who in the October 1964 Election (when Labour led by Harold Wilson won with a majority of four) had gained 4,117 more votes than the Conservative candidate. My first reaction was to decline, but then the challenge began to appeal (did I also want to get my own back on the West Glos people?) and in the end I presented my-self to the city selection committee. I was chosen for the final shortlist of three on the 29th April, but my letter to Ann, who was visiting her parents in France with Max and Juliet, illustrates my continuing hesitation:

'Gloucester do want us on the final short list and we must both appear before the Executive Committee on Friday. I shall be surprised if selected but obviously we must decide beforehand if we really want to try and do it. I have indicated that I would be prepared to stand at least twice if 'allowed off in the middle' for a period of other full-time work and will try to stick to this. (I reckoned that the seat could be won at the second or third attempt). It's a decision we must take together. I am not too sure my-self but I am quite sure that I can not attempt it without your full support. If we do it, it must be because we feel that is the way in which we can serve without adversely affecting the children.'

The drive down to Newhaven, again in the Bristol 400, on Thursday 6th May, 1965 is still remembered. The diary records: 'Leave Midhurst (where I had a snack) 2.15 p.m. Boat arrives Newhaven 4.20p.m.' That car, then twenty years old, as always stimulated on the 170-mile drive back to Compton House. The next evening, Ann and I presented ourselves with two other candidates at Winston Hall in Gloucester. After the then obligatory banalities about suitability and experience, I spoke of my ideas about the wider political scene. These are some of my remarks:

'An aim of politics must surely be to make best use of the country's human resources. Government must try to create the conditions in which all can develop their talents to the full. Yet at the moment there are still too many living in miserable circumstances in our big cities who, in the struggle for existence, have no chance to even think about their talents. And, above this level, our educational and social services lack both financial and human means. I greatly admire professional workers in these fields, teachers struggling in over-filled classrooms, youth employment officers and others concerned in the vital transfer between school and work, voluntary and statutory workers who believe that, given the resources, they could do so much more.

'I have come to realise the limitations of political action; no Government can achieve miracles. I still suggest that more can be done and that Conservative principles are better able to bring about improvements. We do not want Socialism. We do want better Conservatism but what we can do depends on the money that is available and we all know about this problem! In their budget the Socialists have made their intentions quite clear. They intend, through heavy taxation, to redistribute capital and thus achieve equality, to chop it off from the top and give it back at the bottom. Surely this is not the way to create the new wealth we badly need. Business needs to retain control of it's capital in order to finance growth. Growth is a process of nature. There are times when it is advisable to prune but it is surely unwise to hack off great branches.

'I support a free-enterprise capitalist system and suggest that the time may have arrived when Conservatives must defend this system more vigorously. Enterprising and industrious individuals need greater, not smaller, rewards for their efforts. We have got to demonstrate the merit of inequality. With growing awareness, this may be less unpopular than one thinks. Positive benefits can stem from conflict. Too much equality and too little competition can lead to flabbiness and we will soon be losing the cutting edge which Mr Wilson talks about. There are great dangers in mediocre togetherness.

'This idea of inequality is just only if the new wealth which should be produced is used: 1. To promote a system of social security which gives extra help to those who need it most. 2. To alleviate the faults that I have described in educational and social services. The ideal being that no citizen should fall below a minimum level. Above that there should be free competition.

'Inequality is also just if a proportion of those who are successful (and their children) realise that there is a duty to put back into life as much as one gets out of it. We need people with the freedom, which private capital should foster, to think, to stand against the crowd which is not always right.'

This speech reads now as being too idealistic, but British industry was still producing and exporting. A copy of *The Economist* from that period has an advertisement for the Rover 3 litre: 'Tie up a deal in Derby. It's a long way back to town. But you won't feel a thing. Cruise at 70. Easy. Dictate a letter, write a report. Arrive as fresh as you started.' That columns of Mercedes and other German makes would flow down the outer lanes of the planned motorways was then inconceivable. On another page: 'the BOAC VC 10 is triumphantly swift, silent, serene. It is the most advanced, the most powerful, jetliner in the world.' This plane and this company, Vickers, not Boeing, was, we thought, the future. At least we participate in Airbus and can be proud of Rolls Royce. It seemed reasonable to suggest that Britain could produce the revenue which would allow improvement in educational and social services, but I did not realise the quantity of resources which would be needed to achieve my ideals. In accepting and commending inequality, there was no thought that this would lead to today's enormous differences in income and wealth.

What I said seemed to appeal to the selection committee, for Ann and I were then chosen to represent the Conservative cause in Gloucester. At the end of the month I outlined our plans in the adoption speech to all supporters:

'During these first few weeks we want to concentrate on meeting those of you who do the work and keep things going in the Wards and Branches, in your Clubs. Then I would like to get to know and be known by as many people as possible throughout the City. I hope that canvassing will continue until we have visited every street within this Constituency.'

The professionals who advise candidates suggest that rushing round showing oneself to as many people as possible and just asking for 'pledges' is most likely to lead to a good result. I preferred to listen to problems on the doorstep, hoping that people would report favourably to their acquaintances and that a ripple effect might then lead to votes. The diary records speeches made, factories, offices and other organisations visited, all backed up by the continual canvassing. Adopted candidates received encouragement from the Party. Jim Prior (see also Chapter 15) had taken over from Paul Bryan. He took the trouble to write personally to each of us, mentioning individual constituencies : 'I am delighted to send my congratulations on your adoption as prospective candidate for Gloucester and hope you will keep in touch with me and let me know if there is anything I can do to assist.' We were invited to dinners at the House of Commons and made aware of the potential camaraderie if elected. The bond came from common, if disparate, experience in our local Associations. Douglas Hurd (already mentioned and will be again), of whom I was in awe at Eton, was present at one dinner. He was not adopted as candidate for mid-Oxfordshire till January 1972. At that time I was ahead of him on the greasy pole, but, as I slid down, he soon passed me on the way up to a magnificent career, always maintaining good humour. However neither of us have achieved 'One Nation' England. In his books he refers to 'eating and drinking for his country,' evidently a requirement for the job and beyond my capacity!

David Howell, director of the Conservative Political Centre and not yet an MP, though adopted as candidate for Guildford having contested Dudley in 1964, gave an inspiring talk at the Area CPC annual meeting in Birmingham.[1] His theme was that Labour's stock of ideas had run down. This was not a reason for partisan rejoicing on the Conservative side. The party's task was 'to work out the broad approach to the country's dilemmas which really will provide for the whole nation the spark which is at present missing. Talk about the party moving to the right was inadequate and parochial. It is this sectional way of looking at things which the party should now be trying to raise itself above.' After referring to the current new CPC pamphlets[2] David continued: 'a return has to be engineered in public debate to the truth that it is the individual who makes progress and creates wealth. Political emphasis should be turned to encouraging individual men and women to exercise their talents, skills and energies.' Sydney Chapman, then National Chairman of the Young Conservatives[3] supported David Howell in a letter to the *Telegraph* (May 1965) and added another theme which he called 'the just society.' He wrote: 'This means more than protection for the weak and compassion for the unfortunate in reorganised and expanded social services. It means also protection for the individual from the abuses of the State, the inconsistencies in the interpretation of the law, and the intolerance of petty-minded bureaucracy.'

We felt in tune with what the thinkers in the Conservative Party were attempting and wanted to help. But they were not going to win the next Election and I was not going to win Gloucester and achieve a parliamentary salary for maybe five or even more years. We had again toyed with the idea of filling the barns at Compton with carefully selected good old cars. I had thought of trying for the Hispano tourer at the Sword Auction at East Balgray in Ayrshire, then a Bugatti Aravis was for sale locally.[4] Local banks still would not play, that precious family capital could only be used at the discounted value, and what would we do about income? As has proved to be correct, such car purchases were about careful maintenance and storage with the hope of long-term capital growth. Shorter-term sales, subverting the objective, would be necessary to cover living costs. Then there were the strong vibes still emanating from remaining family contact, and even from associates, that other than utilitarian ownership (the Robert Birley well-meaning concern) was wrong, even sinful. Years later, I realised that one answer could have been to use the value of Compton House for membership of Lloyd's. I did not have the foresight or the confidence - and how would we have coped with the Lloyd's problems of the 1990s? More feasible was the invitation to consider paid work, joining the Youth Employment Service in Warwickshire after the next General Election. This had come about through contacts made when working for the Award Scheme, my own experience of the lack of access to this service, my awareness of comparative good fortune and the wish, now clearer after forsaking car trading, to follow on Myrtle's devotion to helping her fellows.

We already realised that Compton was haemorrhaging cash. A helpful local estate agent, who had introduced us to contractors to work the fields and was aware of our concerns, told us about a much smaller house with two fields and an orchard the other side of Redmarley. There had never been cars at The Twynings. The elderly owner, whose husband had died many years before, had till recently used a pony and trap. We thought this property would be a more sensible base if I was going to devote time to Gloucester and there was also the possibility of the work in Warwickshire. Our offer was accepted at the beginning of June and Compton was auctioned at the end of the month. There would be enough money in hand to extend and refurbish The Twynings. In August, Edward Heath became leader of the Conservative Party. We had agreed with the *Sunday Times* leader (25th July 1965):

'The Conservative Party is still the party of Disraeli's novels. It is a good-natured party and Mr Maudling is a good-natured man. It may well be natural for Conservatives to turn to him. Yet once before, with the younger Pitt, the Conservatives were led by a young, reserved, determined, tough-minded bachelor with a gift for economic policy. It would not go against the grain of the party's tradition to make such an out-of-the run choice again. It would be a more realistic assessment of the country's needs.'

I remain a strong defender of what Ted Heath attempted (see Chapter 15). At the 1965 Brighton Conference (13th to 16th October) there was much discussion of the new policy document 'Putting Britain right ahead', the 'achievement of literally thousands of people in our party who took part in the two-way movement of ideas and contributed their own views and thoughts.' Re-reading that conference report nearly fifty years later, I am reminded of my resolution to do all I could to help this man become Prime Minister. With Ann's full support, efforts continued in Gloucester. On the 20th, I spoke to the Women's luncheon club about 'The Conservative Tradition':

'One of the elements of this tradition is the feeling for history and it is therefore a delight and honour to find my-self sitting next to Lady Boyce[5]. Your presence provides the link between the last Conservative Member and hopefully the next Conservative member for this City. Another element is tolerance. If we feel that Conservatism represents thoughts and values which we feel are good, we must not automatically assume that Socialism represents the opposing evil. No party is wholly good, no party is wholly bad. No group of politicians has a monopoly of wisdom. What is important is that the stimulating clash of minds and the ever-increasing store of knowledge is leading us to a more hopeful view of man's future.'

I then referred to the Hailsham Penguin book *The Conservative Case*[6] with its stress on the 'secondary importance of politics':

'Relationships with others, home life, music, creative work, voluntary service, thrift - looking after property and possessions - to the Conservative these things are more important than the political struggle. It is because we value home life, freedom and the ideal of service that we will always oppose attempts to impose a political order. We believe that each of us must work out our own approach to life, must make our own decisions and mistakes.'

It was a long talk, with much about the value of institutions and traditions built up over centuries and I then turned to the land: 'a knowledge of the pace of growth and the rhythms of nature, walking across a meadow or past an old tree, one is aware of the passage of centuries, of past generations and the sense of eternal values.' I referred to Burke, 'a disposition to preserve and an ability to improve', and suggested that 'men and women imbued with Conservative traditions were more likely to take balanced decisions.' I continued: 'some of you may feel this is old-fashioned and out of place in the modern rushing world but Conservative are so often the first to keep in touch with new developments in science and technology.' I concluded with references to 'Mr Heath's inspiring speeches at Brighton last week and how we must show by our own lives that we equate service with Conservatism.'

This speech received good coverage in the local press and I was encouraged by a letter from an influential neighbour, who wrote of his appreciation of 'the search for the historical, fundamental and logical principles of Conservatism, the point made that this Party, although defenders of the best values of the past are none the less likely to make advantageous changes when needed because their approach is less bound by dogma is first rate.'[7] Looking back, this may have been the high point of this time as candidate. It reads now as too idealistic. Too many did not have the freedom to work out their own approach to life. Then, just a week later, I opened a letter from the Chairman of the Association: 'Things have not worked out in my part-time building business and an immediate halt has had to be called. Last week I obtained a senior post in a comprehensive school in the Midlands. I am confident that I hand on an Association in good heart with a first class candidate. I only wish the financial position was stronger.'

The new young Chairman was eventually elected and we pressed on with ward meetings, canvassing and visits throughout the winter. It's all in the diaries, including an encouraging candidate's briefing week-end, more camaraderie, at the Palace Hotel in Buxton. Remembered are the stimulating talks from Messrs Hailsham and Howe, the latter having spent the night in a train after encouraging other supporters in the South West. That amiable man, still contributing in 2013, deserves his later eminence.

Then the General Election was called in April 1966. The Association still did not have an Agent. Ann realised that her help was going to be needed. She took on many tasks and attended meetings with me. Fortunately we then had Margaret Willis to help with the children. She had retired to Redmarley with her husband and they both gave us support in many ways. At the start of the campaign, a young inexperienced Agent was allocated to Gloucester by Central Office. He did his best, but he did not have sufficient knowledge of all the forms, expenses sheets (to make sure that we had not spent more than was permitted) and the like. We had to do much of the work of planning our own campaign, writing articles for the local press, arranging visits to factories and other key places, ward meetings and canvassing, in addition to preparing speeches: particularly remembered is the advice and assistance from Nicholas Ridley, then member for neighbouring Cirencester and Tewksbury. He did not deserve the treatment meted out at Westminster after he had brokered a possible leaseback arrangement for the Falklands which would have prevented the bloodshed in 1982. Then there was the constant flow of written instructions from Westminster, providing suggested answers to be given or policy points to be emphasised. All sorts of organisations and pressure groups - animal welfare, foreign policy, health, safety, transport and many more - wanted the candidate's response and a failure to reply could mean the loss of precious votes. We did not have the well-oiled election machine which would have eased our task. I concentrated on the Conservative manifesto: 'Action, not Words', plus my accustomed way of trying to listen. This did not satisfy some of the activists who, towards the end of the campaign, were muttering about my attitude and the likely bad result for the Party. There had been much talk of economic crisis and divided opinion, including amongst Conservatives, about the need for a prices and income policy. Ian Gilmour's book *Whatever Happened to the Tories*[8] suggested that 'most people did not think that Labour had had a fair chance and tended to blame the Conservatives for what had gone wrong.' Harold Wilson returned to Downing Street with a majority of ninety-six over all other parties. However, the conservative vote in Gloucester increased by 164 when it had decreased in most other constituencies. Jack Diamond, then Chief Secretary to the Treasury, retained the seat and the Liberal candidate, Stina Robson, who had also been candidate in 1964, had her vote reduced by just over a thousand. There had not been a nasty word spoken. Jack was a friendly opponent and kindly congratulated me 'on doing so well in his first election against an established candidate.' A local paper was embarrassing in praise. I diffidently include as contrast to the sentences at the beginning of this chapter.

> 'Mr Balfour's success must have astounded even him-self. Completely raw to the hurly-burly of the political arena, against an opponent of the stature of Mr Diamond, and against a countryside swing to Labour, he held the Gloucester Tory vote steady and even polled more votes than Mr Stokes did in 1964. It was openly being feared by Conservative supporters that the Tory candidate might this time be third. Whatever the reason, however it came about, Mr Balfour confounded the prophets.'

The reason may have been that I had tried to listen to the concerns of all voters rather than fighting a partisan battle and attacking Jack Diamond, but, as a result, some members of the Association felt that I was not sufficiently on their side. Henry Fairlie's *The Life of Politics*[9] was published two years later: 'In spite of all the jokes made about the active constituency worker in spite of the legitimate criticisms of the part they play or appear to play in policy making, it is precisely in their free, fiery and selfless toil that the working of a representative system depends. To encourage and sustain the interest of the active constituency worker is a valuable part of the politician's work and its performance demands peculiar qualities. No politician who fails to retain the support and sustain the enthusiasm of his association can claim to be a good politician. When some disagreement arises between them he can not complain if he is bundled out by his own supporters.' Despite my failings in these areas, the new Chairman felt able to write in September (1966):

> 'Thank you for your very detailed report concerning the last and future election campaign. I am pleased to note that you are prepared to become our prospective candidate again.'

By then I was working full time in the Youth Employment Service. Many of the school leavers interviewed in the Leamington and Warwick schools had parents who worked in, or were associated with, the Coventry factories. This led to being fully aware of union pressures and other productivity issues. The new younger Chairman was reported in the local paper as saying that 'there was an overwhelming decision in favour of my adoption at a meeting of the finance and general purposes committee' and that 'Gloucester was now a winnable constituency.' This led to much reflection during that week in Warwickshire schools and factories. If there was now a chance of getting to Westminster, I felt I must warn Association members that I would want to speak about lessons learnt and might not always accept the Party whip. At the adoption meeting on Friday evening, 7th October 1966, my speech of acceptance may have had some merit in addressing national difficulties, but did not address the concerns of those loyal supporters. Henry Fairlie's book had not then been published, and I might have benefited from studying Politics instead of those tangled years, but study of politics at Cambridge was then less practical than, for instance, PPE at Oxford. Once again I was the poorer for the lack of employment or study guidance.[10] This is what I said:

'You have kindly asked me to become your candidate again. It has not been an easy decision. I am not very good at toeing this thing called the party line, but I remain a supporter of Conservative principles, interested in the future of this country, and with affection for Gloucester. There may be an advantage in having the same candidate for one or more further election, but this consideration must not be overemphasised. I take comfort from the knowledge that you will soon say if you do not like my views. For many years people have realised there are problems in this country that have got to be overcome, but the question has always been how to do this. Alas these problems were not solved during the last period of Conservative government but this was not for want of trying. One of the problems has been what is known as overmanning or underemployment. One of the solutions is in the measures taken by the present Government that have led to redundancies. This solution will, and is, producing the required internal shake-up, but it is also bringing with it many further problems which I hope a Conservative solution would have avoided. I am not prepared to condemn all Mr Wilson's actions and, whether one likes it or not, the Socialist solution is probably the only one acceptable to the electorate at the present time (i.e. after their majority in the election). Rather than getting worked up about the present situation, it was better to concentrate on more constructive things. First in doing all we can to work out the best possible Conservative solutions and then in helping people to understand what is involved in our plans.'

These I outlined on the theme of 'giving people the opportunity to choose' and then spoke of 'building up our association so that it can be run smoothly by busy men and women who also have their own work to do and the need to build up funds to be able, like most other constituencies at that time, to employ a full-time trained and experienced professional Agent. (Fred Davenport had been Labour agent in Gloucester for twenty-one years, the same time as the Tory agent in neighbouring Stroud). I concluded:

'I have purposely tried to talk without emotion and I am well aware that by nature

I am not an attacking man. I ask you to consider that the time has come for a more dignified approach to politics in this country. There is so much at stake in the world today. On the one hand total, or near total destruction. On the other hand a real hope of better things for the human race. Yet the shouting match goes on and on in which Party denounces Party. Somewhere we must have the courage to stop and I believe that there are many men and women who long for a more rational and sensible approach to our political problems. Our institutions, our methods of government have been the envy of the world. They could be again.'

In fact I now realise this is a bit of a naive approach. David Cameron used some of the same language before he was elected but then found that it was a difficult position to sustain against the reality of the tussle in the House of Commons. However 'John Severn' in the *Gloucester Journal* approved:

'Having read the headlines of Mr Balfour's speech I was wanting to slap him on the back and say 'Hear, Hear!' What he clearly accepts is that our present economic plight is not a party political issue, but a national one. It is no good bemoaning the fact that we have lacked strong leadership in the past and squealing the moment we have got it. We can not pass the buck like that. Leaders are useless without support. Tory and Liberal leaders may be in opposition. They may feel it incumbent on them to be as damaging as they can to the Labour government cause but the present situation is one which calls for a rallying of the nation. If any of the Gloucester Tory Party has qualms about Mr Balfour's line, let them take heart. This was the kind of speech which could do the nation - and the Tory cause around here - more good than they imagine.'

This was helpful to read at the time but some of the members did not take heart and did have qualms. They were less interested in my attempt to analyse current problems and did not like my reference to Mr Wilson. In saying that I was not an attacking man and not showing emotion, I was denying them what they wanted to sustain them in their toil for the Party. For some the Labour Party was the enemy. I regarded them as purveyors of different policies with which I did not agree. Anthony Meyer put this well in his book *Stand up and be Counted* published in 1990.

'Party workers, having no time for doubt them-selves, naturally look to their candidate or MP to proclaim the Party's policies with all the eloquence and force that they are expected to possess. When things are going well, a certain measure of dissent is acceptable provided that it is directed away from the centre, that is it is alright for Conservative MPs or candidates to express views which are to the right of the Party line and for Labour people to wander off to the left, but woe betide those who stray towards the middle.'

Twenty-five years earlier, the time I am writing about, the Conservative Party was often referred to as a 'broad church', where those who were not socialists but had differing views on some aspects of policy, could find a home. Whilst I had sympathies for those at the bottom of the pile and those who found themselves at odds with the powerful (this stemmed from my own experiences and family genes may have been at work), I was also already aware of the problems, as for my father, Lionel, of state control and nationalisation. I was on the left wing of the Party as regards educational and social matters, though still on the right on economic policies. This was an acceptable position, as discussed with the likes of Jim Prior at Central Office in London, but by the end of 1966 there were an increasing number of association members including, I think, the new chairman and his associates in Gloucester who were more to the right of the Party. It's in this situation that some political aspirants team up with the Liberals, now Liberal Democrats, a refuge for those - amongst others - who see merit in both sides. Election under the Liberal banner allows well-meaning people to serve and many do valuable work, but, in UK adversarial politics, there are occasions, as in 2010, when a choice still has to be made. I will write more on this in Chapter 15. It isn't an easy road to travel, as I was now finding, but as a middle-of-the roader, it seemed better to make the choice either as a right-wing Socialist or a left-wing Conservative. I chose the latter and would have been publicly labelled a 'wet' in the 1970s.

I should have been more aware of the thinking of those Gloucester right-wingers. A Constituency Agent would have helped in this. Instead, I had invited them to say if they did not like my views and some made it clear that this was so. The words of 'John Severn' were not heeded. Other parliamentary candidates will be aware of this perpetual dilemma. How much are you prepared to modify beliefs resulting from experience to attain and retain a place at Westminster? Compromise is necessary to achieve a position where there can then be a voice for concerns. I could have mollified those Association members, but Ann and I were also reflecting on our priorities. The work in the Youth Employment Service seemed to be important and might deflect others from the mistakes I had made. Whilst the pay was modest, there were allowances and certainly no time to spend other money, so finances were strengthened. The Association wanted more of my time than I was able to give. It seemed to us that what I was learning would be valuable in Parliament. They wanted me to concentrate on the political battle. And then there was the dilemma, which we did not then fully understand. Alcohol and good dining was part of the fabric of House of Commons life. That was one of the ways in which camaraderie progressed. I would often have felt 'out of sorts' and then probably tried to compensate with more stimulants. The basic food, certainly no alcohol, which kept me going through those long days in the schools, was a much better bet.

The Association still did not have an Agent at the annual general meeting in February 1967. An article in the *Telegraph* from that time mentioned that there were then 'just over five hundred full-time agents' and the party chairman was insisting that 'these professional politicians must be treated as managing directors of local associations.' At the meeting I said that a review of candidates was soon to take place at Central Office and wondered whether others were better able to carry the Party's banner at that difficult time. In subsequent questioning, I attempted to give non-partisan answers and confirmed my wish to continue working in Warwickshire till nearer the next election. Looking back, my uncertainty about income, changing Association attitudes and concern about whether I could deliver what they wanted, probably showed. There was a lack of confidence resulting from past happenings, together with the wish to speak openly about the problems I encountered. I wrote to the new Chairman: 'I have been summoned to Central Office. Largely through your efforts a stronger Association is being built up. It is important that you have a candidate with whom you are really happy.' I had a helpful discussion with the ever-friendly Geoffrey Johnson Smith, by then in charge of candidates. A letter sent in March 1967 to Jack Galloway, then West Midlands Area

Agent and another helpful professional, summed up the situation as I then saw it:

'I have realised for some time that some members of the Gloucester Association wanted a more aggressive candidate. The majority of the Officers have changed since I was originally adopted. I have felt the need for full support if attempting the ten (or more) year struggle to win the seat. It was important to settle this one way or other now rather than leaving it till the next election. At the AGM I unwisely answered questions a little too freely. But this may have been a blessing in disguise. The Chairman has made it clear that there are many who would prefer a different candidate. I have discussed this with Geoffrey Johnson Smith. He agrees that I should voluntarily come off the list of candidates and has kindly encouraged me to re-apply in a few years time.'

The Chairman took the right decision in writing the letter, from which there is an extract at the beginning of this chapter. I still clung to the ideal of common endeavour. Many will respond that such thoughts are unrealistic in this difficult human arena: that life is always a battle and that in seeking common endeavour, particularly in politics, one is running away from the facts of existence. Whilst my approach may have appealed to the voters generally, I knew it was important to be in tune with the Party members. If my continuing candidacy had been put to the vote, members would have taken sides. This would not have helped Gloucester Conservatives. I declined the offer of further discussion. On the 7th July 1967 the Association issued the following statement: 'At a meeting last night the Executive Council together with their prospective candidate, Christopher Balfour, mutually agreed that the Association should look for another candidate to represent them. Christopher Balfour fully supports this decision and has resigned which resignation has been accepted by the Officers of the Association. He is, however, continuing his connection with the Association and has accepted the position of Vice-President.'

I have already referred to the lack of funding and that as a result there had been no Agent. This is often a difficulty in cathedral cities where the church organisation sucks in available money and where many who work in the city live in neighbouring constituencies. I then set about using my new position to try and see that an Agent was taken on before the next candidate was adopted. Nothing had happened by the following July. I wrote to the new Treasurer, offering to front an appeal based on my experiences without an Agent. He replied: 'Frankly I am getting towards my wit's end for money raising ideas which I can put into effect and this suggestion comes like manna from heaven.' It was the Chairman who wrote back: 'Your offer is much appreciated and it may well be opportune to get such an appeal under way now since the selection committee have now short-listed three names for presentation to the Executive Council with a view to the adoption of a prospective candidate.' It was Sally Oppenheim who was then selected. My appeal was not necessary. In some way funds were arranged[13] and an excellent Constituency Agent was appointed. Sally had the sort of personality which appealed to those members. This is her message in the 1969 Association yearbook:

'I have called this message 'Into Battle' and this is where I want to lead you. Together we will go into the fight and win. No-one knows how long it will be before Mr Broken Promises Wilson finally has to acknowledge the collapse of his house of

152

cards. That will be our great battle day. Battles are won not only by valiant conduct in the field but by hard work to get troops fit and able to win. For my part I pledge I will do everything in my power to help towards the victory we are all determined to win on election day.'

There were then some appropriate comments about getting known in as many strata of local life and affairs as possible, of identifying with local interests and organisations and going out canvassing on a consistent basis. She concluded with the rousing: 'The glint of battle is in my eye. I ask you all to join with me in the fight with the words 'Up and at 'em.'

It was a different approach to politics. Such words, if I had uttered them, would not have rung true. The value of trying to be true to oneself is one of life's lessons. The problem of pressure from the likes of FG, Eton and others to conform to a particular pattern is that individual make-up may not be taken into account. We each have to decide: in this case to do what was needed to win in Gloucester, or remain in character? Sally did win the 1970 Election and remained an MP for seventeen years, including time in the cabinet as Minister of State for Consumer Affairs[14]. I had been wrong in writing to Jack Galloway and suggesting it might take ten years to win that seat. Jack Diamond, commenting some years later on his ousting from Gloucester, blamed 'the laughable last minute scare over devaluation'[15]. We do not know whether I would have won with a less aggressive approach and trying to explain the merit of Conservative policies. What is certain is that other appreciated experiences would have been missed and there is doubt whether I would have coped with Westminster life.

This chapter has attempted to explain something of a candidate's position. We need those who would like to serve, but they in turn need to be aware of the realities. Apart from aiming for Westminster, there are also all the vital voluntary offices and tasks in the Constituency Associations, including the selection of candidates. If there are those who share my preference for the 'middle of the road' rather than moving to the right, my hope is that these words help to show that, with much patience, influence is possible. The Party mechanisms, continuously honed over the years, exist to be used. There is no need for rebellion. Let us hope that there continue to be volunteers who are better suited and more capable in this task, than I was.

LEARNING FROM DIFFERENCE

Chapter 14

The Youth Employment Services and family life

In April 2012, a new publicly funded 'National Careers Service' started 'online' for those aged 13 and over. Enquirers and those who seek guidance are encouraged to make use of the website where they will find abundant information. There are over seven hundred job profiles, advice on CVs and interviews, and details of qualifications and training. The site is designed to be user friendly. Advisers are on hand to respond in eight languages[1] to telephone calls (though this may be by call-back) and emails - they state within 24 hours. The capacity of the Service is calculated as one million telephone and twenty million online sessions annually. Face-to-face advice is available, but only to those aged 19 and over, or to those aged 18 who are already Job Centre Plus customers, the estimate being that there will be seven hundred thousand such consultations. The thinking seems to have been that those in the 13-18 age group will have sufficient direct contact with advisers, plus some information whilst in full-time education, because of the efforts in recent years to increase career discussion in the schools and the raising of the leaving age.

This new Service is the latest development in the hiatus surrounding career advice which accelerated (there had always been the difficulties resulting from dual control, as will be described) in 1994 and 1995 when Michael Portillo, then Secretary of State for Employment, spearheaded the privatisation of then existing Careers Services through several rounds of competitive tendering.

This is the last letter in the series signed by James Paice, then Under Secretary of State:

'I was heartened by the response to the second round prospectus when more than 100 bids were received. The Government is looking for organisations that can meet rigorous quality standards in delivering careers services and provide value for money to the taxpayer.' The Prospectus with this letter states: 'The Department places no restriction on the kinds of organisations which may bid. We hope that a wide range of organisations, from both the public and private sectors, will consider bidding.'

The Hampshire Careers Service was one of the areas then on offer and we would soon have access to the Winchester house. I had already signed my first book contract (see Chapter 17), but we still wondered about trying to gather some former colleagues and submit a bid. At one of the exploratory briefings attended, I met up with Department staff encountered at the Bridge Project (see Chapter 16) and learnt that a large organisation from the private sector was showing interest. We would not be able to match their resources. The successful bidder turned out to be the shipbuilding and engineering company Vosper Thorneycroft. They ran the Hampshire Careers Service until their contract was terminated in 2002, by which time the Connexions Services, administered by local government and funded by central government, was being established. There had been a change of heart about 'the kinds of organisations', due to increasing concern about the number of young people unemployed. One report explains that this new service 'was not just to be careers advice but also to help the more needy who had personal and social problems which caused them to drop out of the system.' The stated aim was to help with 'money difficulties, health, relationships, housing, leisure and recreation as well as training and careers.' After a few years there were 47 such partnerships employing 7,500 personal advisers. This was not a universal service that was in contact with all school leavers. As the numbers of those 'not in education, employment or training' (now known as Neets) increased, those personal advisers were encouraged to give priority to this group. An Association of Colleges survey found that half of their students 'got no advice from Connexions because of this overarching objective to reduce the number of Neets' and advisers who had previously worked in the Careers Service were not able to make use of their wider professional knowledge.

By the beginning of the new century, careers guidance provision was becoming a muddle. The earlier services with the remit to meet with every pupil before leaving school, which I will soon describe and discuss, were no more. Many advisers tried to do their very best for their clients in Connexions. There is praise and criticism on the web. A comment from a Terry Miles in London hits the bull's eye: 'the problem with Connexions was that it was actually underfunded from the very beginning. The size of the challenge, to engage, listen to, guide, inform, advise and enthuse all young people, whatever their level of skills, whatever their level of exclusion, disaffection or disability, in a working world requiring ever higher levels of technical and people skills was completely underestimated and has been attempted on the cheap.' Prime Minister Cameron is reported on the web as commenting that 'Connexions has not been a great success story.' With the 2012 launch of the web-based National Careers Service, it was announced that 'there will be no expectation that local authorities should continue to provide careers services.' Authorities were free to make their own decisions. Hampshire, as an example, has amalgamated its relevant Connexions web pages into a Youth Tube website for young people. This has information about, and encouragement to use, the National Service and provides other advice and contacts. They have retained some of their advisers and set up a separate 'careers and employability service' whose work is intended to be part of education. Schools can buy adviser attendance in costed packages. The bronze package is one day a week for thirty-six weeks, the gold three days a week.

In January 2013, a House of Commons Select Committee reported their cross-party view that Careers Services were deteriorating. Their conclusions were that guidance by website and phone was not as helpful as a face-to-face discussion with an adviser, that increasing school responsibility for career advice was abdication, not delegation, and there was no enthusiasm for the return of the Connexions service. The Principal of a sixth form college in Worcester is reported on the web as saying: 'Information on line is not the same as a professional guidance adviser exploring the motives and ideas of a student.

You might as well ask why pupils come to school when they could just stay at home and read books.' In all the comments on this present state of guidance to young people, there is little acknowledgement of past efforts. For ninety years it was accepted that face-to-face discussion was helpful. When I was first involved in the 1960s, the concentration was on how to make guidance more effective; the omission that cost and James Paice's 'value for money for the taxpayer' was not at the forefront of discussion. Whilst deficiencies in some of the country's products like cars were recognised, the thought was that design and production in many industries would advance. It therefore seemed sensible to allocate some of the resultant tax revenue to help employers make the best use of the country's human resources, and school leavers to make best use of their talents.

After the 1966 Election, having banished thoughts of buying more Bugattis, Hispanos and their like, I joined the Warwickshire Youth Employment Service. Here was a chance to make use of what, hopefully, had been learnt from all my own mistakes. Experiences in the Army, in the Rootes factory, in the Lanarkshire and on the docks, together with our efforts in the fields at Compton and travel in different countries, had given me some understanding of the realities and pressures of different working situations. Could the sort of help missed at Eton be provided? The value of trying to increase wealth and using it wisely is now better understood, but at the time - probably as a result of previous experiences - I was harnessed to the idea of serving my fellows more directly whilst having sufficient funds for family survival.

Whilst finding my feet accompanying other advisers (we were then called Youth Employment Officers - YEOs), I began to learn about the origins of the Service. As the twentieth century began, the wish was for the State to help with the social problems resulting from the Industrial Revolution, in contrast to more recent years when the concern has been to reduce State-administered services. Employment Exchanges were considered and set up in a few areas. There was discussion of special assistance to 'juveniles'. I was then shown a book about the Service [2] and read that 'a Mrs Ogilvie Gordon had put forward a scheme for the establishment of Educational Information and Employment Bureaux by Local Education Authorities at a meeting of the Glasgow Union of Women Workers in 1904.' Over the following years her scheme, with the aim of 'leading all boys and girls who are physically fit towards employment likely to bring them a livelihood and prove congenial to them', was gradually adopted in many areas.[3] It was to be nearly fifty years later, during research for this book, that I learnt that Great-grandmother Rachel's brother, George Ogilvie, was married to Harriet Gordon, but no direct connection has been found.[4] In 1909 the Labour Exchanges Act provided that 'The Board of Trade may establish and maintain Labour Exchanges and may assist any Exchanges maintained by other authorities or persons.' In the debate on this Bill, it was Winston Churchill who spoke of co-ordinating the exchanges with the educational system for the benefit of school children: 'In some areas the matter would be more in the hands of the Labour Exchange and in others more in the hands of the Education Authority.' Thus from the beginning there was some uncertainty about the responsibilities of the two organisations. In 1927 it was agreed that the Education side could administer unemployment payments.

The more I read, the more I realised how much thought and effort had been given over the years to the provision of an effective Service. The Ince Report in 1945[5] was emphatic that the use of tax revenue for a 'Juvenile Employment Service' was worthwhile expenditure:

'The pivot of life of almost every boy and girl who has left school is the job. The chief function of the Service is to enable them to develop their potentialities through work to the utmost. If it is successful, it will make a contribution of incalculable importance to the life of every worker and the results will overflow into the whole personality of the worker as a citizen. The prime necessity is to enable employment which as nearly as possible matches capabilities. No-one is likely to be happy if the work is beyond their capacity or if on the other hand it fails to stretch their powers.'

The Ince Committee believed that 'it was in the best interest of every pupil to be given vocational guidance before taking employment' and that 'every school should be required to register all leavers with the Service.'

In February 1965, the year before I joined, a Conservative MP - Dr. Wyndham Davies - introduced a debate on the further development of the service.[6] He quoted a report in *Technical Education*: 'Every student interviewed claimed they were unable to get the information to make a rational choice' and even referred to 'Etonians who feel that their career advising is as inadequate as in many other schools.' Dame Joan Vickers spoke of 'the wrong job leading to frustration which may be one of the causes of delinquency' and also mentioned Mrs Ogilvie Gordon's pioneering work. There were many excellent speeches, none critical of the motion. That same year, Lady Albemarle's working party on the future development of the service produced forty ideas and recommendations[7]. The subsequent House of Commons debate on 'Albemarle' in January 1966 noted critically that there had been no decision on the dual system of administration ('this is not the time to make a change') nor any conclusions about another name for the service which included careers advice, not just employment. James Kilfedder, MP for Belfast West, suggested the 'Vocational Guidance and Employment Service' and emphasised: 'I believe part of the reason for the delinquency problem we have to-day is frustration, caused not only by dead-end jobs but by the fact that a youngster has taken up the wrong employment. Most of the young people who appear before our courts have a record of having been in many jobs.' Other speeches mentioned the importance of consulting parents, though this would add to the work of YEOs, who already had large caseloads.[8]

I was starting in the Service at a time when its value was recognised and found in John Skew a Principal who was determined to provide the best possible service with the limited resources. For some weeks, the days were spent learning about local jobs, the contents of the careers library and the then accepted interview techniques. In the files there are fourteen foolscap instructional pages, which included advice on school talks and group discussions, compiled by John and his senior staff. 'Oken' was one of the schools to which I was allocated. The Headmaster wrote to parents:

'As part of his work our Careers Master arranges for parents wishing to do so to meet the Careers Advisory Officer (John Skew opted for this title) so that one or both parents may be present when he talks to a boy at school during his weekly visits.' Appointment times followed then: 'Mr Balfour realises that young people often have difficulty in choosing a career. He will ask your son about his interests, encourage him to find out about different careers and explain the opportunities for further discussion before he leaves school.'

The diaries for those years record lists of interviews on most days, interspersed by visits to employers and colleges. The half-hour allocated never seemed long enough and it was difficult to switch from one discussion to the next. Sympathy for doctors and others with large case-loads has continued. John Skew insisted on a confidential record under the headings: 'Health, physique and appearance; education; interests and aptitudes; personal qualities; family circumstances and parent's views; pupil's choice; summary and recommendations.' The mandatory requirement to see all pupils meant time given to those whose futures were already mapped out, but on the other hand there was contact with those who really could benefit from help, even if not always accepted. One learnt to adjust and use part of the less-needed interview time to catch up on notes or extend other interviews. A regime of only voluntary interviews, though much less time-consuming, could mean that some of the more needy were not helped. As today, potentially helpful assistance may be lost by the lack of face-to-face contact. At the end of the day, records were checked and salient details were transferred (either personally or by an assistant in the office) to wallet-type card documents known as the Y. 1B and Y. 1G, buff for boys and light pink for girls. This card was also the record for issuing national insurance cards, then still paid out by the careers offices and the valuable handle for encouraging young people to visit. Amongst the sections inside the wallet was 'review of progress' through which we tried to keep in touch and help when there were problems. This is another function lost today.

These were good years, which seemed to be more worthwhile than the tussles in Gloucester. Minimal food intake during the day, but making sure there was some nourishment in the car after the interviews, seemed to work. We bought a small house in Leamington while The Twynings was being extended and refurbished. The roads back to Redmarley were well-travelled. We returned for most weekends and sometimes mid-week. Still determined to support British cars, the Austin Westminster (purchased in its cheapest basic form) was one of the few in which my 6' 4" frame was comfortable, but it was a tiring, heavy car to drive and had no power steering. Ann managed to successfully produce our second daughter, Kate, which might not have happened if we had continued in national politics. Our son Max started at the local primary school which, as I was working within the state education system, we wanted to support. The classes were large and discipline was poor. The young teacher accepted that control was difficult. We were faced with the now-familiar parental dilemma: support and try and play some small part in improving the state sector, or find the money for a fee-paying school. The compromise was untidy and meant more disruption and hard work for Ann. I had applied for the odd more senior position and found myself summoned for interview by the London Borough of Merton. This led to the offer of the post of Principal Careers Officer at a three times greater salary, which I then accepted.[9] The Leamington house was sold and a flat was bought in Wimbledon. Juliet became a day pupil at the excellent Wimbledon High School. Max boarded at the fee-paying junior school at Cheltenham, whilst I found myself struggling with some input into the state system.

The appointment at Merton started at the time of the June 1970 General Election. I had coped with Myrtle's death and Nicholas Cayzer's actions, but I have always remembered that evening of the count alone in the flat and the spine-chilling shock when the news came through that Sally had won in Gloucester as part of a Conservative victory, unexpected by many forecasters. It was possible that I too could have got to Westminster if I had fought my corner with the Association, and had had a suitable Agent, but any distress soon vanished when faced with work realities. The politicians had maintained their interest in the Employment Services. Lord Longford had followed Lady Albemarle as chair of the

National Youth Employment Council. The report in his name published in January 1970 had recommended a mandatory local authority service available to all young people up to the age of 22 or still in full-time education.[10] One of the arguments against a national service, which resonates today, suggested that 'the quality of collaboration achieved by an outside agency subject to Whitehall direction could not compare with the teamwork of colleagues who see their careers officer as belonging to the same area and employer as them-selves.' A minority suggestion, mainly from employer representatives, did want 'a national all age vocational guidance service, locally based, which would ensure local control and direction.' In December 1971, the Department of Employment published their conclusions in 'People and Jobs'.[11] Decisions now took over from discussion. Local authorities were to have their power extended to provide a careers guidance and placing service for school leavers and students in colleges of further education, irrespective of age. YEOs were to be renamed Careers Officers. The payment of unemployment benefit for young people under 18 was to be taken away from education authorities and paid out as part of the benefit arrangements administered by the Department of Employment. Many of us disliked the loss of that valuable handle for maintaining contact. This meant that the first port-of-call for a person in difficulties was not to be the adviser linked to the education arena seen when leaving school. Today the metamorphosis is complete. There are no Careers Offices, only the online website. Taxpayers' money has been saved, but at what cost to human aspiration? Many of the issues discussed at the time can be studied in the report of the House of Commons Employment and Social Services sub-committee sessions 1971-2 and 1972-3.[12] The Trades Union Council questioned the transfer of benefit payments: 'advantageous to the individual concerned if he could receive from a single source the advice and help available. Whilst the intended transfer might permit concentration of limited staff resources upon the primary function, a comparable gain could be achieved by more generous staffing.' A far-seeing MP, Timothy Raison, made the point that: 'an education service sees its job as training young people for the work they want to do and are suited to do but not necessarily for the work which is going to be available.' He then referred to the then current period of high unemployment (in no way comparable to the present situation) and suggested that: 'where to put the emphasis is going to be a permanent and very big argument.' This is where we are today with jobs. Personal choice and suitability versus availability. A thoughtful Fabian Society pamphlet had commented: 'It cannot be stressed too much that vocational guidance divorced from the realities of placement can be a grave danger.'

The previous lady Principal in Merton had retired and the Committee had taken their time over finding a replacement. I was shown the proposals for the new Careers Office, which was to be included in the new Merton Technical College then under construction. Meanwhile, we had to cope with the upstairs floor of a house in the middle of a residential road, not the most welcoming location for someone seeking assistance, and Officers did not attend some schools. The sub-office in Mitcham was better situated and looked after by the deputy Principal, whose application to lead the service had been rejected. Understandably, he was not well-disposed to my arrival. A more fundamental difficulty came from the Education Authority's determination not to increase the funding. The choice had to be made if the service was now going to be offered to all schools in the Borough. Should the caseloads of the other Officers be increased, or should I try to combine a full caseload with the administrative work? Looking back, it may have been foolish to attempt the latter. The Labour Government had championed neighbourhood comprehensive schools in the 1960s. The Conservatives, having won that 1970 election, stopped the compulsion to change, but it was too late to reverse the decisions taken in Merton in 1969. Perhaps helped by my background, I was acceptable to upmarket Rutlish, which had been a grammar school when John Major had been a rather unhappy pupil there a decade or so earlier.[13] As a new comprehensive, they needed our assistance with the more diverse intake. Wimbledon College, founded by the Jesuits in 1892, seemed to have more difficulty in adjusting to the new government-maintained voluntary-aided status. The staff, accustomed to teaching able pupils, were finding it difficult to cope with some of the new recruits. Seared in the memory is one of the days when, before talking to all leavers, I was introduced as the person who would soon find jobs for them all. I knew only too well that there were pupils in that large class whose reading and writing abilities were still inadequate.

In the schools three or four days each week and then back to the Careers Office for administration, this was a busy time. There was good support from the other Officers and Employment Assistants and, after a while, understanding with the Deputy Principal. I tried to support and encourage in what was always going to be demanding work and started to make the case for an additional post. There were interesting other activities. All Principal Careers Officers (PCOs) in the London area met up several times each year. They were suspicious of this Etonian, I think the only one in the Service - 'what on earth is he doing here?' etc. I hope those dedicated men and women came to accept me for myself. I had great respect for their commitment to their fellow humans. There was an invitation to talk to all Councillors after one of their meetings. I did not take sufficient regard of my lowly employee status and spoke in 'Gloucester candidate mode', commenting on decisions taken by the Labour Government that affected education and the service. It wasn't particularly critical, but labels mattered and mine now said: 'Do as you are told - you can tell us about what you are doing, but we do not want your views on wider issues.' 'You have earned a black mark,' said one of the Merton Councillors later. All through these years I felt I was the same person, interested in learning and trying to make life a little better, but to others the value of any utterances seemed to relate to that label and the status of the position. We were trying to keep The Twynings in order, hoping that the time might come when we would again be based in that beautiful part of West Gloucestershire near the border with Herefordshire. An adjacent farmer coped with the fields. The older six-cylinder Bristols had been sold and we had bought a secondhand V8, another British car into which I could fit. The power steering and easy response was a great benefit round the roads of the Borough and on weekend visits to Redmarley, but there was a downside. In a 'tea-break' at one of the few meetings attended when some Councillors and the Chief Education Officer were present, there was conversation about the latter's recently acquired Jaguar 2.4, evidently his pride and joy. Because of my interest, I praised the Jaguar and then mentioned the good service we were getting from the Bristol. It was made clear that junior officers did not speak even during refreshment and the thought that an employee of such low status should be driving a Bristol seemed to rankle. This was another black mark.

There was then an invitation to talk to the local branch of the National Council of Women, the organisation with which Mrs Ogilvie Gordon had worked. Janet Fookes MP had been the previous speaker after winning the old Merton and Morden constituency.[14] I felt I was speaking as myself without a restrictive label and there were no scowls when I began by referring to Janet, wishing her well, and mentioning my previous political effort which had led me to conclude that I was better suited to try and do things rather than discuss. I touched on the shortage of resources, how there was never really enough time for interviews, but that budget restrictions had to be accepted. I explained how one learnt to realise that some had already worked out realistic aims, so that more time could be given to the many who were uncertain. Our approach was not authoritarian but rather to explore strengths, weaknesses and interests, to discuss what jobs were available and to explain the qualifications and training which would be required. A particular concern were those who I see I then called 'lame ducks' - probably not an acceptable phrase today - those who could not settle down, or had made a bad start. I mentioned the importance of working with Careers Teachers and Employers and how much one appreciated the invitation and opportunity to spread knowledge of our work. I treasured the subsequent letter of thanks: 'We all very much appreciated what you had to say and wish you every success in what you are trying to do in this important area of education'. The Secretary enclosed a cutting, which as she wrote: 'far from criticising, seems to show awareness of your many problems.' Looking back and re-reading what I wrote at the time, the difficulties stemmed from our position in the pecking order. This was an aspect little discussed in the reports on the Service's future. The Youth Employment Committee was a sub-committee of Education and in addition in Merton all new posts were considered by an appointments sub-committee. Those who took the decisions had no contact with those who did the work. It's all academic now that there is no face-to-face careers service, but it seemed then that if we had been a separate department rather than a junior branch of Education, we might have been able to provide a better service. At least I had control over the budget for the new offices at the Technical College. I had seen other offices where callers were met by a glass window with a notice to ring a bell. A welcoming entrance seemed preferable. By saving on other things, an open-plan reception desk made by a local shopfitter was achieved. Remembering Warwickshire, a comprehensive careers library was built up, available also to all college students. Relations with the new College Principal were good and I persuaded him to set up a course for school leavers who did not soon get a job. I wanted a better deal for those leaving the new comprehensive schools still unable to read or write properly. He was understandably concerned when he realised how much remedial teaching was needed.

After some years of this work, health problems returned. It was difficult to avoid picking up infections in the schools and this led to sinus problems, which were then aggravated by hay fever. In addition, Lionel had confided (with instructions not to tell his third wife) that he had been diagnosed with a weakened heart after some virulent virus and would not live long. There would be much work as executor and trustee. Owning the two houses was becoming more difficult and we had had problems with a tenant. We decided that the time was coming when we should move back to Gloucestershire (Lionel died a few months later). There was the sort of hassle in Merton which I had already experienced, but eventually a new Principal was appointed. It was gratifying to receive some appreciative letters from local school heads, all showing understanding of the difficulties encountered. We then realised that it would be better for our two daughters if they stayed another year at Wimbledon High School. The Merton Service was still short of one careers officer, so I volunteered to work three days a week whilst also coping with the executorship and much else. This was not regarded as an acceptable proposition from a now ex-Principal, but friends in the Service soon told me that there was a shortage of Officers in neighbouring Surrey. They seemed happy with a part-time position. I had an enjoyable year working with some good schools, without the hassles of Merton administration. I was asked to take up permanent posts in Surrey and Kent, but we opted for the return to The Twynings, now free of tenants. Max, after some deliberation, did go to Eton. He had been accepted by Norman Addison, with whom I had got on well when I had been there. Juliet went daily to Cheltenham Ladies' College, soon followed by Kate. There was enough money in hand to start taking control of our own lives and without having to remember one's status before daring an opinion.

LEARNING FROM DIFFERENCE

Chapter 15

Self Employment Again. Defending Ted Heath.
Local Politics

The years at Merton helped me to understand the difficulties of trying to serve humanity in a taxpayer-funded service. Everything attempted had, rightly, to be a compromise and I was not good at this. Money for every sort of public service, including all forms of government, does not grow on trees. It comes from those who make profits through their hard work. I had been too cavalier in my attitude to making and increasing wealth. To be in control, setting my own standards - however small the enterprise - and having more time for the family, was much more satisfactory and more suited to my make-up. As I did all the paper work for Lionel's estate, I began to understand his decision to always work for himself despite all the financial hazards and why he was determined never to be an employee. We knew he had suffered from migraine headaches, that alcohol did not suit and social banter did not appeal. What he had wanted was creative work and to keep busy so that there was less time to dwell on what might have been with Myrtle, the Aerocar and Portsmouth Aviation. As I now know, all this was firmly in the genes. The Balfour and Joachim forebears we have been able to trace were all creative artists or entrepreneurs. It had taken all the diverse experiences recounted in earlier chapters to reach the same conclusion, but how were we to survive when I had given up the profession that had been achieved? The only benefit left in Lionel's estate was a small income deriving from oil royalties resulting from a purchase in Canada by his father, Max. It was difficult for Ann coping with uncertainty but, looking back, she seemed to have had superhuman stamina and never complained. In particular she did much of the school journeying. After unsatisfactory experiences with small British cars, which always seemed to be delivered with assembly faults, we did what so many other car buyers have since done and sought out the best and most economical machine for the task.[1] As Ann recalls, it wasn't the easiest car to drive, but day after day, in and out of Cheltenham, the small Saab (with Ford engine) was consistently reliable and cut costs.[2]

Some property dealing had worked better than others, particularly the Wimbledon flat, and there had been a small profit on Compton. As a result, there was no mortgage on The Twynings and we could do the work in the fields ourselves without incurring a wages bill. There was enough cash for our kind of survival. With relatives no longer around to chide, I turned back to my car interest, making use of knowledge gained and also hoping to achieve some profit. The V8 Bristol was sold and replaced at much lower cost by a six-cylinder Bristol needing work. The 406 was the last Bristol-engined car and we soon found that after fifteen or more years of hard use, their engines could need expensive work. Also, despite the strong chassis, all-year use on British roads had often led to corrosion in the areas above the rear axle. We then found there were 406s lying around half-abandoned because their owners could not afford repair. We purchased three of them, average price £500, two with engines dismantled, one with battered body and no engine. One rescue trip was to Northern Ireland where the Austin Westminster towed the remains onto the ferry. This was not appreciated at Liverpool, where vehicles were not allowed to be towed. I may have remembered previous weakness in that city: now I had learnt to be tougher. I said 'you choose; throw it over the side, take it back to Dublin or let me tow the car off.' That time I won the day. Once it got around that we had two complete sets of engine parts, we soon had some handsome offers from those who wanted Bristol engines for their sports and racing cars.[3] At the time we were concerned that we were taking part in the destruction of potentially good cars, but one of the carcasses was soon used to rebuild a 406 which had been in an accident and now, forty years later, we have plans to install what is now a more suitable engine in the other. The third chassis, with body panels removed, was taken, again by the Austin though this time with trailer, to the school of mechanics at Eton where Max worked away and became a proficient welder. The school's encouragement was an advance on the situation in my time. When Max needed more capital for his business, this then excellent chassis was sold and became the basis of another rebuild.[4] All in all, more usable cars may have been saved than if we had attempted to rebuild the originals. All components were used and the total outcome was profitable for us. The first 406 remains with us in good order, now driven all over Europe and much enjoyed.

The clue to this modest little success was having no money-grabbing factory costs or the like (no Portsmouth or Christchurch). There were enough sheds at the Twynings for our purposes and we did not come into conflict with the then dictatorial local planning laws, a subject with which I later became much involved. We found the wreck of a Delahaye 135 which was gradually restored to working order. The self-proclaimed Delahaye expert of that time offered us a fair reward for our labours, insisting that he had the contacts to finish the car off to a higher standard than we would achieve. Soon after he had taken the car, we learnt that he had sold it on to another owner who intended to strip off the body we had restored and turn the car into a replica racer. That was another lesson about the ways of humankind. It all helped in trying not to be naive or foolish, and always wary of one's fellows, in later life. A Lancia Aurelia B12 saloon found discarded behind a country garage was a happier outcome. Again, we got that delightful car running (see Chapter 16) and some years later it went to a collector in Switzerland. With a little of the profit another wreck, this time a Hotchkiss, was purchased and stored as a project for the future. In all these efforts I was greatly helped by Bill Limb, a knowledgeable and very hard-working engineer, who over the years had built up his own garage in Ledbury. We thought of entering one of the Bristol 406s in the first planned Peking to Paris re-enactment. Bill did a lot of meticulous work on the carcass before we learnt that the event had been cancelled. It is that car which may soon take the road again with another engine. Then Ann's nonagenarian aunt died in Devon, which meant more sorting, and the Austin did useful work ferrying things back to Redmarley.

We were fully occupied and I should have been content with my situation, but the interest in politics still nagged. One can never really judge one's own motives, but I like to think it wasn't the desire for recognition or those MP letters. Maternal relatives (I did not then know about Sir Robert) had been in Parliament. The wish, as I have already written, was to use that education to make things better for one's fellows. A more realistic aim might have been not to make things worse. 1974 was the year in which the Conservatives, led by Ted Heath, lost two elections. Reading many books about those events shows again and again how it could have been otherwise and the Conservative Party today might have been a different animal.[5] As in all politics, which makes that life so fascinating, different decisions by - and advice from - single individuals could have led to a Conservative victory. Looking at the background to 1974, one significant happening was the Labour Party's rejection in 1969, when they were in power, of Barbara Castle's White Paper entitled 'In place of strife'.[6] This followed the Donovan Report[7] which had set out 'a diagnosis of the chaotic state of British labour relations'. (I knew from my time with the Employer's Association in Birmingham that this was not all one-sided.) The story of the tussles within the Labour Party is fully set out in the Conservative Campaign guide for the 1970 election.[8] According to this guide it was Jim Callaghan, later Prime Minister, who found himself caught between the wishes of Harold Wilson, Barbara Castle and others and, as Labour Party Treasurer, the demands of the Unions who financed the Party.[9] The result was that when Ted Heath won in 1970, he and his Party were faced with 'the most politically powerful trade unions in the world'.[10] An incomes policy (the measure I would not condemn which had caused some of my problems in Gloucester) was introduced in 1972 then agreed by 'the overwhelming majority of MPs.'[11] Next came the Arab-Israeli war which led to shortage of oil and increased the bargaining power of the National Union of Miners (NUM). The three-day week was imposed at the end of 1973. Ian Gilmour's book states that there was a possibility of a settlement with the TUC and, through them, with the miners at a meeting on the 9th January 1974 and that 'the Government made a decisive misjudgement.'

Douglas Hurd wrote in his autobiography:

'Discussion of the need for - and value of - a general election increased. Different opinions were voiced by tired Ministers. It is still the opinion of many that the Conservatives would have been re-elected in a 7th February election. Though it can not be proved, I believe we would have won on the 7th.'[13]

The last announcement date was 17th January. Ted Heath, who had also been coping with the Sunningdale agreement on Northern Ireland, a European summit and much else, did not wish to go to the polls. In Douglas Hurd's words: 'Ted believed passionately in reason. Sometimes ministers had come tantalisingly close to agreement with union leaders. One more meeting, one more exposition of the national interest - it might be right to persevere rather than despair.'[14] Then, when the NUM executive called for a strike ballot, the result published on 4th February showed that 81 percent supported the strike call. Douglas Hurd: 'Ted made clear how deeply he disliked the idea of an immediate election, but he could no longer offer an alternative. On Tuesday the 5th February I joined him (and Tim Kitson and Francis Pym) at Pruniers. Ted explained more clearly than ever his desperate worry about the size of the stake. Everything he had tried to accomplish seemed at risk.'[15] The Election was called for 28th February and Labour won with four more seats, though the Conservatives received more votes. Even then, if there had been a different Liberal leader than Jeremy Thorpe, perhaps a coalition could have been formed, a precursor of present times. This is part of the *Sunday Times* leader for March 3rd 1974:

'Mr Heath made a brave try. The electorate has neither voted for the Government nor a simple Labour alternative. It has given a non-partisan mandate for moderation. It has produced a stalemate between two parties without the benefit of a single third party strong enough to hold the balance. One logic of this is to justify Mr Heath in his efforts to stay on'.

(The article continued mentioning the 'transmutation of the eleven Ulster Unionists into political opponents - a self-inflicted but necessary wound -' and referring back to 1929 when Stanley Baldwin resigned in favour of Ramsay MacDonald, even though the Conservatives again had more votes.)

These efforts did not work out and, like Stanley Baldwin, Ted Heath went to the Palace but, unlike SB, never became Prime Minister again. I have always had immense sympathy for him. I met him once at a candidate get-together after I was adopted for Gloucester and when he was fresh to the job of leader. It is often reported that he was uncommunicative and lacked the social graces, but seeing him face to face and aware, from all I had read, of what he was trying to achieve, I felt in tune with his objectives. Here was a man, like self, like Lionel and other Balfours, who was not attracted by banter and gossip - he just wanted to get on with the job. Philip Ziegler's biography tells us so much, both through his own researches and quotes from Ted Heath's own writing.[16] Put together, the following quotes explain his thinking:

'His determination to help articulate and later implement a new brand of Conservatism.'
'Throughout his life he was repelled by the standards of unbridled capitalism and the defeatist philosophy of laissez-faire.'
'The ''One Nation'' approach is the only right approach to social and economic problems in this country today.'
'He did know about people. He took great trouble to know about them and their backgrounds and what they wanted. He enjoys people, but I don't know that he needs them. He's extraordinary self-sufficient.' (This comment when he was a whip).
'Throughout his career, even when the facts pointed most vigorously to the contrary, Heath believed that the uncontrollable could always be controlled, the irreconcilable reconciled.'
'He had a heart full of kindness but there was also an element of reserve and awkwardness which held him back.'
'He had quality and vision. Even if he never dared to show it, he had a softer side which we understood.'

These ideas, carefully working out what needed to be done and then going into action, appealed to me at the time. Now I realise that Edmund Burke was nearer to the mark when he suggested that 'perfection is not given to man so politics is an intrinsically messy business and what is important is trying to govern with the temper of the people.'[17] What would have happened if Reggie Maudling had been chosen as leader? I realise now that there was benefit from the various happenings of my younger days. I came to accept that life is full of problems and disappointments. Apart from the death of his mother (when he was in his thirties) Ted Heath seemed to have had few difficulties. Through application and hard work he had been successful at Chatham House Grammar School and at Balliol. He had survived the war with acclaim. His post-war jobs had gone well. He had been a praised Chief Whip. With all these successes, surely he could succeed as Prime Minister. Why not the outlook suggested by Philip Ziegler? 'He took it for granted that he would serve as prime minister for a decade or so and then retire in glory handing over a healthy and prosperous country to his successor.' What a comparison with the reality; just losing in February, losing again in October and then ousted as leader of his Party in a contest which he and others thought he would win and the challenger 'did not rate her prospects particularly high and was standing to make a point rather than in serious contention.'[18] No wonder that ever after, especially without a family, he found it so difficult to come to terms with what had happened. There is a small family connection in that my mother's younger brother, George Jellicoe, had been close to Ted Heath as Lord Privy Seal and leader of the House of Lords. He had had to resign, as a result of a misunderstanding - one of life's problems again - in 1973. He had proved during the war that he was cool-headed under fire. I have often wondered whether his personality and steady influence at the beginning of 1974 would have led to different consequences.[19]

The chapter about Gloucester is written with hindsight. In truth, in the 1970s I still had not come fully to terms with the difficulties with food and drink. My greater concern was that Ted Heath was no longer leader and that the Conservative Party, now in opposition, might not continue with some of his and other members of the team's 'one nation' ideas. In particular, having been involved with the payment of benefit in the Youth Employment Service, I had learnt about social insurance and some of the flaws of the post-war Beveridge plan. In 1972 the Conservatives had published a green paper proposing tax credits. This was not the same as a partial basic income, the idea which I later defended (see Chapters 16 and 20), but with the same aim of giving some help to those who would benefit. This paper, under the signatures of Anthony Barber and Keith Joseph, can be read in the National Archives.[20] Part of the closing paragraphs read:

> 'To sum up the tax credit scheme does not offer a complete solution to the problems of poverty. It does offer a family support system easier to understand which would provide its benefit largely automatically and would bring significant increases in income to many poor people'.

The year after those 1974 defeats, I wrote to Sir Keith as an ex-candidate with Youth Employment experience, about the potential value of this scheme and received a two-page letter in reply. These are some of his comments in September 1975:

> 'I must warn you that there are unknown dangers of the scheme having disincentive effects. The supplementing of low incomes will encourage some to work less than they might otherwise have done. We shall have to decide whether to keep it in our manifesto next time. There is no chance of it being ignored. Far too many of us are keen on the general ideas'. For me this is one of the more important sentences in this book. 'Far too many of us are keen', but the events which followed meant that this keenness was not followed through.'

Hermione Parker, assistant to Sir Brandon Rhys Williams, a Conservative MP,[21] wrote in her book *Instead of the Dole* published in 1989[22]:

'If these proposals had been put into effect, a large part of the UK personal taxation and security systems would by now be integrated. After extensive debate a select committee of the House of Commons recommended that the scheme be adopted but with a split on party lines Tories voting in favour and Labour against. In 1974 the Labour Government let the matter drop. In theory the Conservative Party remained committed to tax credits but, in practice, under Mrs Thatcher's leadership, the attitude was at first luke-warm and then hostile.'

Instead of being realistic about my own physical situation, I wanted to defend Ted Heath's ideas. On 11th February, Margaret Thatcher became leader of the Conservatives. 'The Party's taken leave of its senses. This is a black day' was the comment by Reggie Maudling, reported by Philip Ziegler.[23] Douglas Hurd summed up what I felt so strongly as a mere spectator:

'Michael Wolff and Sara Morrison and the others were starting a long slow process of humanising the Party.' (They had now been replaced.) He referred to his letter to Humphrey Atkins: 'The team of generous and farsighted men who ran the Party is now dissipated and defeated through lack of political cunning' and at a Party conference in Malvern in November: 'Listened to a talk by a typical Thatcherite - dark-suited, articulate, 55, accountant, full of sourness.'

In April 1976, I wrote to Marcus Fox, then in charge of candidates.[24] This is part of that letter:

'It is rather more than two years since Geoffrey Johnson Smith encouraged me to continue in Politics, but could I still be considered for the Central Office list again, that is if the Party still wants my type. I am not a career politician and do not expect or want a safe seat, but hope you might send my name to the sort of Constituency in which there is an outside chance of winning with the time and effort which I am now in a position to give. I hope I can contribute again to political education and discussion especially as we possibly move towards a post-Beveridge era.'

I asked my successor at Merton to write a reference for Central Office. Having been often criticised for my behaviour, I forgo modesty in this instance to show that some things were achieved. Henry Grainger wrote:

'To all intents and purposes the Careers Service in Merton was virtually dormant in 1969. Schools and Colleges were dissatisfied with what was being provided. Industry and Commerce were apathetic to the needs of young people. When I arrived in 1973, I inherited a well run service. Schools and Colleges were full of praise for the service provided and employers were fully involved in programmes with school leavers. I am sure that this change of attitude was mainly due to Christopher's dynamism and enthusiasm. He quickly sums up a situation and gets on with the job.'

In truth, Henry's reference was over the top. I had enabled other Careers Officers to work well and they had responded. It would also have been better if I had paced myself, and organised other activities, so as to have been able to continue. On the candidate's enquiry form he put 'intolerance of petty bureaucracy' under 'weaknesses'. This was also true. Tolerance is essential. If you cannot do this, it is better to try and work for yourself.

Sally Oppenheim also produced a reference: 'Only too delighted to support your application. I am sure this is an extremely good idea and they will be delighted to have you'. This was the year when Jean Rook had a go at 'rich' Sally in the *Daily Express*. She replied: 'They sneer that I don't know what it's like to be hungry and poor. No M.P. - none of us - lives like the poorest constituent. That does not mean we don't know their problems and work and feel for them.'[25] Later that year we had further contact when I had written about my concerns. She replied: 'I think it is not unnatural that the Party does not at present want candidates who wish to put forward another line of policy from that which the Party is advocating it-self.[26] It was kind of her to support me. I am glad if my efforts in Gloucester helped at all to prepare the way. She has done much good work. Then there was a tussle about not putting Eton on my biographical details sent to constituencies:

'From my own experience especially in local government, (I wrote in May 1977) there seems to be far too much attention given to a person's school when surely how they have tried to make use of their education in subsequent work is more important. This is particularly true of Eton and it seems a pity to flaunt this information in front of the Press, etc, before they have read of the small attempt at service.'

This difficulty continues over forty years later! Whilst waiting for my name to to go before the standing advisory committee on candidates, I had contacted other Conservative MPs about my concerns and experiences, particularly about the growing unemployment among young people. Gerard Vaughan, (prominent in the YES debates recorded in Chapter 14) and Jim Prior, amongst others, acknowledged the points I was trying to make. Peter Walker, MP for Worcester, had been helpful in Gloucester ten years earlier, and that year, 1977, had written a book, *The Ascent of Britain* which is worth seeking out.[27] Peter's writing is good on Burke: 'The arrogance of the intellectual who believes that he can reform society without taking notice of the collective feelings of his compatriots or the history of the society in which he lives' . There are other comments which resonate to-day: 'It is useless for Conservatives to preach freedom unless they can also succeed in creating a fair society'. 'The egalitarian sacrifices efficiency to fairness. Those who only value economic growth sacrifice fairness to efficiency. What is wanted is a middle way. Inequalities are only fair if they benefit those in society who are worst off.' The book also praises Ted Heath: 'Those of us who attended many of the talks will always object to the depiction of Edward Heath as a man who sought confrontation with the Unions. Every union leader who took part in those talks knows that this view of him is completely false. He desired passionately to reach agreement. He believed he could and he very nearly did.' This confirms the words of Douglas Hurd quoted earlier. Peter completely sympathised with my uncertainties and wanted to meet again. I had written (April 1977):

'If I get back on the list, I must decide whether to seek a Constituency Association who might consider a critic of present attitudes which seem to obscure the relevance of Conservative philosophy and 'thought-through' policies to current problems. I do not mind not succeeding, nor being called disloyal or wet, if such a course could be of some small value in the long term. But it's probably not sensible if one would just be a lone voice and potential nuisance - there are other openings and other things in life. If we meet I'd appreciate your comments on the strength of feeling against the present line. I have also got to decide whether those who are not Socialist but of the centre, and temperamentally non-combative, can ever find a place in active politics. My recent 'constituents', clients and colleagues in the Careers and Social Services (who were not committed to Socialism) will only accept Conservatism with a human and compassionate face, and they recoil from words like 'despicable' used by dear Mrs T at Brighton. If there is no prospect of a Liberal - Conservative accommodation, they, as voters, will examine the possibility of a central Social Democrat - Liberal government in preference to a too illiberal Conservatism. It may be that there will be enough Conservative supporters at the next election not to worry about these people's votes, but doesn't the country need the healing spirit - harsh words breed more harsh words. Mrs T's current actions may be in the short-term interest of the Party but I wonder about the long-term national interest.'

We talked at the House of Commons and he then wrote: ' It was good to see you at the House yesterday. I hope it will not be too long before you are there in your own right' (29th April 1977). It could still have happened. When I got home there was a letter from Marcus Fox, dated 27th April, confirming that I was now on the approved list of candidates again and 'wishing every success in finding a suitable constituency.' As Marcus had discarded many candidates and become known as the 'Shipley strangler', here was some recognition of my thinking. The biographical details were agreed, including 'campaigning for compassionate Conservative policies'. Provided a subscription to the party literature service was paid, these details were circulated to all constituencies seeking candidates. The rejection letters flooded in through the rest of 1977 and early 1978. Bournemouth East, Epsom and Ewell, Halifax, Morecombe and Lonsdale, Nottingham, Vauxhall, Wycombe, would not be calling me for interview. All were polite and usually personally signed by the Chairman. There is so much work done by the voluntary side of the Conservative Party. As an example, the Vauxhall Association wrote: 'I regret having to write to say that your name has not been short-listed. By way of consolation you might like to know there were something over 80 applicants'. Then came a letter dated 26th June 1978 from the East Flintshire Conservative Association. I had been short-listed. Would I come to interview on 1st July and 'be prepared to speak on a subject of my own choice and then answer questions'. It was always a long shot. If I had been serious, I should have immediately gone up to Deeside and spent those four days learning about the constituency. Instead I drove up in the tiring old Austin on the Saturday morning, got delayed in heavy traffic going to North Wales, then managed to find a phone box to explain the delay (no mobiles). I was just there in time to deliver my talk, on an empty stomach, about the value of Ted Heath's efforts, the need to reconsider 'Beveridge' and the importance of 'One Nation' policies. Being very hungry, my talk was lifeless and I was certainly not the person they wanted.

That day made me think again about what I was attempting. Did I really want to continue this route when I was less in tune with what the Conservatives were now saying? Years later, I realised that I was then pig-headed, stupid and ignorant. I have wanted to write this chapter in case it is helpful to others, even to students of politics. I wasn't sufficiently aware of Edmund Burke's 'temper of the people'. Mrs Thatcher was leader of the Party. The Constituency Parties wanted to do all they could to help her to win an election. They did not want a Candidate who was harking back to Ted Heath. I had not properly learnt the lessons of Gloucester. If I was serious about still getting to Westminster, I had to work with a local Constituency Association, sharing and working for their concerns. Once there, and after I had proved my loyalty over several years, that might have been the time to carefully voice some of my own causes and interests. Again it needs to be realised that Parliament is about Burke's 'messy business', not a forum for self-satisfied new entrants who think they have the answers. Then three things happened which settled the next ten years. Gloucestershire was extending its Careers Service and made it clear that they did not want to employ an ex-city Parliamentary Candidate. But then there were to be additional posts to concentrate on helping the growing number of young unemployed, and, because they knew of my concern, I was offered one of these positions covering Cheltenham and the Forest of Dean. The house at Redmarley, The Twynings, was within the Forest of Dean Council area. Some progress was made in Cheltenham but - the second discovery - there were far too many unemployed young people in the Forest. The third happening was a vacancy for a new Councillor to stand for the Redmarley and neighbouring areas.

I was asked to stand as an Independent candidate and soon found the required eight people who would sign the form. It remains a decision not regretted. I wrote to Marcus Fox, apologising for having wasted his time, also to Peter Walker who sent an understanding reply. We were to meet again at Tory Reform Meetings and shared our thoughts about what had happened to Ted Heath. Some of my ideas were written down and sent to those MPs with whom I had had contact. They are reproduced in Appendix 2, but I still had not learnt that ideas alone without power have little value, and, if power is achieved, there will be many happenings which will prevent them being implemented. Ted Heath lost that February 1974 Election and its no use lamenting what individuals might have done differently. Forty years on, the country is moving further to the right and the Thatcher legacy has been much praised as the better path to have been taken. Another purpose of this book is to show that there was an alternative. I quote from the fly-leaf of Ian Gilmour's book *Whatever Happened to the Tories* published in 1977.[28]

'Until 1975 the Conservative Party prided it-self on its loyalty to the concept of 'One Nation' and understood that this was more than merely a useful slogan. The success of Thatcherism within the Party have allowed the Right to peddle a story about the post-war Party which is at variance with the truth. Those who have followed the interests of the whole nation throughout their careers have been denigrated as traitors and right-wing philosophers and historians have provided a pseudo-intellectual gloss for an interpretation of history which would have bewildered Churchill and his associates. The desire to preserve One Nation produced a sense of well-being under Conservative rule in the 1950s.'

The local Conservatives then decided to put up their own candidate for Ward 17. I suggested to my supporters that I stood down, but they encouraged me to continue. This was part of my message to the electors of Bromsberrow, Pauntley, Redmarley and Staunton, part of the Forest of Dean District Council:

'I am standing as a candidate because I would like to try and be of some use in a District which has been our base for nearly twenty years. I am standing as an Independent because I believe there is a place at District level for the Independent who is sympathetic to different views and tries to come to unbiased decisions. If pressed I would say I was a little right of centre. I had a short interlude on the fringed of National Politics but came to realise that I could not then sufficiently support a Party line. Having worked in Local Government, I question some of the ways in which things are done. Too often have I seen the apparent needs of the Administration or of political expediency put before the needs of those who use the services. Too often I have seen the efforts of Officers hampered by rules and regulations and those questionable statistics. And who foots the bill for this unwieldy bureaucracy?'

It still reads quite well and this is only half, but looking back, it also proves that it was too idealistic and still not fully accepting Burke's 'messiness' of politics. I then set about trying to visit (Ann again helped with this) every house in the Ward. It was decided to make a point of never asking for a vote or pledge, as instructed by the political parties. I just said I was standing. If they did decide to vote for me and I was elected, I would be there to try and help with any problems. And, if people wanted to talk, I did not hurry on. The general view seemed to be that I would not receive many votes and the ward would be won by my Conservative opponent, a retired Brigadier. There was no Labour or Liberal candidate.

LEARNING FROM DIFFERENCE

Chapter 16

Independent Councillor. Work Initiatives. Benefits

The day after polling day, 4th May 1979, Ann and I drove down to the count in the Forest. We were chatting affably to people we knew when I turned to look at the table on which votes for Ward 17 were being counted. As expected, what I assumed to be the votes for the Brigadier were drawing well ahead. I moved a little closer and someone said 'do you realise those are your votes?' I (or rather 'we' because Ann had done so much) had been elected with a sizeable majority and defeated the Tory machine. An evening of serious talk followed. I had committed myself to four years with many evening meetings. There was no pay, only a £4 allowance per meeting, sometimes a bit more, plus petrol allowance. How were we going to survive financially, pay the school fees, etc? We did not have the solution when I set out the next day for Winchester. David Green, a friend from childhood, whose parents had always been so kind, had invited me to the reception after he had become Mayor of the City. I thought it would be a good outing with happy memories after the probable disappointment of my effort. David introduced me to other councillors and I mentioned my own election that week. I have always remembered one particular bit of advice that evening: 'Don't stay too long, you will be frustrated that you can not do more. Better just to do what you can and then stand down after two terms and let others have a go. If you do stay you will become avid for power, wanting to achieve what isn't really possible'. Although at the time I was only thinking of one term, I did not forget this advice. He was, maybe without realising, hinting at Burke's 'messiness' of politics. There will always be some desperate for power. If you are not of that clay, concentrate on service. Another worry was that this result was a bit of a slap in the face for the Conservative Agent, Angela Darricotte, who had been so helpful at the start of Gloucester. I had to justify my behaviour by what I achieved.

Before recounting some of the efforts as a councillor and particularly trying to do a little about the lack of employment, there was another reminder of the Youth Employment/ Careers Service. Graham Rolls, Area Careers Officer when I had worked in Leamington, had written in December (1978) bewailing the problems in the Service:

'The strain of carrying a case load of some 350, plus now another 150 from the Further Education College, and all the responsibility for 'Special Measures' (similar to what I had been doing based at Cheltenham), statistics, meetings, reports connected with the unemployed, the Press, Councillors, etc, has become such a burden that I can not see my-self carrying on beyond the age of sixty in two year's time. I often wonder how long the Careers Service will continue in its present form before we get taken over by the MSC (i.e. Department of Employment - Manpower Services). Sorry if this letter sounds like a tale of woe, but I thought you would like to hear the latest news. Hope to come over and see you at Redmarley when the longer days come.'

Neither retirement nor visit came about. A few months later, Graham was driving with his wife Fran and stopped the car in a lay-by because he was feeling poorly. A few minutes later, he had a massive heart attack and died. It was Graham's death, worn out in the service of others, which encouraged me to press on with discussions about the service. A few months earlier there had been 'an edited version of Jim Prior's thinking in the Sunday Times'[1]. Some of his comments were:

'Britain has a long tradition of failing to train the right people with the right qualifications for Industry. The advice available to young people is woefully inadequate. An altogether bolder solution would be to found a new unified service which would act as a bridge between schools and employers. The present number of careers officers would be augmented by people coming from the educational and industrial streams. Each school would have a careers officer seconded to it with full-time responsibility for bringing job information and giving job advice to pupils. To entrust this vital task to a single professional organisation seems the only efficient way of improving on past weakness and division.'

I had written, mentioning our previous contact when I had been an adopted candidate and my experiences in the Careers service since then. The reply was typical of many of those still at the helm of the Conservative Party then who, like Ted Heath, wanted to improve the activities of Government:

'I am determined that we should develop a service that is effective in helping bridge the gap between school and industry. I am also determined that as in all public administration we are heavy at the sharp end and light on administration. One of my assistants, Richard Needham, is most interested in the development of the service and I suggest you give him a ring.'[2]

In January 1979, I produced a paper (see Appendix 3) about the service and Richard kindly replied: 'Just what I wanted. A good idea if we both went to see him (Jim Prior). When we are in government your views will be extremely helpful.' Then, as so often in politics, events took over. The country was faced with what has become known as the 'winter of discontent'. Hospital staff and even undertakers joined days of action. Conservative shadow ministers were far too busy to worry about the Careers Service and then Jim Callaghan's Labour Government was defeated in the House of Commons. After the Conservative victory at the polls, Jim Prior became Employment Minister. Richard Needham wrote: 'I am hopeful that a meeting can be fixed in May.' It was not to be. In Ian Gilmour's words: 'The Conservatives were agreed that the Unions must be tamed. The problem was how to do so. Jim Prior adopted a gradualist approach despite opposition from the Prime Minister. His 1980 Employment Act curtailed the main abuses such as the closed shop and secondary picketing. His union reforms benefited the country but did not reconcile the Prime Minister to a moderate who disliked her economic policy.' The Careers Service plans had to wait their turn, but this never came. Jim Prior was sent to Ireland. Norman Tebbit became Employment Minister and he too had other priorities.

By then, Ann and I were beginning to come to terms with this new position as an elected councillor. Redmarley was on the eastern edge of the Forest Council area. The larger towns, Cinderford and Coleford in the Forest, and Lydney down by the river Severn, were all to the West towards the Welsh border across the Wye. It was a lovely place to work, driving through the trees in the different seasons and often late at night. An extra allowance was paid if meetings continued after 9.30pm and those few extra pounds made a difference to some of those older councillors. Sometimes, when very late, I took the single-track road down from Symonds Yat and then galloped up the M50 to the Redmarley turning. The Austin was ageing and I did not want to wear out the Bristol with its mileometer already well round the clock. A search of local paper advertisements produced a silver grey Opel Commodore with a white bonnet. Something had fallen on the front of the car, but the rest seemed sound. It was not British, but £350 produced a machine which coped admirably with both the motorway and the twisting Forest roads. I remember how, on one of those journeys, I suddenly thought of underwriting at Lloyd's. We were aware that the family shares had risen in value. With the land at Redmarley, were there enough funds to become a Lloyd's Name? The tussle with the banks, eventually successful, is described in Chapter 18. There would be no return from underwriting for three years, but here was a plan for survival. On the Council there were separate main committees, not a Cabinet, in those days. I was granted my first choice of Policy and General Purposes, but had to accept Housing rather than my second choice of Planning and Development. For the first few months I kept quiet, no Etonian label, and came to appreciate the qualities and wisdom of those older councillors, some of whom had worked down the coal mines both before and after nationalisation in 1946. Some 770,000 tons had been taken from the Forest mines in 1948. There were also area and county committees on which a Council representative was required; educational, social services, arts, even the county youth employment committee. Some of these were in Gloucester and easier for me, living nearer the city. Involvement in social services was an eye-opener. Whenever I followed up a particular case, the difficulty of the social workers were apparent, always short of time and resources. I was concerned about taking the expenses but the whole package, plus eventually Lloyd's, made the following years possible.

The Manpower Services Commission (MSC) had been established in January 1974, one of the last of the many achievements of Edward Heath's government before their February defeat. The aims of the commission were 'to combat industrial decline, job shortages and strikes by devising policies to value workers both as keys to production and as human beings with their own needs.' It continued under the Labour Government. In the 1977 Review these aims were described as 'ensuring that there is available to each worker the opportunities and services he or she needs to lead a satisfying working life.' There was also obvious sympathy for those who were missing out: 'loss of the sense of personal worth, feelings of degradation, boredom, depression, laziness and inertia. Thus a vicious circle may be established; not only does the individual feel less capable of taking up work again but may be less likely to be given the opportunity' and 'although it is sometimes said that many of the unemployed do not want to work, this view is not supported by a department of employment survey.'[3] There was no blame or 'something for nothing' attitude. An earlier Working Party report had commented on the importance of the Careers Service and the work of those of us who had been extra unemployment specialist officers.[4] This report also noted that 'since they lost the benefit function, especially the weekly attendance to prove unemployment, Careers Offices are not in as regular contact with unemployed young people as they used to be or as they would like to be.' This had been predicted by some of the speakers in those earlier debates about the Service (see Chapter 14). The intention now was to move on from work experience and job creation programmes (it was admitted that there had been criticism of the quality of some programmes) and, in 1978, to support project-based work experience as part of the new Youth Opportunities Programme.

By the end of 1979, after nearly eight months as a councillor, I was well aware of the extent of unemployment, especially amongst young people, in the Forest of Dean. A later report by the Council estimated nearly 22% unemployment in the Coleford area and that this could rise to over 25% after redundancies at Rank Xerox.[5] Declaration of interest and experience soon led to membership of the Employment and Training sub-committee and I was then asked to speak at a meeting of the Forest Trades Council about 'Jobs and training for the Forest of Dean Youth'. The notes for this talk have recently been found. There is much that I would still agree with in the following abridged text:

'I have been accused of sitting on the fence, taking the easy way out. I see it as the only way to go if experiences have left one unable to fully commit to either left or right whilst sympathetic to and critical of both. The advantage is that one can at least try and talk about the realities of a subject like this and hopefully without too much bias. The disadvantage is that one misses the brotherhood and friendship of party politics. After criticism from officialdom, I am grateful for this invitation. After a fortunate, privileged and pampered childhood, suddenly nothing. I still went to a privileged school, but holidays were different to fellows. This was my first contact with that sense of alienation, of not belonging, which also results from unemployment. I could not settle as a student. How many potential talents all around us do not bear fruit because of difficult home circumstances. Young people need stability and encouragement for best performance.

'Eventually I worked in the Youth Employment Service and became involved with the 'disadvantaged', increasingly aware of the need for special provisions and some 'sheltered employment'. In 1977 we returned to Gloucestershire and I was asked to help with the new MSC programmes. I found there were, in fact, vacancies but a pool of less able young people whom employers did not wish to take on and were taking up a disproportionate amount of time of Careers Officers. Yet there was work to be done, watercourses which were not clear, orchards unpicked, firewood unchopped, even, from my own experiences, worthwhile car restoration projects. And how many, given encouragement, could get going on their own enterprises, window or car cleaning, gardening, home maintenance, etc? The ideal would be some form of Centre at which all these activities could be gathered together and which would form a base from which working parties could go out. Many would remain on unemployment benefit or social security, only able to earn a small amount known as disregard, but some might in time be able to make their own way and come off benefit. Of course there would be difficulties, personal problems which upset work, regulations, safety, insurance, etc, etc. But its boredom and loneliness that lead to apathy and frustration and then sometimes destruction. With companionship and involvement these feelings can be dispelled. We need to think about projects where those who are available and want to do something are encouraged and helped.'

This talk seems to have been well received and, perhaps through one or some of those present, came to the notice of the Gloucester Diocesan Council of Education. The Church may have already had ideas in this direction but encouraged by Andrew Banfield, the Diocesan Youth Officer, let it be known that they would be glad to have the redundant school buildings at Broadwell near Coleford, belonging to the Diocese, used as such a Centre. The Council planners agreed a limited change of use. A Committee was formed with Andrew Banfield as Chairman, other Church representatives and a representative of the District Council, the position to which I was elected. I was asked to become Vice-Chairman and Treasurer and, in that capacity, approached the MSC. Their initial response was that there was insufficient training in our proposals, but we could approach them again when established. The District Council did provide a grant and I set about writing to several charities, most of whom responded generously. Paul Marland, then the local MP, was continuously supportive and suggested that he made an application to the European Social Fund on our behalf via the MSC. The reply from the MSC Chairman, then Sir Richard O'Brien, an outstanding leader dedicated to providing opportunities for young people with whom I had had contact in an earlier life,[6] explained that Gloucestershire was not a 'Youth Priority Region'. The County was considered as a whole, rather than specific areas with high unemployment. There were still sufficient funds to start and the draft constitution for what became the Forest of Dean Bridge Project spelled out the aim as 'to educate, train and rehabilitate those people, mainly the young, who through their social and economic circumstances are in need and would otherwise remain unemployed.' This meant that there were no restrictions on age or length of attendance, though the duties of the Committee included the possibility of future involvement with MSC programmes when MSC rules would have to be applied. The ethos of those first years can be explained through part of the illustrated (with workshop pictures) leaflet I then compiled:

'A CENTRE FOR THOSE WHO HAVE NOT BEEN ABLE TO FIND EMPLOYMENT AND APPRECIATE RESOURCES, COMPANIONSHIP, AND SUPPORT WHILST SEEKING ALTERNATIVES OR INVESTIGATING SELF - EMPLOYMENT.

Governments have been concentrating on short-term measures for those under 19. The Bridge is a local partnership between statutory and voluntary organisations and concerned local people, which has set out to provide a longer-term approach with no upper age limit. They are particularly mindful of the needs of those now in their twenties, for whom there was no provision when they left school. By careful house-keeping the project has now for two years provided wood - metal - and vehicle-workshops for repairing and restoring things which would probably otherwise have been thrown away. There is also an arts workshop, a recreation room, a small canteen, and rooms, already let, for other community organisations.'

The Project had started by renovating some of the school buildings. It was encouraging to read comments from participants in the local press: 'I have been doing painting, plastering and putting in windows. I am going to do some carpentry. The girls here do all the jobs that the boys do. We really feel we are achieving something,' or from one of the supervisors: ' Two boys who have stripped and re-felted a roof have done something they never felt they would do.' Amongst other jobs were refurbishing battered jumps for a riding club which also helped the disabled, toys and equipment for a pre-school playgroup, chairs for a nearby Memorial Hall and display stands for the local junior school. There were all these things which could be done with the small subsidy, which begs the question: Is it acceptable to do useful things below the market rate, using public money or voluntarily provided funds, if this helps young people to learn and hopefully later achieve work within the marketplace? There was also a seemingly endless supply of good 50s and 60s vehicles which were worth restoring. The owners had hung on to them, but the expected spare time had not been forthcoming and they were glad to donate to a local project. The MSC then approved of the facilities available and the Committee agreed that we should also provide short-term Youth Opportunity placements, some of which subsequently resulted in jobs. The remainder, with others who had found their way to the project, made up a group of fifteen. Most did not satisfy the conditions for receiving unemployment benefit, having either never worked or not worked recently, so were receiving supplementary benefit with the entitlement to earn another £4 in any one week - the disregard - without affecting benefit. The District Council agreed to underwrite this payment of £4 to ten people for one year and our fund-,raising made up the balance for more than that number. A problem came when one of the group reported that his benefit had been stopped because 'he was attending the project and therefore unavailable for work'. We explained to the benefit office that any of them could attend an interview or start a job at a moment's notice. We suggested that it wasn't realistic to spend the whole week searching or waiting for non-existent vacancies and, after discussion, this was accepted and benefit restored. We found that most of the group did not want to break the law and therefore declined the sort of casual work which became available. If they declared a payment above the £4 of those days, their regular benefit could be altered, with questions and delays. It was the same problem that discouraged the taking up of, say, four weeks' continuous temporary work or attempting self-employment. Many of the younger ones in the group, still living at home, were committed to a regular payment to their parents. If they signed off, or declared enough to lead to an investigation, there could be a wait of three weeks or more before they were again receiving benefit.

It was these experiences that led some of us to try and advance the case for a higher supplementary benefit disregard. (Unemployment benefit disregard was raised to £2 per day. In his 1981 Budget speech, Geoffrey Howe had said this was to encourage unemployed people to work for voluntary bodies - where there might be a small allowance). In July 1982 I wrote to Geoffrey Holland at MSC, whom I had met in Careers Service days[7]. He responded by passing my letter to the Department of Health and Social Security (DHSS) and I had a lengthy reply from one of their Officers (letters were acknowledged if written as an elected member). The kernel of this reply was that 'the object of this benefit was to bring any income a person has, or can manage to earn, up to a particular level' and 'whilst the Government would like the disregards increased still more, bearing in mind the limits on resources, a higher priority must at present be given to maintaining the value of supplementary benefit it-self.' I wrote on the letter at the time 'the difference is that Mr Sayer[8] is writing of this benefit as giving additional support to those who have fallen on hard times, whereas we are trying to help those who have never known better times and receive this form of benefit because there is nothing else.' Now, thirty years later, I better understand what was happening. This was the beginning of the Thatcher era, money did not grow on trees, etc. It was that same year that Richard O'Brien was dismissed by Jim Prior's successor, Norman Tebbitt, some say urged by Margaret Thatcher because Richard's training plans (in his words for a better equipped, better qualified, better educated, better motivated workforce) were reckoned to be excessively expensive. Money could be spent on the Falklands war, but the concept of still more expenditure to prepare the way for future industrial growth was less popular. Employment would increase through financial services, tourism and other non-manufacturing jobs. David Young, the future Lord Young (see Chapter 9, the same names come round) took over at the MSC and projects became subject to many more rules, in particular strict one-year attendance by participants, which was better for the unemployment figures.

It was at this time that I became more interested in the partial basic or citizen's income ideas (see Chapter 20). The magazine *Initiatives* posed the question 'Could a basic income be the answer to unemployment?' It listed in a memo to policymakers: Simplifies and replaces benefit payments and tax allowances, Removes distinction between employed and unemployed, Removes need for special programmes for the unemployed, Removes poverty trap, Legalises black economy, Boosts small firms and start-ups. These ideas were not acceptable as a use of public funds and tarnished as 'something for nothing'. The Conservatives' enterprise allowance concept did catch on and helped many individuals, but not the idea of a mixture of part-time employment, some self-employment, voluntary work, etc, partly subsidised by the State. My thought has been that this more flexible approach would lead to more people working out ways of life which could, in time, become productive and then pay back through tax paid. Many still say that this is unrealistic, too idealistic, and assumes that 'money grows on trees'. At the Bridge Project, I realised that my hope for establishing a long-term Centre for those without work was not going to be possible. I therefore supported the Church when they applied to become part of the Community Programme. The MSC agreed to support 32 places and these were swiftly taken up by people of all ages, though with the bias towards those in their twenties. As I wrote at the time[9]:

'The MSC have gone out of their way to help with the problems and many at the Bridge express their gratitude for the Community Programme, but some of us still question some of the thinking behind short-term schemes. (I was not then sufficiently aware of the political pressures). The quest for higher disregard is only part of the overall quest for partial less-regulated longer term subsidies which can be adapted locally to suit differing needs. The subsidy paid to the Project by MSC is considerably larger than would otherwise have been paid out to most of the individuals on benefit by DHSS. Part of the difference could have been sufficient, with other funding promised, and with the possibilities envisaged through a higher disregard, to keep the Centre running including the cost of encouraging part-time and self-employment ventures.'

I was not alone in this quest for higher disregard. I had kept in touch with Richard Needham and in one of his letters he wrote: 'I absolutely agree with your comments about raising the benefit disregard. There has to be a continuing bridge between unemployment and the world of work.' He had spent some time in America and commented: 'Once a whole generation has got used to living on welfare payments, they create their own sub-culture which rejects working life. As we are not going to solve the problem for many years it is crucial in the meantime we give people the opportunity to earn above the basic level of benefit.'[10] How right he was: 'For many years' and we are still faced with this problem thirty years later. However the Church had made its decision and work could be provided for some people without the worry of running out of funds. I was given the task of interviewing for the 'senior supervisor' post at £128 per week. The advertisement, one of many for the MSC Special Programmes, read:

'The scheme employs over 50 working in one of the workshops - general engineering, wood working, arts and crafts, vehicle repair and the canteen. Your role is to encourage and foster a sense of community purpose and activity.'

I still have the completed application forms for the interviews in August 1983. It was difficult to choose from the eight experienced people who had been made redundant, returned from overseas contracts or who in one case had to give up his business for lack of work. Some of those not appointed helped for a while, but inevitably there was some friction between a paid appointment and the volunteers. I was increasingly concerned that the Project was moving away from the concept of a long-term Centre. I have my written submission for the October 1983 Management Committee meeting:

'Other Committee members have spoken of conflict in the Committee. Is it not more the difficulty of working out the best way of coping with MSC constraints and proposals? The original aims were a long-term Centre more responsive to local needs than current MSC ideas with partnership between Church, District Council, and other concerned local people, and control by the local community. Money has been collected, latterly concentrating on activities separate to and post MSC, for which funds have been readily donated. But now the decision has been taken to concentrate on the MSC role.'

Looking back, Andrew Banfield and the rest of the Committee were realists and it was right to accept what was offered and to concentrate on the employment opportunities which were then made available. I now realise my decision to write to the Bishop of Gloucester, pointing out that funds had been received from Charities and Trusts for the long-term concept, was naive, and I appreciated the sensible reply from that busy man: 'My guess is that you and Andrew have opted for different (though equally honourable) ways out of the dilemma posed to such projects by public funding. If so, it is something of which I have always been conscious in connection with such ventures.'[11] This was exactly right and it is once again the lesson which I hope comes out of this book. In a way it is reminiscent of the Aerocar. Ideas and ideals must lead to profit or be backed by agreed public funding. There is still the argument that if more O'Brien-type public funding had been agreed in the 1980s, if more of the revenue from North Sea oil had been used to modernise industry and infrastructure, the country might have been better placed to retain its manufacturing base. [12] This was not the conclusion of those then in power.

With the paid supervisors in place, I was able to withdraw from Bridge Project involvement. This fitted with other Council work. I had been re-elected without a contest in May 1983. No other candidate had put up to oppose me. I had given much time to trying to help with the lack of employment and wanted to concentrate more of my efforts on the area which I represented. What was pleasing was that the Trades Council had taken the initiative and had established two smaller Centres, at Cinderford and Lydney. Unlike the MSC one-year programmes, these Centres provided continuing care for as long as needed, and helped some participants to become self-employed, making use of the Enterprise allowance. An advance was that DHSS agreed that credits could be earned which could later be used to purchase tools or even finance self-employment. I was still glad to be a member of their Committee and help with fund-raising until I retired as councillor in 1987. The Church continued with the Community Programme at the Bridge for two years and the Council itself established a programme aiding council work throughout the area.

A political complication came with the request to join the local Liberals. This came to its head when I was asked to stand as a Liberal for Gloucestershire County Council. My reply to the Liberal chief, Eric Radley, 24th February 1985, may still be instructive :

'The more I reflect, the more I realise that I must encourage the Alliance (i.e. with the SDP) to adopt their own candidate to trail their colours in Newent. When the chips are down, as increasingly they will be over the next four years, basic philosophy tends to raise its head. I have to accept that I am marginally to the right of centre whereas the Alliance are surely to the left. It's always tempting to come out of the cold and away from the loneliness of independence but I did in fact fight this battle with my-self fifteen years ago when local Conservatives told me I must change my views or get out. The answer to the recurring question - why a liberal Conservative shows reluctance to join the Liberals or SDP - is that mankind has so far only identified two strains of political philosophy. To the right towards a greater or lesser degree of private enterprise, to the left a greater or lesser degree of state control. I'm miles away from the present Conservative Party, not only because of its move further to the right but also because of the increasingly narrow authoritarian views and disinclination to listen. You must also realise that I'm one of those who find it difficult to make the compromises necessary in team or party. The other evening you said something like: 'You can do so little as an independent.' Of course that's true in one sense but in another you can do other things particularly at a personal level. Thank you for forcing me to think.'

Eric's handwritten reply, 7th April 1985, is the best exposition of the Liberal creed I have ever read:

'I do not actually agree with you that politics is divided into those who believe in free enterprise and those who go for public control. There is more to it than that. Broadly speaking for me the dividing line is generosity of attitude. Tories tell us they live in the 'real world' and this I take to mean a world which sees men as inevitably sinners. Liberals accept the sinners bit but not the 'inevitable'. They think goodness just as 'real' as cynicism. For me Liberal is one of the noblest conceptions possible. It has a double connotation of caring for the liberation of the spirit to make life noble and worthwhile and a generosity of attitude in this difficult world.'

This letter, and Eric's kind words about what I was attempting to help those without work, led me to stop ideas of possibly standing for the County Council as an Independent. I still have the draft of my possible appeal to the electorate:

'Whatever decisions are taken at County level over the next four years, they won't please everybody! The problem, as I see it, is that Central Government dictates together with the thongs of National and Local agreements leave little room for manoeuvre. However, if elected, I would try and act as a true independent as likely to vote with the Central as with the right wing group. Some years ago I was involved with local Conservatives, but they are now far to the right of my position. I remain an advocate of private enterprise provided that it is remembered that there are duties as well as rights, and that success is more acceptable when thrift is exercised and compassion displayed.'

I decided that this would have further muddied the electoral choice, so this little missive never reached the public! Eric also wrote of his own position (with other candidates) 'things are a lot less certain for me but hope it will be possible to hold my seat.' He was elected and then for the next five years was Council Chairman.[13]

For the next four years I was a member of my original first choice, the Planning and Development Committee. The memories of those previous four years on the Housing Committee have led to querying the 'sale of Council houses' policy. At that time, it was the task of Councillors to allocate houses at meetings of the Area Lettings sub-Committee. A seven-page booklet explained the rules and how points were to be allocated for different circumstances such as overcrowding, condition of present accommodation, time on list, medical conditions etc. The waiting list was long, with difficult stories of domestic problems. In the whole Forest of Dean District the need was for more, not fewer, Council houses to rent. Then suddenly there was the opposite problem of abundance locally. A whole new estate of houses, initiated by my predecessor - more than were needed in the parishes I represented - was available at the same time. I begged the housing department to allow allocation to some of those on the list from other areas and then, when told this was not possible, I suggested holding some in reserve for the needs which would surely arise. These ideas were rejected. Immediate rental income was required. As a result, some young couples who had not been long on the list, had a windfall when they were able to purchase with a good discount.

Planning was divided between two sub-committees, North and South, then reporting our deliberations to the full committee. 'North' meetings were lengthy afternoon affairs in pleasant offices at Cinderford. The lady chairman believed our task was to precisely apply planning recommendations. We were soon in conflict. I sought to find loopholes to accept applications which seemed beneficial to individuals and did not adversely affect neighbours or neighbourhood. On one occasion there was local uproar because of plans to turn a large but decaying local house into a residential home. There were no immediately adjacent houses, but residents half a mile or so away tried to paint a picture of unrestrained imbeciles running riot. Others in the village saw the application as salvation for the building. The protesters attended the planning meeting and complained that I had tried to express both sides of the argument in a balanced way. I replied that I understood, but that was how I saw my task and they had their remedy at the ballot box when the next election came. The application went to the full Planning Committee and, after a long debate, was in fact turned down. Remembered is the attitude of the Developer, who happened to have been a leading member of the Gloucester Conservatives when I had resigned seventeen years before. He congratulated me on a statesmanlike speech and started talking about my coming back as a replacement to Sally Oppenheim when she retired! I thanked him, but explained we had other plans. Another major issue was the use of redundant farm buildings. Agricultural use was sacrosanct. This all came to a head when the Planning Officer got to hear of a farmer in my area who was using one of his barns for contract metal fabrication and employing local people. I sprang to his defence. I spoke forcefully in Committee and there was considerable press coverage. But it was all to no avail. The activity had to close down. The jobs were lost. At least this attitude has changed and there are now workshops in agricultural buildings all over the country. Site meetings made an interesting day out. A convoy of mainly driver-only cars would seem less responsible today, but this meant that each councillor could be flexible about sites attended. It was interesting to visit remote parts of the Forest District, which otherwise I would not have seen. The mileage allowance covered the cost of even the six-cylinder Commodore.

I tackled particular local tasks, one of which was to combat the frequent flooding in the Playley Green and Staunton areas. Eventually it was agreed that money should be spent on improving the watercourses and ditches and all the work done seems to have helped. In past decades, roadmen would clear grilles over the drains and try to stop the build-up of hedge cuttings. I still look at potential blockage sites when in the area. Policy was an evening meeting at Cinderford. For a while I was Vice-Chairman. On one evening when I was in the Chair because the incumbent was away, I tried to hurry the meeting along. But it was no good. As 9.30pm approached, more and more questions were put to the Chair, or through me to the Officers in attendance. As already mentioned, after that time Councillors received double allowance and who could blame those elderly mainly well meaning and kindly people for wanting a bit more cash for their efforts? The full Council met at Coleford in the Council Chamber, which seemed to lack ventilation. There were no windows and smoking was permitted. By the end of the evening the air was thick with smoke and I became increasingly affected by what is now known as passive smoking. The Officers were aware of this difficulty and kindly installed a small unit which was meant to filter and clean the air. Unfortunately it was noisy and, if switched on, there were requests for it to be turned off! Towards the end of my term I took to sitting at the back and in very late sessions - sometimes they went on till nearly midnight - I wore a mask which also filtered the air. I was later told that this helped the officers when they pleaded for proper air conditioning when the new Council Chamber was planned! But these difficulties are no more, with the changed attitude and legislation about smoking.

By 1986, for many reasons (and not forgetting the advice given after David Green's mayoral election in Winchester!) we decided that I would not stand again at the 1987 Election. Ann had been doing so much and was constantly on the road. Looking back, the little Saab 96 was not the least tiring car to drive. I should have been more aware of this, but it was economical and racked up getting on for 200,000 miles with little trouble. There was the school run to Cheltenham. Her parents wanted some assistance at their Winchester house and their needs were likely to increase. She had helped her nonagenarian aunt to move into a nursing home before she died and then to sort and sell the house at Teignmouth, miles away in Devon. She had also helped Lionel's sister, Rachel, settle at Amesbury after her return from St Helena. As well as the smoking problem, I needed some surgery and was not as fit as I would have liked. There were fewer Independents[14] and there was increasing pressure to stand as either a Conservative or a Liberal at that next Election. We decided to sell the Redmarley house and pass on a little of the proceeds to the next generation, who were - or would soon be - at the start of their working lives in the London area. I had spent nearly twenty-five years helping others with employment. It could not be compared with setting up a company to actually provide new jobs, but it had all been achieved without too much damage to our own resources. Now was the time to concentrate on our own family. Ann would be helping her parents. When I had regained fitness, I wanted to attempt more writing. We would see how things developed, but might in time investigate a family property in London.

LEARNING FROM DIFFERENCE

Chapter 17

Lionel and Portair. Max and Nomad

In Chapter 9 we left Lionel in the workshop at Petersfield with little money but still determined not to become an employee. His files have survived. His efforts seem worth recording: as technology continually develops, many jobs disappear and more people seek the self-employment route. These efforts remain as a lesson in what can be attempted, though in this case he was not living in poverty. PC was prepared to support housing and living costs. Expenses for Karen and myself, including school fees, were covered by the Balfour - Jellicoe marriage settlement. Annual royalties from the Canadian oil interests purchased by his father, Max, seemed to average about £500 and there was an annual consultancy fee of £500 from Portsmouth Aviation (that's near to £9,000 each in 2013). There was some support from past efforts by him and his family, and also from the decision to marry PC. What he seemed to have wanted and achieved was to wake up each day to the challenge of creative work with his own hands plus business activity and decisions, rather than reflecting on past difficulties and losses. He did not seek sympathy. He did not want help from others. He wanted to get on with things in his own way and not to be in conflict with other managers and employers. Looking back, there is much to admire and I understand why he did not want to discuss the past. I also better understand my own difficulties with employers, the tangled path which eventually led to preferring self-employment.

After exit from Portsmouth Aviation, the first step seems to have been to establish L.M.J. Balfour and Co. Patent Development and Consulting Engineers, a one-man company registered at 32 Sussex Road, Petersfield. An edited edition of Lionel's note dated 9th February 1954 titled 'The story of the Balfour Auto-Sledge' follows:

'My wife and I were on a skiing holiday in Austria in 1952. The day after our arrival the cable railway had an accident and remained broken down for the time we were there. Everyone had to do a great deal of climbing to get their downhill running. This led to the idea of a petrol engined device which would take skiers uphill in an ultra light form weighing about 20lbs. It could be folded up and slung across the back for downhill running. An alternative was something larger with a driver which would tow several people on their skis. Propulsion by a sharp edged worm wheel or 'Archimedes' spiral actually engaging with the snow or ice surface seemed to offer the most promise. A remotely controlled tug with one horsepower engine was built and tried in Scotland and at Davos in March 1953 and valuable information gained. Based on this experience an eight horsepower Auto-Sledge unit was built and accompanied the British North Greenland Expedition in 1953.'

Whilst this device was in Greenland, Lionel experimented with a larger spiral worm-wheel within a sledge rather than as an attachment. As I was to discover some years later, my pre-war toboggan was reinforced and pressed into service. This ensemble achieved 12mph when Petersfield lake was frozen over in February 1954. The event was pictured in the local press with an article in the *Hants and Sussex News* on 10th February 1954 and the headline read 'Auto-sledge invention may revolutionise Arctic travel'. Lionel was right when he told the reporter that powered propulsion on snow and ice could have a wide application on frozen lakes and rivers, as well as on snow. As he also wrote in the 1954 note: 'It is expected to be useful in the Scandinavian countries and Canada for the carriage of persons and stores and might also be used by seal-hunters and trappers. With its light weight, it might also be carried by aircraft operating in the frozen North to enable crews to return to civilisation in the event of a forced landing.' The reports from the Greenland Expedition have not been found but it is evident from Lionel's letters of thanks that the propulsion unit was effective attached to the side of a Nansen sledge carrying 1,100 lbs weight. In his letter to Lieutenant Rollitt RN, dated 7th March 1955, he wrote: 'I have found your full and comprehensive report most interesting and helpful'. He then commented: 'your information and other experiences leads me to think that the Auto-Sledge should be like an outboard motor attached to the back so that the whole unit can be turned to steer. I also think the pitch of the propellor was too fine and that it should be greater and the machine geared down accordingly.'

Lionel's thinking and practical efforts to transmit power to winter surfaces were many steps in the right direction. Up to that time, bulky propeller-driven machines, like aeroplane fuselages without wings, had been used. What he did not realise was that, at the same time, Joseph-Armand Bombardier in Canada had been working on another form of transmission. This was a composite plastic transmission band which provided enough friction for forward movement on icy and snowy surfaces. It was the same aim, but simpler and easier to manufacture than Lionel's spiral worm-wheel. Bombardier produced the first 'ski-doo' as it was named, in 1959,[1] and four years later had sold over 8,000. Today these machines are being manufactured and sold in many countries and they are seen in action in most ski resorts. Bombardier Recreational Products has been sold, but the parent Bombardier Company is now a global organisation manufacturing planes and trains throughout the world. It was Bombardier who bought Canadian Car, the company who wanted to build the Aerocar in the 1940s. There is evidence in other letters that Lionel was becoming aware of these developments in Canada and he may then have realised that the transmission band was a better route to his objective. The internet describes earlier examples of other screw-propelled vehicles such as the Armstead Snow Motor in the 1920s and Geoffrey Pryke's experiments in the Second World War. They do work and can move heavier loads than friction bands, but the cost of continuous experimentation with the pitch and make-up of the screw would have been far beyond Lionel's resources. Even if an efficient design had been produced, as with the Aerocar he would have found it difficult to achieve financial support for production in large quantities. The hope must have been, again as with the Aerocar and the approach to

Blackburn and Auster, that he would have found another company or entrepreneur who would take it on.

Once again there is admiration for his efforts and physical hard work - what is needed today but with more realism about finance. Lionel may have also realised this, for he then worked on a product which was more suitable for his situation, did not need finance from others and which he could make himself in small quantities, responding to demand. This was the 'Car Roof Seat' from which to watch the sort of equestrian events which PC attended. It can be seen in the pictures. There are photographs laid out on large display cards all stamped L.M.J. Balfour and Co of office, paint shop and workshop with lathe, press, and cutting, angle-bending and notching machines. In the stores there are lengths of cut timber and some metal components, probably bought out, all neatly arranged on Dexion racking. One can only guess that these pictures were for Inland Revenue or Company House purposes. Their value now is that they show how hard he worked, every day with muscle and brain-power, mostly alone, with no time for regrets. In the 1930s, his father-in-law had remarked that Lionel worked as hard as any man he knew. Francis Luxmoore was a man of the same calibre. If the Aerocar had gained financial support, they might well have succeeded. The grandchildren, like their parents, are showing the same capacity for work. It is to be hoped that this ability can be channelled into effective projects. In November 1954 another company, LB Products and Engineering, was incorporated. This presumably was making use of all previous knowledge about tax matters with the help of the still-supportive Percy Cansdale. Those with whom he had worked remained loyal. There is, for instance, a letter about 1957/1958 tax: 'I enclose the data for the accounts of both L.M.J. Balfour and Co and L.B. Products and Engineering. I think it is policy to get as large a loss as possible agreed for L.M.J. Balfour and any expenses not agreed might be transferred to L.B. Products and Engineering.' For some reason that same year it was LMJ Balfour which sold car roof seats to LB Products. It was obviously a carefully thought-out operation with every single expense carefully recorded. A summary of these expenses includes hand tools, consumable tools and stores, experimental, process and production materials, office, travelling, meals away from home and car repair.

PC's wealthy merchant father had been living in a cottage attached to the garages of the Petersfield house. He died in 1957 and in his will there was enough money for PC to return to the Gloucestershire of her childhood. A house, stables and some land were bought near Tetbury. PC was now able to pursue her ambition to hunt with the Beaufort and, in the words of another letter to Percy Cansdale, 'establish a business buying young horses, bringing them on, training and selling them.' Lionel had to move all his tools and equipment from Hampshire and had the use of one part of the stables for production with an office in the house. A light picnic chair was also made and two years of steady production followed. We have the figures for 1959/1960. Twelve 'Ascot' Car Roof Seats and forty picnic seats were sold, all made with care and patience by Lionel. It was at this time that he took out a patent for 'a collapsible table adapted to be mounted on a wall, door or partition so that the floor space beneath the table is unobstructed. Lazy tongs linkages are mounted on the upright support and extend horizontally to form cantilever supports for the table top'. There is a 180-page file with drawings and patent applications for many countries. Some still criticised: 'Why did he not work for others, take a job?' I see this as the sort of self-employment which more people may have to consider. He was also helping PC with her business finances, looking after the marriage settlement and maintaining some link with Portsmouth. On receiving some funds from the settlement after marriage and wanting to keep the connection, I set about buying any Portsmouth Aviation shares which might be available. The few Cayzer family members who had personally helped in 1932 were willing to sell and I looked forward to attending annual meetings. Lionel wrote that 'he would only be too happy for me to have some association with the company I have spent so much effort and time creating.' It was soon after that I sent him some details of the Rochdale 'Olympic' mentioned in Chapter 12, and his helpful reply contained another reference to the past:

'I take such a poor view of new ideas and pioneer ideas taking on in this country without a tremendous and ruinous struggle that I think it would be well to avoid the pioneer stuff. Improvements to the things which the public already accepts, yes. If you supported Rochdale, it should be in a fairly small way and then cut your losses if it does not come off. It is fatal to be in such a big way that more and more of your capital gets sucked into it to stave off disaster which happened to me.'

This letter is treasured because it shows that he fully understood what had happened to him, did not see it as all his own fault and wanted to warn others of some of the realities of business in Britain.

Then came another bombshell. Lionel's efforts to get back on the board of directors at Portsmouth were not succeeding. Instead it was suggested that he should take over a subsidiary, Portair Products, which was making amongst other things the small Limpet wringer for the domestic market. Whilst Lionel would have preferred to be back with his own foundation, in some ways this was a more suitable conclusion, as he was now based in Gloucestershire. The Escott family wanted to own all the shares which, as a result of their hard work, now had value. They wanted to buy all Lionel's ordinary and preference shares and, in addition, would guarantee a bank overdraft to the extent of £4,000. My problem was that this proposal depended on my agreement to sell the shares which I had so recently purchased. I had not even attended one annual meeting. The last thing I wanted to do was to finally sever the connection with the workshops and hangers of my childhood - though I did not then realise, there was also the connection with Great-grandfather James's efforts in Chile as the source of that capital. But if I did not comply, the chance of a better future for Lionel was gone. This was such a difficult decision and I wish that it had been possible to retain the connection, particularly now when the company continues to prosper. But it was my interest versus my father's need. So the shares were sold and events that I had not anticipated followed.

In the files there is one Portair Products letterhead from early 1962 with Lionel, PC, myself, and my Godfather, Gerald Wood, as directors and the Airport, Portsmouth as address. Perhaps this was some consolation for Lionel. To a degree, he was back where he started. But then, in November 1962, he wrote of splitting up with PC: 'As we no longer enjoy the same things, as our interests and beliefs are now quite different, I think it has become inevitable.' The money from the Portsmouth Aviation shares and the backing for the overdraft enabled the purchase of an old mill in Woodchester, near Stroud in 1963. Lionel rented a room locally and did much of the refurbishment of the mill himself. When not working at Compton or in the Midlands, on Award Scheme activities, I spent quite a few days helping to clear up the sawdust from the previous workings. There is an early report about prospects: 'I do not see Limpet production as an end in itself but, if there is an organisation for manufacture with established sales channels, other products such as the concertina ironing boards and tables for confined spaces (the patent application mention above) and the tool stands can be introduced. I could not take this on without the fullest co-operation of Portsmouth Aviation who will be ordering and paying for the next batch of parts for 10,000 wringers and making them on my account until the physical transfer to Woodchester in May. They will only be charging for parts and materials consumed, they themselves paying for labour and overheads.' Six months later, Dudley Escott was still helping as can be seen in an October 1963 letter: 'There has been no change in Dudley's offer to assist on the tray and he is prepared to finance the manufacture and stocking leaving us the distribution.' This was another potential project, the 'carrywell' tray in which the tray was suspended by a ball linkage from the handle so that liquids in cups or glasses could be carried with one hand. Lionel wrote many letters to me as a director. They are a record of what was achieved and the difficulties of production. There is a further detailed report for the directors, now just me and Gerard Wood. Looking at this again fifty years later, I am in awe of the workload Lionel gave himself. Considering the Limpet wringer, he was responsible for design details and costing e.g. 'the cost of electro tinning on the axles to eliminate corrosion problems can be reduced by painting with a new resin-trichlorethylene preparation from I.C.I.', and the sourcing and collection of components e.g 'the original suppliers of rubber rollers were too expensive. Some fifteen rubber firms were asked to quote and only Hermetic in Birmingham gave a satisfactory price of three shillings per pair.' It was such an achievement from virtually nothing, but the fact remains that they needed to produce and sell five hundred Limpets per week and they were only averaging three hundred and seventy. At least all these were sold, with 'a large proportion bought by Great Universal Stores.'

The report then moves onto the familiar problem of finance. At the time I pencilled in on the front 'another £1,500 needed before the end of the month'. This is all written down because it is another good warning to entrepreneurs. Despite all the merit of the hard work, it can come to nothing unless costs are rigorously controlled - Dudley Escott's achievement at Portsmouth. Closely studying the report again after all these years, I am reminded that nearly £1,000 more than budgeted was spent on refurbishing the building and the shortfall in production meant a nearly equivalent loss. There are even echoes of the Aerocar, where money was spent liberally on publicity. This may have produced provisional orders, but it was all lost when no aeroplanes were built. Lionel understandably wanted that old mill to be in good order. He thought costs would soon be balanced by increasing production, but it might have made more financial sense to rent a more basic industrial unit until he had a better idea of the profit potential. As a director, I was in a difficult position. Lionel wanted me to continue and he knew that I had access to money which had come from the marriage settlement. £1,000 is the equivalent of £17,000 today, and there could well have been more demands. As described in Chapter Twelve, it was only available by selling family shares at considerably below their potential value. All these happenings helped me to realise that the time had come to get back to full-time paid work. Apart from retaining money which could be needed in the future, if I continued with entrepreneurial activities which allowed some independence, my portfolio would have to include helping at Portair. We then learnt from Lionel that he was to marry again, this time to a lady who had helped him with secretarial work at Petersfield. Ann and I concluded that we should provide the money this time, but give notice that I could not continue much longer as a director as there was a chance of returning to full-time work in the Midlands. I was actually only a director in name, as it was clear that Lionel still wanted to take all the decisions. The mill purchase should have been questioned, also the cost of taking out so many patents,[2] but parental authority was then stronger than it is today. The new Mrs Balfour was then able to take my place as director. We also decided that we should, with my sister, help with house purchase. At least we had provided some companionship in the period when he was on his own between marriages.

Lionel now had what amounted to a new family. Remaining letters show that he was kind and helpful to his new wife's two daughters. He did still write from time to time about progress, for I was still an investor in the company, but it would have been difficult in his changed family circumstances for me to have remained a director and challenged the pair of them, Lionel and his new wife, about their decisions. I do not have details of the next few years, then in 1967 came a letter saying that a virus caught that summer had weakened his heart, that he would probably survive only five years, but that I was not to tell anyone - including his wife. I was stuck, not wanting to stop the work in the Careers Service with which I was so fully occupied at that stage. A letter to PC confirms that Portair never made a profit, but in the final years the loss was less than £500. A July 1971 letter sums up the situation and the difficulties of small firms:

'I can do less and have had to take on another hand to do the production I was doing (because of the weak heart). The demand for the Limpet continues to increase. The ticket equipment stoving is also excellent, but the Post Office work for Westinghouse ,whilst technically mastered does not go so well on an output to price basis. In addition they are very bad payers.'

Contracts for others (which did not suddenly cease), and building up a reputation as a reliable provider alongside production of their own products, were the potential salvation of the company. If this stage had been reached before age and ill-health took its toll, Portair might have gone on and prospered. This leads to more reflection on whether I should have resigned from my unpaid directorship. The counter-argument was that, whilst the Careers Service was not well paid, we were able to survive and keep capital intact. Lionel was obviously short of cash. He may not have been drawing out the full salary which we had agreed at early meetings. So I was glad that we were, by then, able to send him some money which he so obviously appreciated. He wrote: 'what a truly pleasant surprise, thank you so much, it relieves anxiety and also means that I can pay my share of our holiday.' We were glad they had an enjoyable three weeks down the west coast of France then across those lovely French foothills of the Pyrenees, visiting Myrtle's sister, Norah, at Sète, and then back through the Auvergne. The next letter of note came in April 1972 and again is valuable about the life of small companies:

'I am afraid it is the end of the road for Portair Products. There was a small loss of around £450 and we shall come to a sticky end unless we stop now. If the Bank puts in a Receiver, he will be quite ruthless, sell the property and any plant to the first comers to cover the overdraft leaving little surplus value to pay off our creditors and a terrible mess for me to clear up both physically and financially. Frankly clearing up Portair with my poor physical capacity is something I dread.'

I began to prepare to try and help and then once again the ever-faithful Percy Cansdale, by now a forty-year relationship since the early days of PSIOWA, came to the rescue. Lionel explained:

'Cansdale has found an alternative in his son-in-law, Roger Cossham, who will take the whole matter off my hands and let me step free almost tomorrow. He will take over the bank overdraft, sell the plant and property, pay off the trade creditors, find the money for the staff's notice period and arrange for the completion of some stock. In return for this he requires the shares transferred to him for a nominal amount and the loans written off. I am more than sorry to have got you involved with this failure but if you can help with parting with your shares for £1 the lot and writing off loans, it will be very much appreciated.'

My reaction, and I think I wrote back to reassure him at the time, was that it was not failure but rather a heroic effort to have kept a small firm with tiny assets trading and providing employment for so long. Because we were by then financially stable, we were able to send him another cheque for his personal use. We were pleased that in July 1972 they had one more holiday, travelling to Switzerland and picking up one of his wife's daughters who had been working there. Lionel died in January 1973. He had been able to drive himself to hospital for some treatment. The next morning he woke and was about to drink a cup of tea when his heart stopped. It was thought that he had no pain at all. He had worked so hard till those final days. He may not have made money but nor had he lived off taxpayer's money as an employee of the State, as I had done during those years in the Careers Service. Many different people have had fruitful working lives because of him. Many others, perhaps grandparents of today's airline passengers, had their first experience of flight because of his efforts. Portsmouth Aviation still flourishes in 2013.

As described in other chapters, I only achieved the fringes of entrepreneurial effort. However our son Max, after graduating from Imperial College and working for computer firms, decided to follow his grandfather's example and establish his own company. The lessons from Lionel's experiences have been put to good use. The first Business Plan for Nomad Software Ltd was drawn up in 1992:

'Nomad Software plans to build and market a software package for electronic retail banking. This will bring the convenience of a system based on point of sales terminals and cash machines to customers of banks in countries where such facilities are largely unavailable. Where such banking is well established, the cost effectiveness of the Nomad software will allow increased penetration. Nomad's solution is radical and only possible because of innovative software and the recent maturing of important technologies. Instead of a large central computer, it uses several smaller, simpler computers connected through a standard communications network. Instead of ATMs (Automated Teller Machines), many of the service points are advanced yet low cost POS (Point of Sale) terminals. The core system is open allowing other programs and modules to share the facilities it offers. There are fast growing markets for such services in Latin America, the Caribbean, Eastern Europe, Africa and India.'

Max and his two founding partners, Tom Hay and Mirek Chelkowski, who had evolved

197

this new system whilst working at a small company called Interlink, were able to produce £50K, with some of Max's input coming from a mortgage on the London house (see Chapter 18). In the 1993 offer document seeking to raise £100K the directors were able to write that they were 'working on ten promising opportunities. Nomad's software package, now named Cortex,[3] allows retailers to save money by polling their own terminals and making a single bulk delivery of all transactions to the bank instead of being charged by the bank for this function.' Family and friends rallied round and the required sum was provided. An approach to the Cayzer cousins was unsuccessful. Whilst some of the younger directors expressed interest in the opportunities for Cortex, the older hands, unfamiliar with this technology and mindful of their responsibilities to the wider family, decided not to support. They also correctly pointed to the lack of business experience in the management team. In some respects it was reminiscent of earlier attitudes to the Aerocar. It was not sensible to take risks when there were many safer and easier to understand investment opportunities. There were still sufficient funds contributed from other sources to be able to press on.

An early Nomad brochure, 'solutions in card transaction processing', included comments from two early customers. Banco Gerencial and Fiduciario in the Dominican Republic wrote: 'We looked at a wide range of packages, many of them from local Latin American suppliers, however none of them provided the in-depth functionality of Cortex.' Kredo Banka in Latvia wrote: 'Cortex offered us excellent integration with our host system at a highly competitive price and gives us a strong advantage over our competitors.' Over the following years more contracts were achieved, but it also became increasingly obvious that more capital would be needed. Each sales prospect took a lot of money and it was impossible to predict which would be successful. Potential clients all had their own difficulties which could affect outcomes. It was agreed to accept investment from two venture capitalist companies who first became involved in 2000. By 2004 it was realised that the sale of Cortex systems to banks and other clients, whilst remaining in profit, could not - just as a licence-selling and servicing business - lead to large growth. With the venture capital money available, it was decided to invest in prepaid card processing so that Nomad would receive a small credit from every transaction. The Newcastle Building Society commented:

'The Newcastle has successfully outsourced the processing of its prepaid cards to Nomad who offer a cost effective and fast route to market. Having previously worked with Nomad on the debit card side of the business, we knew what the company was capable of and that it was well placed from technology, security and market knowledge perspectives to support our prepaid processing needs.'

The Nomad directors' report for 2004 stated:

'A year of transition as we invested heavily in the new Debit Direct service, now known as Nomad Processing Services, which went live with its first customer at the end of the year. Revenues increased 28% on 2003 partly through increased Cortex license and service fees but also through the first fees being generated from Debit Direct.' Another summary confirmed: 'Nomad has already signed its first Debit

Direct member. Islamic House of Britain has a strong pipeline (three banks and four building societies) which it expects to sign up within the next six months.'

Now at last there was involvement in a business which had adequate funding. In 2004 the venture capitalists provided £1,526,000 in loans, the sort of money (though with different value!) with which the Jam Sahib had agreed to fund Portsmouth Aviation Nawanager Ltd in the 1940s. As a result of this deal, Max and the other founders were asked to resign as directors. At least, unlike at Portsmouth fifty years earlier, they remained with the company with all their knowledge and experience.

A new professional chairman, also a chief financial officer, were appointed plus more supporting staff. The fly in the ointment was that the loans would fall due in five years and would then require a repayment of 200% of the original value. Also, we shareholders had no power to prevent Max's dismissal, though if that happened, he would still remain a substantial shareholder. Somehow he managed to tolerate those at the helm who did not always share his vision. As to our family investment, we were in a weak position, but there were good prospects for the company. Then Max heard that Coller Capitol, a leading player in private equity secondaries were keen to sell the small shareholding in Nomad which they had obtained from Abbey National Treasury services. The shareholder agreements prevented individuals connected with the company from purchasing this block of shares. However it was permissible for an investment trust to own shares. Kit Power, Philip Wingfield and I decided to establish a Limited Partnership, in effect an investment trust, to purchase the Coller stake. Assisted by other family members, this entity was able to take on the whole Coller stake and as a result obtained representation on the Nomad Board. We used the name we had thought up years ago at Cambridge for future membership of the House of Lords (as I later realised, not so difficult to attain if the Liberal invitation had been taken up). This was a much more valuable usage of the name. Meondale Ltd was established with Kit, Philip and I as directors.

It was also fortunate that there had been activity within the Cayzer family. Other family members had become more forcefully concerned about the difficulty which we had encountered in the 1960s, namely that we could not sell our shares at anything like their true value (see Chapter 12). As the *Telegraph* magazine had written in August 2001: 'According to Sir James and his advisers family members could realise little more than a quarter of the real value of their inheritance.'[4] This was cousin James Cayzer, who had teamed up with his nephew and heir Nigel and other cousins to dispute the values suggested to potential sellers by Cayzer Trust. Discussions and meetings continued throughout 2002 and part of 2003. What became known as the Minority Group established Cayzer Continuation in Guernsey. In September 2003 the chairman of Cayzer Trust, another cousin - Peter Buckley - wrote of seeking earnestly to come to an agreement on withdrawal of capital on terms which were fair and reasonable to all shareholders. This was part of a letter urging shareholders to reject proposals leading to liquidation.[5] That autumn, the buy-back proposals were implemented. It was made clear that there would not be another opportunity in our lifetime and we accepted, for a portion of our Cayzer shares, some cash and some shares in Cayzer Continuation. In April 2004 Peter Buckley confirmed that a settlement had been reached.[6] We were glad that we had not sold years earlier as part of an attempt to make Portair profitable.

These negotiations were concluded in time for some of this cash and some of the Cayzer Continuation money to be put into Meondale. Other family members, Max's sisters and my sister Karen, gave support, as did the Power and Wingfield families. Friends and contacts chipped in and became Limited Partners. Meondale had collected £280,000, enough for a Meondale director to be in place at Board meetings and be a party to discussions about the future. The next two years were difficult. New customers praised the product, but the cost of demonstrating proposals continued to rise. We also knew the time would come when the other venture capitalists would want their money back. There were not sufficient resources for a management buyout and discussion turned to an outright sale, knowing that Nomad had praised and proven achievements. In September 2007 a merger and acquisitions expert was brought in and before long there were discussions with the American Company, Metavante. Kit Power e-mailed after attending a board meeting in November:

> 'All the signs are that Metavante are pretty serious. They are talking about a formal offer in the range $40-60million. Bryan (the Chairman) thinks it will be somewhere around £27million and that anything over £30million would be a miracle. Bryan thought this was the best opportunity of making a sale. The alternative of ploughing on and hoping for a better offer may not work because, were we to do this, we would need at least £5million new money to take the business to the next stage.'

In early 2008, the deal was done at $58million dollars - that was then just over £29 million. A large chunk of this went to the venture capitalists. It was only a moderate result for the founder shareholders, though they did get some profit on their original stake. They had also been offered the chance, which some had taken, of participating in Meondale. All those Meondale partners received five times their original stake. Had we hesitated, well, the crash came all too soon afterwards and Metavante might have then withdrawn. I don't think we had particular foresight; it was more that we had all had relevant experience. Kit Power had observed the fate of many companies in his days as a 'head hunter', Philip Wingfield - son of Myrtle's sister Norah - had been a banker and I had had the experience of living through the Aerocar saga and much else. I had seen what had happened when loans had got out of hand or unforeseen external circumstances had taken hold. There had been the difficult business of watching Portair always needing a little more. There had been the long drawn-out negotiation for access to the settlement. Now at last there was a positive result akin to what those Balfour brothers achieved in the 19th Century. Soon after the sale, Metavante was bought by another American giant, FIS, whose website[7] describes 'leadership positions in payment processing and banking solutions providing software, services and outsourcing of the technology that drives financial solutions.' Worldwide they employ 35,000 people. Max is one of their consultants. Some of the original Nomad employees also work for FIS. Cortex is now confirmed as FIS's international card management system. It is currently used in Australia, Brazil, the Dominican Republic and India. Max tells of the continuing high cost of each sales pitch and that potential clients, e.g. international banks, prefer to work with a large company with substantial backing. It would have been difficult to develop Nomad into an international competitor. It's the story of this book. The talents of many British people may be best used harnessed to global organisations and there are still plenty of areas in which they can contribute.

The hut at Redmarley

With recent storms, many of the 100-year-old orchard trees have now died. We have compensated with new planting.

The four hard-worked cars, which, with the Saab 96, provided transport 1980s and 1990s. Not all British! Three are still with us and the Opel Commodore has been fully restored by the new owner

We found another wreck in the 1980s, this time a 2.6 litre Hotchkiss, in some ways the best of them with sturdy simplicity, sound design and not too big an engine. Learning the lessons of the Delahaye and the Hispano, and over 25 years, with much work done by Nick Cooper, Tony Curtis, Graham Floyd, Peter Jarvie, Alan and Peter Jones, Philip Goss, Paul Hurley and Richard Williams, Spencer Lane-Jones, the engine and chassis have been carefully rebuilt or repaired and a new strong body has been created. The saloon body is stored. None of the body components have been used, if, in years to come, another owner wishes to build up an original car.

Whilst we do not have the collection which might have been possible if other decisions had been taken, working on the cars we have kept is a restorative pleasure which, also seems to recharge the brain. They are reliable, in use and provide sufficient transport so that it is not necessary to have a depreciating modern car

As a spectator, I was able to follow, the 1988 Coupe des Pyrenees

The late George Milligan in 1929 SSK Mercedes at Foix. Recently sold after his death for millions

Derek Bonzom's 1928 Delage DMS climbing the Col d'Envalira, Andorra

Jean Martinez's Delahaye 135 crossing the bridge at Sabarat

Andorra

Above & above right: View from the flat summer and winter

Right: Saab 96. Looking across encamp to Els Cortals

Bristols in Andorra. 406 on the left. 603, Port de Cabus on the right. The track into Spain

Typical dust from extensive building work in La Massana during the 1980s

The Austin on the track above Pal before it was surfaced

In 1996, we were able to take part in the FIVA World Rally. Here with Shotaro Kobayashi of *Car Graphic*, Tokyo

How often do you see two 37.2 Hispanos together and with a Vauxhall 30/98

A Delahaye 135, also recently sold for many millions

Our neighbours at Ryde, Bill Dallimer, Jim Shaw, John Childerstone and Pete Jarvie who created a good 190 from a scrap-heap wreck and the remains of the red car. Round a bend in a high banked country lane, another car was heading towards us in the middle of the road. There was no escape

The original Hotchkiss Saloon body with disintegrating wood framework

Asia & India, 1930: if you're thinking of motoring home in 1930 and your friends bet you half-crown you won't succeed, what can you do? Messrs Bromage and Stubbs (Imperial civil engineers) serviced their 1926 Armstrong-Siddeley 30 tourer (54,000 miles already on the mileometer), fitted extra petrol tanks and set out from Lahore with their Indian chauffeur (in uniform and peaked cap). Seventy-three days later, after transhipping from Beirut to Athens, here they are for a reception in London given in their honour by JD Siddeley. Mpg was 17. They had no mechanical problems except for broken spring leaves and two punctures

The Overlanders

B efore the Second World War, sea and air voyages were slow, expensive tedious. So the more adventurous used their vehicles to travel across contine Most of the travellers drove the long route via Baluchistan, and then took from the Eastern Mediterranean. It was only the bold, like the Colonel's Phantom p who achieved the Afghan short-cut, and the brave, like Mr Canagaseby and Ju Davies, who attempted Turkey. After the war many continued, including all those trekked across the Sahara to a new life in the British African colonies.

Except for substituting Istanbul for Constantinople, contemporary place-na have been used. For this special picture scrapbook, Christopher Balfour is your gui

Asia & India, 1933: Judge Davies and his chauffeur were among the first to motor across the Sind Desert, north of Bombay, in their 12/50 Alvis which had already done 50,000 miles on Indian roads. This is in Baluchistan (with a locally-used Model 'A' Ford). They tackled Turkey without suffering the indignities of the Vauxhall crew at Dortyol, but the roads and tracks were so bad – broken and pitted surfaces in the dry, deep mud when it rained – that they often had to take to open country, and some days only managed 10 miles. They strayed into a military zone after leaving Istanbul and, like the Trojan party, were arrested at gunpoint. Fortunately the local judiciary discovered their prisoner was a judge and they were allowed to proceed. Wheel studs then sheared when a wheel shook loose. After local repair the otherwise reliable Alvis took them to London

Asia & India, 1930: Charles Agar and his wife (no chauffeur!) motored back from Shiraz to Manchester in a 1923 Vauxhall. They are pictured on the bridge at Antioch. Driving through Turkey had to be abandoned after customs and police encounters at Dortyol. All their tinned f was opened for examination and a financial deposit larger than available resources demande armed officials. The old 30/98's rate of travel still impresses: 596 miles to Tehran in two days From Baghdad, they managed 275 miles in eight-and-half hours to catch up with the regular coach service near Rutba Wells (an unaccompanied crossing of the Syrian Desert to Damasc was not allowed). But the speed and the shaking on poor surfaces took its toll; spring mounti windscreen and hood stays, gearchange selector and petrol tank all needed repair. Back in E they again make good time, Piacenza across the Alps to Lyons in one day, 387 miles in 12 ho

114

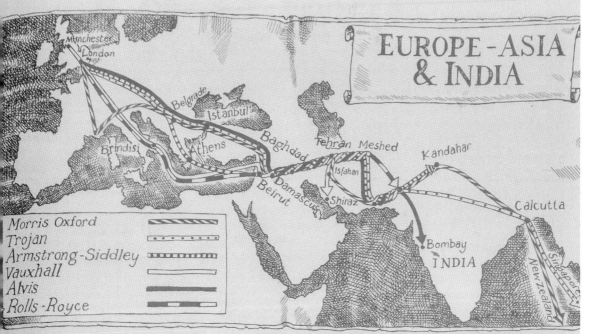

EUROPE-ASIA & INDIA

Morris Oxford
Trojan
Armstrong-Siddley
Vauxhall
Alvis
Rolls-Royce

Asia & India, 1926: would you drive 12 miles in England without the comforting air cushion of the modern tyre encircling your wheels? In 1926 Messrs Canagaseby, De Silva and Scully drove 12,000 miles from Singapore in a solid-tyred Trojan. They were true overlanders all the way from Calcutta to Calais, but they realised their misgivings about Turkey were justified when they were arrested as suspected murderers. They're pictured on the snowy Assadabad Pass, in what was then Persia, and crossing Westminster Bridge accompanied by other Trojan enthusiasts. Before you start a campaign for posthumous medals for the crew, remember that Leslie Hounsfield's unique cantilever suspension went some way towards compensation for the lack of pneumatics and this was one trip without tyre troubles

Asia & India, 1933: in 1933 a Colonel attached to the Indian Political Service, who had observed Rolls-Royce reliability in Imperial conditions, gathered friends to drive two secondhand Phantom IIs (cost: £130 apiece) back from UK leave. When they set out Afghanistan had been firmly closed to travellers. But, at Meshed, they learnt of the death of Nadir Shah and that visas would be granted. They were one of the first to tell the tale of the appalling Afghan roads. Here is a typical encounter with a local bridge between Farah and Kandahar. Then they pushed and dug their way across that devilish sand sea, the notorious short-cut to Chaman, and to Quetta

One of the pleasure of working for Haymarket was that *Classic & Sports Car* asked me to compile some articles on motoring history. These are the first two pages of one of them

LEARNING FROM DIFFERENCE

Chapter 18

Andorra. Authorship. Hut. Highbury.
Haymarket. Lloyd's. Europe

During the latter years in the Careers Service, I had found myself increasingly catching colds picked up in the schools and this had developed into sinus problems. It was a nuisance. Walks at weekends to try and improve the situation made it worse. Then the problem often recurred after attending Council committees. My powers of resistance were weak. There were fewer Council meetings during the summer. Could there be somewhere where I could revive myself when things got bad? With Ann's encouragement I sailed on the ship to Santander, with the Austin and its sleeping platform. The first stop was attractive Castro Urdiales, halfway to Bilbao, where BBC programmes could be picked up even on the ancient Austin wireless. This would allow contact with UK events, but the price of flats was higher than we could afford. Driving east, skirting the Pyrenees and sleeping overnight in lay-bys or in the gateways of fields, the Austin pounded along to Andorra. Much of the central valley was then an unattractive building site with just tracks leading up to what are now fully mechanised ski areas. However, once high up above the construction areas, the mountain views were magnificent. The air seemed immediately invigorating. Breathing was soon better than for many years. To cut a long story short, this experience was not forgotten and in 1985 we were able to buy the large studio which we still so much enjoy twenty-nine years later. During the last two years on the Council, when so much affected by smoking etc, it was a life-saver to take the overnight train from Gare d'Austerlitz and find that breathing was clear again after just a few days.

Ann was finding the distance to Winchester, to see and help her parents, increasingly difficult. Max was working for a computer firm in London, Juliet was training at Bart's Hospital Medical School and Kate was soon to start at John Cleese's firm Video Arts, also in London. We decided to sell the Redmarley house during that last year as a Councillor (I would have temporary accommodation for the remaining few months) and use some of the money to purchase in London. It was Juliet who found the house at Battledean Road in Highbury, which needed a great deal of work. An offer of £80,000 was accepted. Ann would be much nearer to Winchester, with time to see and help her parents enjoy their remaining days surrounded by their friends. She would have a small flat in Battledean Road for when she was not in Andorra or Winchester. We also retained a field and orchard at Redmarley, where neighbour and master builder, Tony Watkins constructed a strong wooden hut as allowed by planning regulations. This has withstood nearly 30 years of English weather. In addition we purchased an Old Dodge camping van which had originally been equipped for Canadian conditions and brought over to Europe as a racing-car tender. This splendid machine, with an engine similar to some of the V8 Bristols, was sufficiently insulated for the occasional winter night. It was also invaluable for carting furniture about.

We felt we had effectively reorganised our life to cope with the changing situation, but then came another of those bombshells similar to those encountered in dealings with Lionel. Ann's parents had gone to visit her brother, Christopher, and his family in New Zealand as they said 'for the last time', (her father was then over 90) before spending their remaining days assisted by Ann at Winchester. Ann had been clearing up in their house whilst I was in Gloucestershire. We were meeting up for an evening party with Nigel and Barbara Hensman (Nigel had been at Highfield, Eton, Catterick and Cambridge) in their house at Hammersmith. I saw the Saab with Ann inside and was able to park the Opel nearby. I saw at once that Ann did not look happy and, when I got to her, she exploded: 'The parents have just telephoned. They say they have found a suitable bungalow and are staying in New Zealand. They are commanding us to sell the Winchester house at once and send out the furniture.' It was not a party that we much enjoyed. Much of what we had done had been based on plans which were now overturned. It was particularly difficult for Ann, but I was still glad that I had stopped the Council and it looked as if the Highbury house was going to be beneficial for the next generation. We also hoped they would enjoy New Zealand. It was just that, as with Lionel's plans, there had been no discussion. It was necessary to re-think. Ann was going to be free of her expected responsibilities. We needed a house together and believed that the Winchester house could be turned into a convenient property. Previous experience had stiffened us in standing up to older generations. This time we did not accept the command, but there was no spare money. It had all been allocated, but our always helpful Solicitor, Richard Eddis at Stephenson Harwood, managed to persuade the Bank that, though I had no earned income at that stage, there was value in Cayzer shares, and I was a member of Lloyd's etc. A mortgage was forthcoming and Ann's parents accepted the reasonable offer which we made for their house.

We had had our share of problems, but then came a bit of luck which made so much difference to the next twenty years, and almost every day I am reminded of - and marvel at - this stroke of good fortune. Ann was having a lengthy session discussing health issues with Aunt Rachel at Amesbury. Having had a short talk with Rachel myself, I was waiting in the car and looking through a current motoring magazine and there it was: an advertisement requesting an archivist to work in the library and sort all the photographic material for Haymarket's motoring magazines. These were mainly colour transparencies - it was some years before much of it became digital - but there were also many historic black-and-white photographs. Why I was chosen from the very many applicants will never be known. Buying that particular magazine was just chance and it must also have been chance that my letter stood out, though it's also true that they wanted an older person to partner the younger applicant they were also taking on. Jon Pressnell, who had previously worked in the Archive, may have put in a good word for me. After much effort and overcoming some difficulties, Jon has gone on to write some magnificent books about the motor industry and it is always a pleasure to visit him in his attractive house west of Cahors. Once again I saw that one can try and plot a course in life, but there are always the actions of other humans. This time they worked in my favour. It was a good thing I did not hesitate, as on arrival, I found that I was to be the junior partner, subservient to the younger man. Lowly status, had to be accepted - no more the occasional Chair of Policy with easy access to MPs and high civil servants! But it was good to be associated with journalists, led by Mick Walsh and Mike McCarthy, who were agreeable company and always appreciative of efforts on their behalf to find appropriate pictures. After a while, my initial partner moved on to become a journalist and I was in charge of the Archive. The pay was also reasonable for those times, which was fortunate as Lloyd's was soon to go through its bad period of losses and we had to cope with that unexpected mortgage.

Then came another unexpected happening. Karen's elder son, Nigel, had a place at Winchester College of Art. With three fellow students, they were happy to pay us rent from their grants and Max, Juliet and Kate kindly agreed that Ann and I could be based for a bit at the Highbury house. This led to experience of nasty travelling from Highbury round to Vauxhall, by underground then a suburban train to Teddington. During college holidays, when the students were not at Winchester, I attempted daily commuting, sometimes driving, sometimes leaving the Dodge at the vast Woking car-park and continuing on the fast train. I even spent a night or two in the van, but it was not the best way to maintain freshness the next day! We stayed for a short spell in the magnificent Twickenham house belonging to Penny and Kit Power (who have been continuously supportive throughout our life) whilst Penny and Kit were away. We are so glad that later (see Chapter 17) they received a small benefit. Eventually we agreed that we must look for a short-term rental near the archives and we were able to find a small flat. Ann was with me as much as possible, and even sometimes helped with filing in the Archive. Courageously, she also frequently coped with the journey right across London to supervise and labour herself on the restoration of the Highbury house in Battledean Road. Gradually, as I got to know kind and encouraging journalist colleagues like Mick and Mike, and later Giles Chapman, I was asked to contribute. For a while I did a monthly history piece for *Your Classic* whilst it remained in print and there were occasional contributions to *Classic and Sports Car* the monthly which flourishes today. All in all, I was earning more than when I had been Principal Careers Officer. Concorde setting off on its daily service from Heathrow was a pleasing sight and sound from the basement windows. Visits to the hut at Redmarley were enjoyed in the summer and, as when I was on the Council, the Andorra studio was just the simple overnight journey away when nasal problems returned or batteries needed a re-charge. It was up to Waterloo after the Archive closed, then the quick journey to Paris, followed by the sleeper to Hospitalet and the bus to la Vella by breakfast-time next morning.

Some of those who have commented on Andorra have been critical of developments since the 1960s. The introduction to the Cicerone guide[1] writes of: ' The bizarre duty-free shopping mall which threads Andorra la Vella, eight kilometres of perfume, hi-fi and booze shops'. Yes, this is true (though those kilometres also include Escaldes and Encamp) but the Andorrans have found a route to survival when traditional tobacco cultivation decreased and in recent years there has been an enormous effort to tidy up and garnish the whole area. Litter is swiftly collected, construction has decreased and most previously derelict areas have been sorted. There are often gorgeous flowers bordering the pavements and all the roundabouts have colourful displays. Trees have been planted where appropriate. Roads have been improved, always with flawless surfaces. Awe-inspiring tunnels have been driven through the rock. Fly-overs and bridges of almost sculptural merit ameliorate intersections. All these constructions have improved traffic flow and, for the moment, there is sufficient multi-storey parking. Cicerone also writes: 'The beauty still exists a short walk away in unspoilt side valleys. The range of walks available in a compact area is breathtaking and much quieter than in the Alps or better known areas of the Pyrenees.' As I write in October, two days ago we took the path above Ransol. The track through the lower trees was well-marked and well-maintained with errant branches cut back, one to a saw sculpture of a duck. Past the treeline, leaves turning to multi-hued autumn colour, we came to the upper pastures with streams of clear water tumbling down from the rugged peaks and imposing rock formations above us. A few days earlier we were above Pal, at the Port de Cabus where the track continues over the border into Spain and the hamlet of Tor and then the village of Alins. It was a gorgeous morning - hardly a cloud in the sky. We were alone in the world except for docile groups of horses. To the east were all the mountains of Andorra and to the west the irregular majestic peaks of the Pyrenees along the skyline. Andorra is also known as a place to reside to avoid some UK taxes. We had some thoughts in this direction when British and Commonwealth shares soared. We realised that this could be an opportunity at last to benefit from the Cayzer heritage. We hesitated because of the need to take on the Winchester house, and then British and Commonwealth collapsed and the shares were of no value. We have still benefited so much from our times in the Principality as visitors rather than residents. We have particularly appreciated the paucity of rules and regulations compared with some other countries. The CISA group, who built this building, Edifici Cabanota, just before we came, and have gone on to construct many other apartment blocks, have always been helpful. Recently, as a result of Nomad and Cayzer developments, we have purchased another flat in the same building. This has been a base for grandchildren to enjoy Andorra's excellent skiing opportunities.

By the middle of the 1990s, when I was approaching 65, I was increasingly aware that my eyes were beginning to protest at the hours spent on the light-box poring over film. Publishers came seeking material and I got to know Charles Herridge of Bay View Books. In conversation, I mentioned my interest in the post-war exploits of British cars and how much material was available. Charles gave encouragement and Simon Taylor, who, as chairman of Haymarket Motoring Publications had overseen my original appointment, kindly agreed that I could quote from any of the correspondence or reports in *Motor* and *Autocar* during those years since 1945. This was a treasure-trove of information from owners all over the world who had had problems with the cars in the post-war period. Then there were all the rally reports, complete with photographs. This was the material which led to my first book *Roads to Oblivion, the Triumphs and Tragedies of British Car Makers 1946 to 1956*. This was published by Bay View in 1996. Charles Herridge found an appropriate photograph of a Riley Pathfinder with Monte Carlo plates rounding a corner, with an upturned Austin Westminster in the background. This was cleverly colour tinted and can be seen on Amazon google entries where there is currently (2013) one new copy on sale at 300 dollars[2]. I had stopped work in the Archive in 1994 and Haymarket had kindly sent me off with the commission to compile the initial 'year by year' texts for *Autocar*'s 100 years celebration issue, to be published in November 1995. Giles Chapman honed my words into appropriate format. We were now able to return to Winchester. With these earnings and better results from Lloyd's, we were able to pay off the mortgage. It was the achievement of *Roads to Oblivion* which led me to Gerald Palmer, designer of the Jowett

Javelin, MG Magnette and Riley Pathfinder amongst other cars, who - then in his mid-eighties - wanted help with his autobiography, *Auto Architect*.[3] Through the Archive, I had also met Malcolm and Andrea Green who ran Magna Press, already the publishers of many MG books and well known in those circles. Gerald's book seemed a good fit. They correctly forecast that it would be popular with the MG clubs. Demand from Jowett owners and then from others interested in the demise of the British owned car companies followed (see Chapter 19).

I am often asked by prospective authors how to get published, especially when they write about specialised subjects for which there are never going to be large sales. There is no simple answer. We each have to find our own path. Mine was the work in those Archives, which led to contact with these small publishers who know they are unlikely to make fortunes but are prepared to work away at the valuable task of making this sort of information available to those who are interested. *Auto Architect* went on to a paperback 'print on demand' edition to which I contributed an additional chapter. It continues to be purchased and consulted by students of the industry. Then, with some diffidence, I mentioned my father Lionel's efforts to Malcolm and he kindly agreed to underwrite the cost of what became *Spithead Express*.[4] This was well-received by aviation historians and led to invitations to talk to aviation groups. PSIOWA now seems to be recognised as a small but important part of the fledgling years of British airlines. My ability to actually complete a text was then recognised. It was Jon Pressnell who kindly suggested to Mark Hughes at Haynes Publishing (who had also previously worked at Haymarket) that I might be the person to attempt a book on Bristol Cars. There was help from many people. Mark was endlessly patient as we tried to achieve a text which would satisfy all the very different, determined and strong characters who had been involved with the company. I was particularly pleased that Mark agreed to the inclusion of comments from owners all over the world. It is good that the book is now in its third edition. I hope that it has contributed to knowledge of the company's achievements.

Membership of the Lloyd's insurance market has already been mentioned, particularly in Chapter 16. We were eventually able to achieve a high-enough value of the Cayzer Trust shares for the bank to offer a guarantee, with these shares as security. Every other asset, including the Gloucestershire orchard, was also valued. In all there was sufficient 'wealth' to be elected as a Lloyd's Name in 1981. In those days it was the task of Members' Agents to offer Syndicate capacity to the Names they looked after relative to the value of the funds (known as 'Funds at Lloyd's' - FAL) which they had deposited. Alastair Leslie, whom I had known since childhood when his parents lived next to FG at Sunningdale, started us off with some good capacity, for which there was then no charge. The risks were constantly emphasised. The membership brochure published in 1986 stated: 'The entire personal wealth of a member is at risk - members must consider whether they can afford to lose what may amount to substantial sums'. Also: 'Underwriting is a cyclical business and membership should be viewed as a long term venture'. Looking back, my early thoughts were probably muddled, but I think we did soon realise that any profits were not a bonus to fund increases in living expenses. Other experiences had taught us to avoid financial advisers. We reckoned that we needed to build up reserves to pay for future losses and be careful about how much we used to assist with our basic way of life. With some income from shares, expenses for various Council-related activities, Ann's careful housekeeping and a little of the Lloyd's profits, we were able to survive.

A few years later we were into a difficult period of Lloyd's history. Membership had soared, reaching over thirty thousand Names. The Advisers had been at work. Some have commented that those in command at Lloyd's had become aware of large claims ahead and wanted to spread the load. As the *Sunday Times* wrote in 1991[5] 'It was the proverbial gravy train reaping thousands of pounds for its names who never had to lift a signet ring. In effect it was outdoor relief for the upper crust'. Except for small losses in the early 1960s and in 1983, there had been continual profit every year from 1950 till 1987. Then came huge losses from the 'London market excess of loss spiral' known as LMX, described by Mr Justice Phillips in 1994 as:

> 'The complex arrangement under which catastrophe excess of loss risks were insured and reinsured often many times - as rather like a multiple game of pass the parcel. Those left holding the liability were those who first exhausted their layers of LMX reinsurance. The effect on individual syndicates was to magnify many times the impact of a particular loss.'[7]

I do not know how much it was luck and how much Alastair's knowledge and good sense, but we were not on the Gooda Walker syndicates which 'were overwhelmed by losses from the Piper Alpha explosion in July 1988, Hurricane Hugo in September 1989 and the European storms in January 1990' (see Note 7 again). Our losses were moderate and by that time I was earning a salary from Haymarket. For one of the years, RBS readily provided us with a 'Lloyd's loss loan', which we were able to pay back within two years. Lloyd's was fortunate to have David Coleridge, (Eton at its best - we had been there at the same time) at the helm, reported in the *Times* as 'remaining calmly and modestly unbowed' and who, partly by chance, had done what I wish I had done - starting work directly after school at the age of eighteen[8]. His 1992 AGM address, reporting on 1989 results, went straight to the point. Short extracts follow:

> 'We meet today in one of the darker chapters in the long history of our Society. No-one in this room is more conscious than I because it is to me that many of you express your feelings. Sentiments include despair, anger and bewilderment and I want to say at the outset that I understand. In short we must enquire, explain, try to help and above all learn the lessons for the future. The total losses in 1989 were £2.063 billion. It is an appalling result reflecting the extreme losses of a handful of excess of loss syndicates. I know most members are already braced for a poor 1990 result. I hope that 1991 may be better than break-even, but any profit is likely to be very modest. Looking ahead, insurance rates have begun to rise as they always do in response to past losses. At last we face more realistic trading conditions. I believe that these will continue to improve and that those who stay will reap the reward of holding fast. For those who decide to take advantage of these conditions there is one absolute priority. To go forward as a business we must demonstrate to the World that that we continue to offer the very best security to all those who buy our policies.'

The speech continued with reference to assistance to those with losses and the findings of the Task Force considering the future. It is worth study by future students of Lloyd's. David Coleridge's response to my letter shows that it can sometimes be worth writing in support: 'I must confess that it does make a very nice change now and then to receive a letter which is supportive and not critical. I share your faith in the future of Lloyd's. Thank you for taking the trouble to write with your kind words.' We decided to continue, remembering the 1986 Membership brochure ' should be viewed as a long term venture.' In 1994 Ann and I decided that I should attempt election to the Council of Lloyd's. As I wrote at the time to a potential proposer: 'I've stuck my head above the parapet, my spirit rebelling against Lloyd's gloom. At Names' meetings in U.K. and Andorra I questioned statements like 'I prophesy that within fifteen years Lloyd's will be wholly corporate.' Result: I have been encouraged to stand for the Council.' We managed to get the sixteen required signatures and I particularly treasured the letter from our former solicitor at Stephenson Harwood, Richard Eddis: ' Yes, of course I'd be delighted to propose you. I'm finding retirement quite blissful. Plenty to do (i.e. local community activities) and the joy of not having to commute to London any more is indescribable.' This is part of the candidate description which appeared in *One Lime Street*, the Lloyd's magazine, in October that year:

> 'Until the mid-70's he worked in the Youth Employment Service then transferred to the elected side of local government always standing as an Independent. As a Councillor he tried to listen and be available to both constituents and officers and if elected he wishes to serve both the members and the market professionals in the same way. He feels that Lloyd's should continue for future generations: its unique system worked for many centuries and has been beneficial to Britain. He is concerned that traditional capital providers may be undervalued and squeezed. He believes there is a place for corporate capital but not at the expense of the continuing unlimited liability sole traders. In the past it was disingenuous to emphasise 'using capital twice'. Lloyd's only makes sense when seen as risking capital with potential for profit and loss. It follows that aspiring Names, besides adequate means, need the temperament to prepare for loss. If those who make up the Lloyd's community all strive to be realists, trust will be rebuilt and it is not unthinkable that younger risk takers, who understand the downside, will again become Names.'

I duly came bottom of the poll but was delighted, as a complete unknown to the Lloyd's establishment and unsupported by any of the Members' Agents, to have received 131 votes. There were also pleasing letters of encouragement from MPs and others. From the MPs, Ted Heath bothered to reply and personally sign a letter that I treasure (see Chapter 15): 'I appreciate the importance of your request, but I have always made it a matter of principle not to take part in any Lloyd's affairs.' Jerry Wiggin: 'If I do have a vote (he was in process of resigning as a name), I shall certainly cast it for you.'[9]. Anthony Meyer (see Chapter 13): 'It is good to know that others think as you and I do.' From others: 'I much laud your willingness to undertake such a task' and: 'I am in sympathy with the views set out and congratulate you on being so public spirited as to put yourself forward'. Afterwards: 'By no means a waste of time and a venture I was happy to be involved with' from a Cambridge friend and, from kind Michael Colvin from the House of Commons: 'We were happy to put our blobs against your name (see Chapter 12). The point of including these letters is to encourage others to play their part in things. I had spoken out on an issue about which I felt strongly and been met with much goodwill. I had also challenged Barry Riley's pessimism (then Investment Editor of the *Financial Times*) and was glad to have his reply: 'I sympathise with your failure to win election to the Council though you wrote your expectations were low.' Barry accepted that 'it is not yet impossible that a core of unlimited liability operations could remain. I gather this is what you are fighting for.'

Lloyd's did then take the decision to allow limited liability companies into the market. David Rowland's Reconstruction and Renewal plan in 1996 gave us what was known as a Finality surplus, though other Names had to pay out. The remaining unlimited-liability sole-trader Names were reduced to around 5,000 by 1996 and there was more talk of a solely corporate future, against which I had argued when I had stood for the Council. The Names organisations, the Association of Lloyd's Members and the High Premium Group, fought their corner. The value of Names as low-cost capital providers, able to quickly respond, has been recognised; also that the annual venture creates a unique level of capital flexibility. Equitas had been set up to deal with asbestosis claims and, as the Wellington Agency explained in their 1996 review: 'Equitas is receiving conditional approval and Names will be asked to pay or receive a given amount to permit the reinsurance of all 1992 and prior liabilities.' Then came 9/11, the attack on the 'Twin Towers' in New York. Disaster for Lloyd's was again forecast by some pundits but they were wrong. A special report in the *Economist* wrote[10]:

> 'The syndicate's collective bill (before receiving reinsurance payouts) ended up at around £5 billion or one quarter of the total for the World Trade Centre. Lloyd's paid up and did not collapse as many feared, indeed the market resumed writing terrorism cover within 48 hours of the disaster. September 11th ushered in a long bull market for insurance. Lloyd's has taken advantage and its financial health has improved. The management team, led by Lord Levene, globetrotting chairman, and the lower key Mr Prettejohn, has impressed many. 'Lloyd's is stronger than at any time in its history' says Robert Hiscox.'

At every meeting organised by the High Premium Group or our Member's Agent, now after many changes and mergers, Hampden, it was confirmed that Lloyd's did want to keep the Names. As I had hoped, younger people did enquire and arrangements were put in place for individuals or families or partnerships to underwrite without unlimited liability. I wanted to continue as sole trader so that I could make use, if necessary, of the funds in what was known as the Special Reserve Fund. Under Lloyd's rules, if I transferred to limited liability I could not continue to use the Special Reserve Fund. Also, when subsequently released, it would be taxed as income in the year of release. Then, after some hospital sessions I became more aware that if I dropped dead as a sole trader, my capacity had to be immediately sold. Our choice was a Lloyd's Limited Partnership (LLP), limited because only the Funds at Lloyd's would be at risk, in which Ann and I became partners and which could continue after my death. By now we had valuable capacity, most of which had come to us many years before without any payment. Those now joining or returning to Lloyd's have to purchase capacity at the auctions. We have to pay tax on relinquishing the Special Reserve, but there is also the bonus of Business Property Relief and the consequent escape from Inheritance Tax on both those funds supporting the underwriting and the value of capacity - that is the amount underwritten. Max, Juliet and Kate have now joined what is known as a family LLP and we are glad that the next generation is involved. As in the past, Giles Berkeley, our contact at Hampden, and his colleagues have been tirelessly helpful, cheerful and encouraging in setting this up. It is gratifying that thirty-three years' involvement has led to being part of a British enterprise whose expertise continues to be in demand throughout the world. We are still prepared for losses and I find myself asking what is the disaster for which Lloyd's is not prepared? How many people foresaw the 'Twin Towers'? What will come next? Some confidence comes from knowing all the effort that now goes into forecasting. Meanwhile we can make good use of profits, whilst also trying to maintain some reserves for what we cannot predict. It has been suggested to me that it is odd that a member of Lloyd's should be concerned about those without jobs. Why? A way of using wealth, which was otherwise unavailable except for receipt of income, seemed worth the risk if it helped to enable involvement in other matters of concern. So it has turned out and the valued increase in freedom reinforces thoughts on the value of a Citizen's Income to others.

To complete this 'rag-bag' chapter, there were two other minor political forays. When we returned to Winchester, we found that friends known for many years were involved with the local Conservative Association. Then a candidate was needed for Hampshire Central in the European elections and they wanted local people to apply. I joined the queue to be interviewed, but a veteran MEP from another area was chosen. This led to the suggestion of attending a Selection Board so that my name went to other Euro-Constituencies. This was a time of hope leading to the 'Single Market' in 1992. An MEP had written earlier of three problems: first, the control of diseases like rabies to allow free circulation of animals; second, the harmonisation of taxes to dismantle customs posts; and third, the stamping out of terrorism and drug trafficking. Alas the third objective has not been achieved and that short period when passports did not have to be examined after crossing the Channel has not continued. Despite previous physical and political difficulties, I had naive ideas that, if elected, I could try and ameliorate some of the workings of the European Parliament, so that British people had more reason to become more enthusiastic about membership. I preferred the semi-circular layout compared with adversarial two-sided Westminster, and from the outside the whole set-up seemed less overtly party-political, with party whips less in evidence and co-operation between parties. It seemed there could also be useful contributions on committees about subjects in which I was interested. How wrong I was. Over the weekend of 12th/13th November 1993, I attended a 'Parliamentary Selection Board' at the Coppid Beech Hotel, Bracknell. We were subjected to two days of interviews, discussions, team debates and games and personal interviews. Aspiring MPs and MEPs were lumped together. There was no consideration of the attributes required by an MEP. Overnight we were requested to write an article suitable for a local newspaper in defence of the recent Conservative decision to privatise British Rail. The 'Joachim' blood revolted. A short note was written, stressing that I was seeking to play a part in European matters, not defend the Party's Westminster decisions, and, anyway, with experience of Europe's state-owned railways, I questioned this privatisation.

The result, in a letter from Tim Smith MP, then Vice Chairman Candidates, was that I was not considered suitable and had received low marks in all scored sessions. It was rather different to the previous single interviews with people like Jim Prior, Geoffrey Johnson-Smith and Marcus Fox when I had received much encouragement and indeed congratulation after the 1966 election result in Gloucester. Which system results in satisfactory Conservative Members of Parliament, I leave others to decide. A few years later, Tim Smith had to stand down as an MP after involvement with Neil Hamilton in the cash-for-questions affair. Was he a good judge of suitability? For the next few years we tried to help in the Constituency with canvassing, fund-raising and literature delivery. After the election of the Tony Blair's Government in 1997, the Conservatives became markedly unpopular. Canvassing was hard work and the front door was often slammed in one's face. By persevering, it was possible to bring a few more into membership and gradually the local Association rebuilt its strength. This was a bit of a pay-back for my win as an Independent in 1979. Whilst in no way accepting right-wing views and sticking to the 'broad church' ideal, I took comfort from an elderly and experienced Party Agent who had been appointed to help out in the Winchester Constituency before retirement. He chided me on too much idealism and I have cherished his remark: 'They are all awful. Its just that democratic politics is better than the alternatives and the Conservatives are the least awful.' In this spirit the request to stand for the County Council, in a division then firmly held by the Liberals, was accepted in 2001. Adopting the same methods as in 1979, I traipsed round nearly every house and concentrated on listening, rather than strong Conservative advocacy. The result was satisfactory in the circumstances of the time when Mark Oaten was the highly regarded Liberal MP.[11] Two elections later, that division has been narrowly won by the Conservatives. All these experiences have helped me to better understand the realities of English politics. The Conservative Party now seems to instruct its members (using emails as well as literature) as to what they should think and support, and expects them to concentrate on fund-raising and electioneering. Gone are the days when those interested in political discussion based on their own experiences, could meet together in local branches and know that those at the centre in Westminster would listen to their thinking and suggestions. Ann valiantly continues to deliver literature, attend some meetings and events and help out at times in the Constituency Office. It's all been a small contribution to democracy whilst maintaining allegiance to 'One Nation' ideas.

LEARNING FROM DIFFERENCE

Chapter 19

The British-Owned Car Industry

I have just walked up our road in Winchester. The tally is: our Bristol, which was made in a then-British-owned factory, two Mercedes, two Audis, two BMWs and four Volkswagens made in Germany, three Skodas from Czechoslovakia, one Renault from France, seven assorted Japanese and two Minis from a now German-owned former British factory. This is what has happened in my lifetime, the change since my childhood when almost all cars, lorries and vans on British roads were made in Britain and, when, as far back as I can remember, I wanted to play my part in ensuring that this country remained a world leader in vehicle production. In three books that I written about the industry, I have touched on the defects in design, production and marketing which gradually led to this decline in market share, as cars from other countries became available. Everything that has happened has been the result of decisions taken by individuals or groups of human beings. Who were these people, why were they there and why did they take these decisions which, with the benefit of hindsight, seem to have been ill-conceived?

From a personal perspective, looking on and unable to see a way of helping to stop the decline, there have been times of despair. Such thoughts now need to be buried. Two years ago I appreciated a lunch invitation from Kamal Siddiqui, the Indian buyer of Bristol Cars.[1] I asked him why he had chosen Britain for his new headquarters. His swift reply was that it was because of the quality and experience of British engineers and technicians. He was less complimentary about British financiers and managers. Whilst some British companies have been unable to compete because of design deficiencies, attitudes and methods on the assembly lines, and insufficient finance, particular products have still established a worldwide reputation and created a valued brand name. The efforts of many individual employees, often in difficult conditions, have led to other nationals believing that they could work out ways and provide investment, including more automated tasks, through which these valued brands like Jaguar, Mini, Bentley, Rolls-Royce, Bristol, Lotus, Land/Range Rover and others still had a future and could flourish in world markets. There may not be another large production British company in the years ahead, but there are jobs for British people as a result of these decisions by these other nationals. Japanese manufacturers are also building cars here. At the same time, smaller British firms like McLaren and Morgan are demonstrating the potential of different methods of production which appeal to those who prefer more personal involvement and the opportunity to use different skills. Other firms contribute massively to the world of racing, and then there is what the British historic vehicle movement referred to as 'a £4 billion hobby' concerned with restoration and maintenance and again with the opportunity for personal involvement.[2]

After writing *Roads to Oblivion*[3] I had the good fortune to be introduced to Gerald Palmer, designer of the Jowett Javelin, the MG Magnette, the Riley Pathfinder and associated Wolseleys. Two years of discussions in 1996 and 1997 led to his autobiography *Auto Architect*.[4] Gerald's wise preface is a good summary of what happened:

> 'It was a period of great activity and innovation, of hopes unfulfilled, of early companies going out of business or amalgamating with others, and of new companies being formed. After an initial upsurge, the domestic industry declined partly - perhaps it must be admitted - from self inflicted wounds. Important amongst these was the lack of investment in an industry which had become increasingly capital intensive as a result of the essential adoption of the all-steel body. There was also insufficient rationalisation of models, insufficient attention to test and development, and excessive demands from labour. These wounds and the intense competition from other countries inevitably led to increased penetration by American, European and Far Eastern interests and personnel into most branches of the industry.'

My only quibble is with the word 'perhaps'. Gerald saw what was needed: a well designed, technically proficient, fully tested and reliable car built in large quantities on automated, clean and well-ventilated production lines allowing reasonable working conditions, the result then sold at a profit and backed by efficient service. There was no advantage in producing - for instance - Austin, MG, Morris, Riley and Wolseley versions of an imperfect design. Gerald realised that his ideas were not going to be accepted and it was Vauxhall which benefited from his later work, but I keep the memory of his regret that he could not achieve his objectives whilst working in a British company.

To set the scene, the reality of life in a British car factory in those post-war years, I begin with a book by David Buckle who became a trade union official in Oxford[5]. He described his first job in 1950 at Pressed Steel's body plant:

> 'My first shock was the condition of the factory. It was filthy, very dark and extremely noisy, with lead dust in the atmosphere, which glittered when the sun shone through the very high, filthy windows. Due to the smoke from gas and arc welding guns it was very difficult to see much beyond fifty yards. All the men looked very pale. Sparks burnt our clothes and woe betide anyone who failed to wear safety glasses because it was very easy to lose an eye. We dreaded being moved from one line to another because it meant we had to use different muscles which proved very painful. Due to lack of investment the dies in the presses were grossly over used and needed to be overhauled or replaced after 100,000 stampings. Instead they were used for up to 500,000. Large amounts of molten lead had to be loaded onto the seams to cover faults then smoothed off with discs which produced the dust.'

Graham Turner, in his book *The Car Makers*[6] gives many more examples of production in that era. There was constant conflict between production numbers and quality:

'The seat is fastened up with rings and a lot are left missing to achieve numbers.'

'Once I used to insist on a quality job' said a man doing electrical repairs, 'I used to think of the bloke who was buying the car. Now I just let it go.'

'The other day we started to get them with heavy clutches and more and more of them piled up until there were about forty. When they found out how many are involved they talked it over, decided they had misjudged and pushed them through.'

'The door-handles may be loose and the man does not notice it. They are forced on. He can't tell whether the clip has connected because the noise in the shop stops him from hearing that little click. Of course they used to be screwed through the side.'

His description reminds me of the time I spent in the Rootes factories. To counter boredom - from time to time a mongrel - part Hillman, part Singer, part Sunbeam came off the line and then had to be taken to bits again. Both David Buckle and Graham Turner described later visits to Volkswagen. David wrote:

'It was very clean with no sign of arc and gas welding fumes and certainly no lead was being used to cover any design faults. Neither were there any air-powered tools which create so much noise. It was a well maintained factory years ahead of England so far as technology and employee rights were concerned. I noticed a huge open space as I was being guided round and was told this was used by the Management and the Union for reporting back on future plans. It was explained that Germany's 'law of co-determination' precludes employers from determining certain matters unilaterally.'

Graham wrote:

'There (at Wolfsburg) you feel planners confident of capturing mass markets have been at work. Sheer carelessness is the thing which appals Volkswagen workers when they see what goes on in British plants.'

In 1997 David, by then Chairman of Oxfordshire County Council, was escorting royalty round the Mini plant, then owned by BMW. The Duke of Kent asked what industrial relations were like compared to the past. At once, before the Plant Director could speak David replied:

'A lot better than when I worked here because it is quieter, cleaner and safer due to the massive investment by BMW (£1 billion) which British Leyland denied it in the past. The conditions you see now are what we begged for in the 1950s and 1960s but could not obtain.'

I am not attempting to add to the books that have been, and will be, written about how other nationals are succeeding. Instead I will attempt a few comments on five groups of people. First there are the British managers. Few of them had had the broad education of the fee-paying schools or leading universities. For good, well-meaning people like Robert Birley at Eton to think of attempting to work in the motor industry seemed somehow regarded as unworthy, as if succumbing to a private indulgence, and not the correct use of what was reckoned to be the best in education. It just did not seem to enter their minds that motor vehicles were going to be used in vast quantities throughout the world and that therefore one requirement of education was to ensure that companies like Austin, Morris and Leyland, amongst others, remained world leaders. Their success and revenue should have been a priority, which would then help to pay for the vaunted public service and intellectual life. Cranwell, Dartmouth and Sandhurst had honed instruction in the business of war. Where was the equivalent discussion on how to lead large companies and without the valuable benefit of the oath of loyalty to the Sovereign? In Geoffrey Owen's words: 'Oxford and Cambridge had played no part in the industrial revolution and had no interest in the world of industry.'[7] I think back again to Great-uncle Fred Balfour and his brilliant career at Oxford before joining the Indian Civil Service. Did he ever think of carrying on his father's work in Balfour Lyon? The Imperial College of Science and Technology was founded in London in 1908 and around that time technical education started to be expanded below university level. Loughborough was founded as a technical institute in 1909, became a college of technology in 1918 and a university in 1996. Cranfield College of Aeronautics was established in 1945 and became a university in 1993. Such routes were only taken by a few Etonians like Desmond Norman. Then there was the Chelsea College of Aeronautical and Automobile engineering, founded in 1924 and attended by Peter Morgan amongst others. This later merged with the West Sussex College of Design. The *Economist* wrote in 1962:

> 'The British Motor Corporation (BMC, the combination of Austin and Morris) has stuck firmly to the motor industry's tradition that managers and engineers should work their way up. It has cut itself off from the mainstream of able young men, something that no large company can afford to do. Compared with Ford, it lacks the bright young graduates in their thirties which now forms the nucleus of that company's middle management.'

My next quote is taken from another of Graham Turner's books *The Leyland Papers* published in 1971 but about an earlier period:[8]

> 'Leonard Lord was a brilliant production engineer. He detested pomp and also distrusted anything approaching sophistication in the running of a business. He regarded both sales men and accountants as overheads: if they were any good, cars sold themselves - make proper bloody products and you don't need to sell 'em'. Nor was he even a believer in the simpler forms of training for industry. When, after he had moved to Austin, one of his senior executives tried to promote an apprentice scheme, Lord strenuously resisted the idea. This was the man on whom the fate of the greater part of the British motor industry was to rest for almost thirty years.'

In contrast there was just one Etonian at Nuffield Products (Morris, Riley, Wolseley) in the war years. Miles Thomas wrote in *Out on a wing*:[9]

'My General Manager was a tall elegant Old Etonian named Charles Mullens. Trained as an engineer, he showed how good manners and human understanding completely bridge the gap between those of high social standing and the men who work on the factory floor.'

Austin and Morris did have a different 'culture'. After their merger in 1952 to form the British Motor Corporation (BMC), came all the subsequent takeovers and mergers:

Jaguar of Daimler, Leyland of Standard-Triumph, both 1961.
Pressed Steel with Fisher and Ludlow then BMC of Pressed Steel Fisher in 1965.
Leyland of Rover 1967.
BMC and Jaguar to form British Motor Holdings (BMH) in 1966.
Leyland and BMC/BMH in 1968 to form British Leyland Motor Corporation (BLMC).

Chrysler had taken over Rootes in 1967, so by 1968 Britain was left with one major British-owned car company, then the second largest in Europe and the fifth largest in the world. Donald Stokes, the successful lorry salesman, was in command but without some of the able people who had by then left the company. Reginald Hanks, vice-chairman of Nuffield after the detrimental departure of Miles Thomas, had wanted to develop the Morris Minor to rival Volkswagen's Beetle. He had lured Gerald Palmer back from Jowett and encouraged Gerald in the design of cars like the still-cherished MG Magnette. He did not have the power to oppose the BMC merger agreed by Lord Nuffield in 1952 and was subsequently ousted by Leonard Lord. Joe Edwards had been dismissed by Lord in 1956, and was then almost immediately asked to manage Pressed Steel. When BMC had taken over Pressed Steel Fisher in 1965, he had been invited back on the BMC board. In 1966 he had become managing director of BMC and subsequently BMH. He had realised that factories had to be closed and employee numbers reduced. He had also been aware of the deficiencies of the Issigonis designs. Yet just over two years later Edwards had lost out in the power struggle, even though Donald Stokes had previously admitted that 'he was only a salesman and could not run the company without the likes of the experienced and competent Joe Edwards.' Stanley Markland had become works director of Leyland in 1953, then managing director of Standard Triumph after the takeover in 1961. He had supported the successful Triumph 2000 and the Spitfire and by 1963 the company was on the way to profit. But that same year he was not, as he had expected, appointed as eventual successor to Sir Henry Spurrier. When Sir Henry died, it was the elderly Sir William Black and then Donald Stokes who had taken over and Markland had resigned. These are just some examples of individuals from those first twenty post-war years who might have saved the British industry if they had not lost out. There were many others.

John Barber was another example of an able manager in the following years. After ten years' experience at Ford, he had joined what became BLMC at the end of 1967. He had wanted to move the company upmarket and produce a higher quality car. In 1973 he had become deputy chairman and, when George Turnbull resigned, managing director. Then came the oil crisis. BL made a massive loss and needed Government money. The Ryder report recommended that BL should receive Government investment, but should remain as both a volume and specialised car manufacture: Barber was out. He was interviewed by *Motor Sport*. These are some of his words in May 1976:

'In any manufacturing business its absolutely vital that top management are keenly interested in their product. In the car business this keenness makes the difference between making motor cars and making properly engineered cars. Its easy to specify 'standard extras' but to make cars that genuinely are better, where the controls fall easily to hand, and everything works smoothly, ah, that's a different matter. To me a refined car is one where everything mysteriously falls to hand just so. The car feels so good that you want to buy it, to drive it, to own it. I decided we needed to slot in a cut above the cheapest models mass produced by people twice the size of Leyland.'

What might have happened if John Barber had been able to continue and encourage at least something of that feel - which is part of the Bristol's appeal - in Leyland offerings, with much higher production quantities? The prototypes of such cars existed. Rover's big 'Mercedes-eater' P8 saloon was cancelled in 1971, six months before it was due to enter production and after it had absorbed many millions of pounds, though at least some of that work seems to have helped the P76 in Australia. Barber also talked about 'Rover's exciting mid-V8-engined sports car remembered as a super car.' The Triumph 'Stag' had potential but was not properly developed. Then there is the wider question of what would have been the result if more of those with the supposed benefits of a wider education had been encouraged to contribute? Would a better understanding of accountancy, economics, geography, history and politics have brought a wider perspective to discussion and decision-making? Such knowledge might have helped, if executive positions had been reached. The bigger problem seems to have been that no single person, even if - like Joe Edwards or John Barber - they realised what needed to be done and had achieved some power, had had the authority and ability to overcome the vested or political interests or achieve the co-operation of other groups which were involved. There is also the reality, often noticed in human affairs, that those who have worked out what needs to be done can be defeated by those who want power anyhow, anyway.

After the Ryder report, and the removal of Donald Stokes and John Barber, Michael Edwardes (with an e and no relation to Joe) was appointed chairman and started off by admitting that he knew nothing about car-making. He closed factories, including MG at Abingdon in 1979, and halved the workforce, but still needed a billion pounds or more of taxpayers' money. The heavily subsidised Metro 'the British car to beat the world' sold over a million but well below the estimate of three to four million. European manufacturers were now offering more attractive brands on the British market. In 1996 there was a retrospective article in *Classic Cars* magazine about the 1976 Rover SD 1. Mark Dixon wrote: 'Despite a new factory, paint rapidly fell off body shells, water leaks through the screens were common, and the interior was made from untried materials that could not last the distance.' Richard Bremner wrote: ' cars often needed replacement back axles and new brake discs then came problems with the central locking and electric windows. I wonder where BL would have been if it had screwed the SD I together properly. Not perhaps in the hands of BMW.' Would these problems have been avoided with John Barber's stewardship? The link with Honda to develop a joint model was agreed in 1979. Graham Day became chairman and in the words of the *Motor Industry Centenary Book*: 'He decided that the company's future lay in the lower volume but potentially more profitable sector. In applying this policy he was reactivating the approach advocated by John Barber ten years earlier but abandoned after the Ryder report.' Ken Gooding from the *Financial Times* explained what happened next [10]:

'In 1986 the British Government was about to sell to American Companies. Mrs Thatcher did not want to put more taxpayer's money into BL, which had absorbed £2 billion of state aid but still accumulated losses of £2.6 billion. Ford had great plans for the MG and Triumph brands. General Motors wanted to rebuild its heavy truck operations on the back of British expertise and planned to give Land Rover a huge worldwide marketing push. Then came Westland[11] and the Conservatives realised that further sales to the Americans would lose votes.'

Graham Day formed a partnership with Honda and sold the lorry side to DAF. With the agreement of Mrs Thatcher, what remained of BL - by then renamed Rover - was bought by British Aerospace in 1988, a business deal with no conditions attached. The lady had prepared the way for the sinking of the British-owned industry. When, five years later, Aerospace had had enough 'it was sold on to BMW cynically excluding Honda from the negotiations.' By then, Ford's offer to buy the already privatised Jaguar had been accepted. Thirty years earlier, BMW had been saved from the clutches of Mercedes largely by the vision of one man, the nearly blind Herbert Quandt. BMW persevered with Land Rover but sought a buyer for the Rover car interest. For a short time there was hope. A sort of Quandt equivalent (with full sight), Jon Moulton of Alchemy, persuaded his partners that they should attempt a slimmed-down business using the MG name to produce globally significant sports cars. BMW were prepared to provide initial financial support. Government approval was needed. The Alchemy offer was rejected by Stephen Byers at Trade and Industry in favour of the Phoenix Four. They offered more work by continuing with a Rover saloon, but in 2005 the company went into administration with debts of £1.4 billion and 6,000 workers lost their jobs.[12] This was the end of the British-owned car industry, with the exception of Morgan and a few very limited production companies. BMW sold Land Rover to Ford and concentrated on the Cowley factory, starting to realise Gerald Palmer's vision of forty years earlier. There was to be one base car which, although larger, made full use of the power of the Mini brand-name. As David Buckle explained during that 1997 visit with royalty, BMW were prepared to spend the money which allowed automated machinery and good working conditions. The German company has been able to do what none of the British managers achieved. Jaguar and Land Rover were then sold to the Indian Tata group. Like BMW, Tata poured investment into the production process. As with the Mini, there is now a huge worldwide demand for these products made by British workpeople in British factories owned by other nationals.

It may be worth looking further at the other four groups involved which played their part in hindering all these efforts. These were the politicians, the workforce represented by the unions, the financiers and the customers. The actions of the politicians which aided the death of the industry have been discussed above, but their actions also influenced the earlier years. Towards the end of the Second World War, the Conservatives warned that the country could not afford the National Health Service and social security insurance recommended by Beveridge. Having won the election, the Attlee government was determined to bring in these measures, but could only do so by imposing heavy taxation and regulation. The motor industry, which would have benefited from assistance and encouragement, was severely handicapped. Miles Thomas commented: 'Mr Dalton is quite wrong when he says that purchase tax on home sales is a stimulus to exports. The reverse is the case because a reduction in factory 'throughput' because of this tax means that the full economies of quantity production are not realised in home or Export markets.' Worse was to come in 1948, when 'double' purchase tax at 66 and 2/3% was imposed on cars costing more than £1,000. (This was imposed on all cars sold on the home market in 1951 and then reduced to 50% in 1953 by the Conservatives). Then on top of the taxation the Minister of Supply, George Strauss, warned companies of sanctions preventing the supply of steel if they did not export 75% of their production. Laurence Pomeroy, a renowned journalist of that period, wrote ten years later:

> 'The high level of UK exports after World War 2 was artificially stimulated by a combination of national needs and Socialist economics at a time when the need for foreign currency was paramount. This led to the sale of large numbers of pre-war or untried designs for which service and spares left much to be desired. Hence, although successful in securing currency, the export first policy has left one and a half million pre-war cars on British roads and a legacy of sales resistance in other parts of the World.'

The post-war British motor industry was handicapped from the start by these actions, but these socialist politicians were only doing what they thought best in the aftermath of war. Reading the magazines of the time, what stands out is that Mercedes waited five years before they started exporting. They had to rebuild their factories, but they also made sure that their offerings did not have faults: not for them a damaging legacy. In 1963 Graham Turner quoted a British designer: 'Mercedes is stiff with Doctors and diploma engineers, and the whole essence of their approach is producing a highly efficient technical product rather than a piece of merchandise which unfortunately has a technical content.'[13] The point is that these brains must have surely have realised that, whilst massive and continuing investment would be required, if they could produce a full range of efficient vehicles - cars, lorries, vans, buses, ambulances, the lot - the eventual return from worldwide markets would be enormous. There were other political events which effected the history already recounted.

In *Empire to Europe* Geoffrey Owen writes: 'Easy access to a fast growing, tariff-free market was an important advantage to German and French car manufacturers. The delay in Britain's accession to the EEC meant that the British car industry largely missed out on the expansion of intra-European trade in the 1960s.'[14] Facing the large tariff barrier, there was little attempt to sell British cars on the European mainland. The De Gaulle veto, and the consequent wait till 1973 to join the Common Market, was not the fault of the British Government, but their actions towards the end of the 1960s are more open to question. In line with socialist philosophy, the praiseworthy priority was to avoid high unemployment. The Industrial Reorganisation Corporation (IRC) was set up. Harold Wilson encouraged the British-owned vehicle manufacturers to discuss merger and the outcome was British Leyland - BLMC. As Geoffrey Owen comments: 'size was no guarantee of efficiency especially where there were deep-rooted managerial weaknesses.' After their 1970 victory, the Conservatives disbanded the IRC and wanted to have more competition. Then came the February 1974 defeat. The Labour Government, still with Harold Wilson at the helm, and with Tony Benn at the Department of Trade and Industry, was again determined to intervene, this time through the NEB. The Ryder Report, mentioned above, which suggested that British Leyland should continue with volume as well as specialist cars, that 'the massive injection of public funds ' (Geoffrey Owen's words) should continue, and that John Barber should be asked to resign. A House of Commons Committee actually supported Barber's views about concentration on specialist cars, but the different Party attitudes before and after the 1974 Election were not helpful to the industry. This takes us back to Ted Heath, as discussed in Chapter 15. Is it too fanciful to suggest that there might still have been a British-owned Rover, and much taxpayers' money saved, if Ted Heath had not been encouraged to call that February election? Would the Conservatives, people like Jim Prior, have listened to people like John Barber? The downside could have been that, without Labour government support, British Leyland might have collapsed earlier, with more unemployment. Then, when privatisation became one of the Thatcher policies, there might have been no factory at Cowley for BMW to eventually take over.

The industry's problems also relate to all that happened in the twentieth century. David Buckle commented on the next group, the workforce - represented by the unions:

'Once the Pressed Steel plant had been built in the 1930s, the Company soon discovered there was no available workforce in the Oxfordshire area. They had to advertise nationally for both skilled and semi-skilled labour. Due to the recession in the 1920s, men from the Welsh, Scottish and Yorkshire coal mines, shipyard workers from the North East and miners from the West of England china clay industry came to Oxford looking for work. Stories are told of ex Welsh coal miners walking to Cowley and dying of hunger and exhaustion on the way. Their friends buried them where they died.'

Many books have been written about the strikes and the strife in those British car factories. Looking back now it seems understandable why those workers, many of whom had experienced the pre-war years and been through the war, struggled for better working conditions. The management, such as it was, first and foremost wanted output. Quality and human considerations were not the priority. There was also an opportunity, just waiting to be utilised, for communist influence on the shop floor. There was no possibility of starting afresh, as with Volkswagen. The class differences I have always disliked still reigned. It was 'them and us', not partners for the national good as at Wolfsburg. During that short period in the 1960s, working with the Employer's Federation in Birmingham, I found myself more in tune with some of the trade union officials than some of the employers . The 2009 *Guardian* obituary of Richard O'Brien, who was a manager rather than an employer and then Director of Industrial Relations at BMC, and with whom I had some contact at that time (see Chapter 16 including note 6), commented: 'He remained convinced that unbalance of status and privilege between shop floor and boardroom was an important factor in the turbulence of industrial relations.' There was also the piecework system of payment, itself partially a legacy of the war years, which meant that shop stewards were involved in determining what the rate would be. This gave plenty of opportunity for disagreement. Later came 'measured day work' where work-study professionals were responsible for timing jobs. The managers had more control, but productivity decreased.

In the Michael Edwardes era, a bonus payment scheme based on the number of cars produced was brought back. Pay negotiations were conducted between national union officials and senior management, instead of at factory and district level. In 1981, before that year's negotiations, Edwardes said on national radio that he had the authority to wind up British Leyland if the meeting failed to reach an agreement. Martin Adeney has written:[15]

'The characteristics of the Edwardes style were now established - give managers the responsibilities they had lacked for years; argue your case with the workforce without relying on the unions; argue it out with the unions but, if they do not agree, go over their heads for a workforce ballot - and when that does not work, argue some more and ultimately threaten to close the place down.'

Agreements were achieved, but often on a knife-edge. The workforce knew that closure could mean years of unemployment. David Buckle was critical of Edwardes. He wrote in the *New Socialist* magazine in 1983:

'My real criticism is that he put commercial success far above human needs, but surely there has to be a balance struck. Edwardes may have thought the crisis he inherited justified an authoritarian industrial relations system, but a different style is required now - more open, trusting and democratic.'

Whatever view is taken of Michael Edwardes' efforts, during which robots and improved conditions were introduced on the production lines, the workforce was halved, fourteen factories were closed and large amounts of taxpayers' money used, the company survived. As written above, there was something for BMW to take over. It seems that BMW have struck the balance which David Buckle suggested. The unanswered questions are what might have happened if Barbara Castle's 'In place of strife' had been accepted and, once again, what might Ted Heath and his ministers have achieved if the Conservatives had not gone to the country in February 1974.

Then we come to the next group. I used to be concerned that the financiers would not give more support to the manufacturers, but they are not free agents. Their task is to provide a return within a reasonable period of time for those who wish to invest their funds. They cannot only think of what might, in the long run, be best for the country. It was the taxpayers' money used without our assent, except later in the 'for or against' in the ballot box, that eventually turned British Leyland into a saleable proposition. It is the car manufacturers that have succeeded which have been the other source of finance for some faltering companies. Thus BMW have breathed new life into Rolls-Royce, and Volkswagen into Bentley. Numerous smaller companies have attempted a better specialist product and run out of money . The Morgan family found their own niche though, at the time of writing, we now learn that Charles Morgan has been ousted. He did not personally own 51%. Bristol was the consequence of the shrewd stewardship of two men who had access to funds from other sources. Then accident and age took their toll. By the time this book is published, it may be known whether the new owners have succeeded.

There is one decision that can be fairly questioned. Jowett was the Yorkshire company for which Gerald Palmer designed the Javelin. The financier Charles Clore sold his stake, purchased from the founders Benjamin and William Jowett, to the merchant bank Lazard in 1947. George Wansbrough, another Etonian in the motor industry, became chairman.[16] Lazard supported the decision that Briggs should build the Javelin body at their factory in Doncaster. The car's early faults were sorted. *The Motor* magazine wrote in 1953: 'The purpose was to check the claim that every weakness had been eliminated. We are pleased to record that the claims for true reliability show every sign of being justified'. Then Briggs was bought by Ford. Problems with body supply resulted. Lazard declined to support body manufacture by Jowett themselves and the existing factory was sold to International Harvester to make tractors in 1954. A potentially world-beating British-built vehicle was lost. Of course it was the right short-term investment decision. The investors received more than the nominal value of their shares. Lazard continues to prosper. Their website tells of forty offices in twenty-six countries and how they are trusted advisers to business. There is no mention of Jowett. It's the same old story. There were no Lazard directors who had the technical knowledge, interest or vision to persuade colleagues and investors that, in the longer term, ownership of a prosperous manufacturing company could be of benefit to all. That's why Lionel was sensible to take up the introduction to the Jam Sahib, who could make his own solo decisions about the use of his wealth. He did not have to persuade others. I talked to the daughter of one of the Jowett managers, nearly fifty years after his dismissal. She remembered the comments in the factory: 'There is no-one on the Board now except the financiers. The money-bags have a one-track mind.'

Jon Moulton of Alchemy Partners, already mentioned, who agreed to take on MG Rover in 2000, is one 'money-bags ' with vision.[17] He believed that, with the initial financial support from BMW, the worldwide renown of the MG brand, fewer workers, and much better housekeeping, a globally significant sports car business could be established. Unfortunately Stephen Byers thought otherwise. We shall never know whether Alchemy would have been a better decision. Even though so much of the motor industry is now in the hands of other nationals, there may still be future opportunities as new technologies develop. Will some of those who have built up large reserves from salaries, bonuses and pay-offs and who perhaps have technical interest, be prepared to follow people like Jon Moulton and Herbert Quandt and offer understanding long-term support? Will the Siddiqui family succeed with Bristol?

The last group are the customers. After the Second World War, Lord Nuffield supported a series of advertisements: 'Buy a British car.' For the following twenty years or so it was considered odd to drive a 'foreign' car, as I noticed with the second Fiat. We came to accept that there would be faults in new British products and struggles with the dealers to sort out these problems. Letters to the manufacturers brought standard replies. 'We note and are grateful for your comments. We are doing what we can do address these issues.' Perhaps, in contrast to today's enthusiastic owners' clubs, many of us should have paraded outside the factories and boycotted the products, insisting on a response from management and the workforce. Britain became more involved with Europe and finally joined the Common Market in 1972. The Volvo estate became the vehicle of choice for aspiring weekenders. Peugeot offered the 504 with all independent suspension. The 5 series BMW was available in Britain from 1972 and then came the W114/115 Mercedes range. The first 'Golf' from Volkswagen was here from 1974. Small Datsun (later Nissan) and Toyota saloons were found to be cheap and reliable. Many British and European garages re-established themselves as distributors for these and other makes.[18] I make a point of asking British motorists why and when they stopped buying British cars. Almost always the answer is that they had had faults, or the lack of reliability in the products of British factories. Then, after experience of a fault-free vehicle produced in another country, that is what they continued to buy. Concern about jobs or loyalty to British workers was not in their minds as part of the purchase investigations. For the following thirty years, customers - including the buying departments of companies who provided cars for their employees, and some central and local government departments -

bought what best suited their needs without worrying about country of origin or the effect on employment. Even many of those who roundly condemned Europe and all its works bought French and German cars.

What would have happened if I had accepted Ford's offer of employment and then been amongst those who were recruited into British Leyland? Of course, it would have been interesting to be there in the 1970s with all the experience and knowledge that I now have forty years later. But that's not how life works. All those managers would have acted differently with the benefit of later hindsight. It would have been a struggle to achieve effective influence. Without influence, it would have been necessary to process orders with which I may have disagreed. It is fanciful to think that I could have been another Charles Mullens. If neither John Barber, Joe Edwards, Reg Hanks, Gerald Palmer, George Wansbrough and many, many others were able to save the British-owned industry, it is unlikely that I would have done so. So, although it led to a tortuous path, I have to be grateful to Uncle Bertie for first warning me of the industry's many difficulties and hinting that considerable wealth, which, he emphasised, could easily be lost, was probably the only route to that influence. Yes, there are times when I regret not leaving Eton and spending the following years learning about mechanical components, accountancy and other business and factory skills. There may have been opportunities through dealing, but, even if I had achieved the initial capital, would I have then had the understanding and tough bartering ability to make use of my knowledge? With a very full share of luck, this could have been the route to workshop or small factory ownership, perhaps to component supply or other avenues. But I did not do this. Why was an alternative to Cambridge, like Loughborough, never mentioned? Instead I was caught, as the Chief Education Officer of United Steel quoted in one of Correlli Barnet's books, explained, 'by the emphasis placed by our public schools and older Universities on building up character rather than imparting specialised knowledge.'[19] Life in industry could have led to family disaster, even to a repeat of Lionel's difficulties, that which I most wanted to avoid, and there would have been the physical problems. It may be that, together with the rescue and preservation of some good thoroughbred vehicles and support to Bristol, writing the books after the fortunate encounter with Haymarket, and the attempt to explain something of what has happened, has been the best use of any ability I may have had. I have also learnt how much of life can be learning about what cannot be done.

Could it be argued that the loss of ownership of the car industry is part of the price that Britain has had to pay as a result of victory in the twentieth-century wars? The unrest and unemployment of the 1920s and 1930s, together with the conditions and methods of payment in wartime impoverished factories, were the precursors of poor productivity through to the 1970s. The 1945 Labour government, another consequence of victory, needed revenue for its social and health service provision, which led to the export of unsatisfactory vehicles. In a very British way, the nation has stumbled over a period of fifty years to overcome these industrial problems and eventually found the answer in preparation for -and eventual ownership by - other nationals. From a perspective of centuries this may be a minor setback, compared with the survival of this valued haven of freedom from which Joachim forebears and many others have benefited. This survival is in part one of the legacies of public school and establishment priorities which I have been reluctant to embrace. The setback can be mitigated if more British drivers reflect before they purchase and support British employees in the factories at least still located in, if not owned by, this country. When the new small Jaguar is available there will be a range of vehicles to suit most needs provided by Mini, Jaguar and Land/Range Rover.

Taken by the author soon after the opening of Leigh Delamere Services on the M4 in the 1970s. Austin, Hillman, Morris, British-built Ford and Vauxhall. Just one non-British car - a Volkswagen.

LEARNING FROM DIFFERENCE

Chapter 20

Creators Not Just Consumers? An Alternative?

This book began by suggesting that ideas are only of marginal value without the power to implement them. Later I described how, as an elected Independent Councillor, I did have that power in a small degree at local level and how it was used. Those were rewarding years, despite the perils of that airless Council Chamber. As I write, I am powerless again but cannot quite banish the hope that someone somewhere might find something of interest in what I have written and in these conclusions. What is it all about? The answer is lifelong support for 'One Nation' Conservative thinking, following up the ideas and words of Benjamin Disraeli and Harold Macmillan, and those I was fortunate to meet or listen to: Ted Heath, Reggie Maudling, Douglas Hurd, Brandon Rhys Williams, James Prior, Peter Walker, David Howell, Ian Gilmour, Anthony Meyer, Richard Needham, Geoffrey Johnson Smith and many others. That is why Ed Milliband's espousal of 'One Nation Labour' was troubling. Though the strength and value of personal, financial and social advancement and success is understood (and there is contribution by tax payments and charitable giving), my own background experiences have led me to value the thinking that those with power should think of all citizens, not just the successful. Cynicism, the feeling of a country and a situation where there is no future, becomes debilitating when there are no job prospects and little hope.

My first contact with ideas for helping all those who live here came from reading a powerful book written by Lord Coleraine in 1970 called *For Conservatives Only*.[1] In the penultimate chapter he suggested those who are able to should pay for education, use of the Health Service, and other services and those who are not - he mentioned 'the old, the disabled and the lower-paid worker' (the unemployed were not in this list) - should be provided not with the services, but with the means to pay for them. He described this system as Reverse Income Tax: 'It uses inequality for the public good. For if the majority is relieved of the heavy burden of taxation and thus in a position to pay (for its own services), it becomes relatively easy to relieve the poverty of the minority and to do so without all the cumbrous expensive and inefficient machinery of over-generous benefits qualified by the claw-back system which still fails to get rid of poverty.' Such ideas about the Health Service would not now be acceptable, but these paragraphs first alerted me to the thought of direct assistance to those with minimal income. Then came the Heath

Government's proposals for tax credits in the 1972 Green Paper (see Chapter 15). Since that chapter was written, Malcolm Torry's comprehensive book *Money for Everyone* about Citizen's/Basic income has been published.[2] He writes of the 1972 Green Paper: 'These Tax Credits would have replaced tax allowances and would have been paid in full if an individual had no other income.' Malcolm explains how these credits would have been withdrawn if earned income was achieved and 'this would have reduced considerably the labour market disincentives (i.e. reasons for not taking work that became available) that many people experienced.'

Malcolm also writes of past Liberal Party commitments. After work by Philip Vince and Richard Wainwright, tax credits became Party policy in the early 1980s. Then, after the merger between Liberals and Social Democrats, Citizen's Income became party policy until their Party Conference in 1994, when the idea was dropped. Then in November 1988, the year after I stopped as Councillor, I just happened to notice the Opinion column in the *Mail on Sunday* under the heading 'The simple way to a more decent country for us all':

'The answer lies within the tax system itself. The Government should move quickly to a system of reverse income tax. Those, as now, who fall in the tax bracket would continue to pay their taxes. Those who fall below a particular level of earning would, instead of paying tax, have money returned to them. There would be but one form filled in by every citizen. There would be just one office for collecting taxes and paying benefits. It would be simple, socially just, and would help towards building a more decent country for us all.'

Was whoever wrote this aware of all the implications? Much has been written since 1988 about why, with the plethora of benefits plus unemployment and incapacity, such a simple system would be difficult to implement. Since 1972 there has been other thought by individuals, rather than political parties or journalists, about the idea of a partial Basic Income or, that word again, a citizen's Income for those who aspire to Citizenship. When Arthur Cockfield was adviser to the Conservatives on that 1972 Green Paper, he also concluded that a partial basic income was 'both technically and economically feasible'.[3] The idea was much in my thoughts during the Bridge Project years (see Chapter 16). Apart from Sir Brandon Rhys Williams and Hermione Parker (see Chapter 15), it has been continually discussed and advocated by the respected journalist Sir Samuel Brittan (see his 2005 book *Against the Flow*[4]). Robert and Edward Skidelski have written about Basic Income in their recent book *How Much is Enough?* published in 2012.[5] In his book *Blind Victory*, written nearly thirty years ago in 1986, David Howell, remembered as a candidate from the 1960s (see Chapter 13), explains the value of, in his words[6]:

'A guaranteed and unconditional basic income for all who have left full time schooling whether they worked full-time, part-time, stayed at home or had no sort of occupation at all. The beauty of it is that it makes the labour market vastly more flexible. Government attempts to ensure adequate living standards for all would shift away from efforts to rig the labour market by complex wage legislation or to devise desperate job-preservation schemes at vast cost since the basic income would take care of all that. People would be free, or freer at any rate, to accept low-wage and part-time jobs. The unemployed would no longer be discouraged from taking some work to top up their basic income. The temptation to join the black economy and work for undeclared income so as to protect state benefits would evaporate.'

This says it all and is why (thinking of 'no longer discouraged from taking some work to top up') we tried so hard to get the disregard increased in Bridge Project days. Lord Howell, as he now is, went on to discuss 'the two huge snags to this idea.' First there would be the incentive for many to be completely and anti-socially idle and second it would be colossally expensive and involve high taxes. A partially supportive income, backed up by other aids to survival, which might not be colossally expensive, was not considered. He also had other ideas. In the following chapters he outlined the preferred route of helping every citizen to own more capital (and income from capital), rather than just being dependent on wages. He referred to a book by Louis Kelso published in America in 1958[7] of the need for a social order based on greatly broadened individual ownership, both of private enterprise and of public utilities and other undertakings. David Howell mentioned that Louis Kelso's insights helped the Conservatives in their planning before the 1970 Election. We wanted: 'a lessening in people's dependence as employees and nothing else. This would mean the spread of personal dignity and individual status and a general rolling back of the rule of officialdom with its master servant connotation which we found so unpleasant and in which we saw a sinister future as Orwell had done before us.' Thirty years later there has been progress and more people do have some ownership through property (helped by council house sales), through shares purchased after privatisation, through insurance schemes, self-invested pension schemes, and so on. Sadly, unemployment in some areas is still as high as it was at the Bridge Project (David Howell referred to the sort of situation which wider ownership might not be able to help: an ex-mining community with 22% unemployment and a scattering of new factories. This was exactly the situation in the Coleford area in the early 1980s) and 'desperate job-preservation schemes at vast cost' have continued. I also take issue with his words about 'incentive to be completely and anti-socially idle'. We had only one person who fitted that description at Broadwell. I am more in tune with what Hermione Parker wrote 25 years ago in *Instead of the Dole*[8]: 'The technical and economic revolution must ultimately cause people to question the continuing relevance of the work-ethic that puts so little value on unpaid work. There is the paradox of high unemployment alongside a growing pile of unmet needs. A small basic income is an alternative to 'workfare' or state compulsion.'

It all comes down to that 'colossally expensive' and the attitude of those in power. The Citizen's Income Trust[9], nurtured by Malcolm Torry and others, has done so much work on this, as have other organisations and - I believe - Government departments. A small basic income, preferred to some form of negative income tax, is not so colossally expensive and was reckoned to be feasible by people like Arthur Cockfield. It is in the minds of politicians and political activists that it still comes into the category of 'cannot be afforded'. This is the mountain which we do not try to climb. Money goes to the Armed Forces because over the centuries that is what we have been good at and employment is provided. Money goes to ceremony and celebration because that is part of the oil which lubricates the whole system. A fund was not built up from North Sea oil, surely the heritage of all citizens. A financial transfer tax is rejected because the City of London must have top priority. Some have questioned 'quantitive easing' and suggested a payment to individuals instead. Will anyone with power consider other priorities? As Barbara Wootton, herself a supporter of basic income,[10] wrote in 1967: 'it is from the champions of the impossible rather than the slaves of the possible that evolution draws its creative force'. Ian Duncan Smith and the present Coalition Government's move to Universal Credit could be a step in this direction, but that word 'conditionality' is still seen as a pillar of the benefit system. The language of 'strivers and skivers', and the whole business of getting people off benefits with an expensive system of testing and checking seems to be having political benefit. I have asked Ian directly at one of those after-dinner question and answer sessions (when there is no opportunity to develop a discussion) whether they could consider going further along the route towards an unconditional benefit. The swift answer was: 'No, we would never consider giving people 'something for nothing'.' I have had the same answer from other Conservative MPs and 'activists' when I rejoined the Party and played some part in the local Constituency organisation attending meetings and committees. Contacts from the past, who remain members of the Liberal and Labour parties take the same view. They all consider that such a policy would lose votes. Only the Green Party referred to the idea in their last manifesto and will, I hope, continue their support. If a forum for discussion could ever be found, I would argue that a small basic income is no more 'something for nothing' than the money the bankers and the rest get in their bonuses. Some of this wealth stems from the labour of those who were shepherded into the new factories at the start of Britain's industrial revolution. Products were sold far and wide, and in all sorts of ways the money which was not dissipated in wars found its way back to London and other British cities. But creative jobs for the descendants of those who were in at the beginning as labourers, and helped to make it all happen, are no longer there. Many of them are in a desert where there is little chance of job satisfaction. Thinking of what we attempted in the careers service, finding work that suits, becomes a joke. There may be the opportunity to fill supermarket shelves, or to spend arid, repetitive and boring days in call-centres, with the threat of losing means of subsistence if they refuse. This is the state compulsion which is the alternative to the suggested small basic income.

It may suit those in power to thus fuel consumerism - consumer fodder instead of the cannon fodder a hundred years ago - but filling shelves so there is enough money to then buy what you have put there is not creative. Would it be realistic to seriously consider other aids to survival, which would permit the cheaper small basic income without leading to starvation? What if, in addition to that small basic income, there was a nationwide assessment of all surplus land? To many this will just sound fanciful, but what might be available through the National Trust, the Forestry Commission, military training grounds, brownfield sites or creating more allotments, where a plot of land might be offered at a small rent to be cultivated by those without work? At first there would only be a few takers, who would accept encouragement to create some of their own nourishment instead of buying from those shelves. Some would be defeated by weather and animal predators. We have watched allotment novices lose their enthusiasm when the weeds proliferate. It is easier to take from the shelves in the supermarket. Realistic encouragement towards such activities could have been another part of Richard O'Brien's thought-to-be-too-expensive plans to point all young people towards a creative life. This would be a continuation of David Howell's thoughts. As he wrote in a later chapter of his book:

'We know that governments can not deliver full-time employment for all. Those who are taught that they can and are then left out naturally conclude that there is a scrap heap of unwanted people in society and they have been left on it. The conventional ethic of dependent employment and the conventional attitudes to wages and salaries are still embedded in the teaching language. Thinking about capital and ownership and the independence they permit to allow a more personal control of work and life hardly enters into the curriculum'.

Allowing more personal control of work and life is also relevant to attempts at partial self-sufficiency, of by-passing the consumer chain with this option of creating some food by personal effort. The potential objections, land availability and human attitude, are understood, but these are more ideas which could 'enter the curriculum' and perhaps - in time - lead to changes in that attitude. What if they were presented as an alternative to being tested, even humiliated, by the likes of ATOS, or that drudgery in those call-centres? What if the pleasures of creativity and potential better health were explained? With mass communication, will email, Twitter, Facebook, etc, slowly engender interest? Initially there may only be a few takers, but such changes always take time. With sensible presentation and a supportive media, this alternative way of life, healthier, fitter and even warmer, could perhaps become acceptable for some. This is what I found had happened in the Forest of Dean in years past. Foresters were in the mines when there was work. At other times they worked their vegetable gardens and were allowed to run a pig scavenging in the Forest scrub. We were able to keep a small orchard when the house in that area was sold. Expeditions to collect firewood for the wood-burning stove and to pick the apples led to feeling the glow from exercise and muscles well-used. Such a concept is far removed from the horizons of those who are stuck in cities and without employment. Many do not want to move from their own communities, but even in cities, more food cultivation may be possible and there could be more encouragement in rural areas. A small basic income could better allow consideration of these alternatives and so much more. The cost of everything rises with inflation, but that's everything except nothing! Nothing does not rise. No comparable wage-rise to balance cost-rise. Benefits may also rise, but if for some reason there is a denial of benefit, for someone with nothing, the gap to achieve survival subsistence just gets wider. As I write, in April 2104, the front page of *The Independent* reads: 'Nearly a million people now rely on handouts to eat and benefit reforms may be to blame'. If the workings of society have led to this inflation, would it not be equitable to make a comparable addition to 'nothing'? This alone seems to me another argument for unconditional basic income. One can not foresee, but could such provision enable ways of life which, with or without cultivation, might then advance through barter, part-time or odd jobs and help to others to the more personal control which David Howell advocated? Better health and less of the depression and despair, which so easily results from poverty, inadequate housing and poor diet and conditions for the family, could mean less pressure on the NHS and hard-pressed Social Services. Only experience would tell whether there would be less crime. There has to be caution about prescription based on personal interests, but could it be that more people would rediscover the pleasure of working with their hands and less time gazing at screens? Perhaps with less pressure, some might even rediscover the pleasure of hand-written communication! With the threat of starvation reduced, more people might attempt the sort of craft industry which can take so long to become profitable. 'Heritage', which brings visitors to Britain, might have more recruits. Even village shops might be possible again with the backing of the basic income. Then there is also so much work available in every community, which may be better suited to the voluntary spirit. Older people cannot be so well served by often harassed employees desperate to achieve their employer's time-table, but volunteers need to eat and pay their household expenses.

As previously commented, I have no power - but how I would like to see a national debate! I have written of a small basic income, hoping that the idea could be more acceptable to the electorate if recipients still had to find some other means to aid survival. In 2013 the Citizen's Income Trust worked out figures to show that what they call a Citizen's Income of £71 per week (less for those under 25, more for those over 64) could be paid for little more than the total cost of benefits, tax reliefs and allowances that it would replace.[11] This suggests that the idea, whether what I shall now call a full Citizen's Income, or a smaller basic income, is no longer fanciful. A pilot project in Madya Pradesh in India has proved to be entirely beneficial, with participants reported having 'more varied diets, improved health, more school attendance, purchasing sewing machines, seeds and fertiliser, and a switch from wage-labour to own-account farming'.[12] The reality in Britain in 2014 is that no political party with a prospect of power, solo or in coalition with the Liberal Democrats, is considering an unconditional basic or Citizen's Income, call it what you will, in any form. That it was included in the Green Party's manifesto at the last Election, and the consequent publicity, is appreciated, but currently they only have one MP. As the 2015 Election approaches, the Conservatives are nailing their colours to the masthead of the Duncan Smith so-called 'universal credit.' It isn't actually universal as it does not continue after earned income rises but - if it all works as hoped - this may be better than the situation when those who do manage to move on from benefits to work can be worse off after taking a job. The fact remains that there are still insufficient jobs and some of those on offer are part-time or subject to what are known as 'zero hours' contracts. Lives are still blighted and potential wasted by lack of work and future prospects. Whilst the resonance for some potential Conservative voters is understood, it does not help those affected when it is put around that unemployment is the consequence of personal failings. 'Buck up and pull yourself together' seems to be the current nostrum. 'Our agencies will sort you out and, if you do not respond, you will find yourself very short of funds.' Some will maintain that there are cases where this is reasonable comment, particularly when several generations appear to have been benefit recipients. I would answer that each case has to be considered individually. When a generation has had hopes dashed and misfortune multiplied, it is thoroughly discouraging for the succeeding generation. Such comment is understandably resented by those who so badly want to improve their situation. It does not help that those agencies charged with achieving job placements and reducing the unemployed count are paid by results. Matching the job to the applicant's abilities and interests is far from the highest priority, a reversal of what was attempted in the Careers Service.

The Labour Party seems now to be committed to finding some sort of work for everyone. With what they call their 'Future Jobs Fund', they are aiming for a placement (which may only be temporary) for all those currently without a job. Of course this policy is appealing to those who hate inactivity and are losing hope. Labour's choice is understandable. It is what many people want and is likely to produce votes. For them this seems a much better bet than the insufficiently understood basic/citizen's income with, at this stage, all its unknowns and not the same immediacy of work - any work - at last. But the problem, as I so well remember from helping to administer similar schemes as an elected Councillor in the 1980s, is the cost (which also falls on the taxpayer and can thus adversely effect those whose efforts do provide more permanent jobs) and the actual difficulty of finding enough work. At first, any activity is appreciated, skills are learnt and the discipline of work experienced. Later, if participants come to realise that their tasks are of doubtful value - what are known as 'make-work' schemes - and there is less possibility of permanent work resulting, the whole idea is questioned. Much depends on whether the Labour Party, if elected, has learnt from past mistakes and, with the assistance of employers and Local Government, can organise sufficient placements with meaning and prospects.

I welcome anything which could help all citizens. It seems a pity that the Conservatives are corralled by the 'something for nothing' barricades, especially when one of their slogans from past years was 'Trust the People.' We know well the pressure on younger members of our family who are working so hard in stressful situations and paying their taxes. In their often exhausting and stressful struggle for survival, and full-throttle well-deserved enjoyment of their recreation, it is understandable that they do not have time to reflect on alternatives which could help those not in their kind of position, or those who - in their view - have opted out from their struggles. As some form of benefit will continue, can we show them that a system which uses their taxpayer money more effectively and is more user-friendly, is better for everyone? Then there are the concerns about continuing growth. Generally in Conservative circles, growth seems to be seen as the route to salvation. As an example, more and more cars and other goods are churned out every day. Higher production is praised as the measure of success, the route to more employment and more tax revenue. But where does this all end? The planet is not growing larger to accommodate these goods. Constant scrapping is a waste of resources. It is difficult to see how manufacturers depending on advancing consumerism and satisfying their shareholders can themselves alter their priorities in the present situation. Change to a basic or Citizen's income would also help this situation. Some of those who adapt to the self-sufficient life may opt (or be encouraged) to repair and recycle all manner of goods. In the case of cars, a consequent decrease in demand need not be disastrous for manufacturers. It would mean trimming the workforce, but in the knowledge that they would have this income in addition to severance pay. This could be creative redundancy. Ex-employees might involve themselves in the burgeoning British restoration industry, rescuing more of the simpler vehicles of past decades, which some drivers still prefer. The Federation of British Historic Vehicle Clubs is working to establish an apprenticeship scheme. Leeds City College plans to begin its classic car restoration course in September 2014.

Such ideas are far removed from current thinking and, if it is the Conservatives who win the 2015 Election, they will be concentrating on matters relating to their promised 2017 referendum. Time will tell whether there will be closer ties to the European mainland, drawing on the gratitude which still remains for all the sacrifice, including all those in this family, which prevented German domination; or whether this in-and-out island will continue, again as with the efforts of family members described in this book, to be a supplier of skills, innovation and inventiveness throughout the world. After the referendum, problems of joblessness may still have to be faced and 'universal credit' may not have been the hoped-for panacea. If the Labour Party has been in power and without a referendum, the taxation needed to fund their schemes may be such that voters are looking for an alternative. In either case, I am suggesting that a basic or Citizen's income will still be worthy of consideration and, as explained above, it has been recognised that it can be financed by changes to the present system. It does not seem to fit with the socialist desire to control and direct. It is in line with the Whig belief in freedom and respect for the individual and reducing government interference in people's lives, though it is also sensible to heed Edmund Burke's warning about how change can lead to creating new difficulties, today's 'unintended consequences.' This is one of the reasons why preparation and explanation in schools would be important, also recognising Tory acceptance of potential human fallibility. There is as yet no sign of a Conservative Member of the House of Commons like Brandon Rhys Williams, who answered the Chair of a Select Committee in 1982 with the words: 'You would not need to register as unemployed. There would be people not in full time work but they would not need to have themselves labelled as unemployed. If they got an opportunity of work or casual work, they could take it and nobody would have to know.' I know from personal experience how difficult it is to oppose the Party line. If one or more younger members saw the merit of basic or Citizen's income, perhaps also encouraged by what might then be happening in other countries, they would, as things now stand, need to have a long-term plan. It is suggested from experience that during their first years in Parliament they would need to establish themselves as loyal, reliable and helpful servants of their electorate and their constituency associations. If elected for a second term, this would be the time to proclaim the value of such a change to benefit and taxation, standing up to the Whips and accepting the possibility of deselection. (Preparation would also need to include provision of other income if pushed out of Westminster!) A few members acting in this sort of way could lead to more recognition of this value. I have attended numerous discussions about these ideas including a conference in Brussels in 2014 where it was suggested that a basic income in all European countries could lead to less 'economic migration'. If funding could ever be agreed, could this be another route to tackling the abundance of UK immigration? It has been comforting to share views with like-minded people. That comfort can be counter-productive in obscuring the realities of power. We have not yet followed Great-aunt Maud Joachim and her fellow suffragettes in taking the hard decisions which might eventually lead to results.

In conclusion, I have not succeeded in my three ambitions. First, thought about in childhood and formulated more strongly when I realised that we had 'lost' Portsmouth Aviation, was to play a part in progressing the British-owned car industry. Second, when at last I realised this was not possible, was to help develop that National Careers and Employment Service, providing effective face-to-face guidance and assistance to those at the start of their working lives. We are what we are, all different in different ways. I still maintain that, where circumstances permit (where life can be more than a desperate struggle for survival and where there isn't an ordained future) it's worth trying to work out weaknesses, interests and strengths before the start of working life. There is an appropriate comment from Confucius: 'Chose a job you love and you will never have to work a day in your life.' For so many this is not possible, but with assistance, people may be able to get nearer to this situation than they might otherwise have done. These were my arguments for the sort of Careers Service which Jim Prior and others wanted. (see Chapters 14 and 16) Whether it could have been afforded and how rated in importance versus the Armed Services or other aspects of Government is another matter. I like to think that a continuing efficient service could, in the end have saved money. Third was to become a back-bench Conservative, attempting to further 'One Nation' policies. The point now is that no-one else seems to have fully succeeded in these objectives. Therefore I have wondered whether it could be of value to try and work out from personal experience some of the reasons why this has happened. Besides the family history, and reflecting on maternal and paternal differences, this is some of the thinking behind the attempt at this book. Of course, it can be argued that the Gloucester challenge was funked. If elected in 1970, would I have been proclaiming some of these ideas and have managed to cope with the physical difficulties? One certainty is that I would not have had all the knowledge and experience gained in the following years. The wish to have both hard-won experience and some power (like Robert Balfour) remains a challenge to all aspirants. As already suggested, voices are much less likely to be heard outside the arena, but all that I am still saying and writing about Citizen's Income, whether or not heard and read, is a continuation of the very words in the Gloucester adoption speech - 'the ideal that no citizen should fall below a minimum level' (see Chapter 13). As the journey to the crematorium approaches, I have to live with decisions taken. It may still have been better to have funked than sunk - with family too? - thus repeating the sinkings of past generations. Lord Coleraine points to the value of the class structure and tradition. Writing this book has helped me to better understand this viewpoint and the lives of those who have co-operated with it all both for their own benefit and often for the benefit of the many others they have helped along the way. Personal circumstances led me to question and for some I have been a sort of non-accepting nuisance with ideas rather than positive achievements. Yet it all points in the same direction: the wish that more citizens are enabled to have more fulfilled lives. I am fortunate to have enjoyed some fulfilment now, 70 years on, having mercifully avoided the sniper's bullet I am back to doing what I did that last summer at Peake, fiddling with wood and metal. I am probably enjoying it all the more because of experience gained in the intervening years.

Appendix 1

Chapter 7: 'it is bad luck on small pre-war operators like our-selves.'

Lord Swinton's own comments on the Swinton Plan, published in 1966, have recently come to light (after publication of *Spithead Express*). They help in understanding why Lionel was not too bothered about the overdraft immediately after the end of the war. Then, when this plan was not taken up by the Labour Government, quite soon there was the agreement for Indian finance, so he could be relaxed about the plans for nationalisation. Two seemingly sound solutions. Would a reasonable man expect them both to fail? Lionel was a member of the British delegation at this conference in 1944:

'I had gone to America in November 1944 as the first Minister of Civil Aviation to lead the British delegation at the International Conference on Civil Aviation. Though my time was fully occupied with the international side of civil aviation, I did work out what I thought should be the pattern of Civil Aviation at home. There were the large state-owned undertakings, the railway companies, then not nationalised which operated a number of inland services, and other inland services operated by a few independent companies. Some of the shipping companies had an interest and wished to extend this. Then there were travel agencies who had no participation in operation but were large customers of air travel. Was not the sensible thing to combine all these interests with their assets in three or four groups which would enable all to participate and operate to their best advantage? I found they were all attracted by this conception. I produced a plan which embraced them all and submitted it to the Cabinet.

'Churchill was attracted to it. I talked to Attlee about my plan and he seemed to be of Winston's opinion. It was agreed that the proposals should be discussed with Lord Leathers and Ernest Bevin. This was approved. They said: 'This is so sensible, let us have a try and to get it as it stands.' The cabinet accepted it. Attlee said: 'You may think this rather odd because this is half-denationalising something that is already nationalised, but Bevin thinks it is so good and sensible that I think we should do it. Then the election came before anything was done. Attlee said to me: 'I hope we do not have to scrap this.' But it was not to be.

The landslide of 1945 was a Socialist triumph. Nationalisation was the watchword. Clause 4 of the Labour Charter was the gospel. There was no place for heretics or deviationists, even in the highest ranks. So the opportunity was lost for having a sensible and commercially realistic policy for civil aviation linked with all the major transport services, a novel experiment in merging public and private enterprise in the national interest.'

Appendix 2

In November 1976 we visited Max at Eton. I had just stopped working in the Careers Service. The contrast was so marked that I decided to write to the then Headmaster, Michael McCrum, after he had spoken to a meeting of parents. The letter was too long but here are some extracts.

'I understand you had your agenda of questions, many put to you by parents, and, whilst you might have welcomed more open discussion, you wished to conclude by 6.30. Perhaps it is not wrong to ask you to glance at this. It does not need a reply. What is the aim of Eton now? What part is the school playing in trying to heal the divisions in our present Society? Itself a potentially divisive force, can it now justify by example and go further to lead the healing?

'Forgive the personal reference but I am perhaps over conscious of the gap between Eton and the 'trouble-filled' comprehensives in which I have until recently worked. Those Eton end-of-term reports, to which reference was made, are superb, but I was reminded of my feeling when comparing them with the almost total lack of such reports in some of the Merton schools. Earlier today I was walking amongst the teenagers in the South Merton Shopping Centre, two hours later I was enjoying Eton's drawing schools. What could some of 'my' ex-pupils have achieved with Eton's encouragement and facilities?

'That discussion was mostly about success within the school - enlightened self-interest. But is this enough in 1976? Is a small privileged group turning in on itself? The successful pupils still have to live in the real world outside the gate. How much is done to help Etonians keep in touch with this reality? I have always hoped that some form of exchange with State schools might be arranged so I was delighted to read the note 'Chez-Feltham' in the Chronicle. Did Feltham pupils come to Eton? Will Etonians go to such schools all over the country and suffer the very real pressures? This may hinder 'A' level preparation but isn't it just as important to learn how to cope with 'A' levels in the conditions prevailing for the majority? It is understandable that some parents paying high fees will not wish their son's chances to be jeopardised in any way. But there are wider issues, not least that some of the Capital paying the fees was built up on the backs of families whose children and grandchildren are in these other schools.

'I do know about the Social Service projects, but these have overtones of protected paternalism. Is there still a relevant ideal of service for Old Etonians, which goes some way towards justifying the privileged treatment? If so, are the practical difficulties of such service, even having motives questioned, discussed? I read about the famous speakers who have been invited to the school. But sometimes the less successful are better aware of the compromises that the successful often have to make. What about inviting those on the lower rungs who are up against the daily pressures in industry and local government? Or is Eton just a preparation for the greatest personal fulfilment? Or for the pursuit of a sort of cultured materialism? Or even for entire concentration on money making to pay the fees for the next generation?

'In my last years at the school, which I left 24 years ago, there was no probing discussion of the Society in which we were going to live and how we might relate to it. It seemed more important to uphold the accepted views and be a good unquestioning team member. An interest in an industrial career was not greatly encouraged and I had quite a struggle with R. Birley to get the Automobile Society and the consequent links with Industry established. Eton has achieved so much since those days. It would be a pity if unrealistic aspirations are still developing by default through lack of discussion.'

To my considerable surprise. Michael McCrum replied two days later with the following two-page letter.

FROM THE HEAD MASTER
M. M^cCRUM, M.A.

ETON COLLEGE,
WINDSOR,
BERKS. SL4 6DL

TELEPHONE: WINDSOR (075 35) 66439

30 November 1976

Dear Mr. Balfour,

Thank you for your most interesting letter.

It is difficult to know what parents want to talk about, and on the whole routine questions are perhaps more easy to deal with, with that number, than the more general and philosophical questions that you raise. I think it would be very interesting to have a general discussion on these lines another year.

Without going at length into my ideas I can say that I am most concerned about the part that Eton plays in trying to heal some of the divisions in our present society, and I am well aware from talking around the country how much we are criticised for our so-called divisiveness.

The problem is not easily solved if there is no source of money to finance boys to come here whose parents cannot afford to pay the fees. Neither the Labour nor the Conservative Party have any intention of providing funds for this. We ourselves have very limited resources. We did, as you probably know, start a small-scale scheme four years ago to provide six free places for boys from primary schools, and the first of these reached us last September and are doing very well; but this is an extremely expensive scheme and in present circumstances I doubt whether the Foundation will be able to afford to keep it up, at this number of awards, for very much longer. And of course six boys, even multiplied by five, is a very small number in a school of over 1,200.

I think that three most effective ways in which Etonians are helped to keep in touch with reality are by all the work they do in Slough on social service, which is considerable, the children's play-groups and other conferences at the Eton-Dorney Conference Centre in the parish of Dorney, and

by fairly frequent exchanges with comprehensive schools. There
are four or five comprehensive schools to whom we send boys and
from whom we receive boys, and these exchanges normally work
very well. They are not limited to Feltham; for example, we
also have an exchange with Ruffwood School in Kirkby, Liverpool.

I do not think that the social service activities are in
the last paternalist but if you would like to make that point
to Stephen Drew, the master who organises it, by all means
write to him. We do our very best to avoid anything
paternalist in all that we do in social service, and the wide
range of activity and the welcome that our boys receive is
evidence, I believe, of genuineness of the service.

There is an endless discussion, formal, informal, and
private on all the issues that you mention. Boys are very
well aware of outside criticism of the privileged treatment
that they enjoy. For our part, those of us who teach here
have to be careful while encouraging them to be sensitive on
these issues, not to make them feel guilty.

Speakers that you see invited to societies are only a
very small proportion of the whole. We have speakers from
all walks of life, not just the famous. For example, when
the Industrial Society visited us after Long Leave and
conferred with boys in B Block, most of the visitors were
from middle management, trades unions in the neighbourhood,
e.g. Slough. We spend a great deal of time and effort on
bringing the needs of industry before the boys here. At
present, for instance, all the recent Oxbridge candidates
(bar a very small number) are on industrial attachment all
over the country.

I do not myself think that there is any connexion
between the present decline in England's prosperity and the
public schools, but if there were it could equally well be
argued that the decline of England's prosperity had gone
hand in hand with the decline of the influence of the public
schools and their products! My own view is that the decline
is far more attributable to what Sir Keith Joseph writes
about in today's _Times_, on the leader page, than anything
else.

Yours sincerely,

C. Balfour Esq
3 Murray Road
London S W 19

This clearly demonstrates how much had changed since I left the school and, given the fact of their existence, the Headmaster and his colleagues were already at that stage trying to meet the concerns which I had outlined. This is part of my reply, written at the beginning of December 1976:

'I am particularly grateful for your letter as, now knowing your obvious personal commitment, I can better defend Eton in the conversations which result from my still straddling-the-two-worlds position. (This was all before the Forest of Dean and the commitment there to those who were unemployed). Alas! It is still two worlds for, however much Eton tries to do, it is hard to appreciate such things from the midst of a large comprehensive school faced with a 14 year old who can't read or write and no remedial classes available, or a potential high-flying engineer where the physics teaching is indifferent. There are perhaps two questions:

1. Could it be that after discussion more parents would be prepared to help finance boys from primary schools whose own parents cannot afford the fees?

2. Could we have some report on the progress of the exchanges with the comprehensive schools?

This absolutely does not need further reply and thank you for explaining more about social service, speakers and present links with Industry.'

The current *Old Etonian Association Review* explains how Eton is now much more involved with other state-provided schools. Eton has become the sole educational sponsor for Holyport College, a non-selective mixed comprehensive near Maidenhead and is also a sponsor of the London Academy of Excellence, a sixth-form college in the East End. There is now the partnership with the Slough and East Berkshire Multi-Academy Trust and Etonians act as mentors in local schools. Some new Eton entrants are supported by bursaries coming from funds donated from previous pupils and others. The *Review* also tells of increasing interest in entrepreneurship, community service, particularly for the elderly, and a careers day in June.

It is so good to learn of all these developments, which obliterate my critical remarks about the school I experienced sixty-five years ago. But it is still true that so much of the country's other potential talent would have benefited - and could still benefit - from similar facilities and treatment. The report of the 1942-1944 Fleming Committee recommended that, after the war, Society should no longer tolerate the social divisiveness of the old public school system and that a minimum of 25% public schoolboys, in the first instance, should be chosen from the state primary schools. The aim seems to have been for more widely spread, though diminished, excellence. The decision-makers may have been mindful of Edmund Burke's concern about change leading to unknown consequences. Instead, Michael Gove and others are now trying much harder to improve the schools funded by the State and other organisations. This is the other route which, combined with a much more open attitude at places like Eton may, hopefully, lead to less social divisiveness.

Appendix 3

This is part of what was sent to various MPs in that period before I came off the candidates list again.

I think I must withdraw my application to be reconsidered for the candidates list. The Party's approach has developed in ways which I would find it difficult to support. Conservative philosophy has always depended on several related ideas. It can not, like Socialism be represented by one easily assimilated word like 'Equality' hence the need to devise ways by which the Conservative concept can be more easily understood.

1. Continuing to advocate cuts in public spending, but at the first stage by carefully pruning to get rid of the wasteful methods of working so well known to those who have been in Local Government, NOT by lopping off whole branches.

2. Admitting that this will lead to more unemployment, but then go all out to say that such unemployment is not a potential disaster, especially with present benefits. Rather it is tremendous opportunity for encouraging so many of our people towards better kinds of employment and better ways of life.

3. Sharing out the existing work, especially the dreary jobs. Introducing more flexible hours and a more flexible attitude to retirement.

4. Some may like the security of part-time work whilst they establish their own small businesses, which in turn will provide more jobs.

5. Others, with the right sort of encouragement, and some initial help, would, I believe, gladly go back to a self-sufficient life in less populated areas (and lower the import bill). Thus, looking back from 2050, the mass migration to the cities might be seen as a temporary phenomenon.

I think back to a recent day in the country. In the morning the fields were a mass of mushrooms just there for the picking. In the afternoon I walked past the queue of unemployed outside the City Labour Exchange. These men and women don't just want dole. They want more effective agencies which link possibilities with people. It may be jobs, it may be money, but it may also be encouragement 'to do one's own thing', to even go out and garner nuts and berries from the hedgerows.

Reading again now, getting on towards forty years later, the reaction is: 'So what? If you believed all this, why did you not press on and get into a position to try and do something about it.' That was my problem. I did not sufficiently understand the slight value of ideas without power. And I did not actually know how many 'would gladly go back to a self-sufficient life.' That was just an assumption.

Appendix 4
Summary of report compiled January 1979.

Careers Advice. A new, unified service. Each school with a full-time advisor.

In 1977 the Fookes Committee recommended further consultation between Department of Employment and Science and Department of Employment to try and avoid duplication of effort. Careers Teachers (often part-time), Careers Officers and Job Centre staff were all helping in different ways. Because some leavers were not getting sufficient help, the MSC had appointed unemployment specialists to seek out those who had missed out.

To build up a unified service, more practising Officers would be needed. Most Officers now attend three or four schools. Where is the extra money? One answer is that it is there already used by the administration instead of used for clients. Should professional advisers collect statistics and carry out other tasks for the Government? Is it necessary to have a separate collection point for vacancies when the Job Centres are already in touch with the same Employers? If these suggestions are accepted, fewer assistants are needed and it may be possible to reduce the number Careers Offices. Thus the Service could fund its own reorganisation.

1. More Careers Officers with higher status and higher salaries. Careers Teachers and others could join.

2. Except for the largest schools where one Officer, perhaps renamed Adviser, required, have one schools based Adviser for a pair of adjacent schools. (Comparison between the two curbs insularity.)

3. Facilities in all schools: Careers library kept up to date, files for records, interviewing room and telephone.

Given manageable case-loads, these revitalised Advisers must accept the responsibility of keeping in touch with all their clients until they are satisfactorily settled or passed to the Job Centre. Advisers can learn as much about local opportunities through keeping in contact with those who they are assisting during the first stages of employment as they can during organised tours of inspection.

Principal Careers Officers are now subservient to Chief Education Officers who, with Education Committees, have the power to block developments including the recommendations of Department of Education Inspectors. It would be better to have Principal Advisers reporting direct to Regional Directors of Careers Service Branches, associating with Education officers as equal partners and making contact with Employers at Board level. If this reorganisation was achieved Advisers would not have to move to other work to achieve higher status.

Thirty-five years later, there is the realisation that this may have been too costly and idealistic. But there is also the thought that, if I and others had been able to work with Jim Prior, if even some of these plans to have experienced advisers keeping watch over school-leavers until they were settled in their working life had come about, we might now have fewer unemployed. Richard O'Brien's preferred MSC plans would have tutored those who had insufficient skills, including those lacking in literacy. Employers would have much less need to prefer some immigrants to those 'homegrown'. The advisory chain would have been reporting back to Government where jobs were scarce. Instead Michael Portillo and others proceeded with privatisation. After problems, the Connexions Service followed and proved inadequate in some areas. Now we are back with the 'National Careers Service' but it is neither face-to-face nor continuing advisory care.

Notes

Chapter 1

Note 1.   George Orwell, born Eric Blair. 1903-1950. King's Scholar at Eton. Animal Farm, 1984, etc.

Note 2.   Eric Hobsbawm. 1917-2012. *Age of Revolution, Age of Capital, Age of Empire, Age of Extremes*, etc.

Note 3.   Letter B Scillitoe to author 20th December 1966. St Lawrence Hall, Ventnor, Isle of Wight, was burnt to the ground soon after being sold by FG in 1946.

Note 4.   Recorded in *Uncharted Waters - The Cayzer Family Firm*. David Sinclair. The Cayzer Trust Company. 2010.

Note 5.   Pablo Picasso. 1881-1973. Painter, sculptor, creator of Cubism.

Note 6.   *Stuff Matters. Genius, risk and the secret of capitalism*. Harry Bingham. Fourth Estate. 2010.

Note 7.   An internet comment from Anthony Black, who was then found to be Professor at Dundee University, the very city of the Balfours and Ogilvies as described in the next chapter. He also wrote 'It is clear that Cameron, Osborne and the Eurosceptics have little clue about the needs of British Industry or of the majority of our people and how they can be met in a global economy'.

Note 8.   See www.bristolcars.co.uk and www.frazer-nash.com. I am glad to have gained some knowledge of their plans as a result of writing the book: *Bristol Cars, a very British story* published by Haynes in 2009.

Chapter 2

Note 1.   Lionel was christened Maxwell Lionel Joachim but he always preferred Lionel after his two godfathers, Lionel Curtis and Lionel Hichens, who were better known to him than his own father.

Note 2.   i. *A Scottish Childhood and What Happened After*, Mary I Ogilvie George Ronald 1952.
ii. *Memoir of Maxwell Balfour* MI Ogilvie Clifton 1916.
iii. Added reminiscences to Anne Ogilvie's memoir MI Ogilvie 1910.
iv. Letter Minnie Ogilvie to Lionel Balfour 1949.

Note 3.   *Spithead Express The pre-war Island Air Ferry and post-war plans*. Magna Press, 1999.

Note 4.   www.ogilviegodfreyfamilytree.com.

Note 5.   In 2010 the company celebrated its bi-centenary. It is now described as a leading supplier of glass-lined equipment with branches in the Americas, Germany, India and China. Robbins and Myers Inc bought Pfaudler and other related businesses in 1994. The Leven plant is still called Pflaudler Balfour. See *A history of Pflaudler Balfour 1810-2010* written by Kristopher McKie. www.pflaudler.com and www.pflaudler.de.

Note 6.   The hull of this ship lies near Garden Island, Port Adelaide, in South Australia. This has been declared an historic wreck, a rare example of an early iron built sailing vessel. www.methilheritage.org.uk.

Note 7.   Alexander Balfour was particularly aware of the conditions sailors had to endure round Cape Horn. In Liverpool he founded the Duke Street Home for sailors, also orphanages for the children of seamen who had lost their lives. In Valparaiso he was a sponsor of the Union Church, founded the Artisan School in 1857 and was one of the founders of the YMCA. *Heirs of Great Adventure. The history of Balfour Williamson and Company* 1851-1951 Wallis Hunt. Jarrold & Sons.

Note 8.   In 1981 after ownership by the Bank of London South America, and then Lloyds Bank, Williamson Balfour was bought by Inchcape retaining the name. As distributors for BMW for the whole of Chile, they are based in Avenida Las Condes, Santiago. In 2012 it was agreed that they would also be responsible for Rolls Royce sales.

Note 9.   The Santa Maria University in Valparaiso is one of the top engineering schools in Chile.

Note 10. This leaves out John and Jean's son, Great-grandfather James's grandfather, William Balfour married to Alison Mitchell.

Note 11. There are further records of the connections between these Dundee families. Anne Maxwell (later Anne Ogilvie), my great-great-grandmother mentions in a memoir written in 1901 that she had met an earlier Rachel Ogilvie when they both worked for the church in the parish of Dr. Roxburgh, Jesse's father. It was through this contact that Anne met her husband John Ogilvie, that Rachel's brother.

Note 12. Consumption was the name then given to what is also known as pulmonary tuberculosis. Tuberculosis is described in the dictionary as 'a nodule or morbid growth'. Pulmonary as 'disease in the lungs'. In other words, my great-grandmother still young, noted as being so helpful to her siblings, and now with three young sons of her own, was finding it increasingly difficult to breathe.

Note 13. The Arica to Tacna rail line was opened in 1856, but there was no connection on to Mollendo. Peru's railway museum is at Tacna.

Note 14. We have long looked at a picture of Westlands, Broughty Ferry, painted by my grandfather Max Balfour without realising its significance. This was George Ogilvie's house. It can still be identified on Google maps though now surrounded by other houses rather than in wooded countryside.

Note 15. Eventually, after other houses in Canynge Square, a location better known from a 2010 murder.

Note 16. Willie himself wrote: 'This excessive mechanical training was a mistake and I would have preferred a wider education'. In practice it seems to have served him well.

Note 17. Both these memoirs can be read on the Ogilvie Godfrey Family Tree (Google Ogilvie Godfrey).

Note 18. www.corpdicyt.cl/homeferroviario.htm or Google santiago railway museum. Locomotive type 57 No. 631 on show similar to Balfour Lyon assembly.

Note 19. To some purpose! Willie married Mary Wolff in Valparaiso. Their eldest son became consultant surgeon at Guy's also to Middle East Forces in 1942 with the rank of Major General. He was knighted as Sir Heneage. Their youngest son became the BBC's second Director General and Principal of Jesus College, Oxford. He was knighted as Sir Frederick. All this without the arm he lost in the 1914-1918 war.

Note 20. *Heirs of Great Adventure. The history of Balfour Williamson and Company.* Wallis Hunt.

Note 21. Archibald Williamson was an MP from 1906-1922 when he went to the House of Lords. He had been created a Baronet in l909. Note *Balfour Williamson and allied firms. Memoirs of a Merchant House.* Archibald Williamson (Lord Forres).

Note 22. It is worth putting 'Sir Robert Balfour Hansard' into Google. Note particularly his speech 18 July 1922. It highlights the conflict between costly warfare seeking to control and creative trade which pays the bill.

Note 23. There is much about Langham Hall via Google.

Note 24. See *Flight* magazine 24th January 1918. Tincort Cemetery is on the Peronne side of the village. Percy Balfour was buried at the Sorel Cemetery which is North of Peronne.

Chapter 3

Note 1. From several internet references, also *The Oxford Musical Quarterly* December 2011.

Note 2. In *The house of Wittgenstein* published 2008, Alexander Waugh writes of Paul's determination to overcome the loss of an arm from a Russian bullet 'an iron will, an inability to dissemble and sometimes unawareness of how the World worked.'

Note 3. Internet reference. Karl Wittgenstein for many accounts of his life. Note especially the article by authors from Frostburg State University and Manhattan College. 'Karl Wittgenstein's rise from self educated engineer to one of the most powerful industrialists of the Hapsburg Empire was entwined with the development of the iron and steel industry and consequently the industrialisation of Austria-Hungary'.

Note 4. Kittsee just to the west of Bratislava and now in Austria. The motorway to Vienna goes past the town. Internet reference. Joseph Joachim. There are pictures of the Kittsee house in which Joseph and his brothers and sisters were born (some records say seven children, others eight).

Note 5. The two settlements became Budapest in 1873.

Note 6. There are still marks in the city today showing the height the water reached.

Note 7. Now the University of Music & Theatre'. The oldest university music school in Germany.

Note 8. Jelli did not marry. She was a friend of the composer Frederick Kelly. He was killed at the Battle of the Somme in 1916. Whilst at Gallipoli he had composed a violin sonata for Jelli which she played at his Memorial Service. Internet reference. 'Lost Gallipoli sonata returns home'.

Note 9. Fanny's youngest children (still babies) would have been looked after by others. Karl, 'the future richest man in Europe' was not born until 1847.

Note 10. This was the final period of stagecoach travel before the railways took over. Much effort had gone into development. Road surfaces were improved. The carriages, many of which were built in Hungary, had some suspension.

Note 11. When there were opportunities elsewhere, many were separated from their families because of the much longer travelling times. The 2012 Michelin map reckons about seven hours today, mostly motorway Leipzig to Budapest.

Note 12. As note 4 internet reference. Joseph Joachim. There is much about his music partners, his teaching at Leipzig, his visits to England.

Note 13. See internet. 'Moving here, migration histories'.

Note 14. Full name. 'The Great Exhibition of Arts and Manufactures' see internet Charles Tomlinson Cyclopaedia of Useful Arts, Manufacture etc. 'The fleeces of Figdor & Sons of Austria presented in high degree the desired qualities of substance in the staple and fineness and elasticity of the component fibres.' After the exhibition closed the whole structure was dismantled and moved to a new site Sydenham Hill. This is now the national sports centre. The Palace was destroyed by fire in 1936.

Note15. Internet references. Henry Smart & Sir George Smart. Henry was organist in Yorkshire and London, finally, although almost blind, at St Pancras Church until his death. He designed an organ for Leeds Town Hall in 1858 and for St Andrew's Hall, Glasgow in 1877. Sir George was knighted by the Lord Lieutenant of Ireland after conducting concerts in Dublin in 1811. Sir Georges's brother, Henry's father and Ellen's grandfather, also Henry, was another well-known violinist and had a business selling music.

Note 16. See Music in *Nineteenth Century Britain* Ashgate Publishing, Gower House, Croft Road, Aldershot GU11 3HR. www.ashgate.com.

Note 17. Reckoned to be around ten million pounds today.

Note 18. Internet reference. Bertram Russell and Harold Joachim by Nicholas Griffin, Mcmaster University, Hamilton, Ontario 2007. 'Bertram Russell's favourite Uncle, Rollo, was a neighbour of the Joachim family and in 1891 married Harold Joachim's sister Gertrude. Harold did not marry until 1907 and at least until that time seems to have spent his summers at Haslemere where he and Russell had plenty of opportunity to meet when Russell was visiting his uncle'.

Note 19. Internet references. Professor Harold Joachim. Biography, accounts of his thinking and writing and obituaries. He, too, was an accomplished violinist who sometimes played in the Joachim quartet. He had not wanted to be in his uncle's shadow so followed his other interest in philosophy.

Note 20. They are buried together in Berlin - Charlottenburg. Internet reference Amelie Joachim.

Note 21. 'With Milner in South Africa'.

Note 22. Internet reference The American Philosophical Society, 105 South fifth Street, Philadelphia, PA 19106. www.manuscripts@amphilsoc.org. Letters of Rollo Russell with a few from Gertrude. Dictionary definition of Temperance 'moderation, even complete absence from the use of alcoholic liquors.'

Note 23. Sylvia had disagreed with her mother Emmeline and sister Christabel.

Note 24. Internet references. Maud Joachim. Whole page ' Spartacus Educational' also www.bathintime. co.uk/image249294/maud-joachin-1910. Also www.amazon/art.com. A picture of Maud on a white horse at a mounted demonstration. Image reference 17251 Collection reference private plate 23.

Note 25. Internet reference Menaggio. Hotels amalgamated as Grand Hotel Victoria. Pictures of interior, gardens and views over the lake. A guest commented in 2011. 'I loved the old world feeling of this hotel in both the presentation and the attentive staff.'

Note 26. Internet reference www.toch.org.uk. Toc H (standing for Talbot House) remains committed to 'building a fairer society by working to promote friendship and service, confront prejudice and practise reconciliation'. It started in the soldier's club at Poperinge in Belgium during the First World War where there was encouragement to mingle and make friends ignoring the rules of rank or status.

Note 27. Gertrude and Rollo's only son John died young, also affected by war wounds. There were no children.

Note 28. Another of Max's friends at Oxford, later Sir Robert Witt of Solicitors Stephenson, Harwood & Tatham.

Chapter 4

Note 1.   Roche Court is now Boundary Oak School just off the Wickham road A32 before Junction 10 of M27. Beaurepaire remained in the family from 1369 to 1873.

Note 2.   Brocas dates.

Note 3.   See many internet references for example: *The Spectator* and *Catholic Herald* archives

Note 4.   Farringford was a hotel but has now been refurbished as an arts-based conference centre also for weddings.

Note 5.   *Life of Earl Jellicoe.* Admiral Sir Reginald Bacon. Cassell 1936.

Note 6.   St John's Church Alresford.

Note 7.   *A Victorian Shipowner.* Augustus Muir and Mair Davies. 1978. *Uncharted Waters.* David Sinclair. 2010.

Note 8.   See internet. Plarrs lives of the fellows. Sir Henry Butlin Bt.

Note 9.   Internet. Many entries for Sir William Butlin.

Note 10. Internet. Notes on the history of Penponds Church.

Note 11. Camborne School of Mines opened in 1888.

Note 12. Trebartha. *The house by the stream.* Bryan Latham. Hutchinson. 1971.

Note 13. Schuyler was returning to the Queen Elizabeth at Portsmouth when, at Portchester, his motorcycle crashed into a lorry. The funeral was attended by Admiral Sir Charles Madden, FG's brother-in-law, then Commander-in-chief of the Atlantic fleet.

Note 14. Internet for the Schuyler family, Schuyler Mansion, Albany, etc.

Note 15. Internet for Heidelberg School, Melbourne.

Chapter 5

Note 1.   Ventnor and District local history Society and Museum. 11, Spring Hill, Ventnor, PO38 1PE Ventnorheritage@btconnect.com Open Tuesday to Friday, May to October. Saturday all year.

Note 2.   Steam Yacht Jeanette. Built 1911 by John Brown. Requisitioned and served in both World Wars

Note 3.   An English lady married to a French Baron who lived at Villa Henrietta.

Note 4.   G-E (G-EBSD) denotes a pre 1928 registration. Later G-A.

Note 5.   For example 67 passengers on 29th May. G-ABIY could only take two passengers so that meant 34 take-off and landings.

Note 6.   Rendezvous still at Dorfstrasse, Grindelwald. 'Decor a little dated', 'cheese fondue best ever tasted', 'large covered patio with great views over the mountains'.

Note 7.   Siddeley Challenge Trophy. Still at Royal Aero Club.

Note 8.   This was a third of capital. £5,000 also from Francis Luxmoore and Alexander Murray.

Note 9.   Hotel on Maximilian Platz 5. A ruin after the war.

Note 10. The album has thirty pages of stuck in press cuttings and many other loose cuttings.

Note 11. It could not have been easy for them. They missed Myrtle and had to cope with me.

Note 12. Admiral Sir Charles Madden, chief of staff at Jutland (then Rear Admiral) and later First Sea Lord. Married to FG's sister.

Note 13. Over a quarter million spectators watched the Royal Air Force Display at Hendon at the beginning of July.

Note 14. Sir Charles Rose 3rd Baronet, whose father had been killed in 1914, worked as a pilot with the airline during the 1930s.

Note 15. We knew Myrtle's sister Norah's husband as Uncle Joe. In this letter Grandfather writes 'Norah and Fred.'

Note 16. Picture in *The Northern Whig* Belfast published 21st November 1935.

Note 17. To me Uncle Bertie, FG's brother, who wanted me to work for the family company.

Note 18. These 188 Admirals were Rear, Vice, and full Admirals. Included Engineer Admirals who were not given the same renown.

Note 19. Leydene became HMS Mercury and has now been sold off as apartments. I remember children's parties and, on a clear day, the views of the Isle of Wight from the windows on the main staircase.

Note 20. Now a more substantial single house with separate garage and garden. But I can still recognise the part which was the cottage. A newer house has been built nearby.

Note 21. Presumably unscrewed from the cabin door of a ship which was being decommissioned or altered. We still have this sign but do not know if it came from the Iron Duke.

Chapter 6

Note 1.   In *Spithead Express* I wrote 'the wireless cabinet in Lionel's workroom.' Since then I have had more recall of Peake and reckon it was the wireless in my room upstairs.

Note 2.   Molly Vesey Holt's husband, Air Vice Marshal Felton Vesey Holt CMG, DSO, had been killed in a most unfortunate accident on 23rd April 1931. At the beginning of April he had been appointed Air Officer commanding fighter forces. He had flown down to Sussex in a Moth with Flight Lieutenant Moody as pilot. After inspecting squadrons they took off on the return flight. A squadron of Armstrong Whitworth Siskins were still airborne and dipped their wings in salute to the Officer Commanding. The Moth was partially obscured by cloud and one of its wings was hit by one of the Siskins. The plane went into a spin. Felton Vesey Holt jumped out but his parachute did not fully open before he hit the ground. Reports at the time write that, if he had been fifty feet higher when he jumped, it is likely that he would have survived. Flight Lieutenant Moody was killed when the Moth hit the ground in Seahurst Park. Myrtle refers to this in her 1931 letter about Helen Stack: 'Poor Mrs Vesey Holt too, did you hear about her husband being killed. Do you remember she stayed for the Schneider Cup'. This was presumably at St Lawrence. 'Aunt' Molly endured a long widowhood and was a kind godmother to me.

Note 3.   'Fynvola', her name written in pencil, was the youngest of the four Maclean sisters. Later the mother of the actor Hugh Grant, whose face always reminds me of Fynvola. There is a strong likeness.

Note 4.   Whinshill was demolished in the 1980s. There are now three blocks of flats and two detached houses on the site of the old house and gardens.

Note 5.   Transported was provided by a new Ford Ten and secondhand Morris Twelve and Hillman Minx. Continual maintenance was needed, but two of these cars were usually in action.

Note 6.   Two sisters who I think lived in Meonstoke but it may have been Exton.

Note 7.   Ivy Bishop helped at Peake and her brother, always Mr Bishop to me, worked in the garden.

Note 8.   The Polygon was built on the site of an earlier hotel towards the end of the nineteenth century. I well remember the revolving doors and the wood panelling as mentioned in one of the Google references. It was the centre of so much civic and social life throughout the twentieth century. Titanic passengers stayed there before their fatal voyage and before D-Day the hotel was headquarters for part of the American army.

Note 9.   The Reverend W R Mills bought the school then located in the Highfield area of Southampton from E A Wells in 1906. He then travelled the surrounding Hampshire countryside on his bicycle and eventually found the present site near Liphook where building began in 1907.

Note 10. Warnford House was demolished in 1956. Amongst previous owners were the Wood family since 1856 (I think there was still a Mr Wood in residence when we first went to Peake in 1938), the Neales whose seventeenth-century monuments are in the Norman church, the Paulets and the de Ports who are recorded as building the church tower in the twelfth century. Over the centuries there were many additions to the house.

Note 11. The first Sir Howard was knighted in 1914 and created a baronet in 1920 for his War service as director of lands for the War Office. He died in 1930. After his elder son, Howard, was killed, his younger son then succeeded to the baronetcy.

Note 12. Air Chief Marshal Sir Arthur Coningham was nicknamed 'Maori' on account of his New Zealand childhood. He was one of the wartime commanders in the Middle East. He then commanded the 2nd Tactical Air Force during the Battle of Normandy. After the war he was Commander in Chief Training Command based at Shinfield Park near Reading. I remember a lunch invitation after which he took me to see a magnificent Lancia Astura which had been appropriated as war booty. After surviving wars he was a passenger on the British South American Airways 'Star Tiger' G-AHNP which disappeared between the Azores and Bermuda in the early hours of 30th January 1948. No trace of plane or passengers have ever been found. Lady Frank/Coningham was widowed for the second time.

Note 13. The Leopoldsburg cemetery with memorial stone to Lieutenant Sir Howard Frank is at Limburg in Belgium.

Note 14. St Lawrence Hall was sold to a builder in 1946 or 1947. It was soon burnt to the ground. Rumours of arson were not proved. The footprint of the house and the surrounding gardens I so much enjoyed is now the site of many houses and bungalows. Those luscious peaches and nectarines on the slope facing toward the sea are no more.

Note 15. He had been appointed a Canon of Portsmouth Cathedral.

Note 16. The attractive Rover came to grief when FG edged out of Cross Road which leads down from the golf course. The story goes that the car was on its side and FG was pulled out of the sunshine roof. The Rover was a write-off and replaced first by a Triumph Renown and then the similar Triumph 2000. After that it was the Armstrong Siddeley Sapphire in which I drove her to Scotland and finally a Rover 105 R with 'Roverdrive'. It is not known whether she kept a car when she moved to a flat in Eaton Square.

Chapter 7

Note 1. *Spithead Express* ISBN 0 9519423 87 published by Magna Press 1999.

Note 2. For full Aerocar story go to www.portav.com downloads P A Aerocar.

Note 3. See *Spithead Express* and Southern Railway discussions page 91. Also Appendix One.

Note 4. He had survived so much and then this. The oak choir stalls in St Andrew's Church, Meonstoke, designed by Sir Charles Nicholson, are a memorial to Major Patrick Chrystal MC King's Dragoon Guards.

Note 5. 'Ranjitsinghi', renowned as a cricketer, died unmarried in 1933. He was succeeded as Jam Sahib of Nawanager by one of his nephews K S Digvijaysinghi who became Lionel's contact. He was an energetic ruler and entrepreneur and also remembered for his camp for Polish refugees during the Second World War. See Google for more about both Maharajahs.

Note 6. Lord Granville of Eye had an adventurous life. As a teenager he went to Australia and then joined up to fight at Gallipoli. He died in 1998 two days after attending the House of Lords on his 100th birthday. Again see Google.

Note 7. See www.britishpathe.com/video/personality-meet-dennis-kendall (in this instance dennis with double n (nn) though newspaper reports are usually only one n).

Note 8. In his first election success in 1942 Kendall as an independent narrowly defeated the official government candidate, Air Chief Marshal Sir Longmore. He won again at the1945 election and was then defeated in 1950. He then went America.

Note 9. See *Motoring News* 8th May 1958.

Note 10. He was one of the five Foster brothers who all played cricket for Worcestershire.

Note 11. Google 'Commonwealth Trimmer'. There are are later planes with same name. This was the amphibian shown flying on film.

Note 12. I loved this pre-war Morris '25' with its 3,500cc lorry engine. Painted green, it exuded simple power. I can picture it now by the garages at Meonstoke House.

Note 13. Remus won at Badminton in 1950 ridden by Tony Collins.

Note 14. Refer to *Spithead Express*. All details therein.

Note 15. See next chapter.

Note 16. Winston Churchill. House of Commons February 1931.

Chapter 8

Note 1. Look at all those names inscribed on the panels along the wall leading to the Chapel entrance.

Note 2. Kevin Ross reports that the new Design Schools rank amongst the finest DT facilities in the country.

Note 3. Rachel had by then left Eton as her husband, Wilfred Tatham joined the British Council after the war.

Note 4. Sir Simeon Bull 4th Baronet.

Note 5. Heathrow officially opened March 1946.

Note 6. A Rolls Twenty, probably 1929, with, I think, a Weymann fabric saloon body. I remember being collected at Tilford station and the comfort of the rear seat. The saloon was taken off and replaced by a wooden utility/shooting brake before they went to Ireland.

Note 7. Brisbane column called 'In the Air' by Stanley Broden.

Note 8. Jamair had several Dakotas. Eventually taken over by larger airlines. Google 'Jamair' for pictures and www.cnac.org/muff01

Note 9. The wings and tail plane were in the packing cases. Are they still there? I was told by an ex-employee from Portsmouth Aviation that he had heard that the passenger nacelle had been dropped into the harbour. If this happened, did they fish it out? If not, there would now be little left.

Note10.   The Privy Purses were taken away by Mrs Ghandi in the 1970s.

Note 11.   The state of Surastha now comprises Rajkot, Jamagadh, Bhavnagar, Porbander, Jamnagar, Amreli, Surendrangar.

Note 12.   This 1930s Lanchester Straight 8 Tourer has recently been displayed in the San Diego Auto Museum.

Note 13.   Other ex-Nawanagar cars are in other Indian Museums.

Note 14.   Comment from Alan Clark in one of the Diaries also page 59 of Ion Trewin's biography.

Note 15.   Lionel's word. It does not exist.

Note 16.   Desmond Norman, who kindly came to the launch of *Spithead Express*, deserves the highest praise. He is on record as saying 'You can make fortunes out of aviation. I am proof having made three. You can also lose fortunes. I have lost four.' He also had experience of dismissal by other directors. One sees why the Cayzers would probably have steered clear if they had been invited in. Desmond was an Etonian who did go straight to a technical apprenticeship (at de Havilland) rather than University and did postpone National Service.

Note 17.   The *Times* 1997

Note 18.   Charles Chenevix Trench. 'The Viceroy's Agent.'

Note 19.   Sir Conrad Corfield. 'The Princely India I knew.'

Note 20.   The Burnelli never went into production so they might have found a good market for the Aerocar. Canadian Car built thousands of buses and trolley buses in the 1950s. After various changes of ownership they are now Bombardier Transportation. Google Canadian Car to see a picture inside the factory where the Aerocar would have been made.

Note 21.   Google www.gmbports.org Gujerat Maritime Board. See the sheds at Bedi in which I saw the crates said to contain the Aerocar wings.

Note 22.   Present Jam Sahib is Shri Jam Sataji living in the bungalow built for J B Muff, the palace having been damaged by earthquakes.

Chapter 9

Note 1.   *The Enterprise Years.* Lord Young of Graffham. 1990. Headline.

Note 2.   *Red Robert.* Arthur Hearnden. 1984. Hamish Hamilton.

Note 3.   Bira, from Siam, now Thailand, was a successful racing drive , mostly in ERAs, in the1930s. After the war he raced OSCA and Gordini cars. He was also a talented sculptor.

Note 4.   Sydney Allard won the 1952 in an Allard Saloon made by his own company. See *Roads to Oblivion*. Balfour. 1996. Bay View Books.

Note 5.   Giles St Aubyn was at Eton, including time as Housemaster, for 35 years. In retirement he has written about Royalty and other matters. For more about Giles, see *Slow on the Feather*. Wilfrid Blunt. 1986. Michael Russell.

Note 6.   Then making Hillman, Humber and Sunbeam Talbot cars and Commer and Karrier lorries.

Note 7.   Royal Electrical and Mechanical Engineers. Royal Army Service Corps.

Note 8.   Catalan is spoken in Andorra and I still have difficulty in catching the swiftly spoken words.

Note 9.   Fleming Committee set up in 1942 'to look into the relationship between the public schools and the general education system.' Relevant issues discussed including: 'if this training was valuable, to confine it to those from a limited social class meant that it was missed by many who would have gained from receiving it.'

Note 10.   Google 'Tornado' to read whole history of this brave venture.

Note 11.   This was Kit Power who has been a staunch friend of the family for nearly sixty years. CKD means Completely Knocked Down. Sunbeam Venezia. More information via Google.

Note 12.   Either static models or attempts to adapt aeromodelling rubber band power units to cars.

Note 13.   *The importance of Eton*. Nick Fraser. 2006. Short Books.

Note 14.   The diminutive Alf, always cheerful, was head boatman at the school's boathouse 'Rafts' . Now being redeveloped.

Note 15.   Could then take the driving test in a 3-wheeler at age 16. If passed then you could drive a 4-wheel car at age 17 without another test.

Note 16.   David Cameron's was part of a group some of whom then worked in the City (i.e. Financial Services). I had different interests.

Chapter 10
Note 1.   See Quakers Wikipedia, etc. Varied reasons for refusing military service. Conscientious objection more acceptable now in some countries especially where alternative civil service. Note *The Quaker Way* by Rex Ambler, husband of Joachim cousin. O Books 2013.
Note 2.   Passage Football was an indoor version of the Wall Game. Two teams, ball in the middle. Which team by pushing and shoving could get the ball to the end of the passage. Preparation for war again. Like going over the top from the trenches, no refusals. If you insisted, wanted to finish an essay or complete a model, well, you would not be shot, but you might be beaten for not showing the right spirit.
Note 3.   The Reverend RDF Wilde MBE MC.
Note 4.   Colonel Sir Hugh Boustead KBE, CMG, DSO, MC. *The Wind of Morning* Chatto and Windus 1971
Note 5.   NCO equals Non Commissioned Officer
Note 6.   *The Sleepwalkers - How Europe went to war in 1914.* Christopher Clark. Allen Lane 2012
Note 7.   *Testament of Youth* by Vera Brittain mother of Dame Shirley Williams.
Note 8.   *Vital Peace, A study of risks* by Wickham Steed. Constable 1936. He also wrote: 'An open-air life, in good physical condition, well fed and well cared for, well paid and with ample leisure when off duty, a care-free life once they had got used to being suddenly despatched to another world. Compared with their humdrum lives in stuffy office or noisy factory, with the fear of unemployment before their eyes and burdened by the care of keeping wife and children on a meagre wage, the one time when they really lived.
Note 9.   Grandfather Jellicoe in the Appendix his book *The Grand Fleet.* Two Admirals and six Captains perished.
Note 10. Alan Clark in his diaries.
Note 11. *The making of the British Army.* Allan Mallinson. Bantam Books 2009.
Note 12. George Wansbrough. Chairman of Jowett in the late 1940s and later helped to finance Gordon-Keeble.
Note 13. Sir Henry Segrave. First Briton to win Grand Prix in British car. First to drive car at 200mph. Held land and water records simultaneously.
Note 14. Rachel had problems which prevented children. Fell out with Lionel over money. Retired to St Helena determined to preserve capital.
Note 15. Nigel Hensman. With me at Highfield, Eton, Catterick and Cambridge.
Note 16. David Green. At Highfield and in the Signals Training Regiment at Catterick.
Note 17. 50,000 Officer Cadets were trained at Mons. We were drilled by the famed RSM Brittain.
Note 18. Singer purchased by PC's father when the ordered Standard was not delivered in 1939. Journalists on *The Motor* were delighted with the performance and cornering characteristics. An attractive machine: see my book *Roads to Oblivion* page 155 Bay View Books 1996.
Note 19. An engine on the Viking cut out after take-off. Pilot brought plane round to land safely. The airport named after King Idris still on the throne.
Note 20. The theatre benefited from maintenance and repair work by the Italians in the 1930s. In 1982 it became a UNESCO World Heritage Site.
Note 21. An expert Army Surgeon screwed on the end of the elbow with a long screw which was taken out the following January. Never any trouble.
Note 22. According to Luke Harding writing in the *Guardian*, six missiles flattened what must have been our camp, but the ruins were not damaged.

Chapter 11
Note 1.   Now expanded for rehabilitation after recent and current wars.
Note 2.   George Maxcy and Aubrey Silberston. *The Motor Industry* 1959. Also quoted in *From Empire to Europe* Geoffrey Owen 1999.
Note 3.   Oliver spoke Persian. Able to converse with similar languages in Northern Afghanistan.
Note 4.   We had then hoped to travel up the Wakhan corridor leading up to the source of the Oxus and the Pamir often referred to as the Bam e Dunya or 'Roof of the World'. We were able to drive to Jurm but then stopped from travelling along the track to Ishkashim. This name is now more applied to the whole of the Pamir area. See below and www.pamir.org
Note 5.   John J Johnson. EPS Lewin and Partners.
Note 6.   *Afghan Interlude.* Oliver Rudston De Baer. Chatto and Windus 1957.

Note 7.   www.archive.org/Afghan Interlude 001981mbp Downloaded 839 times. Also Intermede Afghan.

Note 8.   Wakhan corridor a finger of land East of Badakshan about 140 miles long established as a barrier between Russia and British India in the 19th Century. Now between Tajikstan and Pakistan, the latter boundary along the Durand Line. The Kyrgyz Nomads have wanted a road after Ishkashim to bring in medical and other aid.

Note 9.   Nuristan. An Afghan province on the Southern slopes of the Hindukush and adjacent to the Eastern border with Pakistan. Known as one of the poorer and more remote provinces. Travel not currently advised due to political situation. http://nuristan.info

Note 10.   Built 1919 after third Anglo-Afghan war. Many of building materials bought by road from India. Lawns, swimming pool, squash court.

Note 11.   Shipped to Karachi on SS Warfield covered in petroleum jelly. Delivered on 15th April 1940. www.team-bhp.com Vintage cars and classics in India pre-war. King Zahir Shah's Rolls Royce.

Note 12.   Hind developed from Hawker Hart. Remained with Afghan Air Force till 1957. One now at Shuttleworth Museum.

Note 13.   All in more detail in Oliver's book.

Note 14.   His father, Nadir Shah assassinated 1933 when Zahir 19. Deposed in 1973. 29-year exile in Italy. Returned 2002. Died 2007.

Note 15.   Bamiyan Bhuddas. Built from 544 to 644 AD, hewn directly from sandstone cliffs. Destroyed by Taliban March 2001.

Note 16.   Concern now that the minarets may suffer from the increasingly heavy traffic.

Note 17.   Food and Agricultural Organisation. We might not have survived without these springs.

Note 18.   Toyota's Land Cruiser, a tougher larger vehicle came to dominate these markets.

Note 19.   The Hispano known as the 37.2 built after the first World War. This may have been an early, perhaps 1920, chassis subsequently rebodied. One of the engineers from the previous English agency, Monsieur Briand, was still around and helped us to get the car running well. Remembered as untiring on long drives. Unlike some British cars, vibration and harshness did not intrude.

Note 20.   AEC Associated Equipment Company. Built lorries and buses including Routemaster. Eventually teemed up with Leyland.

Note 21.   Mk1 Six-cylinder Zephyr with short tail. The car was responsive and quiet.

Note 22.   Sir James Cayzer, 5th Baronet, who helped family members to take out some capital at a fair valuation.

Note 23.   Fortunately he recovered and 'lead other survivors back to the British lines for which he was mentioned in dispatches' (see *Uncharted Waters* page 96). Later sent home for surgery.

Note 24.   Factor, the name given to estate managers in Scotland.

Note 25.   For Lanfine today see www.lanfinehouse.com History and present availability.

Note 26.   Lionel's great-grandmother and Ludwig's great-grandfather were brother and sister. Dr. Bevan looked after Ludwig when he had cancer. Ludwig died in his house. I knew nothing of this when Dr. Bevan did so much to help me.

Note 27.   *The Leyland Papers* by Graham Turner. Eyre and Spottiswoode 1971.

Chapter 12

Note 1.   See *Guardian* 9th January 2013. Emma Graham Harrison, also photographs on the web: Veronique de Viguerie.

Note 2.   Alderman Caroll was also Mayor of Ormskirk. When, 25 years later, I became a Councillor, I remembered his comments on the ideals of Local Government Service. This had been our discussion in intervals between the boring tasks.

Note 3.   Michael and Nichola Colvin both incinerated in the fire which destroyed Tangley in 2000. Hopefully they were both overcome by smoke first.

Note 4.   I have been told that Cousin Nicholas had expected me to start other work at once. Vacancies are not always immediately available.

Note 5.   PC again. I acknowledge with gratitude that I was able to keep the MG in one of her sheds. Had I known about the money to come and anticipated a house like Compton, it might have been possible to keep both the MG and the Hispano.

Note 6.   The MG was impractical for commuting. The A35 had a strong frame. As I came out of a drive, I misjudged the distance of another car which then hit the Austin amidships.

Note 7.   Eventually graduate membership of Institute of Personnel Management.

Note 8.   See my book *Bristol Cars. A Very British Story* published by Haynes 2009.

Note 9.   Sir John Hunt, later Lord Hunt. I wish the Award Scheme had been able to reach more of those at the bottom of the pile.

Note 10. We had a cot strapped to the tail of the 406. Both Max and Juliet stayed in a boarding house with Roseann, a kind helper at that stage.

Note 11. The area organisations had these dedicated people who were the heroes and heroines of democracy. Joyce Mann retired mid-1966.

Chapter 13

Note 1.   David Howell was elected for Guildford in 1966, later served as Minister and wrote influential books. Life Peer in 1997.

Note 2.   Conservative 'New Tasks' series 1965.

Note 3.   Sydney Chapman, architect. Elected for Handsworth division of Birmingham 1970-1974. Chipping Barnet 1979-2005. Knighted before retirement. Now Sir Sydney.

Note 4.   The Aravis was on offer at £3,000. Both this Bugatti and the Hispano tourer ended up in the Doune Motor Museum which was closed in 1998.

Note 5.   Sir Harold Boyce who had died in 1955. Brought up in Australia, he had served and been wounded in the First World War and then settled in Cheltenham. He became Chairman of the Gloucester Wagon Company. MP for Gloucester from 1929 to 1945. Later Lord Mayor of London 1951 to 1952.

Note 6.   *The Conservative Case* Viscount Hailsham. 1959. *The case for Conservatism* 1947.

Note 7.   Mr Brooksbank, Squire of Hasfield, Tirley, near Gloucester.

Note 8.   *Whatever happened to the Tories.* Ian Gilmour. 1997.

Note 9.   *The life of politics* Henry Fairlie 1968.

Note 10. Department of Politics and International Studies established in 2009.

Note 11. *Stand up and be counted.* Sir Anthony Meyer. 1990.

Note 12. Geoffrey Johnson Smith. MP for Holburn and St Pancras 1959-1964. Elected for East Grinstead 1965. Later Sir Geoffrey.

Note 13. Whilst a candidate can not directly pay an agent, there is nothing to stop other supporters or associates providing funds.

Note 14. Later in the Lords as Baroness Sally Oppenheim-Barnes of Gloucester.

Note 15. Lord Cromer was criticised for suggesting before the election that the new Government will face 'a very much more difficult financial situation' than the new Government faced in October 1964. Some of the argument is outlined in the *Times* 8th June 1970.

Chapter 14

Note 1.   Farsi, French, Gujarati, Polish, Punjabi, Somali, Sylheti, Urdu.

Note 2.   *The Youth Employment Service.* H. Heginbotham. Methuen 1951.

Note 3.   Fully described in Heginbotham book.

Note 4.   The relationship, if any, has not been established. How was it that this pioneer came to use both names. Her ideas were based on her father's advice to scholars when they left Gordon's College, Aberdeen.

Note 5.   HMSO. *Report of the Committee on the Juvenile Employment Service.* 1945.

Note 6.   Hansard. 5th February 1965.

Note 7.   The future development of the Youth Employment Service. Report of a working party of the National Youth Employment Council. 1965.

Note 8.   Hansard. 25th January 1966.

Note 9.   Salary in Warwickshire about £950. In Merton just over £3,000.

Note 10. Future structure and age limit of the Youth Employment Service. January 1970.

Note 11. People and jobs, a modern employment service.

Note 12. Employment and Social Services sub-committee. 1971/1972 and 1972/1973.

Note 13. *John Major* by Bruce Anderson. Headline 1991.

Note 14. Janet Fookes. MP Merton 1970-1974. Plymouth Drake 1974-1997. Now Baroness Fookes and a Life Peer.

Chapter 15

Note 1. A Mini was reliable. Neither we nor the Agents managed to get a Morris 1300 or a Vanden Plas 1100 to function properly. We did not then know Bill Limb. Both went back to the garage and were replaced by a Triumph 1300. This ran and handled well, but little things went wrong. Eventually part-exchanged for the Austin Westminster which is still with us in 2013.

Note 2. A Saab 96. Precautionary overhaul at 150,000 miles. Balancer bearings had collapsed. Also still with us.

Note 3. Engines used in A.C., Cooper, Frazer Nash, Lotus, etc.

Note 4. This 406 chassis was then used as the basis for a Zagato body.

Note 5. Books about 1974 include: *Edward Heath* by Philip Zeigler. Harper Press 2010. *Douglas Hurd Memoirs*. Little Brown 2013. *Whatever happened to the Tories* by Ian Gilmour and Mark Garnett. Fourth Estate 1997. *The Tories* by Alan Clark. Weidenfeld and Nicholson 1998.

Note 6. Command 3888. 17th January 1969.

Note 7. Donovan Report. 13th June 1968.

Note 8. Conservative Campaign Guide 1970 pages 196, 197.

Note 9.   Jim Callaghan, later Lord Callaghan, Prime Minister when Harold Wilson retired in 1976.

Note 10. Ian Gilmour page 278.

Note 11. Ian Gilmour page 279.

Note 12. Ian Gilmour page 285.

Note 13. Ian Gilmour page 286.

Note 14. *Douglas Hurd Memoirs* page 221.

Note 15. *Douglas Hurd Memoirs* page 222.

Note 16. *Edward Heath* Philip Ziegler.

Note 17. Burke's thoughts and speeches can be digested in *The Conservative Tradition* part of the British Political Tradition series. A and C Black 1950. Also in Jesse Norman's book *Edmund Burke*. William Collins 2013.

Note 18. Philip Ziegler page 485.

Note 19. Philip Ziegler about my Uncle, George Jellicoe, page 409. 'The story was in fact an absurd mistake based on a confusion between Lord Jellicoe and a public house of the same name. He denied that he had ever met Norma Levy but he had in fact made use of the Mayfair Escort Agency. Heath agonised, debated with Douglas-Home, Carrington, Whitelaw and the Chief Whip and concluded that, after the Lambton affair, the Goverent could not handle another scandal. He broke it to Jellicoe that he felt he should resign'. By today's standards there was no scandal.

Note 20. National Archives.

Note 21. Hermione Parker. Research assistant at House of Commons to Sir Brandon Rhys Williams MP. Co-founder of Basic Income Research Group 1984.

Note 22. *Instead of the Dole. An enquiry into integration of tax and benefit systems.* Routledge 1989.

Note 23. Philip Zeigler page 487.

Note 24. Marcus Fox MP for Shipley 1970 - 1997. In charge of candidate selection before the 1979 Election later chairman of 1922 Committee.

Note 25. Jean Rook column in *Daily Express* 3rd November 1976.

Note 26. Sally Oppenheim. 8th December 1976.

Note 27. *The Ascent of Britain.* Sidgwick and Jackson 1977.

Note 28. Part of flyleaf of *Whatever happened to the Tories.*

Chapter 16

Note 1. July 16th 1978.

Note 2. Richard Needham MP for Chippenham 1979-1983, North Wiltshire 1983-1997. Now Sir Richard (also Earl of Kilmorey). Longest serving British Minister in Northern Ireland (see *Battling for Peace* 1999 Blackstone Press). Over 5,000 contributions in the House of Commons, many about benefit and unemployment.

Note 3. MSC Review and plan. November 1977.

Note 4. MSC. Report of the feasibility of a new programme of opportunities for unemployed young people. May 1977.

Note 5. Rank Xerox had decided to move some of their work from Mitcheldean.

Note 6. The reply was to Paul Marland, then Forest of Dean MP and personally signed by Sir Richard O'Brian. See Chapter 19. In the 1960s he persuaded me to have a game of squash. Though somewhat older, he easily won and I have always felt a bit ashamed of my effort. I should have declined but he was very persuasive and always seeking outlets for exercise. The Thatcher Conservatives did not like the MSC's demands for more money for industrial training. When Richard was removed by Norman Tebbit it was 'the end of an era for the kind or progressive manpower and employment policies which O'Brien represented'. Later he chaired 'Faith in the City'.

Note 7. Sir Geoffrey Holland with whom I had had contact when he worked for the department which had serviced the Careers Service in the 1970s.

Note 8. Letter from G M Sayer 31st August 1982.

Note 9. Article in magazine *Initiatives* May 1983.

Note 10. Letter Richard Needham MP 9th February 1983.

Note 11. Letter John, Bishop of Gloucester 30th May 1984.

Note 12. 'North Sea oil revenue was not used to modernise industry and infrastructure'. Ian Jack, *Guardian* 19th April 2013.

Note 13. Comments after the death of Honorary Alderman Eric Radley OBE. County Council Minutes 19th December 1996. 'A gentle kind considerate and tolerant man, politician, teacher, author, farmer, naturalist, sportsman, scholar and preacher. An outstanding and lasting contributor to the Community. His encouragement and inspiration to others, his humour and concern for the welfare of others.'

Note 14. By 2013 there were eight independents and two 'independent alliance' on the Forest of Dean Council.

Chapter 17

Note 1. Originally intended to be 'ski-dog'. The story is told that the name painter for the prototype misheard his instructions and painted 'ski-doo'.

Note 2. We still have many patent specifications, with drawings attached, from the Patent Office in London with others from America, Australia, Canada and France.

Note 3. 'Cortex'. The dictionary defines as 'the outer grey matter of the brain'.

Note 4. *Telegraph* magazine. 11th August, 2001. A five-page illustrated article recounting Cayzer family history.

Note 5. Letter from Cayzer Trust. 15th September 2003.

Note 6. Letter from Cayzer Trust. 8th April 2004.

Note 7. www.fisglobal.com

Chapter 18

Note 1. Cicerone Andorra guide. Details in earlier notes.

Note 2. *Roads to Oblivion*. Bay View Books. 1996.

Note 3. *Auto Architect*. Magna Press. First edition 1998, second edition 2004.

Note 4. *Spithead Express*. Magna Press. 1999.

Note 5. Alastair Leslie who also invested in Nomad and Meondale.

Note 6. Deidre Fernand, *Sunday Times*. 26th May 1991.

Note 7. *Financial Times*. 5th October 1994.

Note 8. The *Times*. 21st February 1992. The Valerie Grove interview states that David had been rejected for National Service and missed out on Oxford. Instead he started at Lloyds at the age of eighteen (would that I had done the same as a mechanic!) and turned his company, Sturge, into a vastly successful one. Valerie continued that he was the type of man Julius Caesar preferred to have about him: 'fat, sleek-headed and such as sleep o'nights' and he was reported as saying: 'There were at least fifteen major catastrophes in the world. At such times people lose money. It doesn't matter whether we are regulated by Parliament, by the DTI or the Almighty. Only the Almighty could determine which catastrophes would occur, when and how many. In fact he would be the best person to regulate us.'

Note 9. Jerry and I were candidates together in the 1960s. He contested Montgomery in 1964 and 1966. Elected for Weston-Super-Mare with a majority over 20,000 in a 1969 by-election. He served for many years and was knighted as Sir Jerry.

Note 10. *Economist.* 18th September 2004.

Note 11. Mark Oaten was Liberal Democrat Winchester MP 1997 to 2010 when he stood down as a result of the earlier *News of the World*'s report about his time with 'rent boys'. He had won by just two votes in 1997 and then by 20,000 after the subsequent by-election. He was well-liked for all his work in the Constituency. His book: *Screwing up. How one MP survived politics, scandal and turning 40* is available via www.independentbooksdirect.co.uk.

Chapter 19

Note 1. The invitation as a result of my book *Bristol Cars. A very British Story* first published October 2009.

Note 2. Research report about historic vehicles in UK. '28,000 people working for 3,800 businesses. Turnover £4.3 Billion, nearly £1 Billion from exports.

Note 3. *Roads to Oblivion.* Bay View Books 1996.

Note 4. *Auto Architect.* Magna Press 1998.

Note 5. *Turbulent Times in the Car Industry.* Parchments of Oxford. 2011.

Note 6. *The Car Makers.* Eyre and Spottiswoode. 1963.

Note 7. *From Empire to Europe.* Harper Collins. 1999.

Note 8. *The Leyland Papers.* Eyre and Spottiswoode. 1971.

Note 9. *Out on a Wing.* Michael Joseph. 1964.

Note 10. The Lost Empire. An article in *Autocar's 100 years Celebration Issue.*

Note 11. The sale of Westland Aircraft to Sikorski which led to the Heseltine resignation.

Note 12. The Phoenix Four who paid themselves and manager Kevin Howe a total of £42 million before the company went into administration with debts of £1.4 billion. 6,000 workers lost their jobs.

Note 13. *The Car Makers.*

Note 14. *From Empire to Europe.*

Note 15. *The Motor Makers.* Collins 1988.

Note 16. George Wansbrough, another Etonian, who was chairman of Reyrolle, a director of other companies and also of the Bank of England. He had been a member of the Labour Party's Advisory Council for the Motor Industry.

Note 17. Jon Moulton who later split up with partners at Alchemy to set up 'Better Capital'.

Note 18. See *Classic and Sports Car* 2004. John Pressnell's interview with Jean-Pierre Richard, Nuffield, later BMC, imported for France from 1958-1970 when: 'Disgusted by British Leyland's reorganisation he turned to Datsun. Speaking of Nuffield exports in the 1970s: 'If there was a problem they hopped on a plane. By midday it was problem solved.' Of the 1970s and the first meeting with fellow Datsun dealers: 'There was the former BMC German distributor who told me he was so messed around with that he made a break. The Japanese distribution was built up on the back of the old British Leyland network. Lord Stokes made some terrible mistakes.'

Note 19. *The Verdict of Peace.* Macmillan 2001.

Chapter 20

Note 1. *For Conservatives only.* Lord Coleraine. Tom Stacey 1970.

Note 2. *Money for everyone.* Malcolm Torry. Policy Press. University of Bristol 2013.

Note 3. Arthur Cockfield who worked on the tax credit ideas for Keith Joseph and Anthony Barber. Later Lord Cockfield and a Commissioner in Brussels.

Note 4. Sir Samuel Brittan. *Against the flow* Atlantic Books 2005.

Note 5. Robert and Edward Skidelski. *How much is enough?* 2012.

Note 6. David Howell. *Blind Victory* Hamish Hamilton 1986.

Note 7. Louis Kelso. *The Capitalist Manifesto* Random House 1958.

Note 8. *Instead of the Dole* page 383.

Note 9. Citizen's Income Trust. www.citizensincome.org

Note 10. Baroness Wootton of Abinger. One of the first 'Life Peers' in 1958. www.barbarawootton.org The full quotation reads: 'The limits of the possible constantly shift, and those who ignore them are likely to win in the end. Again and again I have had the satisfaction of seeing the laughable idealism of one generation evolve into the accepted common-place of the next.'

Note 11. Citizen's Income Introduction. 2013.

Note 12. See *Money for everyone* page 74.

Note 13. House of Commons Treasury and Civil Service sub-committee 1982: 'The structure of personal income taxation and income support.'

With bouquet, Great-aunt Freda, Uncle Bertie's wife (Lady Rotherwick), FG, the author and Myrtle at the launch of HMS Jersey, September 1938. The ship was lost in May 1941

Index

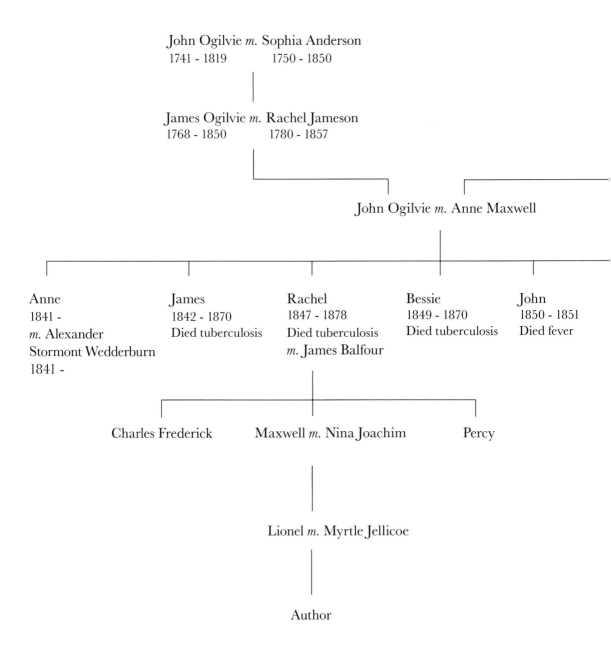

John Ogilvie *m.* Sophia Anderson
1741 - 1819   1750 - 1850

James Ogilvie *m.* Rachel Jameson
1768 - 1850   1780 - 1857

John Ogilvie *m.* Anne Maxwell

Anne
1841 -
m. Alexander
Stormont Wedderburn
1841 -

James
1842 - 1870
Died tuberculosis

Rachel
1847 - 1878
Died tuberculosis
m. James Balfour

Bessie
1849 - 1870
Died tuberculosis

John
1850 - 1851
Died fever

Charles Frederick   Maxwell *m.* Nina Joachim   Percy

Lionel *m.* Myrtle Jellicoe

Author

Ogilvie Maxwell

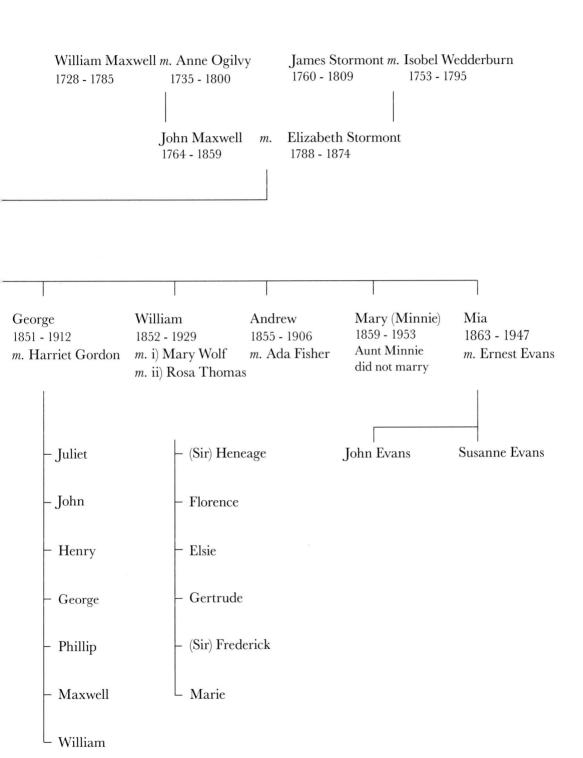

William Maxwell *m.* Anne Ogilvy
1728 - 1785   1735 - 1800

James Stormont *m.* Isobel Wedderburn
1760 - 1809   1753 - 1795

John Maxwell   *m.*   Elizabeth Stormont
1764 - 1859   1788 - 1874

George
1851 - 1912
m. Harriet Gordon

William
1852 - 1929
m. i) Mary Wolf
m. ii) Rosa Thomas

Andrew
1855 - 1906
m. Ada Fisher

Mary (Minnie)
1859 - 1953
Aunt Minnie
did not marry

Mia
1863 - 1947
m. Ernest Evans

John Evans   Susanne Evans

Juliet

John

Henry

George

Phillip

Maxwell

William

(Sir) Heneage

Florence

Elsie

Gertrude

(Sir) Frederick

Marie

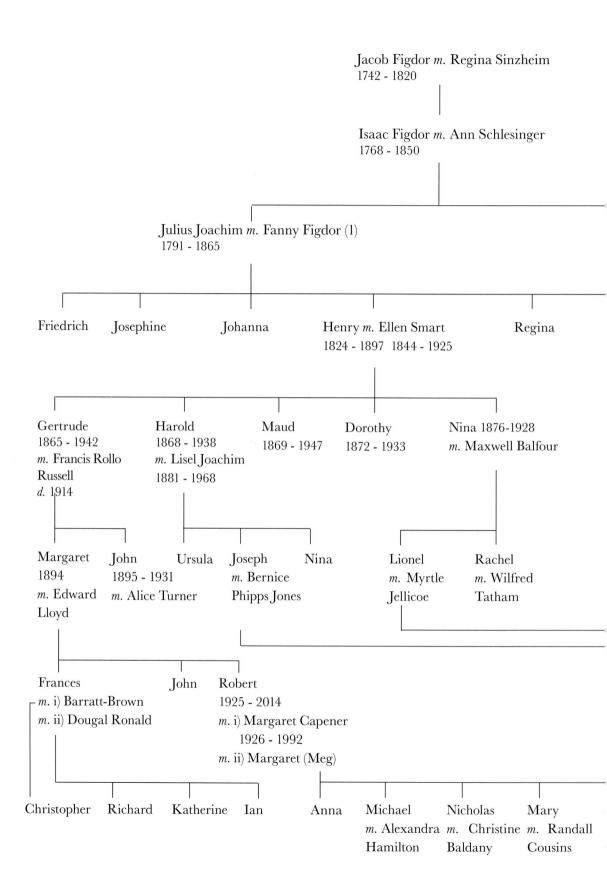

Jacob Figdor *m.* Regina Sinzheim
1742 - 1820

Isaac Figdor *m.* Ann Schlesinger
1768 - 1850

Julius Joachim *m.* Fanny Figdor (1)
1791 - 1865

Friedrich	Josephine	Johanna	Henry *m.* Ellen Smart	Regina
			1824 - 1897 1844 - 1925	

Gertrude
1865 - 1942
m. Francis Rollo
Russell
d. 1914

Harold
1868 - 1938
m. Lisel Joachim
1881 - 1968

Maud
1869 - 1947

Dorothy
1872 - 1933

Nina 1876-1928
m. Maxwell Balfour

Margaret
1894
m. Edward
Lloyd

John
1895 - 1931
m. Alice Turner

Ursula

Joseph
m. Bernice
Phipps Jones

Nina

Lionel
m. Myrtle
Jellicoe

Rachel
m. Wilfred
Tatham

Frances
m. i) Barratt-Brown
m. ii) Dougal Ronald

John

Robert
1925 - 2014
m. i) Margaret Capener
1926 - 1992
m. ii) Margaret (Meg)

Christopher   Richard   Katherine   Ian

Anna

Michael
m. Alexandra
Hamilton

Nicholas
m. Christine
Baldany

Mary
m. Randall
Cousins

Figdor, Joachim & Wittgenstein

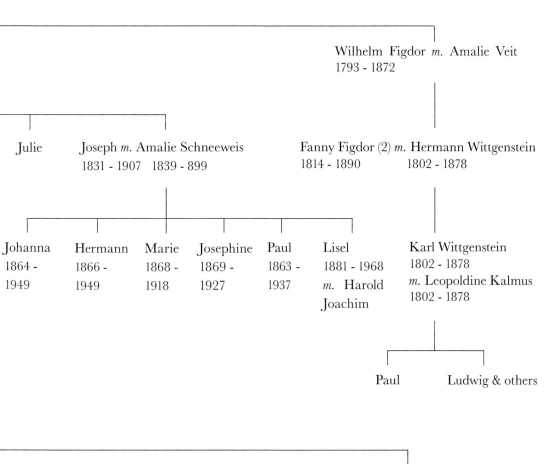

Wilhelm Figdor *m.* Amalie Veit
1793 - 1872

Julie
Joseph *m.* Amalie Schneeweis
1831 - 1907   1839 - 899

Fanny Figdor (2) *m.* Hermann Wittgenstein
1814 - 1890   1802 - 1878

Johanna
1864 -
1949

Hermann
1866 -
1949

Marie
1868 -
1918

Josephine
1869 -
1927

Paul
1863 -
1937

Lisel
1881 - 1968
m. Harold
Joachim

Karl Wittgenstein
1802 - 1878
m. Leopoldine Kalmus
1802 - 1878

Paul

Ludwig & others

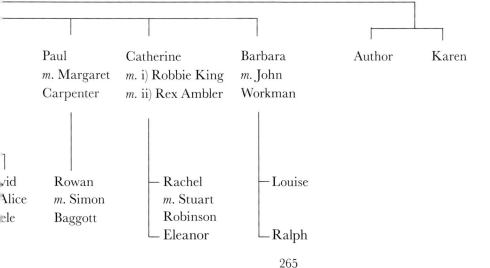

Paul
m. Margaret
Carpenter

Catherine
m. i) Robbie King
m. ii) Rex Ambler

Barbara
m. John
Workman

Author

Karen

vid
Alice
ele

Rowan
m. Simon
Baggott

─ Rachel
  m. Stuart
  Robinson
└ Eleanor

─ Louise

└ Ralph

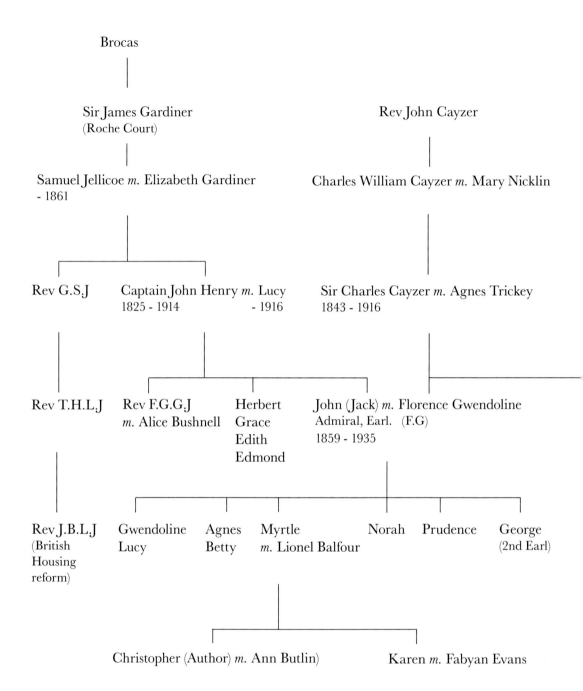

Brocas

Sir James Gardiner
(Roche Court)

Rev John Cayzer

Samuel Jellicoe *m.* Elizabeth Gardiner
- 1861

Charles William Cayzer *m.* Mary Nicklin

Rev G.S.J

Captain John Henry *m.* Lucy
1825 - 1914   - 1916

Sir Charles Cayzer *m.* Agnes Trickey
1843 - 1916

Rev T.H.L.J

Rev F.G.G.J
m. Alice Bushnell

Herbert
Grace
Edith
Edmond

John (Jack) *m.* Florence Gwendoline
Admiral, Earl.   (F.G)
1859 - 1935

Rev J.B.L.J
(British
Housing
reform)

Gwendoline
Lucy

Agnes
Betty

Myrtle
m. Lionel Balfour

Norah

Prudence

George
(2nd Earl)

Christopher (Author) *m.* Ann Butlin)

Karen *m.* Fabyan Evans

Cayzer & Jellicoe

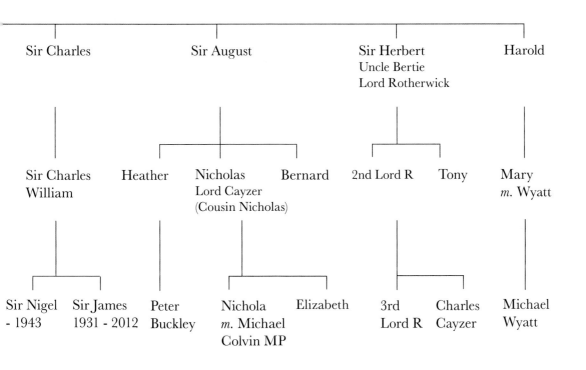

Sir Charles   Sir August   Sir Herbert   Harold
Uncle Bertie
Lord Rotherwick

Sir Charles   Heather   Nicholas   Bernard   2nd Lord R   Tony   Mary
William   Lord Cayzer   m. Wyatt
               (Cousin Nicholas)

Sir Nigel   Sir James   Peter   Nichola   Elizabeth   3rd   Charles   Michael
- 1943   1931 - 2012   Buckley   m. Michael   Lord R   Cayzer   Wyatt
                           Colvin MP

(For other maternal cousins see Cayzer
and Jellicoe trees in other family books)

LEARNING FROM DIFFERENCE

TRICORN

BOOKS